# Creative Industries

*Edited by John Hartley*

**Blackwell**
Publishing

Editorial organization and material © 2005 by Blackwell Publishing Ltd

BLACKWELL PUBLISHING
350 Main Street, Malden, MA 02148-5020, USA
9600 Garsington Road, Oxford OX4 2DQ, UK
550 Swanston Street, Carlton, Victoria 3053, Australia

The right of John Hartley to be identified as the Author of the Editorial Material in this
Work has been asserted in accordance with the UK Copyright, Designs, and Patents Act
1988.

First published 2005 by Blackwell Publishing Ltd

6    2008

*Library of Congress Cataloging-in-Publication Data*

Creative industries / edited by John Hartley.
     p. cm.
   Includes bibliographical references and index.
ISBN 978-1-4051-0147-9 (hardback : alk. paper)—ISBN 978-1-4051-0148-6 (pbk. : alk.
paper)
     1. Culture—Economic aspects.  2. Popular culture—Economic aspects.  3. Industries—
Social aspects.  4. Cultural industries.  5. Mass media—Marketing.  I. Hartley, John, 1948–

HM621.C73 2005
306—dc22

                                                                        2004016925

A catalogue record for this title is available from the British Library.

Set in 10.5 on 12.5pt Bembo
by Kolam Information Services Pvt. Ltd, Pondicherry, India
Printed and bound in Singapore
by Markono Print Media Pte Ltd

The publisher's policy is to use permanent paper from mills that operate a sustainable
forestry policy, and which has been manufactured from pulp processed using acid-free and
elementary chlorine-free practices. Furthermore, the publisher ensures that the text paper
and cover board used have met acceptable environmental accreditation standards.

For further information on
Blackwell Publishing, visit our website:
www.blackwellpublishing.com

# Contents

CONTENTS

# Acknowledgments

Thanks are primarily due to the team at QUT: Ellie Rennie, Jinna Tay, Brad Haseman, Terry Flew, Stuart Cunningham. It was Brad's idea in the first place to collect a set of readings, not least for the information of colleagues in QUT's newly designated Creative Industries Faculty (launched in July 2001), who were not fully confident that they had a clue what the new name stood for. A year later, it seemed that the creative industries had changed, but a general sense of bemusement stubbornly persisted, so Terry Flew and Jinna Tay got together to produce an updated set of readings. These DIY efforts gave us the idea of doing the thing properly, which of course required someone on the team who knew what they were talking about: enter Ellie Rennie and Stuart Cunningham. Thanks to them all.

We've benefited from conversations with many visitors to Brisbane with whom we've shared and contested the idea of the creative industries. They include Peter Beattie, Charles Leadbeater, William J. Mitchell, John Howkins, Kate Oakley, Henry Jenkins, Tom Bentley, Stephen Coleman, Charles Landry, William Uricchio, Jing Wang, Toby Miller, Nick Couldry, Andy Pratt, Don Slater, Sam Chisholm, Brian Johns, Keith DeLacy, Jeffrey Shaw, Terry Cutler, Louise Adler, Andrea Hull, Sue Rowley, Malcolm Gillies, Catharine Lumby, Geert Lovink, Simon Roodhouse, and numerous delegations from universities in China, Taiwan, Singapore, the USA, New Zealand, and Australia. Collectively, I think we're on to something, and I thank you all for your willingness to talk it over.

I owe a special debt of thanks to Jayne Fargnoli at Blackwell, who commissioned the title before the subject was widely recognized in the USA, and to Blackwell's anonymous readers, who put us straight on quite a few things. And an extra mention for Ellie Rennie, without whose critical, tolerant, dedicated and good-humored project management the book would have been poorer (and much later).

John Hartley
Brisbane
February 2004

## Text Credits

The editor and publisher gratefully acknowledge the permission granted to reproduce the copyright material in this book:

1. "Commons on the Wires" from Lawrence Lessig (2001), *The Future of Ideas: The Fate of the Commons in a Connected World*. Random House, New York, pp. 25, 34–7, 39–48, 275–8 (notes). Reprinted by permission of Random House, Inc and International Creative Management, Inc. © 2001 by Lawrence Lessig.
2. "Open Publishing, Open Technologies" from Graham Meikle (2002), *Future Active: Media Activism and the Internet*. Pluto Press, Sydney, pp. 88–91, 92–4, 95–6, 97–8, 103–111, 205–8 (notes). Reprinted by permission of Routledge/Taylor & Francis Books, Inc (pb 0-415-94321-1) and Pluto Press Australia (1-86403-148-4).
3. "At the Opening of New Media Center, Sarai, Delhi, February 2001" from Geert Lovink (2003), *Dark Fiber: Tracking Critical Internet Culture*. MIT Press, Cambridge, Mass. and London, pp. 204–16. Reprinted by permission of the MIT Press.
4. "Multicultural Policies and Integration via the Market" from Néstor García Canclini (2001), *Consumers and Citizens: Globalization and Multicultural Conflicts*, tr. George Yúdice. University of Minnesota Press, Minneapolis and London, pp. 123–34, 179–80 (notes). Originally published as *Consumidores y ciudadanos: conflictos multiculturales de la globalización*. © 1995 by Editorial Grijalbo, Mexico. English translation © 2001 by the Regents of the University of Minnesota.
5. "The Mayor's Commission on the Creative Industries" from John Howkins (2002), "Comments in Response to The Mayor's Commission on the Creative Industries, 12 December 2002", www.creativelondon.org.uk. Reprinted by permission of Creative London.
6. "Delia Smith Not Adam Smith" from Charles Leadbeater (1999), *Living on Thin Air: The New Economy*. Viking, London, pp. 28–36. Reprinted by permission of Penguin Books Ltd and David Godwin Associates.

ACKNOWLEDGMENTS

7. "The Experiential Life" from Richard Florida (2002), *The Rise of the Creative Class: and How It's Transforming Work, Leisure, Community and Everyday Life*. Basic Books, New York, pp. 165–89. © 2002 by Richard Florida. Reprinted by permission of Basic Books, a member of Perseus Books, L.L.C.
8. "Conclusion to *Global Hollywood*" from Toby Miller, Nitin Govil, John McMurria, and Richard Maxwell (2001), *Global Hollywood*. British Film Institute, London, pp. 202–10. Reprinted by permission of bfi publishing.
9. "The Poetics of the Open Work" from Umberto Eco (1989 [1962]), *The Open Work*, tr. Anna Cancogni. Hutchinson Radius, UK, pp. 3–4, 4–5, 13–19, 20–3, 251–2.
10. "Digital TV and the Emerging Formats of Cyberdrama" reprinted and edited with the permission of The Free Press, a division of Simon & Schuster Adult Publishing Group and Charlotte Sheedy Literary Agency from Janet Horowitz Murray (1997), *Hamlet on the Holodeck: The Future of Narrative in Cyberspace*. Free Press, New York, pp. 271–2, 253–68. © 1997 by Janet Horowitz Murray. All rights reserved.
11. "Balancing the Books" from Ken Robinson (2001), *Out of Our Minds: Learning to Be Creative*. Capstone, Oxford, pp. 194–203, 211. Reprinted by permission of John Wiley & Sons Ltd.
12. "Connecting Creativity" from Luigi Maramotti (2000), "Connecting Creativity". In Nicola White and Ian Griffiths (eds.), *The Fashion Business: Theory, Practice, Image*. Berg, Oxford, pp. 3–102. Reprinted by permission of Berg Publishers.
13. "Performing the 'Real' 24/7" from Jane Roscoe (2001), "*Big Brother* Australia: Performing the 'Real' Twenty-Four-Seven." *International Journal of Cultural Studies* 4(4), pp. 482–5, 486–7. Reprinted by permission of Sage Publications Ltd. © 2001 by Sage Publications.
14. "London as a Creative City" by Charles Landry. Paper presented at *Cultures of World Cities*, Central Policy Unit, Hong Kong, July 31, 2001, <www.info.gov.hk/cpu/english/culcities.htm> (accessed February 19, 2004). Reprinted by permission of Charles Landry.
15. "Cities, Culture and Transitional Economies: Developing Cultural Industries in St. Petersburg" by Justin O'Connor (2004). In D. Power and A. J. Scott, *Cultural Industries and the Production of Culture*. Routledge, London. Reprinted by permission of Thomson Publishing Services on behalf of Routledge.
16. "Local Clusters in a Global Economy" from Michael E. Porter (2000), "Location, Competition, and Economic Development: Local Clusters in

a Global Economy." *Economic Development Quarterly* 14(1), pp 15–21, 33–4. Reprinted by permission of Sage Publications, Inc.

17. "Cosmopolitan De-scriptions: Shanghai and Hong Kong" from Ackbar Abbas (2000), "Cosmopolitan De-scriptions: Shanghai and Hong Kong." *Public Culture* 12(3), pp. 772–6, 777–83, 785–6. © 2000 by Duke University Press. All rights reserved. Used by permission of the publisher

18. "Why Cultural Entrepreneurs Matter" from Charles Leadbeater and Kate Oakley (1999), *The Independents: Britain's New Cultural Entrepreneurs*. Demos, London, pp. 10–12, 13–19, 24–5, 26–7, 29–30, 75. Reprinted by permission of Demos, www.demos.co.uk.

19. "Games, the New Lively Art" from Henry Jenkins (2003), "Games, the New Lively Art". In Jeffrey Goldstein and Joost Raessens (eds.), *Handbook of Computer Game Studies*. MIT Press, Cambridge, Mass. Reprinted by permission of the MIT Press.

20. "Harnessing the Hive" from JC Herz (2002), "Harnessing the Hive: How Online Games Drive Networked Innovation." *Release 1.0* 20(9), October 18, pp. 2–8, 9–10, 11–12, 14–21. Reprinted by permission of edventure, www.edventure.com

21. "When Markets Give Way to Networks ... Everything is a Service" from Jeremy Rifkin (2000), *The Age of Access: How the Shift from Ownership to Access is Transforming Modern Life*. Penguin, London, pp. 24–9, 82–95. © 2000 by Jeremy Rifkin. Used by permission of Jeremy P. Tarcher, an imprint of Penguin Group (USA) Inc, and Penguin Books Ltd.

22. "Clubs to Companies" from Angela McRobbie (2002), "Clubs to Companies: Notes on the Decline of Political Culture in Speeded Up Creative Worlds." *Cultural Studies* 16(4), pp. 517–31. Reprinted by permission of Taylor & Francis, http://www.tandf.co.uk/journals

23. "Culture and the Creative Economy in the Information Age" from Shalini Venturelli (2002), *From the Information Economy to the Creative Economy: Moving Culture to the Center of International Public Policy*. Center for Arts and Culture, Washington, DC, pp. 3–16, 37–8. Reprinted here under the title of "Culture and the Creative Economy in the Information Age" by permission of Shalini Venturelli.

Every effort has been made to trace copyright holders and to obtain their permission for the use of copyright material. The publisher apologizes for any errors or omissions in the above list and would be grateful if notified of any corrections that should be incorporated in future reprints or editions of this book.

# Notes on Authors

**Ackbar Abbas** is Professor at the Department of Comparative Literature, University of Hong Kong, and co-director of the Center for the Study of Globalisation and Cultures. He has published essays on photography, cinema, architecture, Walter Benjamin, cultural studies, and Hong Kong culture. He has authored *Hong Kong: Culture and the Politics of Disappearance* and has one book forthcoming, *On Fascination*.

**Néstor García Canclini** is an anthropologist and head of the program of studies in urban culture at the Universidad Autónoma Metropolitana, Mexico. He has published 20 books on cultural studies, globalization, and the urban imagination and his book *Hybrid Cultures* (1995) was chosen by the Latin American Association to receive the first Ibero-American Book Award for the best book about Latin America.

**Stuart Cunningham** is Professor and Director of the Creative Industries Research & Applications Centre, QUT. Known for his policy critique of cultural studies, *Framing Culture*, and for his work on Australian media and film, his recent books include *Floating Lives: The Media and Asian Diasporas* (with John Sinclair, Rowman & Littlefield) and the standard textbooks *The Australian TV Book* and *The Media and Communications in Australia* (with Graeme Turner, Allen & Unwin).

**Umberto Eco** is President of the Scuola Superiore di Studi Umanistici, University of Bologna. He is the author of the highly acclaimed novels *The Name of the Rose* (1980), *Foucault's Pendulum* (1988), and *The Island of the Day Before* (1995), as well as the author of many academic books, including: *The Open Work* (1962), *A Theory of Semiotics* (1976), *Semiotics and the Philosophy of*

*Language* (1984), *Travels in Hyperreality* (1987), and *The Limits of Interpretation* (1990).

**Terry Flew** is Head of Media and Communications in the Creative Industries Faculty, QUT. He is the author of *New Media: An Introduction* (Oxford, 2002) and *Understanding Global Media* (Palgrave, 2005). He has been an editor of special issues of *Media International Australia* and *Continuum: Journal of Media and Cultural Studies*.

**Richard Florida** is currently the Hirst Professor of Public Policy at George Mason University and a visiting fellow at the Brookings Institution. He was previously the Heinz Professor of Economic Development at Carnegie Mellon University. He is the author of *The Rise of the Creative Class*, and co-author of five other books and more than 100 articles in academic journals. His new book, *The Flight of the Creative Class*, which examines the global competition for creative talent, will be published by Harper Business in March 2005.

**Nitin Govil** is Assistant Professor of Sociology and Media Studies at the University of Virginia. He is the co-author of *Global Hollywood* and is completing a co-authored study of the Indian film industry for the British Film Institute. He has published articles on race and US television, digital television technology, in-flight entertainment, and the globalization of labor in digital media production.

**John Hartley** is Professor and Dean of the Creative Industries Faculty at QUT and a director of CIP Pty Ltd. He is author of over a dozen books in the field of media, journalism, and cultural studies, including *A Short History of Cultural Studies* (Sage, 2003), *Communication, Cultural and Media Studies: The Key Concepts* (Routledge, 2002), *The Indigenous Public Sphere* (with Alan McKee, Oxford, 2000), *American Cultural Studies* (edited with Roberta E. Pearson, Oxford, 2000), *Uses of Television* (Routledge, 1999), and *Popular Reality* (Arnold, 1996). His books have been translated into ten languages. He is editor of the *International Journal of Cultural Studies* (Sage).

**Brad Haseman** is an Associate Professor and Head of Postgraduate Research Studies in the Creative Industries Faculty at QUT. He has worked as a teacher, researcher, director, and dramaturg for over 30 years, during which time he has pursued his fascination with the aesthetics and forms of contemporary performance. His text *Dramawise* has been translated into four languages.

**JC Herz** is the author of *Joystick Nation: How Videogames Ate Our Quarters, Won Our Hearts, and Rewired Our Minds* (1998) and *Surfing on the Internet* (1995). She was the *New York Times'* first computer game critic and serves on the National Research Council's committee on Creativity and Information Technology.

**John Howkins** is a partner in The Creativity Group, deputy chairman of the British Screen Advisory Council, and the UK representative of the Transatlantic Dialogue on Broadcasting and the Information Society (TADOBATIS) which brings together leading US and European policy-makers. He is chairman of Tornado Productions Ltd, director of ITR Ltd, Equator Group plc, Television Investments Ltd, and World Learning Network Ltd. He is the author of *Understanding Television* (1974), *Communications in China* (1982), *New Technologies New Policies* (1983), *Four Global Scenarios on Information and Communication* (1997), and *The Creative Economy* (2001).

**Henry Jenkins** is Director of the Comparative Media Studies program and John E. Burchards Professor in the Humanities at Massachusetts Institute of Technology. His books include *Science Fiction Audiences: Doctor Who, Star Trek and their Followers* (co-author, 1995), *What Made Pistachio Nuts: Early Sound Comedy and the Vaudeville Aesthetic* (1992), *Textual Poachers: Television Fans and Participatory Culture* (1992). He is editor or co-editor of *Hop on Pop: The Politics and Pleasures of Popular Culture* (2003), *The Children's Culture Reader* (1998), *From Barbie to Mortal Kombat: Gender and Computer Games* (1998).

**Charles Landry** is an international authority on city futures and the use of culture in city revitalization, cultural planning and heritage issues, strategic policy development and the cultural industries. He has been based at the World Bank in Washington advising them on their strategy for culture and cities worldwide, and is responsible for over 180 assignments for national and local authorities and funding agencies in the UK and abroad. He is one of the founders of the cultural planning consultancy, Comedia, and author of *The Creative City: A Toolkit for Urban Innovators* (Earthscan, London, 2000); *Riding the Rapids: Urban Dynamics in an Age of Complexity* (CABE/RIBA, London, 2004); and, with Marc Pachter, *Culture @ the Crossroads: Culture and Cultural Institutions at the Beginning of the 21st Century* (Comedia, Bournes Green, 2001).

**Charles Leadbeater** is an ideas generator, independent writer, and adviser to leading European companies. He is "Tony Blair's favourite corporate thinker" and his books include *Living on Thin Air: The New Economy* (1999) and *Up the Down Escalator: Why the Global Pessimists Are Wrong* (2002).

Leadbeater was Tokyo correspondent for the *Financial Times*. He writes regularly for the *Industry Standard* magazine as well as contributing to the *New Statesman*, the *Financial Times*, and the *Guardian*. (For further information see the London Speakers Bureau website.)

**Lawrence Lessig** is a Professor of Law at Stanford Law School and founder of the school's Center for Internet and Society. He is the author of *The Future of Ideas* (2001) and *Code and Other Laws of Cyberspace* (1999). He also chairs the Creative Commons project and is a board member of the Electronic Frontier Foundation, a board member of the Center for the Public Domain, and a commission member of the Penn National Commission on Society, Culture and Community at the University of Pennsylvania.

**Geert Lovink** is a media theorist, net critic, and activist, based at the University of Amsterdam. He is also an Honorary Research Advisor in the University of Queensland's Centre for Critical and Cultural Studies. His recent titles include *Dark Fiber* (2003), *Uncanny Networks* (2002), and *My First Recession* (2003).

**Luigi Maramotti** is President of the MaxMara Fashion Group. With an annual turnover in excess of £600 million and with over a thousand stores worldwide, Max Mara is one of the best known and most successful names in fashion. He was awarded an Honorary Degree of Doctor of Design by Kingston University in 1997.

**Richard Maxwell** is Associate Professor of Media Studies at Queens College, City University of New York. He is author of *The Spectacle of Democracy* (Minnesota, 1994), and editor of *Culture Works: The Political Economy of Culture* (Minnesota, 2001).

**John McMurria** is a Ph.D. candidate in the Department of Cinema Studies at New York University. He is working on digital television policy, transnational television programming, and Hollywood's international financing. He is co-author of *Global Hollywood* (BFI, 2001).

**Angela McRobbie** is Professor of Communications at Goldsmiths College, University of London. She is author of *British Fashion Design* (1998) and *In the Culture Society* (1999). She has written extensively on young women and popular culture, and about making a living in the new cultural economy.

**Graham Meikle** is an Associate Lecturer at Macquarie University in Sydney. He worked in Japan, Spain, Ecuador, and Scotland before moving to Australia in 1994. He is the author of *Future Active* (2002).

NOTES ON AUTHORS

**Toby Miller** is Director of the Program in Film and Visual Culture and Professor of English, Women's Studies, and Sociology at the University of California, Riverside. He is the author and editor of over 20 books and is currently editor of the journal *Television & New Media*. His work has been translated into Swedish, Japanese, Chinese, and Spanish.

**Janet H. Murray** is the director of Georgia Tech's graduate program in Information Design and Technology and of the Laboratory for Advanced Computing Initiatives, and a member of Georgia Tech's interdisciplinary GVU Center. She is the author of *Hamlet on the Holodeck: The Future of Narrative in Cyberspace* (Free Press, 1997; MIT Press, 1998).

**Kate Oakley** is an independent consultant and writer on the knowledge economy and regional development, and an Adjunct Professor in the Creative Industries Faculty, QUT. She is an Associate Director of the Local Futures Group, a consultancy specializing in the geography of economic and social change, and an associate of the independent think-tank Demos. She previously held research and consulting posts with the Policy Studies Institute and Manchester Business School, where she had a fellowship in the Knowledge Industries.

**Justin O'Connor** is Director of Manchester Institute of Popular Culture at Manchester Metropolitan University. He has published widely on the city, consumption, cultural policy in music and urban planning and cultural industries. He is a co-editor of *The Clubcultures Reader, from the Margins to the Centre: Postmodern City Cultures* and series editor of *Popular Cultural Studies Arena* (9 vols., Aldershot). He has a forthcoming book on *Cultural Industries and the City*.

**Michael Porter** is the Bishop William Lawrence University Professor at Harvard Business School. He is the author of 16 books and over 100 articles on competitive strategy and international competitiveness. He is author of *Competitive Strategy: Techniques for Analyzing Industries and Competitors* (1980), *Competitive Advantage: Creating and Sustaining Superior Performance* (1985), and *The Competitive Advantage of Nations* (1990). He led a project on clusters and innovation (2001) to investigate new theory and data about the sources of innovation and prosperity in regional economies, and co-authored *Can Japan Compete?* (2001).

**Ellie Rennie** is a Postdoctoral Research Fellow Queensland University of Technology and author of the forthcoming book, *Community Media* (Rowman & Littlefield). Ellie is currently co-vice chair of the Community Communications section of the International Association of Media Communication Research.

**Jeremy Rifkin** is president of the Foundation on Economic Trends, and the author of 16 books on the impact of scientific and technological changes on the economy, the workforce, society, and the environment, including *The End of Work* (1995), *The Biotech Century* (1998), and *The Age of Access* (2000).

**Sir Ken Robinson** is Senior Advisor to the President of the J. Paul Getty Center in Los Angeles and an international expert, consultant, and speaker on educational renewal. He was previously Professor of Education at Warwick University in the UK. His book *Out of Our Minds* was published in 2001.

**Jane Roscoe** is Head of Screen Studies at the Australian Film, Television and Radio School. She is the author of *Documentary in New Zealand* (1999) and co-author of *Faking It: Mock-Documentary and the Subversion of Factuality* (2001).

**Jinna Tay** is a Ph.D. candidate at the Creative Industries Research and Applications Centre at QUT. Her research focuses on fashion magazines and modernity in Asia, specifically the cities of Singapore, Hong Kong, and Shanghai.

**Shalini Venturelli** is Associate Professor of International Communication Policy at the American University, Washington, and chairs the Communication and Human Rights Committee of the International Association of Media and Communication Research (IAMCR). She is author of *Liberalizing the European Media: Politics, Regulation and the Public Sphere* (1998).

*John Hartley*

# CREATIVE INDUSTRIES

## Creativity – a Class Act

The background to this book is the need to respond to the challenges posed in a world where creativity, innovation, and risk are general necessities for both economic and cultural enterprise, where knowledge and ideas drive both wealth creation and social modernization, and where globalization and new technologies are the stuff of everyday life and experience.

> "Creativity . . . is now the *decisive* source of competitive advantage."
> (Florida 2002: 5)

Creativity will be the driver of social and economic change during the next century. John Howkins, author of *The Creative Economy* (2001), argues that thinking about an "information society" (see, for example, Castells 2000) is no longer enough. He suggests that the information age is already beginning to give way to something much more challenging:

> If I was a bit of data I would be proud of living in an information society. But as a thinking, emotional, creative being – on a good day, anyway – I want something better. We need information. But we also need to be active, clever, and persistent in challenging this information. We need to be original, sceptical, argumentative, often bloody-minded and occasionally downright negative – in one word, creative. (In this volume)

The **creative industries** – variously defined – are already significant components of advanced economies. In 2001 the US the core "copyright" industries were estimated at $US791.2bn, representing 7.75% of GDP and employing 8m workers. Their share of US foreign sales/exports was $US88.97bn – outstripping the chemical, motor vehicle, aircraft, agricultural, electronic components, and computer sectors (Siwek 2002). In the UK in the same year (but differently defined), the creative industries were estimated to have generated revenues of £112.5bn, employing 1.3 m people, with £10.3bn exports and over 5% of GDP (DCMS 2001). In Australia, they were valued at $A25bn, and the most dynamic areas, such as digital media content, were growing at twice the rate of the overall economy (NOIE 2003: 12). Creative inputs into other service industries such as finance, health, government, and tourism were increasingly significant.

In addition to scale and growth, the creative industries are significant because they are claimed to be drivers of the knowledge economy and enablers for other industries or services – for instance through the provision of digital content which "translates directly into the competitive advantage and innovation capability of other sectors of the economy" (NOIE) as well as through the nurturing of creative capital and creative workers generally.

Richard Florida has identified a new economic class – the **Creative Class** – that he says will dominate economic and cultural life in the century to come, just as the working class predominated in the earlier decades of the twentieth century and the service class did in the later ones. While the creative class is not as big numerically as the service class, it is nevertheless the dynamo of growth and change for the economy as a whole, and incidentally for the temper of the times too. American workplaces are evolving from blue- and white-collar environments to "the no-collar workplace":

> Artists, musicians, professors and scientists have always set their own hours, dressed in relaxed and casual clothes and worked in stimulating environments. They could never be forced to work, yet they were never truly not at work. With the rise of the Creative Class, this way of working has moved from the margins to the economic mainstream. (Florida 2002: 12–13)

Florida describes how the no-collar workplace "replaces traditional hierarchical systems of control with new forms of self-management, peer-recognition and pressure and intrinsic forms of motivation, which I call *soft control*":

> In this setting, we strive to work more independently and find it much harder to cope with incompetent managers and bullying bosses. We trade job security for autonomy. In addition to being fairly compensated for the work we do and the skills we bring, we want the ability to learn and grow, shape the content of our work, control our own schedules and express our identities through work. (Florida 2002: 13)

Not least because they attract "artists, musicians, professors and scientists," the creative industries broaden the social base of enterprise culture, extending opportunities to sections of the population previously characterized by low entrepreneurial activity and various forms of social dependency. They include a good proportion of micro-businesses and SMEs, and simultaneously involve some of the world's largest corporate brands, from News Ltd to Time Warner or the BBC. But the creative industries are not just capitalist wannabes and corporate giants. They require a new mix of public and private partnership. Economic success stories such as Silicon Valley and the creative industries in London are always accompanied by the substantial involvement of universities and government agencies, which take up some of the burden of pre-competitive R&D, and provide a milieu in which creative clusters can flourish.

In such a context the value of the creative industries is not confined to economic activity as such, but extends also to new models of social development that are at the cutting edge of international practice. Sir Ken Robinson, senior education advisor to the Getty Trust, makes the connection between economic and educational imperatives:

> The economic circumstances in which we all live, and in which our children will have to make their way, are utterly different from those of 20 or even 10 years ago. For these we need different styles of education and different priorities. We cannot meet the challenges of the 21st century with the educational ideologies of the 19th. Our own times are being swept along on an avalanche of innovations in science, technology, and social thought. To keep pace with these changes, or to get ahead of them, we will need our wits about us – literally. We must learn to be creative. (In this volume)

Instead of working for a single industry or even a single employer throughout their career, people entering the workforce now can look forward to several changes of career, whether they are part of Florida's creative class or working in the service, industrial, or primary sectors. To prepare for it they need new skills and capabilities in education, but they also need to be avid lifelong learners, returning to education – formal and informal, accredited and non-certificated – as they navigate their individual **portfolio career**.

Educators are a part of this universe: they too are part of an emergent creative class within a global knowledge economy. But schools and universities are not necessarily best placed to respond to the need for innovative, creative, adaptive, and curious consumer-citizens to make that economy prosper. Twentieth-century educational modernization, based first on massively expanding formal institutions and more recently on increasing their productivity with centrally regulated performance targets, has certainly strengthened the education *system* of schools, universities, and government departments. But inadvertently it has had a negative effect both on the kind of knowledge imparted and on the wider social desire to learn:

> This approach to modernization also reinforces a deeply conservative approach to education, as a body of knowledge imparted by organizations with strong hierarchies and demarcated professional disciplines. . . . Two traditions are reflected in this culture: the monasteries, which were closed repositories for knowledge in the form of precious manuscripts, and Taylor's factory, which encouraged standardized, easily replicated knowledge. The result is a system that is a curious hybrid of factory, sanctuary, library and prison. (Leadbeater 1999: 110)

Instead of *providing* disciplinary knowledge in a controlled environment, Charles Leadbeater argues that education should inspire a yearning for learning:

> The point of education should not be to inculcate a body of knowledge, but to develop capabilities: the basic ones of literacy and numeracy as well as the capability to act responsibly towards others, to take initiative and to work creatively and collaboratively. The most important capability, and one which traditional education is worst at creating, is the ability and yearning to carry on learning. Too much schooling kills off the desire to learn. (Leadbeater 1999: 111)

To what kinds of people and institutions should the mission of creating a society that is "yearning for learning" be entrusted? Merely expanding the formal education system is not the answer. Individuals and families can and will take more responsibility for their own knowledge needs. Learning services will be provided by private as well as public organizations, for purposes determined by the needs of the learners themselves rather than for formal accreditation and certification. In short, **learning will become a distributed system**, dedicated to creativity, innovation, and customized needs and networked across many sites from the family kitchen to the business breakfast as well as the classroom, café, and workplace.

It is in this context that the idea of the creative industries makes most sense; not merely as an area of economic development but more as an idea – namely that creativity can have decisive social and economic effects. Creativity doesn't stop being an attribute of individual people. It turns up wherever humans think, do, and make things. But in this context it can be seen as something more. The "industry" part of "creative industries" links that human attribute with large-scale organized enterprise. It sees imaginative innovation as the very heart – the pump – of wealth creation and social renewal.

# What Are the Creative Industries?

> The idea of the CREATIVE INDUSTRIES seeks to describe the *conceptual and practical convergence* of the CREATIVE ARTS (individual talent) with Cultural Industries (mass scale), in the context of NEW MEDIA TECHNOLOGIES (ICTs) within a NEW KNOWLEDGE ECONOMY, for the use of newly INTERACTIVE CITIZEN–CONSUMERS.

The "creative industries" idea itself is a product not of industry but of history, both immediate and long-term. Long-term, the creative industries concept has evolved from previous conceptualizations of the "creative arts" and the "cultural industries" going back to the eighteenth century, and it also picks up some long-term changes in the idea of "the consumer" and "the citizen." More immediately, the idea of the creative industries arose from recent changes in technology and the world economy, especially during the 1990s, and the beginnings of broad uptake of interactive media forms. It found favor in the framework of national and urban or regional policy formation, in countries where creativity caught the imagination of politicians and policy-makers who wanted to promote "jobs and GDP" (as the economic development mantra has it). Increasingly the creative industries are also named as such in higher education in the same countries, especially in universities with a direct stake in educating creative personnel, nurturing the next generation of wealth creators, and researching cultural and media policy.

Because it is historical rather than categorical, the "creative industries" idea varies geographically, depending on local heritage and circumstance. Most notably, in the USA creativity is consumer- and market-driven, whereas in Europe it is caught up in traditions of national culture and cultural citizenship. In jurisdictions that are porous to both America and Europe, the idea of the creative industries has developed with both of these extremes in play – consumer and culture, market and citizenship. Such places include the UK, Singapore, Australia and New Zealand, and other Commonwealth countries, as well as Taiwan and Hong Kong, and these intermediate countries have been the early adopters of the term. Elsewhere, notably mainland China, the idea has remained relatively quiescent for the time being, with creative enterprise and innovation subsumed into other development policies (Wang 2004).

It may be argued that the more porous or intermediate countries have seen the creative industries as a chance to bring together the two extremes of public art and commercial market in order to move beyond them and grasp new possibilities. Certainly the "creative industries" idea combines – but then radically transforms – two older terms: the *creative* **arts** and the **cultural** *industries*. This change is important for it brings the arts (i.e. culture) into direct contact with large-scale industries such as media entertainment (i.e. the market). It suggests the possibility of moving beyond the elite/mass, art/entertainment, sponsored/commercial, high/trivial distinctions that have bedevilled thinking about creativity in policy as well as intellectual circles, especially in countries with European traditions of public culture. To understand why the idea of the creative industries is conceptually innovative in this context, it is worthwhile considering where the previous terms came from, and how they have become attached to a number of other terms that divide the field of human endeavor into opposed pairs: citizen and consumer, freedom and comfort, public and private. The promise of the creative industries idea is that it picks up the extent to which these oppositions have been and might further be resolved in creative activity itself. At the widest horizon of analysis, then, the concept focuses attention on how contemporary communications and corporate media may be reconfiguring fundamental cultural structures like narrative, story and code on an international scale.

## Creative Arts and Civic Humanism

**Creative arts** is a term associated with the subsidized or sponsored "public" arts. It is derived from the early modern philosophy of **civic humanism**, espoused by people like the earl of Shaftesbury and Sir Joshua Reynolds in the 1700s (see Barrell 1986, to whom this account is indebted, and Hartley 2003: 69–77 for a fuller discussion). Shaftesbury was a theorist of painting and sculpture as noble arts, suitable pursuits for members of the gentry and aristocracy. If paintings conveyed abstract ideas about moral values and civic virtues, then both creative practice and connoisseurship in the arts would form part of the skill-set of government, especially for scions of prominent families who had to learn the discipline of *self*-government while avoiding any ignoble activities that might smack of "trade." Shaftesbury, Reynolds, and others constructed an intellectual ideology for "public" art, which linked it with the community of taste capable of understanding and appreciating it, and conflated that community of taste with the political public (Barrell 1986: 70).

It was not enough to claim that the "liberal" arts were vital contents of the kit-bag of rulers – it was equally important to separate out the governors from the governed. The opposite of "liberal" (pertaining to a free citizen) was "servile" (pertaining to a servant); and the opposite of "intellectual" was "manual." Shaftesbury revived a classical distinction between "liberal" *arts* and "mechanical," "useful" or "servile" *artisanship*. This schema was firmly based on the idea that trade — commercial activity including creative work — was "servile" or even "slavish," as in "slavish imitation." A rather telling double standard was in operation. For Lord Shaftesbury, the "mere Vulgar of Mankind," as opposed to the landed gentry, i.e. families who were wealthy enough not to need paid employment, could not act virtuously out of public spirit, but only out of "*servile* Obedience." To ensure that obedience, they "often stand in need of such a rectifying Object as *the Gallows* before their Eyes." Another such "rectifying Object" was of course penal Australia. But a gentleman educated by the liberal arts into civic virtue was in a different position. A contemporary of Shaftesbury wrote: "publick Virtue makes Compensation from all Faults but Crimes, and he who has this publick Virtue is not capable of Crimes" (quoted in Barrell 1986: 8, 19).

Commercial creativity was deemed unworthy of "free" citizens, who needed an independent income and leisure in order to pursue "public service." It was honorable to be a philosopher, but servile to be a potter. It could be an expression of taste to *collect* "pots" — in the form of Sèvres or Minton — but those who *made* them remained artisans and therefore servile. Gentlemen could only engage in creative work if it was dedicated to public rather than private ends, and only then if it represented abstract intellectual ideas, rather than merely decorated things. You could be an oil painter or a house painter, but you were unlikely to win national honors for the latter (unless you were Adolf Hitler).

Despite its aristocratic provenance, civic humanism remains to this day a strong driving force in the rhetoric and the infrastructure of creative arts, even in countries with long histories of political democratization. It has persisted in the distinction between intellectual "higher education" (universities) and artisanal "further education" (vocational skills training). It motivates the distinction between "fine" or "serious" arts and "commercial" entertainment. And it has resulted in the chronic oversupply of individual artists to an economic sector that can't support them, sustaining a myth of the struggling artist in the garret, made noble by creativity even while subsisting in a condition of dependent beggary that is the very opposite of freedom.

Civic humanism underpins a cultural climate that still, after more than two centuries of democratization, encourages the mass of anonymous but sovereign voters to assume that they are excluded from the world of art. They don't "get" its underlying "political" rationale, which is not about the expansion of creativity but the abstraction of ideas. They remain unemancipated into that artistic or intellectual "freedom" that is taken to be the prerequisite for "liberal humanist" citizenship.

Public support for the arts has continued to flow from this hierarchical topography. Creativity was rationalized as worthy of ongoing subsidy from taxation, or in the USA from philanthropic foundations but with the same rationale, only because of the arts' humanizing and civilizing influence over the populace. Civic humanism was *nationalized*, as it were, and from the Victorian period onwards noble artworks duly began to migrate from aristocratic halls and country houses into national institutions, museums, and galleries for the civic education of the general public. Instead of slavish obedience, the increasingly sovereign "Vulgar of Mankind" were to be taught self-control, and they would learn it via the "rectifying Object," not of the Gallows, but of Art.

One consequence of this migration was that art was protected from some of the modernizing fury of the Industrial Revolution and the growth of "mass" democracies, certainly in Europe. Although many artists responded to industrialization in their works, the system of public art did not have to reinvent itself in the image of the newly ascendant industrial societies over whose collective national mantelpiece it hung. Indeed, it was often proposed as an antidote to that society. Creativity – "culture" – was a bastion *against* "civilization," which in the hands of cultural critics of the early twentieth century – such as Lewis Mumford, F. R. Leavis, and T. S. Eliot – became synonymous with mechanization, standardization, and the cheapening of aesthetic and ultimately of human experience (see Carey 1992). Needless to say, the fact that America waxed rich upon this very ground – radically lowering transaction costs for participation in aesthetic pursuits, and turning creativity, culture, and art into a mass market – meant that "Americanization" became synonymous with everything European critics found most distasteful. The creative practices most characteristic of the industrial era on both sides of the Atlantic, from engineering and transportation to popular aesthetics including shopping (department stores), the press, cinema, photography, fashion, and recorded music, had a hard time gaining acceptance or even recognition *as* art.

It became commonplace, possibly even a required ideology among arts activists, to express contempt for the "Americanized" aesthetic pursuits of their own populations. Root-and-branch opposition to the values and experience of popular culture and consumer tastes was fostered among those who pursued "true" creativity within nationalized "public" institutions – whose ostensible purpose was to *express* the civic humanism and "liberal" freedom of those same despised populations.

Such a long and institutionally entrenched history cannot be undone in a day. But there is an argument for re-purposing the very idea of "creativity" to bring it into closer contact with the realities of contemporary commercial democracies. "Art" needs to be understood as something *intrinsic*, not *opposed*, to the productive capacities of a contemporary global, mediated, technology-supported economy. Both art and creativity need to be looked for within the living practices of a multi-cultural, multi-valent population that is neither aristocratic nor dumb. In short, how could "European" notions of the public and civic value of creativity conjoin with "American" willingness to test such values in the market?

## Citizen and Consumer – Freedom and Comfort

While almost everyone in modernized countries is a consumer, no one is *just* that. The consumer has never been alone. Two figures, the **consumer** and the **citizen**, have grown up together throughout the modern period. Indeed, they express the twin energies of modernity, neither of which can be understood without both of them being present. These energies are: the desire for freedom, and the desire for comfort (Hartley 1996).

- The desire for **freedom** is expressed in citizenship, which is of course the domain of government, and has been evolving, not always steadily and certainly not without great struggle, since the English (1642), American (1776), French (1789), and Russian (1917) revolutions. During those events and their aftermath, individual civic rights and mass political sovereignty were more generally established. Since then, citizenship has been extended to include social rights – for instance to education, welfare, and social security. Latterly, these political and social rights have extended again to encompass cultural rights of various kinds. The modernist desire for freedom is still evolving, toward what I've called "DIY citizenship" (Hartley 1999).
- The desire for **comfort** – for freedom from want, for plenty not scarcity, on the scale of the entire population not just for privileged classes or castes – is the dream that propelled the Industrial Revolution of the nineteenth century. It is the domain of business. Again, not without struggle, the desire for comfort has evolved. The mass, industrial model of consumption, i.e. a disciplined industrial workforce consuming mass entertainments via spectator tourism, media, and sport, has developed into a customized, interactive partnership based not on mass persuasion, manipulation, and passivity but on difference, affinity, and informed choice.

The history of freedom and comfort involves both divergence and convergence between these twin energies. Historically, the distinction between

**public** (freedom) and **private** (comfort) has been one powerful way of keeping these two sides of modern identity distinct from one another:

- In the **public sphere**, where citizenship is formed, lies government, politics, security, justice, debate and democracy, public service and the public interest, human and civil rights; and more recently public rights to some forms of welfare, education, social security, and cultural identity. These various aspects of citizenship are expressed in substantial institutions which are also often publicly owned, although that can no longer be assumed.
- In the **private sphere**, where consumers are formed, lies both "private enterprise" and "private life," often at odds with each other since the distinction between public and private was first theorized in the eighteenth century: business, the market economy, the family, private life, and property; and more recently consumer rights and even "consumer sovereignty."

Selves are formed in both spheres. Our individual identity results from both public and private elements. Furthermore, the two spheres appear to be converging, even while there is controversy and contestation designed to keep them clearly separated. One place where the changes themselves and the issues raised by them are especially prominent and insistent is in the field of creativity.

## Culture Industries

The **culture industries** is a term originally associated with the radical critique of mass entertainment by members of the Frankfurt school in and following the 1930s and 1940s – the era of mass totalitarian politics and total war. Theorists such as Theodor Adorno, Max Horkheimer, Hannah Arendt, and their more recent successors such as Herbert Marcuse and Hans Magnus Enzensberger, used the concept of the "culture industries" to signal their disgust at the success of fascism, which they partly attributed to the use of the media of "mechanical reproduction" for propaganda and mass ideological persuasion; the so-called "aestheticization of politics." They feared that in ostensibly democratic countries like the USA, where some of them emigrated to escape fascism, the entertainment media were culpable, responsible for dumbing down the population, making it politically docile, and softening it up for demagoguery and worse. Indeed, it was the culture shock of comparing European (cultural) politics with the poolside culture of the Roosevelt or Ambassador hotels in Hollywood that sparked Adorno's famous critique of popular culture:

Life in the late capitalist era is a constant initiation rite. Everyone must show that he wholly identifies himself with the power which is belaboring him. This occurs in the principle of jazz syncopation, which simultaneously derides stumbling and makes it a rule. The eunuch-like voice of the crooner on the radio, the heiress's smooth suitor, who falls into the swimming pool in his dinner jacket, are models for those who must become whatever the system wants. Everyone can be like this omnipotent society; everyone can be happy, if only he will capitulate fully and sacrifice his claim to happiness. (Adorno and Horkheimer 1997 [1947])

The same shock of looking at California with European eyes sparked Raymond Williams's critique of US television a generation later (Williams 2003).

The production and distribution of cultural commodities on an industrial scale in "dream factories" like Hollywood was seen as a disaster. Instead of applauding standardization as the guarantee of affordable quality, the Frankfurt school intellectuals joined with conservative intellectuals such as T. S. Eliot to disapprove of it as "cheap" and inauthentic. The industrialization of culture was denounced as the commodification of "the human mind." The term "culture industries" began life as an expression of contempt for the popular newspapers, movies, magazines, and music that "distracted" the masses from their duty to progress the class struggle (left-wing intellectuals) or kow-tow to aristocratic legacy values (right-wing intellectuals) (see Carey 1992).

The radical difference of view between European and American perspectives on culture has remained forceful. Writing about "strategic culture," Robert Kagan caused a stir in policy circles and opinion pages with this:

On the all-important question of power . . . American and European perspectives are diverging. . . . on major strategic and international questions today, Americans are from Mars and Europeans are from Venus: they agree on little and understand one another less and less. (Kagan 2003: 3)

Kagan's own interest was confined to *strategic* power – military might and the willingness to use it. He did not expand his analysis to include other spheres in which the USA and Europe have diverged during and since the Cold War. But it may be argued that a parting of the ways had occurred much earlier in the sphere of culture. Europeans persisted in seeing culture in national terms (e.g. "French culture") and therefore also in the context of transnational negotiation governed by law, to preserve and promote national cultures without overwhelming the national culture of others. Americans on the other hand defined culture in market terms, and saw no reason why the market shouldn't prevail. Market might matched military might – it was

America's "manifest hegemony," as it were. So "globalization" came to be seen by activists on both sides of the Atlantic as "Americanization" by another name, and people frequently conflated colonization with commerce, seeing the international expansion of American consumerism (not least via international trade agreements) as a global threat to freedom and democracy.

## Corporate Critique and Critical Analysis

A feature of the creative industries is that they try to create wealth on the site of a universal human attribute. And not a few humans are predisposed by ideology or income (i.e. they're pissed off or poor) to oppose or avoid activities whose purpose is to make someone else wealthy. (This book recognizes that antipathy by starting from the "human" rather than the "industrial" perspective, because it is important not to dismiss the creative industries idea as a mere ruse of big business.) In both creativity itself and in the new interactive media upon which innovation in the creative industries depends, there are some decidedly *anti*-industrial folk. Here can be found everything from the open source movement to amateur dramatics, DIY and folk culture, third-sector volunteerism, as well as the possibilities for new modes of expression and communication arising from new media technologies of rapidly declining cost. With interactivity, customization, and the evolution of media from "read only" to "read and write," relations between audiences and creative content have irrevocably changed, even while existing forms persist. Among the changes must be counted the vociferous refusal of some among the potential audience to play with corporate creativity at all, even while they poach the possibilities. The culture jamming movement, anti-globalization activists, and environmental groups have proven themselves adept at using new media to criticize new media, drawing popular attention to the continuation in the creative industries of some of the most notorious features of the "culture industries," including the connections between brands and sweatshops, new communications technologies and call-centers, and the impact of the "new economy" on human and cultural ecology as well as on the natural environment. The creative industries, like any other field of endeavor, have entailed costs as well as benefits, downsides as well as up. New investment in creative talent has left in its wake displaced practices which are highly valued by individuals and communities, contributing further to the "digital divide." Creative industries have reordered international power flows in ways that certainly don't advantage everybody.

So **corporate critique** and **critical analysis** are needed even where people are persuaded of the overall benefits of these developments (Uricchio

2004). Critique is perhaps most explicit in the "culture industries" tradition, which has certainly turned a skeptical, jaundiced, and critically practiced eye on the idea of the creative industries (Pratt 2004; Miller 2004). But at the same time many on the left who have been trained in Frankfurt-style critique have turned up working directly in the creative industries, and in the policy, educational, and government support agencies that serve them. A turn toward practical engagement, in other words, is not an alternative to critical analysis but its outcome, and seeking to make the most of the opportunities offered by the creative industries, even in the form of private enterprises, is not an abandonment of critique but its implementation.

One increasingly evident outcome of such critical engagement is that policy consultants, especially those working near labor governments, have begun to adopt terms like "ecology" and "sustainability" in policy discourse. They've understood from social and environmental activists that economic development requires a new approach, based less on large-scale industrial and public works (dams and factories), more on sustainable activities in a context of multiple obligation; the so-called "triple bottom line" of social and environmental as well as financial outcomes. Because of miniaturization and customization of hardware, and the fact that their stock-in-trade is intangible (it's the information or entertainment, not the disc or player), industries based on creative content and new communications technologies are well suited to environmentally and socially sustainable development, and are often peopled by innovators and entrepreneurs who themselves share sympathies with counter-cultural values. They don't mind creating "sustainable" wealth, but seek to tread lightly on the environment and deal fairly with fellow humans. They share with the Frankfurt school an antipathy to the "mechanical reproduction" of standardized mass culture.

## Cultural Industries Policy

Stripped of its Marxism, the term "cultural industries" re-entered the policy lexicon in the democratizing and egalitarian 1970s and 1980s. It was used for provincial promotionalism. It became useful to persuade local, state, or federal governments to support arts and culture for the economic benefits they delivered to regional communities. Also in this period, *media* industries were taken in the direction of "culture" in public policy discourse. Popular commercial industries such as TV, film, and music were branded as "cultural industries" so that they could come under the umbrella of a state's cultural policy regime.

Countries like France that were reasonably relaxed about free trade in manufactured goods and armaments were bitterly opposed to it in the cultural sphere. "National culture" had to be protected from "Americanization" – otherwise known as "cultural imperialism." So much the better if the "cultural industries" were defined as "national culture." It was one way to maintain a local audiovisual production industry in the face of international competition, even while the same protectionist countries were active in international commercial competition via companies like Vivendi (France) and Bertelsmann (Germany).

In Australia, the acceptance of the term "cultural industries" into state policy-making saw the conjoining of arts with communications and media in one federal portfolio. More recently IT has been added too, resulting in a Department of Communications, IT, and the Arts (DCITA). In the UK, another ministry took IT, but sport went in with culture and the arts, resulting in a Department of Culture, Media and Sport (DCMS). This take on the cultural industries helped justify continued regulation and subsidy, even as it became harder to use direct industry development arguments, with the forces of globalization working against the state "picking winners" and protecting industries from free trade flows.

But even the morally neutral use of the term "cultural industries" has proven limiting in the policy context, because it failed to *combine* art and culture, culture and creativity. It failed to take advantage of social, technological, and cultural changes that evolved in the cultural ecology and have continued to do so: "creative arts" remained one thing; "cultural industries" like media and movies remained another. Creative arts were a form of Veblenesque conspicuous waste; cultural industries a form of commercial exploitation. Never the twain could meet, because one side was "honorific," the other "utilitarian" at best.

## Public and Private Ownership

Modern media institutions have displayed a long-established distinction between **public** and **private ownership**, which was only challenged following the deregulatory politics of the Thatcher/Reagan era. In Europe and former colonial countries like India and Australia, although not in the USA and not in relation to the daily press, there was a strong tradition of public ownership of media going back to the invention of broadcasting in the 1920s. The rationale for such a regime was precisely civic – publicly owned media were thought to be needed to inform the citizen in the service of democratic debate and decision-making, and sometimes to counter an overly partisan (usually right-wing) commercial press. In many countries this argument was so successful that the entire range of broadcasting, not just news and current affairs, was held in public ownership in organizations such as the BBC (UK), ORTF (France), RAI (Italy), and so on. This meant that civic education extended to entertainment formats. And for many years it worked. Sitcoms like *Yes, Minister* in the UK proved conclusively that publicly funded civic education could be as entertaining as anything produced for a commercial market, a lesson that the BBC learnt in the 1940s during the popular heyday of radio. The long-running radio serial *The Archers*, which began life in that era as a slot for dramatized government advice to farmers, has survived as a national British institution in its own right. So much so that after the fall of the Soviet Union, the BBC and other broadcasters exported this expertise. Via schemes like the "Marshall Plan for the Mind" (bankrolled by George Soros) they made radio soap operas for civic education purposes in former Soviet countries, blurring the distinction between public and private, education and entertainment, as a first step to contemporary citizenship.

However, even in countries with strong public service broadcasting policies the grasp of government traditionally became more relaxed the further one went into the more obviously private world of fiction, fantasy, and fun. Thus film industries were rarely publicly owned in democratic countries, even where TV channels may have been. Totalitarian regimes were less squeamish about getting into private dreams as well as public affairs. The biggest film production facilities of the era began life as "public" (or rather state) instrumentalities: Mosfilm in Russia (nationalized in 1920, it became Mosfilm in 1935) and Cinecittà in Italy (1937) were founded to serve Stalin and Mussolini respectively. Latterly both had to navigate the deregulatory rapids from public to private ownership and transmogrify into contemporary corporations (see <http://www.cinecitta.com> and <http://www.mosfilm. ru/index.php?Lang=eng>).

In the USA, where there was no public ownership of media, there was still a clear understanding of the idea of the public, especially in relation to journalism. They may have been privately owned, but some of the most influential outlets – for example, the *Washington Post* and *New York Times* – have survived for decades and longer as "public good" organizations. And, at times of crisis, the entertainment media in general were quite happy to take on "public" responsibilities; such as Humphrey Bogart's wartime propaganda movies (of which *Casablanca* was only the best). Post-9/11, US politicians, including the governor of California, declared that commercial consumption itself was a patriotic act – citizens could oppose terrorism and a jittery stock market with brave and selfless shopping (see Uricchio 2004).

In creative arts, the distinction between public and private ownership is older and has been even more pronounced than in media, at the level of both institutional and discursive structures, because of the idea of "public arts" discussed above. To the publicly owned museums belonged fine art, while private life was served by commercial utilitarian, mechanical, or decorative arts.

Such public/private distinctions have never been stable, however, and there's every sign that in the post-broadcast era of mediated democracy the ground is shifting again. Various institutions that were once entirely in public hands, serving citizenship, have been privatized, and now serve consumers, including many national broadcasters in Europe like ORTF and RAI. Conversely, increasing public policy attention to the creative, content, and copyright industries is evidence that the state has begun to take new interest in these most private of enterprises. Meanwhile, commercial companies strive to be good corporate citizens and much of what any community would regard as public information passes through private channels.

## Consumption and Identity

As **consumers** we're presumed to be interested in comfort, beauty, and price; as **citizens** in freedom, truth, and justice. But freedom and comfort, truth and beauty, justice and price, have become ever more clearly integrated. The formation of self occurs at that point of integration: the experience of citizenship has begun to feel like the experience of the consumer.

In practice, and not just since deregulation, the powerful public/private distinction that has been evident in the structure of production (ownership and control) did not carry through so clearly to the experience of consumption. What people watched, listened to, and read was likely to be a mix of publicly and privately originated content, and in many cases they may not have been able to recognize the difference. Public corporations made you laugh while private companies taught you civics. Content originated in one regime was frequently distributed via the other; for example, news footage originated by the BBC was broadcast on commercial TV, especially internationally.

Nowadays individuals are addressed in all media as both consumers and citizens, both public and private. Media platforms that are all commercial one day may be all citizenship the next – as was the case with TV channels and the internet on September 11, 2001. That transformation was led by consumers, not simply imposed by public-spirited providers. For instance, on September 10, 2001 internet search engines were groaning under the usual weight of requests to know more about sex and Britney Spears. The next day their agenda had completely changed, to patriotic searches for the US flag and news about the terrible events and their perpetrators. Google was "private" one day, "public" the next, because millions of consumers made it so.

The pursuit of comfort has converged with the desire for freedom, to the extent that the consumer has accrued civil rights and public-sphere championship. Since the Ralph Nader era in the USA, a complex web of consumer rights has been established. Even in countries where the labor market is much more regulated than it is the USA, the public voice of the consumer protection regulator (e.g. Alan Fels in Australia or "Ofcom" in the UK) has more or less supplanted that of the union leader of the industrial period (e.g. Bob Hawke in Australia or Arthur Scargill in the UK).

Journalism, the textual system of public affairs, by means of which the modern public was discursively created, has for its part turned increasingly to "private life" and "non-news" forms, blurring the line between citizen and consumer still further by expanding news coverage beyond its standard diet of politics, business, culture, and public affairs to style, fashion, travel, home and garden, leisure and consumption. Celebrity – the textual form taken by identity in media – has colonized whole formats.

The drift from public culture to private life has been accompanied by a vigorous and extended struggle about **identity**. Throughout modernity various forms of identity politics have advanced their cause in the public domain, bringing into the realm of citizenship important attributes of what had until then been thought of as entirely private matters. Thus, for instance:

- **Gender** – women's rights, dating back to the suffragists at the turn to the twentieth century, through to various waves of feminism and the women's movement to date, and latterly men's rights activism too;
- **Ethnicity** – Indigenous and first peoples' rights, minority civil rights, Black Power, multiculturalism;
- **Sexuality** – gay, lesbian and transsexual rights;
- **Nationality** – rights for sub-national peoples such as the French in Canada, or the Welsh and Scots in the UK;
- **Age** – children's rights, youth rights, gray rights.

All of these rights had to be established by taking the identities and practices to which they referred out of the privacy of the bedroom, the family, and the community, and establishing in law and legislation that people's very identity – their subjectivity as persons not just their status as subjects of the state – was part of citizenship.

The ongoing struggle to achieve these outcomes, and also the often much more militant reaction and continuing opposition to them, were both recorded blow by blow in the media in both factual and fictional formats.

JOHN HARTLEY

Compulsively almost, over recent decades, the media made the struggle for and between identities its front-page story. In the process, news itself drifted from a concern with decision-makers (public policy) to an obsession with celebrities (private identity), and the private lives of public figures were regularly used to judge their political fitness. Identity, often in "bodily" form, irrupted into history. The politicization of private life and the personal has been a notable feature of the past couple of generations. It interconnected identity politics with other sectors of the so-called "new social movements," including the peace and environment movements. These too were initiated outside the traditional political sphere, gaining recruits, ideologies, leaders, and an activist agenda via commercial media and consumer events such as the record industry and rock festivals. Notions of citizenship, including rights and community obligations, began to infiltrate communicative networks ("netizens") and even taste cultures based on affinities for certain kinds of music or other aesthetic, cultural, or lifestyle domains. In each case, the boundary between citizen and consumer became harder to discern.

## The Emergence of the Creative Industries

Latterly a new term, **creative industries**, has emerged from this mix that exploits the fuzziness of the boundaries between "creative arts" and "cultural industries," freedom and comfort, public and private, state-owned and commercial, citizen and consumer, the political and the personal. It was partly a case of democratizing culture in the context of commerce: "my.democracy.com," as a 2001 advertisement for business consultants Accenture had it. And was also a case of creativity as an enterprise sector. Creative industries were the commercial, or commercializable, applications of creativity within a democratizing "republic of taste." "Creative industries" as a term emerged out of the political, cultural, and technological landscape of these times. It focused on the twin truths that (1) the core of "culture" was still creativity, but (2) creativity was produced, deployed, consumed, and enjoyed quite differently in post-industrial societies from the way it used to be in the time the earl of Shaftesbury.

This reconceptualization was a product not of the industry players themselves but of high-level public policy-making in countries and regions that wanted to win economic benefit from the IT and stock-market boom of the 1990s. However, the creative industries sector as a whole – however defined – proved to be a troublesome partner for both government and education institutions, which were more used to dealing with large-scale industries or well-organized professions. What they faced in the creative media especially was a market-oriented sector whose biggest players, especially television and

18

the daily press – normally the major creative industries in any city – generally sought to minimize their exposure to both government and formal education. Beyond these public policy-averse corporations, who owed more to head office in another city or country than to their local situation, the creative industries seemed to comprise a jumble of entities of radically differing scale: international corporate giants working the same turf as local micro-businesses – kid-in-garage at one end; AOL/TimeWarner at the other. Some enterprises were at the cutting edge, using technologies, skills, and business plans equal to any in the world, while others were rebadged subsidy-junkies from the community arts sector, and it was very hard to tell these types apart at the beginning of their career. Some providers were hopelessly dependent on bigger players, others were engaged in a game of provincial over-competitiveness, with all their energies focused on the local rival rather than on global opportunities. It was a disorganized Hobbesian universe, each entity at war with all the others, with no higher sense of organization or purpose.

Despite the difficulty of working with volatile, market-driven, mutually competitive and generally small-scale players, however, the advantages of developing creative industries seemed clear: jobs and GDP. The "creative industries" idea brought creativity from the back door of government, where it had sat for decades holding out the tin cup for arts subsidy – miserable, self-loathing and critical (especially of the hand that fed it), but unwilling to change – around to the front door, where it was introduced to the wealth-creating portfolios, the emergent industry departments, and the enterprise support programs. Win, win! Creative industries might help to revitalize cities and regions that had moved out of heavy industry (Scotland, England), or had never developed a strong manufacturing base (Queensland, New Zealand), or who were over-exposed to declining IT industries (Taiwan, Singapore). And at the same time they might transfer creativity itself from the spending departments – arts, education – to the Treasury, where the fruits of public investment in enterprise development would eventually be reaped via taxation.

## The New Economy and the Creative Industries

Why did policy-makers and educational institutions turn their attention to the creative industries, rather than to some other service sector? The answer to this was in the logic of the **new economy**. During the Clinton presidency the world economy – especially its American "locomotive"– appeared to be completing an epoch-making shift from manufacturing industry to consumer services. Value came not from processing *things* (e.g. steel into automobiles) but *information* (e.g. computer-operating systems). Where the stock market had once been dominated by companies like General Motors and General Electric, it came to be dominated by Microsoft and giant telcos. Technology played a leading role in this shift, underpinning the development of what became the "Information Society." And indeed, information technology was migrating out of organizations and into people's homes, cars, and pockets. Society as a whole, not just the stock market, was saturated with information based on code.

During the mechanical manufacturing era of the twentieth century, a company like IBM (International Business Machines) prospered by making mechanical information-processing machines like typewriters and comptometers. IBM dominated the early period of computer technology too, with giant mainframes like the 360-50 and 360-65, which sent humans to the moon. "Big Blue's" dominance appeared unassailable. In those days, among computer companies across the world, it was said to be a case of "IBM and the seven dwarfs." IBM even entered the cultural consciousness of the age via Stanley Kubrick's dysfunctional computer Hal (whose name is I, B, M, shifted one letter to H, A, L) in *2001: A Space Odyssey*.

IBM was essentially a "b2b" (business-to-business) company – its computers were designed for organizations to use, not for retail to individual consumers. Despite its international corporate dominance, its self-image, customer-base, and business plan had not evolved from the manufacturing era. Eventually IBM's very existence was threatened, and Bill Gates became the richest person in the world after the Sultan of Brunei, by challenging this view of information. Microsoft promoted the idea of the personal computer or PC, not only for individual workers within an organization, with the result that everyone had the equivalent of a mainframe on their desk in the office, but for the retail and consumer market too. And what made Bill Gates rich was not that he manufactured the computers – other firms did that – but that Microsoft controlled the operating system inside – wealth was created from information, not manufacturing.

*Infrastructure → Connectivity → Content → Creativity*

These moves coincided with a larger shift in economic activity from goods to services, from producers to consumers. For a while it seemed enough. The boom sector was IT. Everyone was investing in IT **infrastructure**, which in effect meant computing power at the command of every individual in an organization: a PC on every desk. Through the 1990s there was an astonishing and eventually unsustainable level of investment to achieve just this by firms and other organizations in government and education throughout the developed world.

But infrastructure was not enough. Upon it was built the next level of the IT economy – **connectivity**. This was the stage that evolved "IT" to "ICTs," adding "communications" to "information" and pluralizing the "technologies." Here the goal was not computing power but interactivity: computers that could talk to each other. Again, the success of connectivity in the marketplace was phenomenal – this was the period when the telcos, the internet, the World Wide Web, email, chat rooms, MOOs, MUDs, and other manifestations of interactivity gained popular as well as corporate acceptance.

At this point it became clear that connectivity had unleashed what looked like almost infinite opportunity for **content**. It was here, at a third level of development in the IT boom, that *creativity* became a market asset. The progression from infrastructure through connectivity to content was an investment strategy as much as a technological trajectory. Companies that provided infrastructure were the first giants of the IT revolution; then connectivity brought the telcos to the fore – Microsoft then Nokia. The shift from connectivity to content was symbolized in the – subsequently troubled – merger of two of the biggest corporate players: AOL (America On-Line) and TimeWarner.

The dot.com crash of 2000 was in its own way a driver toward a further focus on content. The infrastructure market had matured – businesses began to feel that they may have over-invested in IT, and market growth (if any) relied on equipment rollover not expansion. Soon the IT industry was shedding jobs. Meanwhile, the overall stock-market boom had generated more investment capital than people knew what to do with, and much of it went into irrational and unsustainable schemes that sought to emulate early connectivity successes: Yahoo, Hotmail, Amazon, Ebay, Google. Indeed, the "bubble" was in share prices and take-over figures; few if any of these companies made a trading profit throughout this period. After the crash it was clear that connectivity was no longer the key to instant riches.

Content and **creativity** were a better long-term bet. It was evident that information – IT and code – was no longer a driver of economic activity by itself. People were interested in ideas and knowledge rather than information as such, and in experience rather than connectivity alone. Those who wanted to build viable enterprises on top of the now mature levels of infrastructure and connectivity included producers and brokers of creative content. The "new economy" retained certain characteristics that made this an attractive direction for policy-makers. Costs of access for new entrants were not prohibitive as they were in broadcasting, and literally anyone could play, allowing marginal individuals, regions, and countries to hitch their locality to the world economy. In this context, locally specific skills, ideas, and heritage were valuable means to stand out in the pack. So although the new economy was characterized by "weightlessness" and innovation, there were also new opportunities for local culture and enterprise, including music, Indigenous arts, or locally based craft skills to support global industries, such as fashion in Italy. Conversely, some new economy enterprises like the games industry could follow lifestyle choices rather than needing to rely on local infrastructure or markets, and so it showed decidedly non-metropolitan tendencies, with significant producers on the Gold Coast in Australia, attracted by lifestyle, and major consumer uptake and innovation in Korea, for instance.

## Public Policy

At this point the "creative industries" came to be seen as a worthwhile investment in **public policy**. The term was picked up in diverse settings and adapted to meet various national and regional agendas. The way in which the idea traveled to countries like Taiwan, Hong Kong, and Singapore indicated its expanding usefulness in describing changes and priorities not previously named, which perhaps bore little relation to the origins of the term itself in the "third way" strategies of the Australian Keating and British Blair governments of the mid-1990s (Howkins, in this volume). Taiwan, for instance, launched its creative industries strategy in 2003 after the return of the relevant minister from a fact-finding trip not to London or Sydney but to France. Taiwan was looking to diversify its economy and strengthen its cultural output – from indigenous cultural expression to games. In Korea, the term described linkages between government and big business, which also provided infrastructure for local content production. In Hong Kong the effort was to maintain a well-regarded film and television industry. Singapore attempted to embellish its world-class infrastructure with quality content which it sought to encourage at the education level. In New Zealand the focus was on screen production and national branding. In Queensland it was movies and games. National policies in Australia focused on broadband content and the articulation of creative applications into health, education, and business services. In the US and Europe, where the term itself had enjoyed less strategic application, the components and characteristics that came under the creative industries received ongoing attention – innovation, IP, local cultural outputs, etc.

What this means is that the creative industries should be seen as a useful idea to investigate and explain, even where it has not been taken up directly (as yet). It illustrates some of the most important recent changes in consumption and production, in global flows of capital and culture. And while it has its corporate aspect, the creative industries idea allows for a broadening of participation in the possibilities offered by new interactive media in the so-called new economy. It can mean new cultural engagement rather than homogenization, a chance to contribute, participate, and challenge. It means seeing success in collaboration and ingenuity rather than big business and capital. However, this is dependent upon a supportive environment and education.

## Consumption and Production

Most advanced economies have witnessed a major turn from manufacturing industry to consumer-led enterprises. The creative industries are "services" where the **consumer** is causal. They don't present themselves for analysis in a way that fits with accepted understandings of **manufacturing industry**. In the past, industry has been depicted as:

- large-scale enterprise (creative industries are often micro-businesses or SMEs)
- industrially organized (creative industries are organized around the project not the factory or office)
- led by entrepreneurs (creative industries are consumer-led – not to mention the number of creative businesses based on individual artists such as musicians, producer-directors, authors, etc.)
- where production is the key to added value (creative industries harvest value from the consumption end of the value chain)
- in a defined sector of the economy (creative industries are increasingly dispersed into other service sectors: finance, health, education, government).

The creative industries are so varied in scale, organization, and sector of economic activity that they are barely recognizable as a coherent object of analysis within this framework. As a result, they don't always show up well in the places where industry policy is habitually discussed, in government or in business. Such forums are organized around an image of industry, and business more generally, that is devoted to the entrepreneur as the cause and agent of economic success. "Emergent industry" policies, business forums, tax breaks, lobbyists, and consultants are concentrated around these figures – they're the ones whose talents are valued, nurtured, competed for, and often subsidized.

In this model consumers are not seen as causal. They exist only in relation to the entrepreneur via the cash nexus; they are treated as the effects not the agents of business success. They are the province of marketing executives, not development agencies or even most CEOs. The technologies that have grown up to understand and influence consumers belong to marketing not manufacturing, and the fundamental discipline that still rules the roost in marketing is psychology. In other words entrepreneurs "act," but consumers "behave." Industries "make," but consumers "use." The trick is to get consumers to recognize that they need whatever it is you're capable of offering. They're the desirable other.

This psychological model of markets doesn't work simply (or simply doesn't work) in the creative industries. Indeed, the creative industries offer a compelling reason for revising that model wherever it still holds sway. Where the consumer remains a separate category that is understood via psychological methods, no matter how sophisticated the understanding gets, while "industry" is courted in terms of action and productivity, then something fundamental has been missed. For the consumer has evolved. She is no longer Vance Packard's easily distracted housewife who needs to be propelled by psychologically tested methods of behavior management toward a particular shelf in the supermarket. She is "a thinking, emotional, creative being" (Howkins, in this volume) and she expresses this in the way she designs her life. As much as she is a consumer, she is also a citizen. Her desire for freedom (citizen) goes hand in hand with her desire for comfort (consumer).

The creative industries can only be understood when we dump the behavioral model of the consumer, and instead begin an analysis that is sited on consumption as much as production – but consumption as action, not behavior. It is a theme that runs through this book. JC Herz describes the army of citizens who contribute to games development through their use and participation. Alternative styles are taken up by the mainstream. Cities reinvent and market themselves through the tastes and culture of their citizens. In all of these examples, consumption is part of the creative industries cycle rather than its destination.

## Education

One aspect of the creative industries that isn't often mentioned in policy discourse is the extent of their reliance on **education**. Not only are "workers by brain" needed in much higher proportion here than in other sectors, but so is R&D, and in cities where there are large numbers of students and educational workers there is also a large concentration of people who are trend-conscious, early adopters, curious about the new, and relatively unencumbered by family commitments. In short, here are customers as well as recruits for creative industries, which cluster in neighborhoods also favored by students because both are looking for cheap rents and have the confidence to take their culture where they go rather than venturing only into suburbs designed for them. Universities are not just destinations, but hubs, and young people with time on their hands who are just hanging around are just as important to the creative sector as more traditional forms of investment (Leadbeater 1999; Florida 2002; Hartley 2003: 69–77).

Educational institutions are routinely excluded from policy discourse because they're not understood as "industry partners," even where they contribute substantially to the revenues of a city or town. In many countries the fact that they are funded or supported from the public purse means that other departments of government – emergent industry sections especially – find them hard to deal with for fear of "double dipping" or granting state funding to state-funded organizations. But in fact education is a major player in the creative industries, both directly, in producing creative personnel, products, and services, and indirectly, by providing employment for many who can then use that security to support their "creative habit" in a multitude of different fields.

Internally, universities are grappling with the question of whether and how they can educate for the new economy. Traditional large-class teaching based on the provision of standardized knowledge is modeled on industrial production and labor, but there are definite moves in another direction. Teaching creative specialists is a model, because there's much to learn in addition to nurturing and training individual talent in some branch of design, performance, production, and writing. Creative workers need to learn how to manage a career which is likely not to be with a single employer or even the same industry for life, but to be a "portfolio" career, self-employed, freelance or casualized, project-based, part-time, working in teams with multiple partners who change over time. They need to understand an international environment with changing cultural, technical, and business imperatives, where continuing education is necessary, project management a core skill, and their own "life design" an increasing priority. They need to be mindful of the fact that entry-level "workforce" jobs (editing copy) are quite different from aspired-to destinations (editing *Vogue*), which are themselves very different from "wealth-creating" positions (owning Condé Nast). Learning itself is "just-in-time," outcome-oriented, continuing, self-motivated, and self-monitored, and increasingly sought from commercial learning services rather than from traditional certification institutions with disciplinary silos and a "provider" mentality. All this requires a response from formal education; major changes in pedagogy, curriculum, assessment, and the experience of education for both teachers and learners. Instead of seeing students as not quite fully-formed persons, betraying a "lack" or "need" that can be remedied by providing them with knowledge that is in the authorized possession of the professional, learning becomes a creative experience driven by the student herself. It's a transformation with high stakes: "It's not a country's size, its population, endowments of raw materials or even access to technology" that limit "social processes of learning and creativity" as Charles Leadbeater has argued. "The vital constraints are in our hands, and depend on how we organize ourselves to spread education and promote creativity, entrepreneurship and innovation" (Leadbeater 2003).

## Defining the Creative Industries

Perhaps because they don't fit the model of entrepreneur-led industrial enterprises with behavioral consumers, the "creative industries" have proven to be shy birds, not drawing attention to the fact that they may constitute an entirely new species of cultural and economic enterprise. This may simply be a matter of their relative youthfulness in this regard: at this stage of their development they wear the self-effacing plumage of the chick rather than gaudily self-advertising their fully-fledged productive glory. In fact (if I may be allowed an Australian comparison) they're more "tawney frogmouth" than "rainbow lorikeet" – which simply means that if you look at them directly you might have a hard time seeing them at all. The creative industries, in short, have been rather slow to *name themselves* as such.

Is this because no such sector can be identified, or are they perhaps an emergent entity whose shape and extent has yet to be properly mapped and understood, even by the people involved? In fact it is public institutions in government and education that have made the early running in identifying the creative industries, not the industries themselves. They are like perturbations on the surface of the landscape that cannot be discerned by the apparently obvious method of walking over them and having a look. Their shape, interrelationships, and trends can only be observed from a bird's-eye view, where larger patterns can be seen. To understand them you need to get above the horizons of those most closely involved.

### Industry

They're not like old-style industries, which could be named easily after what they produced: the steel industry, automobile industry, airline industry, because industrially, creativity is an input not an output. It's not even completely clear where creative industries might be slotted into the chain of primary (farming and mining), secondary (manufacturing), and tertiary (service) industries. Creative products and processes are found across all of them, and although creative industries have most in common with the services sector, the value of what they make and supply is not readily captured by comparison with professional or remedial services like accountancy or laundries, which has led some to talk of an "experience economy" that goes beyond the tertiary sector.

## The organization

People apply their individual talent to the creation of something else (including steel, automobiles, airlines). Creativity is not confined to one industry, and what it means in engineering, education, health, or finance may differ markedly from what it means in fashion or entertainment or to a phone company. So businesses are slow to identify it as their defining characteristic, even among those most obviously devoted to creative products, like publishing and media. In short, the "creative industries" cannot be identified at the level of the *organization*.

## The association

Creative businesses have proven slow to recognize common interest with other creative enterprises. Unlike the automobile industry, for example, which has a well-developed set of national and international associations of manufacturers and traders, the creative industries have not formed cartels or lobby organizations in which the interests of each are understood and promoted to government and the public as the interests of all. Publishers don't see what they have in common with gaming companies, who have little contact with newspaper owners, who can't stand the sight of creative artists, who disdain theme parks, whose operators actually employ creative performers, designers, and writers but who see themselves as belonging to quite a different industry (tourism).

Organizations do crop up that are devoted to exploiting the interests of different industries, including creative ones. But their purpose may not be to promote creativity as such. An example is the American Coalition of Service Industries, founded in 1982 "to ensure that US trade in services, once considered outside the scope of US trade negotiations, would become a central goal of future trade liberalization initiatives" (<http://www.uscsi.org/about/>). It lobbies "aggressively" for the liberalization of world trade in

JOHN HARTLEY

forums like the WTO, NAFTA, and GATS, to press the advantage of American companies across a wide range of services – an incoherent but presumably pragmatic amalgam of the interests of their subscribers, but one which clearly overlaps the creative industries with other services:

> travel, transportation, air freight, energy, financial, insurance, advertising, health care, legal, accounting, telecom, construction, engineering, architectural, information technology, tax, education, electronic commerce, environmental (<http://www.uscsi.org/>)

## The statistician

Official statistics in most countries, which all parties in government, business, the academy and the community need to rely upon to identify, quantify and track any economic sector, have not isolated and mapped the creative industries sector as such. The relevant activities appear under a series of other, overlapping categories, including arts, leisure, sport, culture, services, media, and the like. Furthermore, there is as yet little agreement within individual countries, let alone internationally, about which activities should count and how they should be counted: methodologically the creative industries are very fuzzy. As for their scope and extent, no commonly accepted baseline has been established using reasonably rigorous research, as opposed to "boosterist" business development rhetoric, to determine whether they're growing, in which regions, and at what rate (Oakley 2004).

## The person

Creativity can be found just about anywhere that people do, make, or think things. Everyone is creative. But, just because everyone (more or less) can cook an egg, sew on a button, and think, it does not follow that everyone is a chef, a tailor, or an intellectual. The same applies to creativity. Everyone's got it, but only some *function socially* – by means of their employment, vocation or calling – to create economic or cultural value from it. The social function of creativity is achieved not by individuals being creative, but only where such persons find places where access, capital, infrastructure, regulation, markets, property rights, and large-scale processes can monetize that creativity. Individual artists, musicians, designers, and writers – the stars of stage, screen, and studio – are the most obvious beneficiaries of the social organization of creativity, but they don't determine its shape or structure, and most identify with their particular craft rather than with the industry as a whole.

## The worker

**Creative workers** include a vast multi-national workforce of talented people applying their individual creativity in design, production, performance, and writing. They range from fashion designers in Milan to shoe-factory operatives in Indonesia. They do the work of combining creativity and value. But historically creative workers have been very weakly unionized, usually around mutually divided specialist occupational groups – journalists, screen actors, technicians, printers, and the like. Something like a unified workforce is emerging among creative professionals, so that an individual with the right talents, a freelance designer for instance, might gain employment in more than one industry. But these workers have very little bargaining power, beyond the laws of supply and demand, operating as self-employed satellite suppliers of professional or technical services. And the factories which make creative products, from sportswear to animation, tend to be located in developing countries with weak labor protection. So although the creative industries may be integrating at the level of workforce, that workforce is increasingly casual, part-time, freelance, and relying on a "portfolio" career with many jobs and employers, and it is increasingly internationalized too, so that individual workers see little common cause with each other (McRobbie, and Miller et al., in this volume).

## The user

Creativity is very much in the eye of the beholder – the economist Richard Caves asserts that "innovation" in the creative industries comprises nothing more mysterious than novelty-seeking consumers "changing their minds" about what they like (Caves 2000). The consumer (or market, more accurately) is "sovereign" to the extent that the *value* of creativity as an input can't be gauged until it is used. Publishers and media companies don't know in advance which one of their creative works will be this season's hit, or flop. Consumers are the vital determinant of success, but they play very little direct part in the productive process. Users are more prominent in some sectors, such as games and interactive software, than in others, such as movies, and this trend is widening. But the creative industries can't be recognized as such at the level of the user.

## Creative industries defined from the outside

In these circumstances, there has been little incentive for people in particular structural positions to scope out the overall situation – both industrial and international – in a systematic way, and few industry-based organizations were capable of doing the job. If there was to be a sense of purpose, strategic direction, and development in the creative industries, it had to come from the outside. One reason for making such an attempt is that there are so many terms in play that the untutored observer would be forgiven for thinking that this was a field characterized only by category confusion. But in fact the confusion is more apparent than real – it results from the different perspective of various players. A report for the National Office for the Information Economy in Australia summarized the different usage adopted in different analytical contexts (see figure 1).

In Singapore, an interesting attempt was made to integrate the cultural, creative, and copyright industries by showing them in relation to the value chain – where the cultural industries are clustered around the point of origination, while the copyright industries extend to the distribution industries, with the creative industries somewhere in between. The resulting pyramid would have an even wider base if it included "service" as well as "distribution" industries, but it would also require the extension of the creative industries into that base (see figure 2).

| Creative Industries | Copyright Industries | Content Industries | Cultural Industries | Digital Content |
|---|---|---|---|---|
| *largely characterized by nature of labour inputs: 'creative individuals'* | *defined by nature of asset and industry output* | *defined by focus of industry production* | *defined by public policy function and funding* | *defined by combination of technology and focus of industry production* |
| Advertising Architecture Design Interactive software Film and TV Music Publishing Performing arts | Commercial art Creative arts Film and video Music Publishing Recorded media Data-processing Software | Pre-recorded music Recorded music Music retailing Broadcasting and film Software Multimedia services | Museums and galleries Visual arts and crafts Arts education Broadcasting and film Music Performing arts Literature Libraries | Commercial art Film and video Photography Electronic games Recorded media Sound recording Information storage and retrieval |
| *Source*: NOIE 2003. | | | | |

**Figure 1.** What are the creative industries – category confusion or focus of analysis?

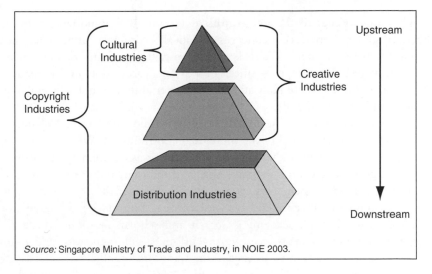

Source: Singapore Ministry of Trade and Industry, in NOIE 2003.

**Figure 2.** The value chain of content industries

## How To Read This Book

It is at this point that the idea of the present book becomes useful. The question that eludes those in the thick of the action – "What and where are the **creative industries**?" – can be answered, at least provisionally. The book brings together various perspectives that, taken together, begin to map the conceptual terrain within which the active players mentioned above are operating. That terrain is far from settled, and like any new enclosure its boundaries, occupants, and uses have all been contested.

This introduction has emphasized the historical and contingent nature of the idea of the creative industries, but the sections and readings that follow are not organized chronologically. The sections zoom in progressively from "human" or universal perspectives on creativity to a more narrowly economic focus – from the world, identity, and creative practice, through the city and region, to the level of the enterprise and the creative economy.

In **intellectual** terms, this strategy corresponds with what Rita Felski has written about the *appeal* of cultural studies as a field of inquiry – the "amalgam of concerns, the simultaneous and sometimes contradictory emphasis on both the particular and the universal" (Felski 1998: 169). She recommends a *pragmatic* rather than a *positioned* approach, resulting in "politically informed eclectic scholarship that includes both specific, empirical studies and broader, more speculative approaches." Such an approach is appropriate for this book, which applies it both in the argumentation and in the evidential aspects.

The same applies to the **geographical** terrain. It is important to move between global ("universal") concerns and local ("particular") difference, not to choose between them. We seek to demonstrate that many regions in the world, not just the European-American axis, are participants in the changes we trace, and not as mere illustrations of a universal theme, but as irreducibly "particular" objects of study.

Another such aspect is the **interdisciplinary** and inter-sectoral character of the book as a whole and of the individual contributions. We have sourced material "pragmatically" rather than on the basis of its disciplinary "position," choosing good writers on important aspects of the topic rather than a succession of like-minded disciplinary clones. Because part of the argument is that creative industries fuzzy some well-established boundaries we have not selected materials from academic research and scholarship alone; there are also policy writers, activists, creative practitioners, commentators, and journalists. Nor have we wanted to restage the traditional conflict between "critical" and "celebratory," "left" and "right," "corporate" and "community" positions. Each of these is represented here, but not in order to defeat an opponent. Instead, the book attempts to appeal to readers across a range of specialisms. Whether such an approach constitutes a "new paradigm" remains to be seen, but in the meantime what it says is of interest to – and in the interests of – people in business administration, communication, creative arts, cultural studies, economics, geography, IT, media studies, sociology, and urban studies, as well as non-academic readers interested in business and policy as well as creativity. If there is in the creative world itself a "convergence" and even "integration" among economics, creativity, expression, and production then the framework of explanation needs to reflect that convergence.

Naturally, such a project presents its difficulties, not the least of which is the wide disparity of **disciplinary languages**, methods, assumptions, anecdotes, and allusions that any reader will have to navigate. In order to facilitate the translatability of contributions from across the disciplinary divide we've done our best to find (and practice) accessible writing as well as good analysis. The "silo" that contains each disciplinary, intellectual, and creative specialism also notoriously keeps all the others out. These mental silos, which have served modern disciplines for a long time and are harder to dismantle than anyone wants, nevertheless have to be breached and interconnected in order to understand the nature and scope of the changes we're mapping. Some version of a **vernacular** language is required where a "convergence" between different ways of seeing, speaking, and learning is desired.

Silos exist in the **industrial** landscape too. Indeed, the creative industries sometimes look like a collection of silos with little in common. The difficulties associated with the AOL–TimeWarner merger stand as an important lesson in how incommensurate cultures grow up in different specialist areas. But still, a taxonomy that simply lists creative industries in their existing silo-fortresses – *Advertising, Architecture, Arts and antiques market, Crafts, Design, Designer Fashion, Film, Interactive Leisure Software, Music, Performing Arts, Publishing, Software, Television and Radio, Heritage, Hospitality, Museums and Galleries, Sport and Tourism* (DCMS 2001) – pre-empts any attempt to understand how things may be changing and what interconnections may already be forging among them. So here again the book adopts the strategy of moving between the "particular" (individual sectors like fashion or music) and the "universal" (the creative industries as a whole), because the categories overspill into each other and into the wider knowledge economy. There's little to be gained by describing the creative industries one by one.

The readings and perspectives selected here are symptomatic of the field as it has developed to date. There are encouraging signs that a phase of critical analysis has already begun, using these materials as the basis for discussion (see *IJCS* 2004). In time such critical reworking will in turn feed back to the activities of those working in the field as academics, policy-makers, or cultural entrepreneurs, at which point a more integrated conceptualization of the creative industries may emerge.

In the field of cultural and media studies there has been a shift over the years in the analytical attention devoted variously to *production, content,* and *reception* in creative media. This book does not try to choose a primary or causal site among these, or to argue a shift from one research preoccupation to another. Instead, it aims show how content-creation itself links production, distribution, and consumption, and that each plays a distinctive role in determining outcomes. The creative industries idea recognizes that economic (production) and audience (consumer) issues are crucial to the understanding of creativity (content), and that each of these areas plays some causal role in each of the others.

# The Sections

The readings are grouped into six sections, each edited and introduced by a member of the editorial team (all of whom are colleagues at QUT Creative Industries Faculty, the first of its kind in Australia and perhaps internationally). Each section encompasses a different aspect of the creative industries, beginning with broad issues of society and the self (**world, identities, practices**), and developing toward the areas that have taken center stage in creative industries policy (**cities, enterprises, economy**).

I **Creative World**, introduced by Ellie Rennie, with readings from Lawrence Lessig, Graham Meikle, Geert Lovink, and Néstor García-Canclini

The readings in the first section, "Creative World," describe the emergence of a creative ecology that reaches beyond formal definitions of the creative industries. The creative spaces described in this section are only just beginning to be named and theorized, yet they speak of the context, use and transformative capacity of creativity as an organizing principle. These include the spaces of the amateur, the alternative, and local communities. Seeing these as sites for creative opportunity questions the marginal status that they have been dealt in the past and opens up new possibilities for social and economic regeneration.

II **Creative Identities**, introduced by John Hartley, with readings from John Howkins, Charles Leadbeater, Richard Florida, and Toby Miller et al.

The creative industries are grounded in personal ideas, talent, experience, and work – and those personal attributes are important right through the value chain from source to destination. This requires attention not just to the creativity of the artist (see next section) but also of the consumer, understood not as a set of behaviors caused by more or less successful corporate and marketing stimuli, but as an autonomous, communicative, interactive citizen whose identity, personality, experiences, and labor are the ground upon which the creative industries are nurtured. Identity itself has become a major focus of political, cultural, and business activity over the past half-century. It has been expressed as much in cultural expression and commercial entertainment as in traditional civic terms. The readings in this section focus on how identity and creativity have intersected in commercial democracies. They explore how attributes of identity – ideas, know-how, experience, and the work of consumption – connect (or not) with commercial enterprise in a knowledge economy.

III **Creative Practices**, introduced by Brad Haseman, with readings from Umberto Eco, Janet H. Murray, Ken Robinson, Luigi Maramotti, and Jane Roscoe

The "Creative Practices" section casts a net across the diverse activities and disciplines which fall within the creative industries. After an introduction which seeks to rewrite the often hostile relationship between the arts, the cultural industries, and the creative industries, the section then characterizes the predominant forms and creative processes in play – from fashion to film, from the BBC to the DVD. The readings included in this section have been selected because they offer evidence and argument to support the claim that five distinctive attributes are inflecting the creative practices of our age. As these attributes become more pronounced they will become the drivers to unsettle even further the categories and definitions which once comfortably accounted for and explained what artists and other creative workers did at work and how they did (or didn't) earn their daily bread.

IV  **Creative Cities**, introduced by Jinna Tay, with readings from Charles Landry, Justin O'Connor, Michael E. Porter, and Ackbar Abbas

The "Creative Cities" section focuses on four cities – London, St. Petersburg, Shanghai, and Hong Kong. It is organized around two thematic strands. First, there is the status of cities in the world; global, regional, and emerging. Each selected reading (apart from Michael Porter's) relates to one of these categories, which also convey a sense of the developmental/planning aspect surrounding cities. Second, a global/local tension takes shape in the move from general to specific examples, played out on cityscapes. The section also addresses the need to balance the competing claims of developmental cultural policies and grass-roots problems. The articles work to convey a sense of "uses of creativity" in city studies, and the local strategies that are co-opted by cities, communities, and individuals in working toward sharing and renewing their city.

V  **Creative Enterprises**, introduced by Stuart Cunningham, with readings from Charles Leadbeater and Kate Oakley, Henry Jenkins, and JC Herz

This section makes an argument for considering the creative enterprise from the viewpoint of policy and industry development perspectives. Taking both a descriptive and normative approach, it divides the policy and industry development perspectives into "culture," "services," and "knowledge." Part of the challenge of the concept of creative industries is that it is addressing the shift from seeing creativity as principally embodied in cultural activity ("culture") to perceiving mainstream industry sectors as increasingly influenced or indeed driven by creative inputs ("services"). So much so good; but the additional wrinkle is the emerging trend stries      to regard creative enterprises – or at least certain high-tech sectors such as games – as R&D-based innovators that should be treated like the new sciences and information technology ("knowledge").

VI   **Creative Economy**, introduced by Terry Flew, with readings from Jeremy Rifkin, Angela McRobbie, and Shalini Venturelli

The "Creative Economy" section begins with a discussion of how the concept of a creative economy can be seen as bringing together creative industries discourses with those surrounding the knowledge economy. It reflects on the impact of the dot.com crash of the early 2000s, but notes that theories that we are now in a "new economy" rest upon more intellectually robust foundations than the more "boosterish" prognoses about the impact of information technologies that gained currency during the late 1990s boom in technology stocks. The rise of a creative economy is related to what has been termed the "culturalization of economic life," as well as the turn toward networked organizations and the revaluing of creativity as an input into wealth creation in the global economy. At the same time, it critically reflects upon the often precarious existence that creative people have in increasingly flexible labor markets. The section concludes with a discussion of the relationship of creative industries to cultural policy and the globalization of cultural markets. It is observed that public investment in the promotion of creative activity is increasingly being seen, not through the modernist prism of preserving national cultures, but as a part of local and regional innovation strategies in the global creative economy.

## Reading Against the Grain

Recurring themes and questions are present within the creative industries literature and its critique. We have not attempted to resolve all of these questions, but to draw attention to them as areas for further investigation. Because many cut across the sections in this book, the following "reader's guide" is intended to help you to navigate your way through various issues by reference to the chapters which address them:

*What is the role of government and policy in shaping the creative industries and how does this activity structure and intervene in the cultural sphere?*

- Howkins – the scope of the creative industries
- Canclini – national cultural policy shaping local creative activities
- O'Connor – difficulties in transferring policies to different geographical settings
- Landry – challenges and guidelines for creative city development
- Leadbeater and Oakley – supporting "creative entrepreneurs"
- Cunningham – comparative approach to policy models for creative enterprise

*What is the relationship between not-for-profit and commercial activity in the creative industries?*

- Rennie – the role of the amateurs and activists in the development of creative industries
- JC Herz – consumers as producers: armies of users contributing to commercial products
- Meikle – activist, non-profit activity
- Lovink – a new media center as a strategy for economic growth in a developing country setting

*The creative industries are not evenly distributed across the globe, or in terms of demographics. How have factors such as ethnicity and generation influenced the rise of the creative industries historically? What is the relationship of creative industries to cultural diversity?*

- Porter – distribution of creative activity more effective in clusters
- Hartley ("creative identities") – diversity of identity required for creative industries development, and the role of consumers
- Florida – "creative class" depicted as an affluent, young demographic
- McRobbie – creative workers need to be young, single, and able to freelance. This raises new industrial relations issues and disenfranchises some from the benefits of the creative economy
- Canclini – trade agreements and ethnicity
- Venturelli – prospects for overcoming global inequality

*The arts are not the subject of this book and so are not covered systematically – for instance dance and publishing are neglected. However, traditional live arts like theatre appear alongside contemporary entertainment such as games or* Big Brother.

- Hartley ("Creative Industries") – history of the shift from creative arts to creative industries

- Haseman – case study on the live arts of Robert Lepage
- Eco – the creative process in the production of artworks
- O'Connor – St. Petersburg's tradition of high culture in conflict with creative industries initiatives
- Murray – digital TV
- Maramotti – fashion
- Roscoe – *Big Brother*
- Jenkins – computer games

*What is the "new economy," and is a theory of globalization and cosmopolitanism important in understanding the creative industries?*

- Tay
- Abbas
- Porter
- Flew
- Leadbeater
- Rifkin
- Venturelli

*How do the creative industries fit within traditional political economy debates, for instance, concerns over ownership and control and cultural homogenization?*

- Miller et al.
- McRobbie

*What is the importance of education and training?*

- Hartley ("Creative Industries")
- Robinson
- Lessig

This book's own architecture is intended to show how the creative industries can be understood as an interdisciplinary nexus, bringing multiple voices to consider the question of how creative talent and industrial scale can be organized, combined, and used for social and economic development. It is thus something of a "narrative of progress," and doubtless there will always be reasons to be skeptical about that, but at the same time it does seem important to think about how new developments in business, government, and technology can be used to "enfranchise" more people, regions, and activities than were served by the industrial and service economies.

If it seems to you that despite the diversity of opinion and position among the 30-odd contributions the book as a whole feels over-optimistic, then perhaps that is because its purpose is to explore the *capacity* of this new system, not simply to point out the pitfalls. Even where serious problems remain, what Charles Leadbeater calls "militant optimism" is required, because creative innovation offers more hope than did the totalizing utopias of left and right in the twentieth century (Leadbeater 2002: 328–53). Innovation depends upon diversity, openness, social and global interdependence, cumulative (not revolutionary) progress, and experimentation (including failure, mess, and disequilibrium). But these components of hope all entail uncertainty: "constant innovation makes the world uncertain, unsettled and unpredictable. We can only have hope because society is unfinished, still developing and learning. That in turn means that we have to endure uncertainty about what might be in store" (Leadbeater 2002: 348–9). The tenor of this book, then, is an attempt at Leadbeater's "politics of hope." That is how the idea of the creative industries feels at this stage in its development – an impression that may need to be corrected in later editions.

# References

Adorno, T. and M. Horkheimer (1997 [1947]) *Dialectic of Enlightenment.* Verso, London.

Barrell, J. (1986) *The Political Theory of Painting from Reynolds to Hazlitt: "The Body of the Public."* Yale University Press, New Haven.

Carey, J. (1992) *The Intellectuals and the Masses.* Faber & Faber, London.

Castells, M. (2000) *The Information Age: Economy, Society and Culture*, 3 vols (millennium edn). Blackwell, Oxford and Malden, Mass.

Caves, R. (2000) *Creative Industries: Contracts between Art and Commerce.* Harvard University Press, Cambridge, Mass.

Couldry, N. (2004) The Productive "Consumer" and the Dispersed "Citizen." *International Journal of Cultural Studies* 7(1).

DCMS (2001) *Creative Industries: Mapping Document 2001.* Department of Culture, Media and Sport. HMSO, London, <http://www.culture.gov.uk/creative/mapping.html>.

Felski, R. (1998) Images of the Intellectual: From Philosophy to Cultural Studies. *Continuum: Journal of Media and Cultural Studies* 12(2), 157–71.

Florida, R. (2002) *The Rise of the Creative Class.* Basic Books, New York.

Hartley, J. (1996) *Popular Reality: Journalism, Modernity, Popular Culture.* Arnold, London.

Hartley, J. (1999) *Uses of Television.* Routledge, London and New York.

Hartley, J. (2003) *A Short History of Cultural Studies.* Sage Publications, London.

Howkins, J. (2001) *The Creative Economy: How People Make Money from Ideas*. Penguin, London.

*IJCS* (2004) *The New Economy, Creativity and Consumption*. Special issue of the *International Journal of Cultural Studies* 7(1). Sage Publications, London.

Kagan, R. (2003) *Paradise and Power: America and Europe in the New World Order*. Atlantic Books, London; Knopf, New York.

Leadbeater, C. (1999) *Living on Thin Air: The New Economy*. Viking, London.

Leadbeater, C. (2002) *Up the Down Escalator: Why the Global Pessimists Are Wrong*. Viking, London.

Leadbeater, C. (2003) Seeing the Light. *RSA Journal* 5505 (February), 28–33.

Miller, T. (2004) A View From A Fossil: The New Economy, Creativity, and Consumption – Two or Three Things I Don't Believe In. *International Journal of Cultural Studies* 7(1).

NOIE (2003) *Creative Industries Cluster Study*. National Office for the Information Economy; Department of Communications, IT and the Arts, Canberra, <http://www.govonline.gov.au/publications/NOIE/DCITA/cluster_study_report_28may.pdf>.

Oakley, K. (2004) Not So Cool Britannia: The Role of the Creative Industries in Economic Development. *International Journal of Cultural Studies* 7(1).

Pratt, A. C. (2004) The Cultural Economy: A Call for Spatialised "Production of Culture" Perspectives. *International Journal of Cultural Studies* 7(1).

Siwek, S. (2002) *Copyright Industries in the U.S. Economy: The 2002 Report*. International Intellectual Property Alliance, Washington, <http://www.iipa.com/copyright_us_economy.html>.

Uricchio, W. (2004) "Beyond the Great Divide: Collaborative Networks and the Challenge to Dominant Conceptions of Creative Industries." *International Journal of Cultural Studies* 7(1).

Wang, J. (2004) The Global Reach of a New Discourse: How Far Can "Creative Industries" Travel? *International Journal of Cultural Studies* 7(1).

Williams, R. (2003, rev. edn) *Television: Technology and Cultural Form*. Routledge Classics, London.

# PART I
## Creative World

# Ellie Rennie
# CREATIVE WORLD

Two hundred years of American technology has unwittingly created a massive cement playground of unlimited potential. But it was the minds of 11 year olds that could see that potential.
(Craig Stecyk, 1975)

The creative world might not look much different from what came before. But as with the skateboarders who took the architecture of the city and saw in its shapes the potential for speed and style, creativity is about repurposing, subverting, and improving what is already there. Even now, as those who invented the term "creative industries" review its boundaries and inroads, the creative world is doing what it likes with the idea.

The general introduction outlines how creative industries came about through the forces of globalization, including changes in national and international economic patterns and in culture and communication. "Creative industries" suggests a new organizing principle to fit a reorganized world, where opportunity is located in unusual spaces: in knowledge, ideas, relationships; and in both local and global communities. Policies that seek to expand and mobilize creativity display a new awareness of how selection, sanctioning, and control can inhibit as well as support. It is therefore as much about the creative conditions and spaces where creative participation can occur as it is about the products themselves. It is also an acknowledgment that creativity is not just for the talented few, but a dynamic being picked up and pursued by people and groups in a range of contexts. So although "creative industries" deals with the vast, prevailing ramifications of a global economy, it is also an idea that works from the ground up.

Craig Stecyk, whose words open this chapter, is an artist, writer, and photojournalist who took his passion for skateboarding and used it to redefine youth culture. The quotation is from a series of articles that he put together under a range of pseudonyms about a group of street kids called the Z-Boys. In the mornings the Z-Boys (and girl) would surf through the ruins of the dilapidated theme park at Pacific Ocean Park, Venice Bay – the "seaside slum" they called Dogtown. When the ocean died down they would find concrete waves to ride: asphalt ditches around schools and later swimming pools in wealthy areas (locate, drain, skate, and clear out before the cops arrived). When they formed their team in the 1970s, skateboards were the equivalent of the hoola-hoop. Now the graffiti images that marked out their territory and decorated their boards are the symbols of a massive skateboarding industry. You can learn more about the Z-Boys in a documentary that tells their story from their origins as surfers and skateboarders of "aggressive localism and outcast behavior" to their fame as leaders in sport and style (*Dogtown and Z-Boys* 2002). Not only did they "employ the handiwork of the government/corporate structure in a thousand ways that the original architects could never dream of" (Craig Stecyk in *Dogtown and Z-Boys* 2002) they also turned it into a creative industry. The documentary *Dogtown and Z-Boys*, which won two awards at the Sundance film festival, was directed and co-written by Stacy Peralta, one of the original Z-Boys members. The production designer and co-writer? Craig Stecyk, of course.

# Open Source

Innovation from the ground up is an idea that is catching on. Charles Leadbeater has written in one of his thought-pieces:

> Open source is a new model of networked, citizen-led innovation, which could have huge implications for other fields, in which knowledge and creativity are highly dispersed. For instance, the Natural History Museum, working with Lancaster University, is recruiting a small army of citizen naturalists to help it monitor biodiversity among unfashionable invertebrates, algae, ferns and lichen. The Museum has 350 scientists. Its aim is to augment its capacity by working with a fieldwork force of several thousands. (Leadbeater 2003b: 25)

Suddenly, amateurs – even people who love algae – are important: "In the future, people will have to work with, learn from and sometimes compete with them" (Leadbeater 2003b: 25). This activity arises from non-commercial spaces, where people engage in activities for personal fulfillment or community involvement. "Creative industries" recognizes that there is a "world" of ideas out there where creative pursuits are born. Leadbeater takes inspiration for this new creative arrangement in the phenomenon of open source. Open source is a design feature that enabled participation in the internet by as many people as possible, resulting in its rapid growth. To some it is a technological device, for others a hobby, for many a movement. For thinkers such as Leadbeater who are concerned with the future of innovation it is also a blueprint for economic and social advancement.

---

## Commons on the Wires: Lawrence Lessig

In the first reading of this section, Lawrence Lessig explains how the internet was designed so that control of the network lay with the end users rather than at the center, allowing for greater participation in the innovation of the technology. He endorses a model of innovation that is not dictated by big business or the talented few, but by the interest and time of enthusiasts everywhere. The architecture Lessig describes, end-to-end (e2e), is made possible through "packet-switching" – a system of protocols that shift packets of data by labeling and routing them to their destination along whatever pathway is most convenient at the time (see also Froomkin 1997). No central machine is necessary as control lies at the "ends" of the network (with the end user via the protocols they send). As a result, no one needs to get permission to participate in the internet (Leiner et al. 2000).

"Open source" means that the code used to construct a computer program is visible to all users, not just the creators. During the internet's early development, open source code was used to construct the architecture of the internet, which in turn inspired openness at the applications layer. If code is visible to all, then anyone can build new layers of protocols, and thereby develop new applications or produce new versions of existing ones. If, on the other hand, the code is hidden (as it is in much proprietary software), users are unable to copy, refigure or adapt the application. Lessig argues that a degree of "openness" is necessary for a technology to grow and develop. The two principles of e2e and open source meant that the internet could develop in any direction its users wanted it to develop. As David Reed puts it in Lessig's excerpt, the design was about presuming as little as possible, and not "running a bake-off." The internet needed to be "out of control" so that as many people as possible could contribute to its growth. For Lessig this is a key to innovation.

---

Despite this simple idea, the internet's early contributors had a hard time persuading the telecommunications industry to pay attention. What the experts *didn't get* was that the old business model of centralized network control, managed by a core group of highly trained professionals, was not necessarily the best path to technological growth. Business and government were still important in the rise of the internet, as Lessig explains at length in the book. But his argument also represents a significant shift in the role of creativity that occurs outside of these structures. For the creative industries, activities that might have once been considered "below the radar" in terms of the economic wealth of cities and nations have become important.

Perhaps the best known example of open source innovation is the operating system Linux. Before Linux there was Unix, invented by computer scientists at the US telecommunications company AT&T. As Unix could not be sold owing to legislation that prevented AT&T from participating in the computing industry, its inventors convinced the company to give it away, retaining its open source design. However, when the legislation changed in 1984 and the barrier was lifted, the company decided to make Unix proprietary, removing the ability for others to distribute and develop it. By this time, "a generation had devoted its professional career to learning and building upon the Unix system" (Lessig 2001: 53). Understandably they felt betrayed. Computer programmer and free software advocate Richard Stallman decided to develop a free version of Unix, which was later linked to a concurrent project developed by Finnish computer science student Linus Torvalds, creating GNU/Linux (otherwise known as just Linux). Linux is now the fastest-growing operating system in the world and it is estimated to be the result of the efforts of over 100,000 independent and voluntary enthusiasts. Due to its transparency as open source code, Linux is considered by many to be a far more robust system than Windows. This is an example of one not-so-"small army of citizens" that contributed to the growth of a technology. As JC Herz (in part V) points out in relation to the games industry, credence should be granted "to the collective intelligence of the network – the fact that a million people will always be smarter than 20 people and that there is a business value in that differential."

## Open Commons

If this is how creativity begins, then where does it end? The main argument of what has become known as "the commons" debate is that as much as innovation can be encouraged by providing spaces within which people are free to use technology, the same technology can also become restrictive.

Code can be built that hides the architecture of the technology, thereby restricting people's capacity to adapt it and build new technologies. For Lovink, "the image of World Wide Web ghost town pops up, abandoned home pages, bored avatars, broken links, switched-off servers, controlled communities, spam-flooded email lists, and newsgroups. The freedom is there, but no one cares and no one will be able to find the counter-information through the corrupted portals and search engines at any rate" (Lovink 2002: 239). The fear within Lovink's dark vision is that the inter-creativity that defined the early internet will be dramatically reduced as old business structures take over – hardly what we could call a "new economy."

One example of this prospect is given by Lawrence Lessig and Mark Lemley (1998) in their submission to the FCC's investigation into the AT&T/MediaOne merger. Their concern was over the bundling of internet service providers (ISPs) with access to broadband infrastructure (note what is not allowed):

> The consequence of this bundling will be that there will be no effective competition among ISPs serving residential broadband cable. The range of services available to broadband cable users will be determined by one of two ISPs – @Home and RoadRunner, both of whom would be allied with the same company. These ISPs will control the kind of use that customers might make of their broadband access. They will determine whether, for example, full length streaming video is permitted (it is presently not); they will determine whether customers might resell broadband services (as they presently may not); it will determine whether broadband customers might become providers of web content (as they presently may not). These ISPs will have the power to discriminate in the choice of Internet services they allow, and customers who want broadband access will have to accept their choice. Giving this power to discriminate to the owner of the actual network wires is fundamentally inconsistent with End-to-End design. (para. 52, p. 11)

By determining the way in which the technology would be used and developed through the ISP, the end-to-end principle is potentially compromised. This suggests that in the new economy, fundamental concepts such as property and ownership require rethinking. Owning an idea (copyright) can add value, encourage distribution of an idea, and provide recompense and incentive for its author, but it can also restrict use of that idea by others (see also Meikle's discussion on open source licences in this section). The "creative industries" idea requires thinking about how intellectual property can create value and reward, but it also requires a conscientious approach to corporate enclosure that may restrict the emergence of new creative ideas.

When it comes down to it, this necessary balancing act alerts us to the fact that the new economy is not a natural equality. This is despite the fact that involvement in creative pursuits, individual flair, and good judgment seem as if they *should* benefit everybody; and even if recipes and software can be used again and again without being depleted (see Leadbeater's piece in part II). Castells (1996) writes of the nodes in the network where it is good to be and where success seems to strike out of nothing, but he also tells of nodes which are unlit, disadvantaged places. We also know that where knowledge plays a significant part in the economy, the gaps between rich and poor are likely to be greatest (Leadbeater 2003a). In such an economy success comes down to the provision of education and an environment for good ideas to flourish. It needs to be asked what else can be done for the creative world to be realized.

For Lessig, government has a role to play in ensuring that some spaces provide access to anyone – a portion of US broadband cable bandwidth, for instance. David Bollier writes that:

> Any sort of creative endeavour – which is to say progress – requires an open "white space" in which experimentation and new construction can take place. There must be the *freedom* to try new things and an unregimented workspace in which to imagine, tinker and execute new ideas. When all the white space is claimed and tightly controlled through commercial regimes that impose quantitative indices and quarterly profit goals, creativity is bureaucratized into narrow paths. There is no room for the visionary ideas, the accidental discoveries, the serendipitous encounters, the embryonic notions that might germinate into real breakthroughs, if only they had the space to grow. An argument for the commons, then, is an argument for more "white space." (Bollier 2001: 5)

For Lovink, it is about economic competence and diverse participants: "if we still have the naïve idea that an open and diverse cyberculture can somewhat influence the course technology is taking," the best approach is to "start up businesses and pollute the concepts used under the umbrella of the term New Economy" (in Meikle 2002: 177). The "creative industries" brings new ideas to old issues of inequality, primarily centered on what can be done to provide opportunities for creative participation. Even if it is the case that creative success is a luxury of the talented or entrepreneurial minority (see Howkins, in part II), a larger creative ecology can be seen to be emerging. The "white space" within which this can flourish is not just a matter of technology, but of resources and culture.

## Self-Creating (not "Developing") Countries ──────────

### At the Opening of New Media Center, Sarai, Delhi:
### Geert Lovink

Geert Lovink's article tells of a creative space in Delhi, India, where media tools are provided to assist the creative efforts of artists, activists, and theorists. The media producers at Sarai draw their content from the city itself – for them a place that is much more than a node in a global economy. This is a picture of creativity that is intimately tied to a space and culture, where Delhi's stories are told and listened to, but where any predictable form of cultural representation gets challenged. It shows how creative development involves more than policy choices around sustainability, resource provision, or information dissemination. Creative production allows the people involved to determine their own discourses – to describe themselves and articulate that locally and globally. As a creative center, Sarai is actively engaged in the intellectual and policy debates that it finds itself implicated in, including the role of new technologies, the crisis of development and the discourse of the digital divide.

The development aspects of the creative industries endorse creative participation as a means towards post-scarcity. This promotes an open-ended view of culture in which people can pursue opportunities through self-expression and creative production. Critique and inventiveness are likely outcomes of such a development rationale – where people and groups such as Sarai have the means to articulate and promote their own views and ideas. Where development policies in the past have focused on the alleviation of need – implying lack and helplessness in the receiver – groups such as Sarai actively refute (and disprove) connotations of powerlessness. Lovink quotes Jabeesh Bagchi, a Sarai member also from Raqs Media Collective:

> Development often implies the notion of victims of culture. I don't think in those terms. People live, struggle, renew, invent. Also in poverty people have a culture. I feel a little lost in this terrain, knowing that Sarai, to a large extent, is financed through development aid programs. I would never use a term like "digital divide." We have a print divide in India, an education divide, a railway divide, an airplanes divide. The new economy in India is definitely not

conceived as a divide. It is a rapid expansion of digital culture. The digital divide is a "social consciousness" term, born of guilt. We should interpret the media in different terms, not just in terms of haves and have nots. (Jabeesh Bagchi in Lovink 2002: 210)

The assertion of local culture and ideas in groups such as Sarai, through the use of communications technologies, challenges the way that Asia, Africa, and Latin America are understood in the global trajectory. This is not about bringing technology to the poor (although Sarai and other such groups admit to being dependent upon development funds for their survival); it is about the creative expression of places and communities – something which, as Bagchi puts it, is not a matter of "haves and have nots." If a new economy is about ideas, knowledge, and creativity, then new configurations of development arise that can be constructed upon existing knowledge rather than need. Post-development theorist Arturo Escobar has written that

We need to consider how a postdevelopment frame of communication practice may be linked with the idea of place as project, that is, with the potential to elevate local knowledges into different constellations of knowledge and power through enabling networks. (Escobar 2000: 171)

Sarai, Delhi, is one such place.

These ground-up initiatives can be helped at a national level through policy initiatives. Creative industries approaches seek policy solutions that allow communities to assert their cultural uniqueness. This involves both small-scale, community-empowering projects as well as nationally implemented schemes (see also Stuart Cunningham's introduction to part V of this volume).

## Multicultural Policies and Integration via the Market: Néstor García Canclini

Néstor García Canclini argues that the failure to achieve greater political and cultural integration in Latin America has been a failure of policy. In particular he argues that cultural policy in Latin American nations has remained confined to officially sanctioned monuments, heritage, and fine arts and has remained largely nationally based. Therefore, attempts to achieve cultural policy on a continent-wide scale have remained confined to high culture and to monuments and folkloric heritage, giving preference to "a conservationist vision of identity and to an integrationist view based on traditional cultural goods and institutions."

At the same time, there has been a rapid expansion and uptake of electronic communications media in all of its forms – both US-based transnational media organizations as well as the expansion of Latin American-based conglomerates. This means that, "for the first time in history, the majority of commodities and messages received in each nation has not been produced in their own territory, do not result from the particular relations of production, and do not convey messages connected exclusively with given regions." They operate "according to a transnational, deterritorialized system of production and diffusion."

Importantly, Canclini does not propose a defensive cultural nationalism or a reversion to the "strong state" as an alternative to globalized media culture disseminated by transnational media corporations. The privatization of broadcasting and communications has weakened the capacity of Latin American states to intervene to ensure cultural diversity and equal opportunities for participation in communication. However, Canclini also recognizes that popular media are a source of cultural dynamism in Latin America, as are the large networks of independent educational, cultural, and communications organizations that operate largely outside of the domain of the nation-state. Canclini instead proposes the development of a "Latin American audiovisual space" that could enable the expansion of production and markets for domestic producers while having some capacity to regulate the flows of capital and product from outside of Latin America – most notably, of course, from the United States – and which could enable a greater degree of harmonization of development of the corporate, state-funded and independent sectors in forms compatible with the development of democratic citizenship in multicultural societies.

Both Canclini and Sarai see the possibilities for creativity in India and Latin America as existing beyond the binary opposition between the state and the market. It lies instead in a newly constructed idea of public space – not unlike the commons – spaces where civil society initiatives can flourish: "social movements, artists' groups, independent radio and television stations, unions, ethnic groups, and associations of consumers, radio listeners, and television viewers. Only the multiplication of actors can favour a democratic cultural development and the representation of multiple identities."

## Resistance is Fertile

Spaces that once did not fit comfortably with ideas of progress and development are now where new ideas of progress and development can be found. Creativity can be the result of resistance and local culture.

> ### Open Publishing, Open Technologies: Graham Meikle
>
> Creative producers sometimes work in isolation, but more often as part of a group, and sometimes for a cause. Graham Meikle's *FutureActive* tells of the development of Indymedia (an open publishing web forum) from its origination as a calendar of events and actions for Sydney's community groups to a network of over 70 locally based sites around the world. Meikle shares Lessig's concern over the future of the internet, advocating open and non-proprietary spaces (what he calls "Version 1.0") over market enclosure ("Version 2.0"). His focus on the activist uses of the internet gives the sense of an information commons that is inhabited by groups and individuals with something to say – be that through electronic art, radio, open publishing, blogging, or hacking. Meikle grounds the technological achievement of the internet with a sense of place, demonstrating how innovation arises out of locally significant communities and cultures.

The emphasis on the local has ramifications for the way we see cultures of resistance and community-based media more generally. Compare this to a 1984 report by the UK research and development agency, Comedia, which found that the alternative press failed because it was not aggressive enough in positioning itself within the market, either through unwillingness or inability (discussed in Atton 2002: 33). The survival of the alternative press, in their opinion, was only due to subsidy in the form of "self-exploited labor" and benefit gigs donated by the music industry. The report found that the volunteerism that sustained the publications was merely the result of a "commitment to squatting and claiming as a way of life" (Comedia in Atton 2002: 36). The implication was that volunteerism was a pursuit to be associated only with extremist behavior. What is interesting about Comedia's findings in retrospect is the way in which "squatting and claiming" has become a creative pursuit that has been legitimated by the open source/commons movement. It is a shift towards acknowledging the places where creativity arises and seeing within that "natural" activity an opportunity for new ideas, and sometimes industries, to grow. Moreover, it suggests that the traditional binaries around work and personal fulfillment are shifting (see Angela McRobbie in part VI of this volume).

The creative industries approach is interested in how a creative world works as a seed-bed for new ideas. The idea of increased participation sits better with creative policies that seek to expand creativity than with previous cultural policies more concerned with its improvement and status (high art and culture). But although the radical, oppositional, and local are recognized as sites from which creative industries might develop, does "creative industries" leave room for dissent and critique? Is it true, as McRobbie (2001) argues, that creative industries is a policy that wants to turn "angry social critics" into successful commercial artists with little time for thinking about other matters? The creative spaces described by Meikle – alternative or tactical media – are a field of creative production that fits uneasily with ideas of commercially driven creativity intended to exploit global flows of capital and culture. These cultures pose a direct challenge to the idea that knowledge should be commodified, often to the idea of property itself. The argument that alternative culture inspires the music industry to new heights or gives the design industry a new (street) style, will grate with some. It appears that "creative industries" and its governmental, industry, and intellectual frameworks co-opt alternative culture into a commercial box that it resists by its very nature. Geert Lovink argues that:

> Alternative has been effectively reduced to style. In the media context, this means that we can no longer sell a certain forum – website, radio station, zine – as subversive or even revolutionary. It will have the immediate danger of being turned into a fashion, a lifestyle item. (Lovink in Meikle 2002: 112)

The reality is that the alternative and mainstream are getting more difficult to delineate, at least in an aesthetic sense, and this is part of the forces of the new economy. But this does not cancel out resistance. What is left is a series of critiques and alternative visions that seek to interrupt and challenge presumed knowledge and authority, described increasingly in alternative media theory as the "tactics" of the weak (de Certeau 1984; Couldry 2000; Klein 2000).

Linux, for instance, is not just an operating system, it is also a movement – best summed up by writer Neal Stephenson (1999) through his analogy of car yards. As he explains it, 90 percent of people will go to the biggest car dealer and buy the Microsoft station wagons, passing by the group who are camped by the road giving away free Linux tanks "made of space-age materials and sophisticated technology from one end to the other" (p. 7) – tanks that never break down and can be used on any street. But despite the tanks' superior qualities, most people won't go near a bunch of "hackers with bullhorns" trying to give stuff away by the side of the road. So what is the value in this activity? As much as alternative cultures can produce new ideas and systems, they will still present *alternatives* even within a creative approach to culture. In this way, the issue is bigger than Lessig's point about innovation. It is important to remember that what attracts some people may also alienate others. There is a dialogue going on within those choices about where our creative pursuits should take us.

Creative industries would be a one-dimensional concept if it did not take this activity into account. Moreover, it would be incomplete in its understanding of creativity, denying the creative invention that exists in dissent and the imagining of alternative futures. Just as creative industries are a response to globalization, so are the new social movements that Meikle is describing. Joshua Karliner (2001) from the group Corpwatch describes the anti-globalization movement:

> the vast majority of our movement can be characterized as engaged in a debate with the corporate globalizers as to the direction modernity should take, rather than across the board opposition to it and advocacy for a return to strict, traditional values.

Alternative media is the site upon which much of this critique occurs. It is the creative manifestation of new economy critique that is not separate from it but a part of the self-reflexiveness of a knowledge society.

Creative production that arises out of amateur and alternative spaces (the "third" space beyond industry and government) has generally received little attention in cultural policy settings outside of the confines of community development. Some of the readings in this volume maintain that it cannot fit well with the creative industries framework either – at least where that is defined as government-designed initiatives directed at intellectual property go-getters (see Howkins in part II). Under such a remit there is not much room for creativity that is less capitalistic in its pursuit, and especially not for that which is outright disruptive. Indeed, it is doubtful that some of the radical and oppositional groups that are included under the banner of "alternative" would sit down to a government review on cultural policy anyhow. But in terms of the broader fate of innovation and creativity, this activity does figure. At one level it generates ideas, images, and styles that have commercial significance, as well as new methods of organization, collaboration, and training. Perhaps more importantly, the alternative and the amateur have signaled some critical themes in the social and economic dynamics that the creative industries term was invented to respond to and describe – tensions between property and freedom, work and personal fulfillment, dissent and government.

# References

Atton, C. (2002) *Alternative Media*. Sage, Thousand Oaks.

Bollier, D. (2001) *Public Assets, Private Profits: Reclaiming the American Commons in an Age of Market Enclosure*. New America Foundation, Washington, DC.

Castells, M. (1996) *The Rise of the Network Society*, vol. 1. Blackwell, Massachusetts.

Couldry, N. (2000) *The Place of Media Power: Pilgrims and Witnesses of the Media Age*. Routledge, London.

de Certeau, M. (1984) *The Practice of Everyday Life*. University of California Press, Berkeley.

*Dogtown and Z-Boys* (motion picture; 2002), Sony Pictures Classics. Director Stacy Peralta, producer Agi Orsi, written by Stacy Peralta and Craig Stecyk.

Escobar, A. (2000) Place, Power and Networks in Globalization and Postdevelopment. In K. G. Wilkins (ed.), *Redeveloping Communication for Social Change*. Rowman & Littlefield, Lanham, 163–74.

Froomkin, A. M. (1997) The Internet as a Source of Regulatory Arbitrage. In B. Kahin and C. Nesson (eds.), *Borders in Cyberspace: Information Policy and the Global Information Infrastructure*. MIT Press, Cambridge Mass., 129–63.

Karliner, J. (2001) Where Do We Go From Here? *OpenDemocracy*. <http://www.opendemocracy.net> (accessed November 6, 2001).

Klein, N. (2000) *No Logo: No Space, No Choice, No Jobs*. Flamingo, London.

Leadbeater, C. (2003a) Seeing the light. *RSA Journal* 5505 (February), 28–33.

Leadbeater, C. (2003b) Amateurs: a 21st-century remake. *RSA Journal* 5507 (June), 22–5.

Leiner, B. M., V. G. Cerf, D. D. Clark, R. E. Kahn, et al. (2000) *A Brief History of the Internet*. ISOC, <http://www.isoc.org/internet/history/brief.shtml> (accessed October 2, 2001).

Lessig, L. (2001) *The Future of Ideas: The Fate of the Commons in a Connected World*. Random House, New York.

Lessig, L. and M. A. Lemley (1998) "In the Matter of AT&T/Media One."

Lovink, Geert (2002) *Dark Fiber: Tracking Critical Internet Culture*. MIT Press, Cambridge Mass. and London.

McRobbie, A. (2001) "Everyone is Creative": Artists as New Economy Pioneers? *OpenDemocracy*, <www.opendemocracy.net> (accessed August 30, 2001).

Meikle, G. (2002) *Future Active: Media Activism and the Internet*. Pluto Press, Annandale NSW.

Stephenson, N. (1999) *In the Beginning was the Command Line*. Avon Books, New York.

# 1    *Lawrence Lessig*

# COMMONS ON THE WIRES

The Internet is a network of networks. In the main, these networks connect over wires. All of these wires, and the machines linked by them, are controlled by someone. The vast majority are owned by private parties – owned, that is, by individuals and corporations that have chosen to link to the Net. Some are owned by the government.

Yet this vast network of privately owned technology has built one of the most important *innovation commons* that we have ever known. Built on a platform that is controlled, the protocols of the Internet have erected a free space of innovation. These private networks have created an open resource that any can draw upon and that many have. Understanding how, and in what sense, is the aim of this chapter.

[ . . . ]

The Internet is not the telephone network. It is a network of networks that sometimes run on the telephone lines. These networks and the wires that link them are privately owned, like the wires of the old AT&T. Yet at the core of this network is a different principle from the principle that guided AT&T. [ . . . ]

First described by network architects Jerome Saltzer, David Clark, and David P. Reed in 1981, this principle – called the "end-to-end argument" (e2e) – guides network designers in developing protocols and applications for the network. End-to-end says to keep intelligence in a network at the ends, or in the applications, leaving the network itself to be relatively simple.

"Commons on the Wires" from Lawrence Lessig (2001), *The Future of Ideas: The Fate of the Commons in a Connected World*. Random House, New York, pp. 25, 34–7, 39–48, 275–8 (notes). Reprinted by permission of Random House, Inc and International Creative Management, Inc. © 2001 by Lawrence Lessig.

There are many principles in the Internet's design. This one is key. But it will take some explaining to show why.

Network designers commonly distinguish computers at the "end" or "edge" of a network from computers within that network. The computers at the end of a network are the machines you use to access the network. (The machine you use to dial into the Internet, or your cell phone connecting to a wireless Web, is a computer at the edge of the network.) The computers "within" the network are the machines that establish the links to other computers – and thereby form the network itself. (The machines run by your Internet service provider, for example, could be computers within the network.)

The end-to-end argument says that rather than locating intelligence within the network, intelligence should be placed at the ends: computers within the network should perform only very simple functions that are needed by lots of different applications, while functions that are needed by only some applications should be performed at the edge. Thus, complexity and intelligence in the network are pushed away from the network itself. Simple networks, smart applications. As a recent National Research Council (NRC) report describes it:

> Aimed at simplicity and flexibility, [the end-to-end] argument says that the network should provide a very basic level of service – data transport – and that the intelligence – the information processing needed to provide applications – should be located in or close to the devices attached to the edge [or ends] of the network.[1]

The reason for this design was flexibility, inspired by a certain humility. As Reed describes it, "we wanted to make sure that we didn't somehow build in a feature of the underlying network technology . . . that would restrict our using some new underlying transport technology that turned out to be good in the future. . . . That was really the key to why we picked this very, very simple thing called the Internet protocol."[2]

It might be a bit hard to see how a principle of network design could matter much to issues of public policy. Lawyers and policy types don't spend much time understanding such principles; network architects don't waste their time thinking about the confusions of public policy.

But architecture matters. And arguably no principle of network architecture has been more important to the success of the Internet than this single principle of network design – e2e. How a system is designed will affect the freedoms and control the system enables. And how the Internet was designed intimately affected the freedoms and controls that it has enabled. The *code* of cyberspace – its architecture and the software and hardware that implement that architecture – regulates life in cyberspace generally. Its code is its law. Or, in the words of Electronic Frontier Foundation (EFF) cofounder Mitch Kapor, "Architecture is politics."[3]

To the extent that people have thought about Kapor's slogan, they've done so in the context of individual rights and network architecture. Most think about how "architecture" or "software" or, more simply, "code" enables or restricts the things we think of as human rights – speech, or privacy, or the rights of access.

That was my purpose in *Code and Other Laws of Cyberspace*. There I argued that it was the architecture of cyberspace that constituted its freedom, and that, as this architecture was changed, that freedom was erased. *Code*, in other words, is a *law* of cyberspace and, as the title suggests, in my view, its most significant law.

But in this book, my focus is different. The question I want to press here is the relationship between architecture and innovation – both commercial innovation and cultural innovation. My claim is that here, too, code matters. That to understand the source of the flourishing of innovation on the Internet, one must understand something about its original design. And then, even more important, to understand as well that changes to this original architecture are likely to affect the reach of innovation here.

So which code matters? Which parts of the architecture?

The Internet is not a novel or a symphony. No one authored a beginning, middle, and end. At any particular point in its history, it certainly has a structure, or architecture, that is implemented through a set of protocols and conventions. But this architecture was never fully planned; no one designed it from the bottom up. It is more like the architecture of an old European city, with a central section that is clear and well worn, but with additions that are many and sometimes confused.

At various points in the history of the Net's development, there have been efforts at restating its principles. Something called "RFC 1958," published in 1996, is perhaps the best formal effort. The Internet was built upon "requests for comments," or RFCs. Researchers – essentially grad students – charged with the task of developing the protocols that would eventually build the Internet developed these protocols through these humble requests for comments. RFC 1 was written by Steve Crocker and outlined an understanding about the protocols for host ("IMP") software. Some RFCs specify particular Internet protocols; some wax philosophical. RFC 1958 is clearly in the latter camp – an "informational" document about the "Architectural Principles of the Internet."[4]

According to RFC 1958, though "[m]any members of the Internet community would argue that there is no architecture," this document reports that "the community" generally "believes" this about the Internet: "that the goal is connectivity, the tool is the Internet protocol and the intelligence is end-to-end rather than hidden in the network."[5] "The network's job is to transmit datagrams as efficiently and flexibly as possible. Everything else should be done at the fringes."[6]

This design has important consequences for innovation – indeed, we can count three:

- First, because applications run on computers at the edge of the network, innovators with new applications need only connect their computers to the network to let their applications run. No change to the computers within the network is required. If you are a developer, for example, who wants to use the Internet to make telephone calls, you need only develop that application and get users to adopt it for the Internet to be capable of making "telephone" calls. You can write the application and send it to the person on the other end of the network. Both of you install it and start talking. That's it.
- Second, because the design is not optimized for any particular existing application, the network is open to innovation not originally imagined. All the Internet protocol (IP) does is figure a way to package and route data; it doesn't route or process certain kinds of data better than others. That creates a problem for some applications (as we'll see below), but it creates an opportunity for a wide range of other applications too. It means that the network is open to adopting applications not originally foreseen by the designers.
- Third, because the design effects a neutral platform – neutral in the sense that the network owner can't discriminate against some packets while favoring others – the network *can't* discriminate against a new innovator's design. If a new application threatens a dominant application, there's nothing the network can do about that. The network will remain neutral regardless of the application.

The significance of each of these consequences to innovation generally will become apparent as we work through the particulars that follow. For now, all that's important is that you see this design as a *choice*. Whether or not the framers of the network understood what would grow from what they built, they built it with a certain philosophy in mind. The network itself would not control how it would grow. Applications would. That was the key to end-to-end design. As the inventor of the World Wide Web, Tim Berners-Lee, describes it:

> Philosophically, if the Web was to be a universal resource, it had to be able to grow in an unlimited way. Technically, if there was any centralized point of control, it would rapidly become a bottleneck that restricted the Web's growth, and the Web would never scale up. Its being "out of control" was very important.[7]

[ . . . ]

The Internet isn't the only network to follow an end-to-end design, though it is the first large-scale computer network to choose that principle at its birth. The electricity grid is an end-to-end grid; as long as my equipment complies with the rules for the grid, I get to plug it in. Conceivably, things could be different. In principle, we might imagine that every device you plug into a grid would register itself with the network before it would run. Before you connected, you would have to get permission for that device. The owner of the network could then choose which devices to prohibit.

Likewise, the roads are end-to-end systems. Any car gets to enter the highway grid (put tolls to one side). As long as the car is properly inspected, and the driver properly licensed, whether and when to use the highway is no business of the highway. Again, we could imagine a different architecture: each car might first register with the grid before it got on the highway (the way airlines file flight plans before they fly).

But these systems don't require this sort of registration, likely because, when they were built, such registration was simply impracticable. The electronics of a power grid couldn't handle the registration of different devices; roads were built stupid because smart roads were impossible. Things are different now; smart grids, and smart roads, are certainly possible. Control is now feasible. So we should ask, would control be better?

In at least some cases, it certainly would be better. But from the perspective of innovation, in some cases it would not. In particular, when the future is uncertain – or more precisely, when future uses of a technology cannot be predicted – then leaving the technology uncontrolled is a better way of helping it find the right sort of innovation. Plasticity – the ability of a system to evolve easily in a number of ways – is optimal in a world of uncertainty.

This strategy is an attitude. It says to the world, I don't know what functions this system, or network, will perform. It is based in the idea of uncertainty. When we don't know which way a system will develop, we build the system to allow the broadest range of development.

This was a key motivation of the original Internet architects. They were extremely talented; no one was more expert. But with talent comes humility. And the original network architects knew more than anything that they didn't know what this network would be used for.

As David Reed describes, "[T]here were a lot of experiments in those days," and "we . . . realized that [there] was very little in common [other] than the way they used the network. There were sort of interesting ways that they used the network differently from application to application. So we felt that we couldn't presume anything about how networks would be used by applications. Or we wanted to presume as little as possible. . . . We basically said, 'Stop. You're all right' as opposed to running a bake-off."[8] These designers knew only that they wanted to assure that it could develop however users wanted.

Thus, end-to-end disables central control over how the network develops. As Berners-Lee puts it, "There's a freedom about the Internet: as long as we accept the rules of sending packets around, we can send packets containing anything to anywhere."[9] New applications "can be brought to the Internet without the need for any changes to the underlying network."[10] The "architecture" of the network is designed to be "neutral with respect to applications and content."[11] By placing intelligence in the ends, the network has no intelligence to tell which functions or content are permitted or not. As RFC 1958 puts it, the job of the network is simply to "transmit datagrams." As the NRC has recently concluded:

> Underlying the end-to-end argument is the idea that it is the system or application, not the network itself, that is in the best position to implement appropriate protection.[12]

[ . . . ] We can now see how the end-to-end principle renders the Internet an *innovation commons*, where innovators can develop and deploy new applications or content *with out the permission of anyone else*. Because of e2e, no one need register an application with "the Internet" before it will run; no permission to use the bandwidth is required. Instead, e2e means the network is designed to assure that the network cannot decide which innovations will run. The system is built – constituted – to remain open to whatever innovation comes along.

This design has a critical effect on innovation. It has been, in the words of the NRC, a "key to the explosion of new services and software applications" on the Net.[13] Because of e2e, innovators know that they need not get the permission of anyone – neither AT&T nor the Internet itself – before they build a new application for the Internet. If an innovator has what he or she believes is a great idea for an application, he or she can build it without authorization from the network itself and with the assurance that the network can't discriminate against it.

At this point, you may be wondering, So what? It may be interesting (at least I hope you think this) to learn that the Internet has this feature; it is at least plausible that this feature induces a certain kind of innovation. But why do we need to worry about this feature of the Internet, If this is what makes the Internet run, then as long as we have the Internet, won't we have this feature? If e2e is in the Internet's nature, why do we need to worry about e2e?

But this raises the fundamental point: The design the Internet has *now* need not be its design *tomorrow*. Or more precisely, any design it has just now can be supplemented with other controls or other technology. And if that is true, then this feature of e2e that I am suggesting is central to the network now can be removed from the network as the network is changed. The code that defines the network at one time need not be the code that defines it later on. And as that code changes, the values the network protects will change as well.

The consequences of this commitment to e2e are many. The birth of the World Wide Web is just one. If you're free from geekhood, you are likely not to distinguish the WWW from the Internet. But in fact, they are quite distinct. The World Wide Web is a set of protocols for displaying hyperlinked documents linked across the Internet. These protocols were developed in the late 1980s by researchers at the European particle physics lab CERN – in particular by Tim Berners-Lee. These protocols specify how a "Web server" serves content on the WWW. They also specify how "browsers" – such as Netscape Navigator or Microsoft's Internet Explorer – retrieve content on the World Wide Web. But these protocols themselves simply run on top of the protocols that define the Internet. These Internet protocols, referred to as TCP/IP, are the foundation upon which the protocols that make the World Wide Web function – HTTP (hypertext transfer protocol) and HTML (hypertext markup language) – run.[14]

The emergence of the World Wide Web is a perfect illustration of how innovation works on the Internet and of how important a neutral network is to that innovation. Tim Berners-Lee came up with the idea of the World Wide Web after increasing frustration over the fact that computers at CERN couldn't easily talk to each other. Documents built on one system were not easily shared with other systems; content stored on individual computers was not easily published to the networks generally. As Berners-Lee writes:

> Incompatibility between computers had always been a huge pain in everyone's side, at CERN and anywhere else. . . . The real world of high-energy physics was one of incompatible networks, disk formats, and character-encoding schemes, which made any attempt to transfer information between computers generally impossible. The computers simply could not communicate with each other.[15]

Berners-Lee thus began to think about a system to enable linking among documents — through a process called "hypertext" — and to build this linking on top of the protocols of the Internet. His ideal was a space where any document in principle could be linked to any other and where any document published was available to anyone.

The components of this vision were nothing new. Hypertext — links from one document to another — had been born with Vannevar Bush, and made famous by Bill Atkinson's HyperCard on the Apple Macintosh. The world where documents could all link to each other was the vision of Robert Fano in an early article in the *Proceedings of the IEEE*.[16] But Berners-Lee put these ideas together using the underlying protocol of the Internet. Hyperlinked documents would thus be available to anyone with access to the Internet, and any document published according to the protocols of the World Wide Web would be available to all.

The idea strikes us today as genius. Its success makes us believe the idea must have been obvious. But what is amazing about the story of the birth of the World Wide Web is how hard it was for Tim Berners-Lee to convince anyone of the merit in the plan. When Berners-Lee tried to sell the plan at CERN, management was unimpressed. As Berners-Lee writes:

> What we hoped for was that someone would say, "Wow! This is going to be the cornerstone of high-energy physics communications! It will bind the entire community together in the next ten years. Here are four programmers to work on the project and here's your liaison with Management Information Systems. Anything else you need, you just tell us." But it didn't happen.[17]

When he went to a meeting of hypertext fans, he could get few to understand the "ah-ha" of hypertext on the Net. For years he wandered from expert to expert, finding none who understood the potential here. And it was only after he started building the Web out, and started informing ordinary people on a hypertext mailing list about the protocols he was developing, that the Net started to grow.

*The experts didn't get it.* Someone should put that on a bumper sticker and spread it around. Those controlling the resources of the CERN computer lab wouldn't support the technology that would give the world the Web. Only those innovators outside of the control of these managers saw something of the potential for the Web's growth.

Berners-Lee feared that competing protocols for using the Internet would wipe away interest in the WWW. One protocol built about the same time was called Gopher. Gopher enabled the easy display of a menu of options from a site. When you went to a Gopher-enabled site, you would see a list of links that you could then click on to perform some function. Gopher was extremely popular as an Internet application – running on the Internet protocols – and use of Gopher took off in the early 1990s.[18]

But for the purposes that Berners-Lee imagined, Gopher was extremely limited. It would not enable the easy construction of interlinked documents. It was closer to a universal menuing system than a system for linking ideas. Berners-Lee was afraid that this inferior standard would nonetheless stick before the new and better WWW became well known.

His fear, however, was not realized, both because of something Berners-Lee did and because of something the creators of Gopher did – and both are lessons for us.

Berners-Lee was no bully. He was not building a protocol that everyone had to follow. He had a protocol for displaying content on the World Wide Web – the HTML language that Web pages are built in. But he decided not to limit the content that one could get through a WWW browser to just Web pages. Instead he designed the transfer protocol – HTTP – so that a wide range of protocols could be accessed through the WWW – including the Gopher protocol, a protocol for transferring files (FTP), and a protocol for accessing newsgroups on the Internet (NNTP). The Web would be neutral among these different protocols – it would in this sense interconnect.[19]

That made it easy to use the Web, even if one wanted to get access to Gopher content. But the second doing was much more important to the death of Gopher as a standard.

As Berners-Lee describes it, high off its success in populating the world with Gopher, the University of Minnesota – owner of the right to Gopher – suggested it might exercise its rights to charge for the use of the Gopher protocol.[20] Even the suggestion of this terrified developers across the world. (It was, Berners-Lee writes, "an act of treason."[21]) Would developers be hijacked by the university once they depended upon their system? How much would they lose if the platform eventually turned against the developers?

Berners-Lee responded to this by convincing CERN to release the right to the Web to the public. At first he wanted to release the protocol under the GPL, or General Public License (the "GNU General Public License"). But when negotiations over that bogged down, he convinced CERN simply to release the rights into the public domain. Anyone had the right to take and use the protocols of the WWW and build anything upon them that they wanted.[22]

The birth of the Web is an example of the innovation that the end–to–end architecture of the original Internet enabled. Though no one quite got it – this the most dramatic aspect of the Internet's power – a few people were able to develop and deploy the protocols of the World Wide Web. They could deploy it because they didn't need to convince the owners of the network that this was a good idea or the owners of computer operating systems that this was a good idea. As Berners-Lee put it, "I had designed the Web so there should be no centralized place where someone would have to 'register' a new server, or get approval of its contents."[23] It would be a "good idea" if people used it, and people were free to use it because the Internet's design made it free.

Thus two networks – the network built by AT&T and the network we call the Internet – create two different environments for innovation. One network centralizes creativity; the other decentralizes it. One network is built to keep control of innovation; the other constitutionally renounces the right to control. One network closes itself except where permission is granted; the other dedicates itself to a commons.

How did we get from the one to the other? What moved the world governing our telecommunications system from the centralized to the decentralized?

This is one of the great forgotten stories of the Internet's birth. Everyone knows that the government funded the research that led to the protocols that govern the Internet. It is part of the Internet's lore that it was the government that pushed network designers to design machines that could talk to each other.[24] The government in general, and the Defense Department in particular, had grown tired of spending millions for "autistic computing machines."[25] It therefore wanted some system for linking the systems.

Yet we are practically trained to ignore another form of governmental intervention that also made the Internet possible. This is the regulation that assured that the platform upon which the Internet was built would not turn against it.

The physical platform on which the Internet took off came prewired. It was the telephone wires that linked homes to homes. But the legal right to use the telephone wires to link to the Internet did not come preordained. That right had to be earned, and it was regulation that earned it. Nothing guaranteed that modems would be permitted on telephone lines. Even today, countries in Asia regulate the use of modems on telephone lines.[26] What was needed before the revolution could begin was permission to connect the Net to this net.

And what made that permission possible? What made it possible for a different use to be made of the telephone wires from that which AT&T had originally imagined?

Here a second kind of regulation enters the story. Beginning in force in 1968, when it permitted foreign attachments to telephone wires, continuing through the 1970s, when it increasingly forced the Bells to lease lines to competitors, regardless of their purpose, and ending in the early 1980s with the breakup of AT&T, the government increasingly intervened to assure that this most powerful telecommunications company would not interfere with the emergence of competing data-communications companies.

This intervention took many forms. In part it was a set of restrictions on AT&T's permissible businesses. In part it was a requirement that it keep its lines open to competitors.[27] In part it was the general fear that any effort to bias communications more in its favor would result in a strong reaction from the government.

But whatever the mix, and whichever factor was most significant, the consequence of this strategy was to leave open the field for innovation in telecommunications. AT&T did not control how its wires would be used, because the government restricted that control. By restricting that control, the government in effect created a commons on AT&T's wires.

In a way analogous to the technical requirements of end-to-end, then, these regulations had the effect of leaving the network open and hence of keeping the use of the network neutral. Once the telephone system was used to establish a circuit, the system was kept free for that circuit to send what-ever data across it the user wished. The network thus functioned as a resource left open for others to use.

This is end-to-end operating at a different layer in the network design. It is end-to-end not at the layer determining the connection between two phones on the telephone system. That connection may well be formed by a system that does not comply with the end-to-end rule.

But once the circuit is connected, then the environment created by the mix of technical principles and legal rules operating upon the telecommunications system paralleled an end-to-end design at the network layer. This mix of design and control kept the telephone system open for innovation; that innovation enabled the Internet.

Are there costs to the e2e design? Do we lose something by failing to control access to the resources – the bandwidth – of the network?

Certainly the Internet is not without its weaknesses. The capacity of the Net at any one moment is not infinite, and though it grows more quickly than the demand, it does at times get congested. It deals with this congestion equally – packets get transported on a first-come, first-served basis. Once packets leave one end, the network relays them on a best-efforts basis. If nodes on the network become overwhelmed, then packets passing across those nodes slow down.[28]

For certain applications, "best efforts" is not enough. Internet telephony, for example, doesn't do well when packets carrying voice get delayed. Any delay greater than 250 milliseconds essentially makes the system unusable.[29] And as content on the Net moves to real-time, bandwidth-demanding technology, this inability to guarantee quality of service becomes increasingly costly.

To deal with this problem, technologists have begun to propose changes to the architecture of the Net that might better enable some form of guaranteed service. These solutions generally pass under the title "Quality of Service" (QoS) solutions. These modifications would enable the network to treat different "classes" of data differently – video, for example, would get different treatment from e-mail; voice would get different treatment from the Web.

To enable this capacity to discriminate, the network would require more functionality than the original design allowed. At a minimum, the network would need to be able to decide what class of service a particular application should get and then treat the service accordingly. This in turn would make developing a new application more complex, as the programmer would need to consider the behavior of the network and enable the application to deal with that behavior.

The real danger, however, comes from the unintended consequences of these additional features – the ability of the network to then sell the feature that it will discriminate in favor of (and hence also against) certain kinds of content. As the marketing documents from major router manufacturers evince, a critical feature of QoS solutions will be their ability to enable the network owner to slow down a competitor's offerings while speeding up its own – like a television set with built-in static for ABC but a clear channel for CBS.

These dangers could be minimized depending upon the particular QoS technology chosen. Some QoS technologies, in other words, are more consistent with the principle of end-to-end than are others.[30] But proponents of these changes often overlook another relatively obvious solution – increasing capacity. That is, while these technologies will certainly add QoS to the Internet, if QoS technologies like the "RSVP" technology do so only at a significant cost, then perhaps increased capacity would be a cheaper social cost solution.

Put differently, a pricing system for allocating bandwidth solves certain problems, but if it is implemented contrary to end-to-end, it may well do more harm than good.

That is not to argue that it *will* do more harm than good. We don't know enough yet to know that. But it raises a fundamental issue that the scarcity mentality is likely to overlook: The best response to scarcity may not be a system of control. The best response may simply be to remove the scarcity.

This is the promise that conservative commentator George Gilder reports. The future, Gilder argues, is a world with "infinite" bandwidth.[31] Our picture of the Net now – of slow connections and fast machines – will soon flip. As copper is replaced with glass (as in fiber optics) and, more important, as electronic switches are replaced by optical switches, the speed of the network will approach the speed of light. The constraints that we know from the wires we now use will end, Gilder argues. And the end of scarcity, he argues, will transform all that we do.

There is skepticism about Gilder's claims about technology.[32] So, too, about his economics. The economist in all of us can't quite believe that any resource would fail to be constrained; the realist in all of us refuses to believe in Eden. But I'm willing to believe in the potential of essentially infinite bandwidth. And I am happy to imagine the scarcity-centric economist proven wrong.

The part I'm skeptical about is the happy progress toward a world where network owners simply provide neutral fat (or glass) pipe. This is not the trend now, and there is little to suggest it will be the trend later. As law professor Tim Wu wrote to me about Gilder's book:

> I think it is a "delta dollar sign" problem as we used to say in chemistry (to describe reactions that were possible, but not profitable). Private actors seem to only make money from infrastructure projects if built with the ability to exclude. . . . [H]ere in the industry, all the projects that are "hot" are networks with built-in techniques of exclusion and prioritization.[33]

Here *is* a tragedy of the commons. If the commons is the *innovation* commons that the protocols of the Net embrace, e2e most important among them, then the tragedy of that commons is the tendency of industry to add technologies to the network that undermine it. [ . . . ]

The Internet was born on a controlled physical layer; the code layer, constituted by the TCP/IP, was nonetheless free. These protocols expressed an end-to-end principle, and that principle effectively opened the space created by the computers linked to the Net for innovation and change. This open space was an important freedom, built upon a platform that was controlled. The freedom built an innovation commons. That commons, as do other commons, makes the controlled space more valuable.

Freedom thus enhanced the social value of the controlled: this is a lesson that will recur.

## Notes

1. National Research Council, *The Internet's Coming of Age* (Washington, DC: National Academy Press, 2000), 30.
2. Telephone interview with David P. Reed (February 7, 2001), who contributed to the early design of the Internet protocols – TCP/IP – while a graduate student at MIT.
3. Lawrence Lessig, *Code and Other Laws of Cyberspace* (New York: Basic Books, 1999), 243, n. 19 (citing Kapor).
4. Network Working Group, "Request for Comments: 1958, Architectural Principles of the Internet," Brian E. Carpenter, ed. (1996), available at http://www.ietf.org/rfc/rfc 1958.txt.
5. Ibid., §2.1.
6. Ibid.
7. Tim Berners-Lee, *Weaving the Web: The Original Design and Ultimate Destiny of the World Wide Web by Its Inventor* (San Francisco: HarperSanFrancisco, 1999), 99.
8. Telephone interview with David Reed.
9. Berners-Lee, 208.
10. National Research Council, 138.
11. Ibid., 107.
12. Ibid., 36–7.
13. Ibid., 37.
14. Douglas E. Comer, *Internetworking with TCP/IP*, 4th edn., vol. 1 (Upper Saddle River, NJ: Prentice-Hall, 2000), 691 (HTTP stands for "hypertext transfer protocol" and is "[t]he protocol used to transfer Web documents from a server to a browser"), 713 (TCP stands for "transmission control protocol"), and 694 (IP stands for "Internet protocol)."
15. Berners-Lee, 35.
16. See Robert M. Fano, "On the Social Role of Computer Communications," *Proceedings of the IEEE* 60 (September 1972), 1249.
17. Berners-Lee, 46. See also James Gillies, *How the Web Was Born: The Story of the World Wide Web* (Oxford and New York: Oxford University Press, 2000); Hafner and Lyon, *Internet Dreams: Archetypes, Myths, and Metaphors*, Mark J. Stefik and Vinton G. Cerf, eds. (Cambridge, Mass.: MIT Press, 1997).
18. Berners-Lee, 40 (describing Gopher and WAIS growing faster).
19. Ibid. (interconnect).
20. Ibid., 72–3.
21. Ibid.
22. Ibid., 74.

23    Ibid., 99.
24    John Naughton, *A Brief History of the Future* (London: Weidenfeld & Nicolson, 1999), 83–5.
25    Ibid., 84.
26    See, e.g., <http://www.asiapoint.net/insight/asia/countries/myanmar/my_spedev. htm>.
27    Steve Bickerstaff, "Shackles on the Giant: How the Federal Government Created Microsoft, Personal Computers, and the Internet," *Texas Law Review* 78 (1999), 25.
28    National Research Council, 130–1, n. 18 (describing best efforts as consequences of uniformity).
29    "Humans can tolerate about 250 msec of latency before it has a noticeable effect," <http://www.dialogic.com/solution/Internet/4070Web.htm>.
30    They are described in Mark Gaynor et al., "Theory of Service Architecture: How to Encourage Innovation of Services in Networks" (working paper, 2000, on file with author), 14.
31    See G. Gilder, *Telecosm: How Infinite Bandwidth Will Revolutionize Our World* (New York: Free Press, 2000), 158–64.
32    See, e.g., Bill Frezza, "Telecosmic Punditry: The World Through Gilder-Colored Glasses," *Internet Week* (December 4, 2000), 47; Rob Walker, "The Gilder-cosm," *Slate* magazine (September 11, 2000), available at <http://slate.msn.com/ code/MoneyBox/MoneyBox.asp?Show=9/11/2000&idMessage=6030> (Gilder runs "against the current wisdom that sees bandwidth shortage as a problem"); Julian Dibbell, "From Here to Infinity," *Village Voice*, September 5, 2000, 65 ("It takes either profound sloth or transcendent faith to persist in voicing such breathless sentiments."). For a more favorable review, see, e.g., Blair Levin, "Review, *TELECOSM: How Infinite Bandwidth Will Revolutionize Our World*," *Washington Monthly* (September 1, 2000), 54.
33    E-mail from Timothy Wu to Lawrence Lessig, February 16, 2001.

# 2    *Graham Meikle*

# OPEN PUBLISHING, OPEN TECHNOLOGIES

*12 September 2000: The Opening Ceremony of the Olympic Games is just three days away and an estimated 22,000 journalists have descended on Sydney for the largest programmed media event on the calendar. During the Games, journalists will be able to draw on the resources of the International Broadcast Centre at Homebush Bay, with its 3200 staff, 70,000 square metres of TV broadcast facilities, 700 cameras and 400 video machines. And that's just for broadcasters, with hundreds of additional staff and thousands of volunteers deployed to assist print journalists. But not everyone has such resources. In a converted warehouse in the inner-western suburb of St Peters, the Sydney Independent Media Centre (IMC) is also gearing up for the Games.[1] Sharing the building with an anarchist bookshop, an office of Friends of the Earth and some residents, a dozen computers line the room. Some are hand-painted or stickered, having been donated or salvaged from dumpsters. Volunteer contributors cluster around terminals, typing up stories and helping each other upload video and audio files. Spare monitors and disk drives in various states of repair are piled on shelves, jostling for space with Linux penguin dolls, an anti-uranium mining flag, and banners reading 'do-it-yourself media' and 'cause for comment'. With its scraps of taped-down carpet and mismatched chairs, the IMC resembles a garage band rehearsal space, a model of DIY culture, makeshift and make-do. The IMC, observes volunteer Gabrielle Kuiper, 'runs on the smell of a burnt-out modem'.*

The Sydney IMC is a Net-based vehicle open to all to exchange information, contribute stories and discuss ideas. Initially set up to provide coverage of Olympic-related issues other than the medal tallies, it was still going strong

"Open Publishing, Open Technologies" from Graham Meikle (2002), *Future Active: Media Activism and the Internet*. Pluto Press, Sydney, pp. 88–91, 92–4, 95–6, 97–8, 103–111, 205–8 (notes). Reprinted by permission of Routledge/Taylor & Francis Books, Inc (pb 0-415-94321-1) and Pluto Press Australia (1-86403-148-4).

many months after the closing fireworks of the Games. Its main feature is a web page that automatically publishes submissions from participants, who can contribute text, photos and graphics, video clips and audio files. Its database automatically updates the site to make each new submission the lead item. While the website is the virtual centre, and anyone can contribute items from home, work, libraries or Net cafés, the physical office space offers volunteer support for the more technically demanding submissions, such as uploading audio and video clips.

The IMC software represents a confluence of interests, influences and experiences which makes it, in many ways, the state of the art in Internet activism. Building on our earlier analysis of alternative media, in this chapter we'll look at two key aspects of the IMC movement: its advocacy of open publishing and its links with the open source software movement.

Open publishing is the key idea behind the IMC. There are no staff reporters as such – instead, the content is generated by anyone who decides to take part. There is no gatekeeping and no editorial selection process – participants are free to upload whatever they choose, from articles and reports to announcements and appeals for equipment or advice.

'We wanted people to be active participants, not passive readers,' explains Gabrielle Kuiper, recalling the ideas behind the Active Sydney project that led to the IMC. 'They are the ones with the knowledge of their events, groups and news, not us – why should we be gatekeepers? If you come from this philosophy – basically respecting the intelligence and creativity of your fellow human beings – then good communication practice and making the site easy to use follows from that.'

Contributing a story, as IMC programmer Matthew Arnison says, is no harder than using Hotmail – type your article into an online form and click on a button to submit. And in an important use of the conversational dimension of the Net, each story includes an option that allows others to add their own follow-up comments, so that each story can be the catalyst for an online discussion as well as a stand-alone item. Before the IMC was even officially launched (on 7 September 2000), more than 300 items had already been posted; over 120 people had subscribed to the main mailing list; and the site was receiving around 1000 hits per day, with most of this traffic coming from word-of-mouth, incoming links and the existing global network of more than 30 other IMCs.

[ . . . ]

The first IMC was established in Seattle for the World Trade Organisation events of November 1999. In the ten months following Seattle, a network of more than 30 such IMCs had been set up, each using the same freely circulated software, and each relying on individual participants or visitors to submit content. The Sydney site was only one of five new IMCs to go online in September 2000. By March 2002 there were more than 70. IMCs have been established for one-off events, such as May Day in London, and as part of longer-term, localised political campaigns, from India to the Czech Republic, from Italy to the Congo. The Brazilian IMC, for instance, offers ground-level analysis of trade issues in a choice of three languages, while the Israeli site offers eyewitness accounts of conditions in the West Bank and Gaza.

This dispersed network is a key to thinking about the opposition to globalisation which the contributors to IMCs tend to share. First, we should note that the 'anti-globalisation' label is reductive – globalisation is a complex matrix of processes, but the content of the IMC sites tends to address opposition to global *corporations* rather than to *all* aspects of globalisation. Second, it's entirely consistent that this opposition to dispersed global capitalism is itself dispersed and localised, rather than centralised. If corporate power is everywhere and nowhere, nomadic and dispersed, then opposition to that power needs to be likewise.

The routine emphasis on the global nature of the Net means it's easy to overlook the significance of *local* applications of computerised communications. In fact, activist groups have been capitalising on this potential since well before the Internet took off in the mid-1990s. In the early 1980s, for instance, community groups in New York established computerised databases to calculate the risk of arson attacks by landlords intending to claim on insurance policies, number-crunching such variables as a landlord's fire history, tax arrears, and record of building code violations.[2]

By the late 1980s, local government and civic network infrastructures were establishing computerised presences, and homeless people in Santa Monica used local library connections to the city's Public Electronic Network to mount a successful campaign for improved access to showers and lockers, both essential in finding work or accommodation. In Wilmington, North Carolina, the residents of the Jervay Place housing project used public access Net terminals to secure a more active, participatory role in its proposed redevelopment. Through discussion lists, they made contact online with architects who analysed the redevelopment plans (sent to them as email attachments) and offered advice, which the residents then took to negotiations with the housing authority.[3]

[ . . . ]

The IMC format is a development from a local site called Active Sydney.[4] Like the IMCs, Active Sydney is an open publishing forum, though it has an additional emphasis on co-ordinating direct actions and discussing tactics. Gabrielle Kuiper, a PhD student at the Institute for Sustainable Futures, first had the idea for this site at two o'clock one morning while she was supposed to be thinking about her research (although she stresses that creating Active Sydney became very much a collaborative process and evolved through the input and ideas of the site's volunteers). The initial inspiration was a monthly photocopied listing of local social change events, the 'Manic Activist' calendar. Compiled by student environmentalists, the calendar listed direct actions, lectures, seminars, meetings and screenings.

'As a compulsive reader of noticeboards, all-round information junkie and email addict,' Kuiper says, 'it was obvious to me that this sort of information should be online. While it originally focused on events, Active is attempting to be more than a subversive newspaper or a community bulletin board. It aims to be a meeting place, an online autonomous zone, a hub of active information where a whole variety of social change movements connect. What we hope is that participants can connect their talk to action, either by discussing events on the calendar or using the discussion to facilitate future events or actions – even things as simple as using the forum to write a joint letter to a politician or corporation or bank.'

Kuiper had an extensive network of connections to activist groups in Sydney, including to Critical Mass,[5] but the technical expertise needed to bring them together online was co-ordinated by Matthew Arnison, also a PhD student, researching physics at Sydney University. Arnison was a co-founder of the Community Activist Technology group (CAT) in 1995 – CAT's orientation can be seen in its slogan 'pedestrians, public transports and pushbikes on the information super hypeway'. Among other projects, CAT offers training and geek help to those who want to take progressive causes online;[6] in helping to devise Active Sydney, Arnison was able to bring this experience to that of the two programmers who'd begun the project.

In his landmark essay on open source software, 'The Cathedral and the Bazaar', Eric S. Raymond suggests that 'Every good work of software starts by scratching a developer's personal itch'.[7] The itch that was to lead to the IMC software was a frustration with the unproductive hierarchies and group politics of other alternative media. Like many in the city, Matthew Arnison had been unhappy when the previously Sydney-focused Triple J radio station went national, leaving a community gap which smaller local stations, such as 2SER, struggled to fill. Missing the underground feel of the old Triple J, Arnison gravitated towards community TV, but became frustrated by management and top-heavy group politics and moved on to the Net. With CAT he built connections with independent groups working in both old and new media, developing software to enable online coverage of an Australian community radio conference in 1995; the group's first piece of automated software was developed for the 1997 conference. This software enabled continuous updates from correspondents at the event, extending information and participation to those who couldn't attend. But Arnison again became frustrated by hierarchical management, an experience which would be pivotal in the development of the horizontal Active software.[8]

Active Sydney first went online in January 1999, using most of the features of the subsequent IMC software – open publishing, email alerts and events calendars. By March 2000, the site hosted contact details for more than 100 organisations in the city – community TV and radio groups, organic food co-ops, public transport activists, disability rights discussion lists, sexuality collectives, legal advisory services, local branches of Amnesty and Friends of the Earth, and Ecopella – 'a community group that performs modern choral works about environmental issues'.[9]

[ . . . ]

As plans for the Seattle actions took shape, Arnison met some American activists who were planning a site to cover the events. They envisioned an online newswire for alternative media outlets, such as community radio stations in the US, but were planning to use commercial software to build it. Arnison persuaded them that the technical advantages of a site based on free software would make international collaboration more possible. The Active Sydney software offered the basis.

Working from Sydney, Arnison was instrumental in getting the Seattle IMC online from scratch in the two weeks before the events. As the protests began, physical distance from Seattle turned out to actually be an advantage: Arnison was able to focus on programming and systems administration problems more clearly than could the geeks on the ground, who were stretched by helping contributors digitise their video footage and post their stories. It also meant he didn't have to deal with the tear gas which intermittently wafted into the Seattle IMC office.

## DIY Media and News Narratives

[ . . . ]

In this sense, the IMCs are part of a long tradition. Downing's historical surveys of alternative media enable us to trace this tradition back hundreds of years. But a key root of the IMC approach is in the tradition of the fanzine (now generally abbreviated to zine). In his punk history *England's Dreaming*, Jon Savage writes that 'Fanzines are the perfect expression – cheaper, more instant than records. Maybe THE medium. A democratization too – if the most committed "new wave" is about social change then the best fanzines express this.'[10]

If the sound of punk was fossilised by the time the Sex Pistols released their second single, the more lasting impact was in the spread of the DIY aesthetic typified by the zine – the rise of indie record labels and distributors changed music more than any of the records they released; and, as Savage suggests, the boom in zines enabled by photocopiers opened up new possibilities for self-expression. Mark P, of seminal punk zine *Sniffin' Glue*, claimed he would write each issue in a straight draft with no revisions, with the final copy including crossed-out lines. 'I didn't really care about the magazine,' he told Savage, 'it was the ideas that were important.'[11] There's a direct line from early zines to the open publishing philosophy of the IMCs.

This access principle – here's three chords, now form a band – is the central pillar of what cultural studies academic George McKay terms 'DiY Culture'. McKay defines this as 'a youth-centred and -directed cluster of interests and practices around green radicalism, direct action politics, new musical sounds and experiences'.[12] The contributors anthologised in McKay's collection *DiY Culture* flesh this out, with their participant accounts of setting up indie newspapers and video magazines, of Reclaim the Streets and Earth First!, of free parties and traveller culture. Central to all of these is the circulation of ideas: this is not just a precursor to activism, it is activism – writing *is* action, open publishing *is* a direct cultural intervention.

Stephen Duncombe, in his book on zines, confesses to an anxiety that the cultural space of indie publishing is a retreat from actual engagement, from physical action: DIY media, in this analysis, are only 'a rebellious haven in a heartless world'. What good is all this subcultural creation, Duncombe asks, if it remains 'safely within the confines of the cultural world'?[13] The current state of development of Net-based activist media, as represented here by the Sydney IMC, offers an opportunity to rethink this separation of writing and action, of commentary and participation.

Questions about alternative media are usually framed in terms of their political economy, around issues of ownership and access; the DIY impulse of the online zine lets us think of alternative media in terms of *content*, in terms of the ways in which that content is framed and presented.

[ . . . ]

## Getting Determined

[ . . . ]

To understand the open source movement we need to recognise that in the worlds of computing and the Net there are also in-built technological politics. This was the serious point behind Umberto Eco's playful claim that the differences between the Macintosh and DOS computer operating systems were analogous to a religious schism. The Mac interface, Eco suggested, was Catholic, with its ease of use making it possible for all to enter the kingdom of spreadsheet heaven; the difficulty of DOS, by contrast, was a more demanding faith, which assumed that some would not make it all the way.[14] The Mac interface certainly took many people to spreadsheet heaven who might otherwise not have made the trip. In his history of Apple computers, Steven Levy enthuses about their desktop visual metaphor, describing it several times as 'brilliant' – 'What better way to emulate the sort of work that most of us do with computers – deskwork – than by making a virtual desk, with virtual drawers, virtual file folders, virtual paper?'[15] And indeed, in terms of popularising computers, an interface that the initial corporate target market could quickly get to grips with was an undeniably smart idea. But as for the rest of us? Whether we're using our machines at home, or at school, or on the beach, we're also still using that same office metaphor – a Version 2.0 interface.

But while the Version 2.0 corporate imagery remains dominant on desktops more than 20 years later, the web adds an extra layer of metaphor. In commercial web design, a common current interface is based on the newspaper front page. For some Internet critics, such as Geert Lovink, this is 'a regressive move, back to the old mass media of print'.[16] In such an analysis, the newspaper metaphor conceives of the Internet *participant* as an information *consumer* – we may read newspapers in many different ways, but we don't generally have many opportunities to contribute or interact with them, beyond letters to the editor. But for Matthew Arnison, the combination of newspaper imagery and the open publishing potential of the web is reinventing the idea of the newspaper. Not as a medium of consumption, but of intercreativity.

'Most people spend most of their web surfing time making their own newspapers through email, egroups, instant messaging, and personal web pages,' he argues. 'I see Indymedia's identification of open publishing as part of a broad pattern of how people use the Net. Time and again, parts of the Net that take on aspects of open publishing prove to be enormously popular. Geocities is in the top ten websites, and the big thing about Amazon is the community of book reviews it fosters – Amazon has a strand of open publishing at its heart. It's interesting to me that we are moving from a highly *corporate* model for computer use, the cubicle, to a much more *community* space – the newspaper. When you turn on most people's computers you get a corporate desktop, but within seconds the Net whacks a funky wallpaper over the top. The Net is the space where people are seriously messing with the way we interface with computers. And it's feeding back.'

In other words, the shaping of technology is not just down to governments and business, but also to the rest of us – we can *adapt* technology as well as *adopt* it; the best description of this remains novelist William Gibson's observation that 'the street finds its own uses for things'.[17] We might think, for instance, of hip-hop's adaptation of the turntable, turning an instrument of reproduction into one of new production. Or of early house music producers' use of the Roland 303, taking what was designed as a home practice aid for guitarists and turning it into the creative centre of an entirely new style of music. Such examples cause problems for a number of the most common assumptions which have featured in cultural responses to new technologies – among them the hard determinist notion which Langdon Winner, in criticising it, summarises as follows: 'technological innovation is the basic cause of changes in society and . . . human beings have little choice other than to sit back and watch this ineluctable process unfold'.[18] In fact, the open source software movement – which underpins online open publishing in both technical and philosophical senses – shows that many people spend every day proving this inevitability to be false.

'This is why the Internet and the free software behind it is great,' argues Arnison. 'There is a reason for this inherent decentralisation in the technology. The tools were designed by geeks who wanted to chat with other geeks, not by Microsoft to maximise their profits, and really not by the military either, despite their role in funding it. The geeks didn't want bottlenecks, editors, censorship. [This decentralisation is] in the very low-level workings of the Internet system. To "fix" this, global corporate giants [would] need to get control of enough of the hardware and software that runs the Internet, and change the rules.'

When Microsoft suddenly noticed the Net in early 1994, this looked, in Arnison's words, 'like a snack'. With its existing dominance of the PC software and operating system markets, it appeared all too likely that the company could use these virtual monopolies to gain another. But the emergence of the Linux operating system and the corresponding wider interest in free software – or open source – has dented this scenario.

When Arnison talks about 'free software' he doesn't just mean applications which are available without charge, although this is often the case, but applications where the actual programming code is openly accessible rather than masked, so people are both allowed and encouraged to adapt and customise it for themselves. More than this, the software itself cannot be privatised for commercial exploitation: it can be sold, but only if buyers are allowed to continue the modification process, should they want to. This stimulates innovation, experimentation, improvements, which are then passed along for others to build upon. New developments are continually being tested and either built on or rejected. Among other consequences, this means that open source software is extremely reliable, continually going through a kind of peer review process. It's free, as the saying goes, as in free speech *and* as in free beer.

'I find this whole process a total inspiration,' says Arnison. 'A lot of it hinges on the idea of copyleft, where you include a GNU Public Licence with the source code, which means no one else can ever privatise the software. It's like a virus that enforces caring and sharing on people who use your software. All of the tools we use [in IMCs] are free software, which means anyone has the right to use, copy, or change them. This includes access to the source code, the blueprint behind the software, which means we can customise it or add features with wild abandon. Having reaped the benefits of free software, pass them on.'

This idea of non-proprietorial invention is not a new one. Salk refused to patent his polio vaccine, and Benjamin Franklin left his many inventions unpatented, arguing that 'we should be glad of an opportunity to serve others by any invention of ours, and this we should do freely and generously'.[19] And it's important to underline that this is far from a fringe movement – Matthew Arnison points out that the open source Apache web server has double the market share of any competitor, including Microsoft. Apache has even been used to run Microsoft's own Hotmail.[20] And key IT corporations, including IBM, Netscape and Hewlett-Packard, have embraced the principles of open source software to greater or lesser degrees. In February 2002, *New Scientist* magazine published an article about developments in this area which extend the principles beyond computing, from OpenLaw to Open-Cola. But perhaps the real significance of that article was that the magazine issued it under an experimental licence, encouraging readers to copy, re-distribute or modify the text – the article itself was open source.[21]

Such open source software is not only a powerful armoury for activists – it's an activist movement in itself.

'Free software,' says Arnison, 'is the main resistance against the privatisation of the Internet. This is a huge struggle for the future of mass media. I like to think the free software movement is a very strong activist movement, but somewhat hidden. This is because the people involved don't really think they are activists, and other activists don't realise what is going on. The organisation of the movement is highly decentralised, with people all over the place spontaneously starting new projects, and placing them out there to see if people like them. One big reason the people making free software don't realise they are activists is because they are having so much fun! For once they can write software to do what they want, rather than what they can get paid to write, and they get to join a huge family of other people sharing the process of writing software.'

The IMC philosophy of open publishing is, then, entirely consistent with its technical foundations in the open source movement. Both essentially argue that anyone can and should be trusted to be both creative and responsible. And both are the Version 1.0 Internet in action. In yielding editorial control in favour of relying on participants to be responsible in their contributions, the IMCs trust that a self-selection process will keep the projects on track.

'If you provide a space,' says Gabrielle Kuiper, 'where people can be intelligent, imaginative and creative, they will be. We've had no problems with people writing inappropriate or even boring news, for example. If you look at the news stories, you'll see that a lot of thought and effort has gone into most of them.'

The open source and Independent Media Centre movements are not, of course, the only Net projects with a stake in the in-built properties of technology. At the level of cultural activism, some interesting Net art works to raise awareness of the fact that our sexy new tools are not neutral. One example is Word Perhect (sic),[22] a web art project which displays a crude, hand-drawn word processing interface. We are invited to choose a surface to write on – the back of a phone bill, an old calendar, scraps from a cigarette packet – and then to select either messy or tidy handwriting. While the icons on the toolbar are mainly familiar, clicking on them produces messages which call attention to our increased dependence on certain kinds of technology to shape our writing, our correspondence, our thinking. Select the spell-check button and you're told to go and look the word up in a dictionary. Ask to open a saved document and you're told 'you should close your eyes and remember about it yourself'. And the 'undo' button urges you to take responsibility for what you've just written.

What's this all about? It teases us about our reliance on automated functions, but it also points to the in-built values in word processors, to a potential gulf between the automatic functions which toolbar programmers decide we want, and the reality of the writing process (Word Perhect includes a kettle icon for tea breaks). As Jeanette Hofmann argues, learning to write with a word processor involves learning a kind of new language.[23] Word Perhect draws our attention to this and to the degrees of skill and autonomy that programmers allow us.

A more sophisticated project than this, though, is Natural Selection. Natural Selection is a search engine mind-bomb, created in response to racist, white supremacist material online.[24] It works to undermine the supposed objectivity of mainstream search engines, interrogating the ways in which they select and rank their results. As Matthew Fuller, one of the creators of Natural Selection, argues, 'The apparent neutrality of these technologies and their inbuilt cultural biases need to be taken apart'.

Created by members of the Mongrel art collective in the UK, Natural Selection offers a conventional search interface. But if we enter certain search strings, we land in a parallel network of content created by Mongrel and their collaborators. The idea is that anyone searching for, say, neo-Nazi writings would find themselves instead at a site which ridiculed their views. But the engine is not only activated by searches for what could be considered offensive key words. Let's take 'cats' as a harmless example. When we run our search, the engine retrieves a list of matches to cat-related sites – all of which are aliases for links to Mongrel's own content. Click on our cat choice and we might find ourselves reading a self-assessment questionnaire to gauge our chances of being accepted for immigration into the UK. Fill it in, and an article appears about Jamaican woman Joy Gardner, who died on 28 July 1993 after being forcibly restrained with a 'body belt' while she was being issued with a deportation order. Other destinations include an article about neo-Nazi rock bands by post-Situationist author Stewart Home and an essay about Islam and globalisation by Hakim Bey.

The result? Nothing returned by the search engine is what it seems, nothing can be taken at face value, and we may be left to question the processes by which our usual search mechanisms select and organise their material. Matthew Fuller argues that the project points to the in-built cultural politics and assumptions that regular search engines exhibit; that their methods of selecting and presenting results mask intrinsic biases towards the world views of the kinds of users that their programmers imagine. There may be no way around the use of such assumptions, of course, but one point of Natural Selection is not to criticise programmers for doing this, but to ensure that we are aware that they do it when we go to use a search engine.

'The authority of the mainstream search engines is derived from the relative accuracy of their ability to crawl and order the Internet,' Fuller says. 'There are a variety of ways in which they do this. Yahoo!, of course, trades on having a legible view of the world, a way of ordering things and dividing them up into neat little definitions. Let's just say there's not much poetry going on here. This is the Internet made into a filing cabinet. For the other two techniques, when their crawler hits a search engine, they organise what they find in different ways. Either a fixed view of where words or contents fit, or a system of ordering that is determined according to the choices users make about where they go from a list of search results. The first is really a hidden, automated form of directory; the second is more subtle, but seems largely to be determined by associations of search terms with search results determined by whatever is the demographic majority of Net users. This has obvious implications."

Natural Selection is also significant because it engages with one of the central scare stories attached to the Net – the claim that information found online just can't be trusted. It's a common argument – that there's no central quality control, no peer review, and no editorial selection. This is a typical journalistic response to the open publishing model of the IMCs. In fact, it's striking how often those articulating this position are those with a stake in older media and in those media's self-appointed role as the Fourth Estate: journalists who, trained to work in certain ways, for certain kinds of institution, want to convince us (and maybe themselves) that those ways and institutions work better than they in fact do. This despite the fact that it's only too easy to find fault with the established media, from the specious veneer of objectivity to the blatant cross-promotions. Anyone who consumes enough media can write their own list.

In his history of the Internet, John Naughton – himself a journalist – reminds us of the established media's less-than-spotless record on addressing Net issues, reviewing *Time* magazine's legendary 'cyberporn' beat-up, in which a crude undergraduate research project was brandished as evidence of the need for censorship in cyberspace.[25] Perhaps, then, to appropriate some corporate-speak, the status of information on the Net is not so much a problem as an opportunity. Perhaps the IMC open publishing model offers – or demands – a new way of looking at older media: a Version 1.0 lens through which we can view Version 2.0 media. Rather than just reminding ourselves not to be too trusting of what we see online, perhaps we should extend this scepticism into a more active engagement with other media forms as well.

## Notes

1   Sydney Independent Media Centre, http://www.sydney.indymedia.org.
2   Alison Cordero (1991) 'Computers and Community Organizing: Issues and Examples from New York City', in John Downing, Rob Fasano, Patricia A. Friedland, Michael F. McCullough, Terry Mizrahi and Jeremy J. Shapiro (eds), *Computers for Social Change and Community Organizing*, Haworth Press, New York and London, pp. 89–103.
3   Christopher Mele (1999) 'Cyberspace and Disadvantaged Communities: the Internet as a Tool for Collective Action', in Marc A. Smith and Peter Kollock (eds), *Communities in Cyberspace*, Routledge, New York and London, pp. 290–310.
4   Active Sydney, http://www.active.org.au/sydney.
5   Originating in San Francisco in 1993, Critical Mass is not an organisation, but a regular 'organised coincidence' in which as many cyclists as possible ride together through peak-hour traffic, advocating a range of aims, including sustainability, clean air and car-free public spaces.
6   Community Activist Technology, http://www.cat.org.au.

7   Eric S. Raymond (1997) 'The Cathedral and the Bazaar', http://www.tuxedo.org/esr/writings/cathedral-bazaar.

8   A map of its development, 'The Roots and Shoots of the Active Software', is at http://www.active.org.au/doc/roots.pdf.

9   Full list at http://www.sydney.active.org.au/groups.

10  Jon Savage (1991) *England's Dreaming: Sex Pistols and Punk Rock*, Faber & Faber, London, p. 401.

11  Ibid., p. 202.

12  George McKay (1998) 'DiY Culture: Notes Towards an Intro', in George McKay (ed.) *DiY Culture, Party & Protest in Nineties Britain*, Verso, London, pp. 1–53, quote from p. 2.

13  Stephen Duncombe (1997) *Notes From Underground: Zines and the Politics of Alternative Culture*, Verso, London, p. 190.

14  See the interview with Eco in Lee Marshall (1997) 'The World According to Eco', *Wired* 5.03, March, http://www.wired.com/wired/archive/5.03/ff_eco.html.

15  Steven Levy (1994) *Insanely Great*, Penguin, Harmondsworth, pp. 68–70.

16  See Geert Lovink (2000) 'Cyberculture in the Age of Dotcom Mania', posted to the nettime list 15 April. Archived at http://www.nettime.org.

17  William Gibson (1986) 'Burning Chrome', collected in (1995) *Burning Chrome and Other Stories*, HarperCollins, London, p. 215.

18  Langdon Winner (1986) *The Whale and the Reactor*, University of Chicago Press, Chicago and London, pp. 9–10.

19  Franklin, quoted in Merritt Roe Smith (1994) 'Technological Determinism in American Culture', in M. R. Smith and L. Marx (eds), *Does Technology Drive History? The Dilemma of Technological Determinism*, MIT Press, Cambridge, MA, pp. 1–35, quote from p. 3.

20  On open source software see http://www.opensource.org, http://www.gnu.org and http://www.slashdot.org. For an accessible history of the movement see John Naughton (1999) *A Brief History of the Future*, Weidenfeld & Nicolson, London. See also Lawrence Lessig (1999) *Code*, Basic Books, New York.

21  Graham Lawton (2002) 'The Great Giveaway', *New Scientist*, 2 February, is also at http://www.newscientist.com/hottopics/copyleft/copyleftart.jsp.

22  Tomoko Takahashi and Jon Pollard (2000) *Word Perhect* http://www.frieze.com/projects/perhect/frame.html.

23  Jeanette Hofmann (1999) 'Writers, Texts and Writing Acts: Gendered User Images in Word Processing Software', in Donald MacKenzie and Judy Wajcman (eds), *The Social Shaping of Technology* (2nd edition), Open University Press, Buckingham and Philadelphia, pp. 222–43. On the politics of word processing, see also Matthew Fuller (2000) 'It Looks Like You're Writing a Letter: Microsoft Word', at http://www.axia.demon.co.uk/wordtext.html.

24  Natural Selection http://www.mongrelx.org/Project/Natural. See also Matthew Fuller's accompanying essay, 'The War of Classification', at http://www.axia.demon.co.uk/woc.html.

25  Naughton, *A Brief History of the Future*, pp. 32–3. The *Time* magazine cover story was: Philip Elmer-DeWitt (1995), 'On a Screen Near You: Cyberporn', 3 July, archived at http://www.time.com/time/magazine/archive. The Electronic Frontier Foundation website has a good archive of material on the case at http://www.eff.org/Censorship/Rimm_CMU_Time.

# 3    *Geert Lovink*

# AT THE OPENING OF NEW
# MEDIA CENTER, SARAI, DELHI

During the last weekend of February, Sarai, arguably the first new media center in South Asia of its kind, opened its premises with a three-day conference on the Public Domain. Sarai, a word which means in various South Asian and Middle Eastern languages an enclosed space, tavern or public house in a city, or, beside a highway, where travelers and caravans can find shelter, is located in the basement of a newly erected building in Delhi (India). The Sarai initiative describes itself as an alternative, non-commercial space for an imaginative reconstitution of urban public culture, new and old media practice and research and critical cultural intervention.[1]

[ . . . ]

Sarai is a unique blend of people and disciplines. The main background of the initiators of Sarai is in documentary filmmaking, media theory and research. Historians, programmers, urbanists and political theorists have subsequently joined them. One of the founders, Jeebesh Bagchi, describes Sarai as a "unique combination of people, practices, machines and free-floating fragments of socially available code ready for creative re-purposing. Here the documentary filmmaker can engage with the urbanist, the video artist jam with the street photographer, the film theorist enter into conversations with the graphic designer and the historian play conceptual games with the hacker."

Sarai is a program of the Center for the Study of Developing Societies (CSDS), an independent research center founded in 1964. CSDS is funded by the Indian state and a range of international donors. The center has

"At the Opening of New Media Center, Sarai, Delhi, February 2001" from Geert Lovink (2003), *Dark Fiber: Tracking Critical Internet Culture*. MIT Press, Cambridge, Mass. and London, pp. 204–16. Reprinted by permission of the MIT Press.

welcomed dissenting voices in South Asia and it is well known for its skepticism towards received models of development. Sarai is a pilot project for the Dutch Ministry of Foreign Affairs. So far most of that money was spent on building water pumps in rural areas. For decades Dutch policy had been to only support the poorest of the poor. However, recently more and more NGOs in the field started using the Internet. There is a growing awareness of the importance of IT use within development projects – and society as a whole. New media are becoming an important part of the rapid growing and diverting process of urbanization.

With a public access space full of terminals and a cafe, Sarai neither has the feel of an isolated research facility, nor does it have the claustrophobic agenda of many new media arts institutions. Nor does it equal an IT company, even though the place is flocked with young computer hackers. Monica Narula (another founder of Sarai, member of the Raqs Media Collective) is a filmmaker, photographer, and in charge of design at Sarai. She is responsible for the look of both the web site and the internal network interface. She says: "Delhi is a polarized space. Young people and students have nowhere to go. Either places are too expensive for them or nothing happens. So, the idea here is that people can come to Sarai, use the internal network interface via one of the terminals in the public space, and also have coffee and interact. In principle and execution the internal Sarai interface is much more sophisticated compared to the web site. This is because in India download time means money; people often can't be bothered to have plug-ins installed. After a fierce internal debate we decided to develop the heavier, creative interface for the public terminals and keep the web site really light."

The atmosphere during the opening was one of an exceptionally high intellectual level, the air filled with lively debates. The Sarai community, now employing 13 staff members, is open for everything, ready to question anything. Jeebesh, himself a filmmaker and another member of Raqs Media Collective, says: "I was not happy with the way in which classic research feeds back into society. I don't like being specialized. The idea is to proliferate and multiply, creating a new hybrid model in order to discover something and not get stuck with the form in which we are producing it."

Sarai has a number of research areas: ethnographies of the new media, the city and social justice, film and consciousness, mapping the city, free software and "language and new media" to do with the role of Hindi. The Internet provides an occasion for a new form of Hindi language expression, different from the culture of the Hindi literary establishment. The "CyberMohalla" free software project is under construction. It will focus on tactical, low cost hard- and software solutions for web authorization, scanning, streaming of audio and visual material. Sarai will provide schools and NGOs with solutions that are resulting from this project. From early on, Sarai has been collaborating with the Delhi Linux user group which led to the Garage Free Software project whose aim it is to set up a gift economy, working on alternatives to expensive proprietary software. It will also develop user-friendly interfaces and develop Linux-based applications in Hindi.

[During 2002–3] all those working at Sarai have been busy creating the space, installing computers on an entirely open-source network, designing and uploading the web site (www.sarai.net), doing basic construction work in order to prevent the monsoon storm water from entering, and setting up the groundwork for the Sarai archive so as to enable it to hold a variety of platforms, from books to DVDs, and connect it to a database with material accessible to visitors of the public access area. The Sarai database is best accessed via Sarai's internal network interface.

Monica Narula says: "We have worked on three versions of the site. The first was basic, the second one visually interesting but slow and somewhat linear. The newest and present version is faster and more complex. In our design, what we started working with was the idea of multi-perspectives. We wanted to combine elements from traditional work with contemporary street feel and its bright colors. Here in Delhi we experience simultaneous time zones. 'Old' representations show up in the most unexpected places. Therefore also the urge to work with a multi-perspective approach to representation."

Already before Sarai started, Monica had the idea of the computer taking you on a journey through the city. Monica: "The experience would be interactive but would also give you a path. Icons representing concepts would lead you through a narrative space around a concept using image both still and moving, text and sound. That idea is fairly ambitious. We realized that such a difficult design was all about coding, and we are working on it. In such an experience a sense of discovery remains important. You click on a certain motive and reach somewhere else. You think you know the city, but you discover you don't. By looking at it you start seeing new elements. That's the basic motivation behind the Sarai interface, even the form it has now."

For the handful of international guests visiting the opening, the quality of the Internet connection was a surprisingly stable 128K ISDN leased line, supported by back-up battery systems in case of "load shedding" which indeed frequently happens. On one occasion, last year, North Delhi had a 36-hour electricity power cut. The batteries for the Sarai servers are worth more than the servers themselves and can hold for up to $4\frac{1}{2}$ hours. Apart from that each PC has its individual UPS system.

Using both old and new media is a key element in Sarai's design program. Monica Narula: "It's about being interpretive and subjective. Our 'Mapping the City' project is not meant to present a demographic or ethnographic account. For us the question is: how does the city feel to us? Questions of class and gender are involved in this. There are so many untold stories, from people that usually do not matter. And we want to tap into the oral world of telling and listening to stories as well. Even me – I like reading but I also like talking and listening. We will focus on the dialogue aspects, looking into storytelling and oral traditions. For example, using film, photography and sound we would like to do an anatomy of one specific location, a little zone, making a cross-section from the rich trader to the man who is pulling the street car, all within a square kilometer. Such as an area in Old Delhi, where at one place someone once registered twenty-one different ways of transport."

The city of Delhi, with its approximate 10 million inhabitants, is an end-less source of inspiration for the Sarai members, lacking the disgust for poverty, pollution and noise of the elite and innocent Western tourists. The setting is post-apocalyptic. Shuddha Sengupta, also a member of the Raqs Media Collective and one of the Sarai founders: "In Delhi we are in some ways living in the future. In a situation of urban chaos and retreat of the public and the state initiatives. Tendencies that are currently happening in Europe. The young generation in Europe will face some of the realities that many of us are accustomed to in India, whereas we may leave some of these realities behind. The difference between a contemporary moment in India and Europe is one of scale rather then of an essential nature. There is more of everything here. More people, more complexities, and also more possibilities."

I asked Shuddha whether he would therefore say that Delhi is a global city as Saskia Sassen defined it in her book "Global Cities," as Delhi looks more like a national metropolis than a node for global finance. Shuddha replied: "Earlier Delhi was not considered a global city because it did not have a harbor, unlike Calcutta and Bombay. In global capitalism that doesn't count any longer. What's important is the capacity of a city to act as a network with other cities. Delhi is a center of the extended working day, providing the global market with back office accounting and call center services. There is an emerging digital proletarian class which is connected to the world."

Ravi Sundaram, a Sarai founder and now a co-director, and fellow at CSDS, added: "Saskia Sassen's book *Global Cities* came out right after the rise of finance capital in the late 1980s. I think we have to rework that notion. The new phase of globalization in the 1990s does not only depend on financial nodes anymore. They are complex networks of flows. Delhi is a new global city and there are many of them. In the new economy people are trading in global commodities, using global technologies, increasingly using the net, surrounded by an empire of signs. Delhi used to be like Washington DC. That was 15 years ago. Now it is a mixture more reminiscent of LA South Central with its urban chaos, migration, and uncontrolled growth of suburbs, informal networks and capital flowing everywhere. In that sense I would not limit global cities to financial nodes and labor flows. The narrow definition of global cities borders the sociological. We should move to a more cultural, political and engaged form."

I met Ravi Sundaram for the first time in June 1996 at the fifth Cyberconf in Madrid. He delivered a paper about the difference between the coming of cyberspace in India and previous national industrialization policies such as the building of dams. Ravi's research topic within Sarai is electronic street cultures, the gray economy of hardware assembly and the role of software piracy and cyber cafés in the spreading of PC usage and the Internet. The aim of Sundaram's investigations into the local "ethnographies of new media" is to add complexity to the view that computers are a conspiracy of the rich against the poor with only the upper class benefiting from information technology. Sarai rejects such clichés. Ravi: "The elites in the West and India share a culture of guilt. In the view of these elites, 'their' technology and creativity cannot be a property of daily life. Rather, the domain of the everyday is left to state and NGO intervention for upliftment." Sarai does not share that agenda. "We live in a highly unequal, violent society. But there are very dynamic forms of technological practice in that society. We speak to that, and not just in national terms. We speak equally, within transnational terms, which marks a difference to earlier initiatives in cinema, radio or writing. We are not the third new media (like in third cinema)."

How does Sarai look at the development sector? Jeebesh Bagchi, also from the Raqs Media Collective and a Sarai member: "Development often implies the notion of victims of culture. I don't think in those terms. People live, struggle, renew, invent. Also in poverty people have a culture. I feel a little lost in this terrain, knowing that Sarai, to a large extent, is financed through development aid programs. I would never use a term like 'digital divide.' We have a print divide in India, an education divide, a railway divide, an airplanes divide. The new economy in India is definitely not conceived as a divide. It is a rapid expansion of digital culture. The digital divide is a 'social consciousness' term, born out of guilt. We should interpret the media in different terms, not just in terms of haves and have not."

Sarai rejects the "Third World" label altogether. Jeebesh: "Within arts and culture, the human interest story usually comes from the Third World whereas formal experimentation is done in Europe and the United States. That's the international division of labor between conscience and aesthetics. It would be unfortunate if this would happen with Sarai. Working within the net, with different forms of knowledge, there are no longer discrete spaces. Working from within a so-called developing country means that you are constantly put under the techno-determinist pressure to be functional. At present there is no other domain to be creative outside of the development realm of sanitation, water and poverty. The pressure will always be there. But what worries us more is what discourse critical minds in Europe and the States will construct around Sarai."

Being the South Asian early bird on the global screen comes with certain responsibilities – and pressures. The threat of being instrumentalized, having to act within Western parameters, is a real one. Sarai members are aware of the danger of exoticism. Jeebesh: "I am afraid of over-expectation and burn out. Ideally Sarai should not become representative of its country or the region it is located within. We should break with the tradition of national cinema and the national filmmaker going to international festivals, saying 'I am from India, I am from Germany, etc.' We can lose focus if that's happening. We are interested in a dialogue among equals and do not want to get caught in the curated festivals of the world."

Monica: "Showing work abroad has a good side. It gives you deadlines, to start with! But I am not interested in becoming an authentic Third World voice. The aesthetics have to be driven from here. If there are collaborations, they have to be equal and have to integrate the smell and texture of a city like Delhi. Sarai is also aware of the danger of supremacy of text. You can say a lot with images. Images can be called either highbrow art or kitsch from the street, but they are also much, much more than that."

It's not all that easy to combine the busy excitement of new media production with more reflective research activities. Demanding programming and design of new media works can easily take over from theoretical reflections. Sarai is in the first place a research facility, but the pressure will be strong, from both in and outside, to show concrete results in terms of interfaces, software and new media titles. I asked Jeebesh how he would stop a hierarchy between new media production and research from happening. "It's a deep, institutional tension. There is an academic codification of research. In India there are only a few independent researchers. The academy here is creating systematic knowledge, but it's not creating dynamic public forms. In the early 20th century most of the brilliant thinkers were independent researchers, creating a dynamism of thought which we still carry on."

According to Jeebesh, Sarai should create media forms, which the academy cannot neglect. "Feature film has been respected as an equal, artistic art form, whereas the documentary form has been patronized by the academy. We should create such a dynamic tactical media form that it becomes equal to academic knowledge." Sarai does not intend to become a production house.

Jeebesh: "We are into experimenting. Still, there is certainly slackness among documentary filmmakers. We shoot and there is an equation between what has been shot and the film itself. The claim to be the makers of reality bites has created a climate which is not very self-critical. There is a crisis of representation. I do not want to represent anyone. So what then is an anti-representational documentary? With new media we would like to emphasize that intellectual crisis."

Where in Delhi does Sarai look for collaboration? Jeebesh: "Some of the intellectuals are experts, a technocracy which is being taken serious. After 1989 you can more freely say what you feel because the burden of state socialism and communism is no longer there. We will therefore see more interesting things happening. It will not only be about talking but about doing. From the beginning Sarai did not want to network with people who have already established themselves. We can collaborate with individuals, on a mutual basis. More challenging is how you engage with the popular design sensibility. What kind of dialog with this strange and eclectic world do we want to create, not based on domination or populism? How does a programmer create software for a non-literate audience?"

So far in India popular culture has been defined by film. There is a tradition in India to interpret society through film. Jeebesh: "Film will remain an important reference. Till the mid-1980s film was looked down upon. In the 1990s different readings of film and social inequalities were created. These days film has a strange presence through television culture. The music video clip does not exist here. What we have is television relaying film songs. India is a song culture and visual sign board culture. It is deeply embedded in the stories you tell. New media are reconfiguring narration and codes of self-description. There is interesting science fiction now. The problem is that film and television may be imaginative but it is not creating a productive culture. There is a tension with new media, from which potentially something new could grow. We are still surrounded by 20th century broadcasting concepts – inform, educate and entertain. New media should not follow that rubric."

There are numerous obstacles for Sarai in building public interfaces. Will the general public find its way to Sarai and how will Sarai reach out? Jeebesh: "Let the practice speak over time. We must become a place where young people feel at home and become confident so that they will start using it. An intellectual place where different opinions can be articulated, not a ghetto where people feel they have to say correct things." The balance between dissent and power is a delicate one, constantly having to question and re-invent itself while slowly becoming an institution. Co-director Ravi Sundaram: "One has to be deeply skeptical of all institutions, including our own.

Being part of an institution means being part of power, whether we like it or not. Both universities and arts institutions are strong nodes of power. In India both of them are in a financial and intellectual crisis. For a long time arts institutions were a monopoly of the state. That's over now."

Jeebesh: "Recently an American media artist was visiting Sarai and at a certain point the conversation focused on the question of how to map a database onto a surface, if I want to see the content of a database as an image? What is the aesthetics of a database? That's productive discussion. If people take that as an art form, and see it as an art work, that's fine, as long as it comes from an internal curiosity. In a non-visual, non-literate culture we have to somehow work out how the database relates to the surface, which is not text based."

Shuddha: "People may be interested in such arts-related issues on an individual basis. There should be an open space for the creative pursuits that people wish to follow on their own instinct without taking away the concerns that Sarai has as a collective body. We are not here to provide a platform for Indian new media artists to engage with the international community. Nor is it in our interest to stop it."

It is Sarai's explicit wish not to create a new discipline. A brave statement in times in which artists either have to buy themselves into the IT industry or, as in the case of net art, are bailing out by writing themselves into art (history) discourses and their institutions. Shuddha: "Sarai is not going to become an arts institution. There are many of us who are practitioners, working with images, text and sound. We look at those practices from different points of view. We would like to find hybrid forms, beyond the categories of the artist, activist, theorist or critic. Some of the work will take on the form of the aesthetic. Other work will engage with the realm of the political, of knowledge, and with the realm of understanding. None of these elements will have a primacy because we don't see it in those terms. Which is not to say that we will not have an engagement with the aesthetic or the realm of pleasure. We certainly will."

Jeebesh does not want to identify himself with any artist specialization. "That's the problem of net art or net culture. It limits cross-conversations. We will be very sensitive about that. We should not establish formal identities and disciplines. This can create structural divisions between us. That's why I like to call Sarai a post-institutional space where the public is always present, pushing you to be different."

Ravi Sundaram: "I never understood most of net art. I have always been interested in avant-garde practices but I have not yet identified net art as such. These are complicated aesthetic translations and we at Sarai still have a lot to discover. Two years ago we never imagined what and where we would be today. We have a shared language and a lot of creative disagreements and we would like to share that with outsiders too. If dialogue is a transparent, honest process, not rendered in national, Indian/Western terms, it becomes easier. It is a cruel, historical baggage that we are born into. It is marked on us that you are from the Third World. We abandon that old baggage."

Shuddha: "Working with sound, text and images over the past years we have found that the taxonomic regime of people being described as writers or film makers has been an inhibition of our work. We wanted to do more interesting work than 'filmmaking' allows. Funding wants to classify your practice and organize it in certain modes of qualifications. Having said that we do not want to enter into another regime of qualification of ourselves as net artists. One of the reasons why we entered the new media is because we felt that it allows for a certain liberation in which qualification regimes can be put aside." Ravi Sundaram adds: "All of us want to break out of disciplinary forms. I come out of formal academic institutions. Yet Sarai is a program of an academic research institution, CSDS." Jeebesh interrupts: "I like the tradition of public intellectuals, such as Ashis Nandy of CSDS who has a disdain for academia. He says 'I don't write, I think.' " Ravi Sundaram interrupts again: "There might be an avant-garde urge to mock institutions. But the money and recognition will come from that very same place. We have to recognize that tension. If we do not recognize the tension we will become rhetorical. We want to be in both places. We are not innocent of power. We live in a highly unequal society. But it is important to render this public, straight."

Let's go back to Sarai's original drive, to develop its own language of new media. What would it be based on? Shuddha: "The communication imperative is an important one for us. Media technologies in India so far have only been one to many. That should not happen to the net. The relation between communication and power should be investigated and challenged, even only conceptually to begin with. In order to get there we need to establish a truly international sensitivity. With that I do not mean national or regional identities. New media culture is not yet international. What goes on elsewhere has to be taken into account. When I used to look at the Internet and the new politics of communication that emerged earlier, I thought: our space, our city should be able to create this. I hope it will be possible for someone living in Teheran or Rangoon, in parts of Asia and Africa to think that something like Sarai should also be possible there. At one time it was impossible for us to imagine a Sarai. For me, after coming back from the Next Five Minutes 3 conference (Amsterdam, March 1999, www.n5m.org) it seemed possible. Before we were unable to bring together the energies that were necessary. There is a process of discovery of such energies."

## Notes

1   Sarai, The New Media Initiative, Centre for the Study of Developing Societies, 29 Rajpur Road, Delhi, 110054, India. Phone (00) 91 11 3951190; email dak @sarai.net; URL http://www.sarai.net. For the opening a reader was produced, entitled The Public Domain, with a variety of texts about new media in South Asia. For more information on how to order, please write to dak@sarai.net. There is also a Sarai list, called reader, discussing IT culture and politics in India and elsewhere: http://mail.sarai.net/mailman/listinfo/reader-list.

# 4    Néstor García Canclini

# MULTICULTURAL POLICIES AND INTEGRATION VIA THE MARKET

In 1994 the Latin American presidential summit held two meetings in two emblematic cities to try to reanimate a project that had languished for some time: regional integration. The first, held in June in Cartagena de Indias, included a representative of the Spanish government; the second, held in December in Miami, included Clinton but not Fidel Castro.

The first attempt to include this continent in the world economy took place five hundred years ago. Homogeneous labor-control methods in different regions facilitated the unification of local styles of production and consumption. The Christianization of the Indians, their introduction to literacy in Spanish and Portuguese, the design of colonial and subsequently modern urban space, the uniformization of political and educational systems engendered enabled one of the most effective homogenizing processes on the planet. With the exception, perhaps, of the Arab countries, there is no other area of the world where such a large number of independent states share the same language, history, and dominant religion, or have occupied for more than five centuries a more or less shared position in their relation to metropolitan countries.

Nevertheless, this historic integration contributed little to consistent economic development or to competitive participation in global exchange. In the cultural sphere, despite the multiplication of integrating organizations since the 1950s – Organization of American States (OAS), Economic Commission for Latin America and the Caribbean (CEPAL), Latin American Free Trade

"Multicultural Policies and Integration via the Market" from Néstor García Canclini (2001), *Consumers and Citizens: Globalization and Multicultural Conflicts*, tr. George Yúdice. University of Minnesota Press, Minneapolis and London, pp. 123–34, 179–80 (notes). Originally published as *Consumidores y ciudadanos: conflictos multiculturales de la globalización*. © 1995 by Editorial Grijalbo, Mexico. English translation © 2001 by the Regents of the University of Minnesota.

Association (ALALC), and so on – Latin American countries have not even been able to establish lasting forms of collaboration and reciprocal knowledge. It is still almost impossible to find Central American books in Montevideo, Bogotá, or Mexico. We can learn through US news agencies that Argentine, Brazilian, and Mexican films have won prizes in international festivals. But such news sources do not distribute them throughout the continent. Our publications, films, and musical works have just as much difficulty entering North America and Europe as do our steel, our grain, and our crafts.

Two decades ago, developmentalism – like other evolutionary modernizing tendencies – attributed Latin American disintegration and backwardness to "cultural obstacles," that is, to those traditions that differentiated the region. There was confidence that with industrialization our societies would be able to modernize homogeneously and establish fluid linkages among themselves. This did happen, in part. It is now easier to communicate via television networks than through books, or via fax than through the mail.

Nevertheless, there persist marked ethnic, regional, and national differences among Latin American countries. And we no longer believe that modernization will do away with them. On the contrary, the social sciences tend to accept Latin America's heterogeneity and the coexistence of diverse historical temporalities that are articulated to a degree but not dissolved in a uniform style of globalization. Multitemporal and multicultural heterogeneity is not an obstacle that needs removal but a necessary piece of information for any development and integration program.

However, the free-trade agreements that promote greater economic integration (such as NAFTA among Mexico, the United States, and Canada; MERCOSUR and other accords among Latin American countries) have little interest in the possibilities and obstacles presented by greater social disintegration and the low level of cultural integration in the continent. The cultural policies of each country and their exchanges with others are still programmed as if economic globalization and technological innovations had not already begun to reconfigure identities, beliefs, conceptualizations of what is one's own, and one's connections to others.

## Indigenous Peoples and Globalization

In order to understand the current challenges of the multicultural character of Latin American development projects, we should distinguish between two of its modalities: on the one hand, its multiple ethnicities; on the other, the multicultural outcome of modern forms of segmentation and the organization of culture in industrialized societies.

Indigenous rebellions and mobilizations bring home the importance of Latin America's multiethnic relations. Their complexity, however, is quite evident in everyday life circumstances. Many branches of our economies cannot develop without the participation of the 30 million indigenous people who live in Latin America. These groups possess differentiated territories, their own languages (whose speakers are increasing in certain regions), and work and consumption habits that distinguish them. Two and a half million Aymaras, 700,000 Mapuches, more than half a million Mixtecos, 2 million Mayas, 2 million Nahuas and 2 million Quichés, and approximately 10 million Quechuas have remained a fundamental part of Chile, Bolivia, Peru, Ecuador, Guatemala, and Mexico throughout their five centuries-long resistance.

There is no dearth of research on what these multiethnic relations represent in processes of modernization and integration. As modernization becomes problematic and it is obvious that metropolitan models of development are not applicable mechanically in Latin America, that version of history that considered modern technologies incompatible with non-Western traditions is no longer compelling. It is thus feasible to focus on the sometimes positive role of cultural diversity in economic growth and in popular strategies of resistance. On this view, ethnic and religious solidarity is seen as contributing to social cohesion and production techniques and traditional consumption habits are understood to be the basis of alternative forms of development.[1]

In some societies, consensus is achieved through multicultural policies that recognize diverse modes of economic organization and political representation. Some examples are ethnodevelopment programs in various Latin American countries, legislation to guarantee the autonomy of indigenous peoples on Nicaragua's Atlantic Coast, and juridical reforms of ethnic issues that are currently being negotiated in Mexico. These are examples of a partial shift from paternalistic *indigenismo* to modes of greater self-determination.[2] But these attempts at reformulation are not instituted without resistance from racist elites, who still see indigenous cultures as antiquated remnants or mere survivals that are of interest only to folklorists and tourists. On the other hand, many indigenous groups refuse to be integrated, even in pluralist societies, because they consider ethnicities to be "potential nations," completely autonomous political unities.[3]

Neoliberal economic policies have intensified these conflicts. In the past decade, they accentuated poverty and marginalization among Indians and mestizos, and they continue to aggravate migration, displacement, and struggles over land and political power. Intercultural conflicts and racism are on the increase in many national border areas and in all large cities on the continent. Never before has it been so necessary to develop education, communications, and labor-regulation policies in the interest of greater interethnic democratic coexistence. In countries such as Peru and Colombia, peasant and urban economic conditions have deteriorated, spurring guerrilla movements, alliances between peasant struggles and narcotraffickers, and other explosive expressions of social disintegration. The segregationist fundamentalism of ethnic or paraethnic movements such as Sendero Luminoso only makes it more difficult to implement integration projects. In the United States, the restructuring of labor conditions and increasing racism have led to intensified repression of Latin American migrants, contradicting the integrative tendencies of free-trade agreements.

Despite the social upheavals that continue to vex intercultural relations, an analysis of the issues raised by these relations cannot be understood only in terms of the antagonism between dominant and subaltern groups. There are also promising changes in some government policies and new modes of relating traditions to modernization among indigenous groups.

Presently there are movements that balance their energetic claims for cultural and political autonomy with demands for full integration in modern development. They appropriate modern forms of knowledge as well as technological and cultural resources. They combine traditional healing procedures with allopathic medicine, ancient techniques of artisanal and peasant production with international credit and the use of computers. They seek autonomous democratic changes in their regions and egalitarian integration in modern nations. Guatemalan, Mexican, and Brazilian peasants send fax reports on the violation of human rights to international organizations. Indians from many different countries use video and E-mail to lobby for the defense of alternative ways of life.

At least in these cases, the problems of socioeconomic integration do not seem to ensue from the incompatibility between tradition and modernization. The failure of globalizing policies stems from a lack of flexibility in modernization programs, cultural incomprehension in their application, and, of course, the persistence of discriminatory habits in institutions and among hegemonic groups.[4] State reform in the guise of deregulation of services and subordination of public responsibilities to private interests does very little to expand the social agency of these multiple styles of life and the various forms of participation of marginalized sectors.

## The Failure to Coordinate Cultural Policies and Consumption

The problems raised by multicultural phenomena at the end of this century cannot be reduced to multiethnic conflicts, nor to the coexistence of diverse regions within each nation. The forms of thought and life connected to local or national territories are only one part of cultural development. For the first time in history, the majority of commodities and messages received in each nation have not been produced in their own territory, do not result from the particular relations of production, and do not convey meanings connected exclusively with given regions. They operate, in our view, according to a transnational, deterritorialized system of production and diffusion.

Since the 1950s, the principal means of access to cultural commodities, aside from schooling, are the electronic communications media. The number of homes with radio and television in Latin America is equal to, and in some areas even greater than, that of homes in which family members have completed primary school. Although textbooks have provided a modest integration of Latin America, they are usually limited to a national-historical perspective and often distort the history of neighboring countries. These shortcomings are not overcome by the historically weak information and "up-to-the-minute world reports" on television and radio. Our enormous consumption of the mass media, greater than that of the metropolitan countries, as pointed out earlier, is not nourished by endogenous media production with better information and greater potential to bring Latin American countries together. Like cinema, television – and radio to a lesser degree – gives priority to information and entertainment that originates in the United States. The representation of the diversity of national cultures is low in all of our nations, and there is even less airtime given to the cultures of other Latin American countries.

As we near the end of the century, we must turn to the actions and decisions of those responsible for cultural policies if we are to deal effectively with the problems raised by the culture industries (the primary agents) and globalization (the main tendency) for our multicultural societies. We also need to ask who can be integrated into these processes and what are the conditions for the democratization of transnational integration.

The following summarizes the approaches taken by those organizations most involved in dealing with (or neglecting) these problems:

1. State cultural policies are still focused on the preservation of monuments and folkloric heritages, and in the promotion of the fine arts (visual arts, theater, classical music), whose audiences are diminishing. Public action regarding electronic industries has been reduced to the privatization of radio and television stations as well as other circuits of mass diffusion, precisely those in which there have been attempts to sustain – almost always with little success – artistic and information programs that represent cultural diversity.

2. In contrast, large transnational private corporations (mostly US-based, but also Latin American-based conglomerates such as Televisa and Rede Globo) have dedicated themselves for decades to the most profitable and most influential communications media. They have thus penetrated into family life and become the principal organizers of mass entertainment and information. Some Latin American corporations have produced recreational programs with broad transnational coverage, thus favoring a greater presence of national or "Hispano-American" themes and styles. Recent audience surveys show that they have high receptivity among the popular classes. More educated people prefer US TV series, films, and music.[5] But the main question today, in my view, is not how many foreign or national messages circulate (although this may still be important), but rather the disdain or apathy of all programs (whether *Dallas, Cristina*, or *Siempre en domingo*) toward minority or regional cultures that have not been sanctioned by world folklore. Also deplorable is the censorship of debates about society itself and the lack of a diversity of information indispensable for the construction of citizenship and integration with other countries in the region.

3. The cultural actions of international organizations and those promoted by the meetings of ministers of culture reproduce on a Latin American scale the view of states, which gives priority to high culture, on the one hand, and monuments and folkloric heritage, on the other. They give preference to a conservationist vision of identity and to an integrationist view based on traditional cultural goods and institutions. For example, of the sixty-seven projects recognized by UNESCO as activities of the "World Decade for Cultural Development" in Latin America in 1990–91, twenty-eight were dedicated to conservation of cultural heritage; seventeen to participation in cultural life and development; ten to the cultural dimension of development; eight to advancement of creativity and activity in the arts; three to the relation between culture, science, and technology; and only one to the mass media.[6]

Some Latin American governments have recently signed accords to facilitate the exchange of books, works of art, and antiquities through customs houses. Mutual cooperation programs have also been created. Worthy of mention are book collections such as the Biblioteca Ayacucho and the Biblioteca Popular de Latinoamérica y el Caribe; the journal supplement series Perio-libros, which includes works by prominent writers and artists; the decision to create a Latin American Fund for the Arts and another for Cultural Development; Latin American endowed chairs and Latin American and Caribbean Culture Houses in each country. All of these are definite advances in the mutual knowledge of the continent's nations. But these measures are limited to the field of written culture and "classical" plastic arts and music.

Meanwhile, the Working Group on Cultural Policies of the Latin American Social Science Council (CLACSO) has carried out research on cultural consumption in large Latin American cities that offers data similar to ours in Mexico City. For example, audiences for high culture do not exceed 10 percent of the population.[7] It is no doubt necessary to expand support for literature and the nonindustrialized arts, but at the end of the twentieth century it does not seem convincing to say that we are promoting cultural development and integration if we lack public policies for the mass media through which 90 percent of the inhabitants of this continent inform and entertain themselves.

4. Cultural resources involving everything from traditional artisanal knowledges to radio and video programs also circulate in nongovernmental organizations and associations of independent artists and media workers. Festivals, exhibitions and workshops, networks of alternative audiovisual programs, magazines, and books in which cultural development is documented – all of these are sponsored with scarce local funding and a great amount of free work, sometimes with subsidies from universities and international foundations. According to a directory put out by the Institute for Latin America, there are more than five thousand independent groups of education, culture, and communications producers in our region. We value their contributions toward the formation and organization of popular sectors in defense of their rights, and toward the documentation of their life conditions and cultural production. But their actions are strictly of local scope and cannot be taken as a substitute for the actions of states. These independent groups almost never include the mass media and consequently have little influence over the majority's cultural habits and ways of thinking.

That states, corporations, and independent organizations work in isolation hinders the development of multicultural societies in Latin America; instead, it produces greater segmentation and inequality in consumption, impoverishment of endogenous production, and discouragement of international integration. In recent years, the reduction of public investment and weak action on the part of private enterprise have produced the following paradox: greater trade among Latin American countries and with metropolitan ones is promoted at the same time that we produce ever fewer books, films, and records. Integration is encouraged at the same time that we have fewer things to export and lower salaries reduce what majorities can consume.

The drawbacks are even more dramatic with regard to Latin America's access to cutting-edge technologies and communications highways: satellites, computers, faxes, and the other media that provide information necessary to make decisions and innovate. The subordination of Latin American countries will get even worse with the elimination of free-trade agreements, trade barriers to foreign products, and the few surviving subsidies for local techno-logical development. We will be left more vulnerable to transnational capital and cultural trends devised outside the region as there is an increase in cultural and scientific dependence on cutting-edge communications tech-nologies, which require high financial investments and generate more rapid innovations. The multiculturalism generated by these trends does not repre-sent diverse historical traditions but rather stratification resulting from the unequal access to advanced communications by countries and sectors internal to each society.

How do the modes of access to transnational communications systems produce new forms of sociocultural stratification? The incorporation into global culture of the great majorities, especially in peripheral countries, is limited exclusively to the first phase of audiovisual industries: free entertain-ment and information on radio and television. Small sectors of the middle and popular classes have updated and upgraded their information as citizens through access to the second stage of the media, which includes cable televi-sion, environmental and health education, as well as political information on video, and so on. Only small fractions of the corporate, political, and aca-demic elite are connected to the most dynamic forms of communication, to that third stage that includes fax, e-mail, satellite dishes, as well as the infor-mational and playful interactivity of aficionado videomakers and horizontally organized international networks. In some cases, a handful of popular groups gain access to these latter circuits through the dissemination of community newspapers, radio stations, and video production.

The extension of the last two models of communication is a key condition for the development of democratic forms of citizenship today. People need access to international information and must have the capacity to intervene in meaningful ways in global and regional integration processes. The multi-national complexity of problems such as environmental contamination, drug traffic, and technological innovations requires information that transcends local spaces still circumscribed by nations, and coordinated action in a supra-national public sphere.[8]

What is being done in Latin America to develop the forms of citizenship that require the most advanced and interactive forms of cultural diffusion and consumption? If we believe that endogenous production and the representa-tion of regional interests in these fields require not only the organization of civil society but also state initiatives, then we need to keep track of the amounts invested to this end.

Latin America has more than 8.3 percent of the world's population but only 4.3 percent of engineers and scientists active in research and develop-ment, and it only invests 1.3 percent of all the resources in this field.[9] These figures raise questions about the participation of a continent such as Latin America in international markets and about its capacity for self-management in the future.

## Cultural Integration in an Era of Free Trade

The multicultural integration of Latin America and the Caribbean requires constitutional and political reforms that guarantee the rights of diverse groups in the context of globalization, that promote understanding and respect for differences in education and in traditional forms of interaction. But it is also the responsibility of public institutions to develop programs to facilitate reciprocal information and knowledge in culture industries that provide mass communications – radio, TV, film, video, and interactive electronic systems – to different peoples and subgroups within each society.

We need policies to promote the formation of a Latin American audiovisual space. In an era in which film, video, records, and other industrial forms of communication are unable to recoup their high costs if distributed exclusively in a given country, the integration of Latin America becomes an indispensable resource for the expansion of markets, thus facilitating our own production. I would like to mention three proposals that adumbrate what these policies might look like:

1. The creation of common Latin American markets for books, film, television, and video, accompanied by concrete measures to promote production and favor the free circulation of cultural commodities. (The steps taken in this direction, more declarative than practical, demonstrate the need for more fine-tuned diagnostics of the consumption habits in Latin American countries as well as their most determined public policies.)

2. The establishment of quotas for minimum screen time, radio airtime, and other Latin American cultural commodities in each country of the region. (Notice that we do not recommend returning to the narrow policy that established a 50 percent quota for national music and cinema; this new suggestion is inspired by a 1993 Spanish law that took into account regional conditions of production and circulation and decreed that movie houses in cities with more than 125,000 inhabitants should show 30 percent European films.) The promotion of a Latin American market for cultural commodities will not be effective unless it is accompanied by measures that protect that production through its circulation and consumption.

3. The creation of a Latin American Fund for Audiovisual Production and Diffusion. Its role would be to finance in part film, television, and video

production, to provide smooth coordination of state, corporate, and civil institutions, to imagine new channels of distribution (video rental outlets, high-quality cultural programs, mass audiences for national and regional television networks, a Latin American cable signal).[10]

Free-trade agreements should not foment an indiscriminate opening of markets, but take into consideration the unequal development of national systems as well as the protection of the rights of production, communication, and consumption by ethnic and minority groups. It is necessary to regulate the participation of foreign capital, including that of larger Latin American economies or of transnational corporations based in the region, in order to prevent monopolies from strangling the cultural industries of the smaller countries. But more important than restrictions, it is necessary to seek collaboration agreements that balance the relations between "truly exporting countries (Brazil, Mexico), emerging exporters (Argentina, Chile, Venezuela), and those that only import (the rest)."[11]

A democratic multicultural development will be realized in each nation only if there are favorable conditions for the expansion of regional, ethnic, and minority radio and television stations; or at least of programming designated for the expression of different cultures, subject to collective public interest rather than commercial profitability.

The promotion of these policies requires a reformulation of the role of the state and of civil society as representatives of the public interest. It has been said that it is necessary to put an end to overly protectionist populist states in order to reduce the risks of centralization, clientelism, and bureaucratic corruption. But after a decade of privatization we have not seen private corporations make telephones or airlines function any better, or even elevate the quality of radio and television programs. Rather than mire ourselves in the quagmire of the state versus the market, we have to create policies to coordinate the diverse actors who participate in cultural production and intermediation.

The goal is not to reinstall the proprietary state, but to rethink the role of the state as an arbiter or guardian against subordinating collective needs for information, recreation, and innovation to the profit motive. To guard against the risks of state intervention and the frivolous homogenizaton of diverse cultures by the market, it is necessary to get beyond the binary option between the two and to create spaces where the multiple initiatives of civil society can emerge: social movements, artists' groups, independent radio and television stations, unions, ethnic groups, and associations of consumers, radio listeners, and television viewers. Only the multiplication of actors can favor a democratic cultural development and the representation of multiple identities. The new role of states and international organizations (UNESCO, OAS, SELA [Latin American Economic System], ALADI [Latin American Association for Integration], etc.) will be to reconstruct public space, understood as a multicultural collective space where diverse agents (states, corporations, and independent groups) will be able to negotiate agreements for the development of public interests. Such changes in communications and cultural policies are necessary for the exercise of diverse forms of responsible citizenship, as conditioned by transformations in sociocultural settings, current forms of consumption, and transnational integration.

## Notes

1   Lourdes Arizpe, "Pluralismo cultural y desarrollo social en América Latina: elementos para una discusión," *Estudios Sociológicos* 2:4 (Mexico City, January–April 1984); Rodolfo Stavenhagen and Margarita Nolasco, *Política cultural para un país multiétnico* (Mexico City: Universidad de las Naciones Unidas, 1988).

2   [In Latin America, and especially in Mexico, Central America, and the Andean countries, *indigenismo* is the name for a literary and artistic style that represents the circumstances and struggles of indigenous peoples. It is also the name for political movements and state policies regarding indigenous peoples. – *Trans.*]

3   Guillermo Bonfil Batalla, ed., *Hacia nuevos modelos de relaciones inter-culturales* (Mexico City: Consejo Nacional para la Cultura y las Artes, 1993).

4   On these topics, see José Jorge de Carvalho, *O lugar da cultura tradicional na sociedade moderna* in *Seminário folclore e cultura popular. As várias faces de um debate* (Rio de Janeiro: INF Coordenadoria de Estudos y Pesquisas/IBAC 1992), 23–38 [Spanish translation: "Las dos caras de la tradición: Lo clásico y lo popular en la modernidad latinoamericana," in *Cultura y pospolítica*, ed. Néstor García Canclini (Mexico City: Consejo Nacional para la Cultura y las Artes, 1995), 125–65]; and Roger Bartra, *Oficio mexicano* (Mexico City: Grijalbo, 1993).

5   Emile McAnany and Antonio C. La Pastina, "Telenovela Audiences: A Review and Methodological Critique of Latin American Research," paper presented at the Eighteenth Convention of the Latin American Studies Association (LASA), Atlanta, March 1994. See also Joseph D. Straubhaar, "Más allá del imperialismo de los medios. Interdependencia asimétrica y proximidad cultural," *Comunicación y sociedad* 18–19 (Guadalajara, May–December 1993).

6   Fernando Calderón and Martín Hopenhayn, "Educación y desarrollo en América Latina y el Caribe: tendencias emergentes y líneas estratégicas de acción," Third Meeting of the World Commission on Culture and Development, San José, Costa Rica, 22–26 February 1994.

7   See Carlos Catalán and Guillermo Sunkel, *Consumo cultural en Chile: la élite, lo masivo y lo popular* (Santiago: CLACSO, 1990); Néstor García Canclini, ed., *El consumo cultural en México* (Mexico City: Consejo Nacional para la Cultura y las Artes, 1993); and Oscar Landi, A. Vacchieri, and L. A. Quevedo, *Públicos y consumos culturales de Buenos Aires* (Buenos Aires: CEDES, 1990).

8  The Economic Commission for Latin America (CEPAL) is one of the few international organizations of the region that has begun to deal with these questions. See *La industria cultural en la dinámica del desarrollo y la modernidad: nuevas lecturas para América Latina y el Caribe*, LC/G. 1823 (14 June 1994).

9  Ibid., 47.

10  Manuel A. Garretón, "Políticas, financiamiento e industrias culturales en América Latina y el Caribe," Third Meeting of the World Commission on Culture and Development, San José, Costa Rica, 22–26 February 1994.

11  Rafael Roncagliolo, "La integración audiovisual en América Latina: Estados, empresas y productores independientes," paper presented at the symposium on Cultural Policies in Processes of Supranational Integration, Mexico City, 3–5 October 1994.

# PART II
## Creative Identities

# *John Hartley*
# CREATIVE IDENTITIES

## Creative Industries: A Contradiction in Terms?

Two elements are crash-merged in the term "creative industries." "Creative" seems to preclude organization on an industrial scale, emphasizing instead the aspect of individual imaginative creative talent. "Industries" seems to preclude most human creativity from consideration. In short, if creativity is part of human identity, then what has it got to do with industries? Most people do not "identify" with industries as part of their sense of self, even if they work in an industrial environment – which most people in the world do not. So if there is such a sector as the creative industries, does it not follow that most of what human beings recognize and practice as creativity is excluded?

This section of the book explores this problem from different perspectives by showing how the creative industries sector connects with broader aspects of human creativity. How do human imagination, innovation, experience, creative labor, and consumption underpin the creative industries? How does everyday activity connect with large-scale enterprise, and vice versa? Why are the creative industries different from traditional manufacturing or primary industries?

Meanwhile, on the other side of the equation, it is probable that most industries from engineering to biotechnology believe that their own processes, products, and personnel are creative, and few would want to argue with that. So what might a distinctly creative sector have that the others don't? And how does the creative sector of the economy make use of human creativity more generally?

The readings for this section represent how a number of writers, all highly influential in their different ways, have intersected with these issues. None of them has addressed the issue of "creative *identities*" directly; indeed none of them is entirely happy with the idea of creative industries as a concept. And of course they address different problems arising from different contexts. Two of the extracts are by writers whose frame of reference is chiefly Europe and the UK (Howkins and Leadbeater); the other two refer primarily to the USA (Florida, and Miller et al.).

But in the course of their arguments about other matters they all do bring to life the main issue this section seeks to address: that the creative industries are grounded in personal ideas, talent, experience, and work. They show that the development of a sustainable economic sector upon that ground is a complex and challenging task, but in each case what emerges is that the creative industries, however defined, depend on individual identities, the growth and diversification of which remain the larger context within which creative industries themselves may grow and prosper.

## The Mayor's Commission on the Creative Industries: John Howkins

John Howkins begins with the definition of the creative industries, which he finds unsatisfactory and even contrary to common sense. This is because the term has arisen in the environment of public policy-making, and has been shaped by that. Howkins returns to first principles, which for him are that there's a fundamental difference between "information" (as in IT) and an "idea" (as in IP), and that completely different industries, even societies, follow from information and ideas respectively. In Howkins's view, the capture of the notion of creative industries by government agencies has not been entirely helpful, as it has tended to narrow the definition of creative industries to those which might benefit from government assistance. By this definition, art is in but media are out. Furthermore, and even more fundamentally, as it has become established, the notion of creative industries does not include all of those that are based on ideas. Science may develop IP and patents – the commercializable application of ideas – but the term creative is not extended to cover these. CP Snow's "two cultures" (arts–humanities and sciences) remain separated.

Howkins wants to get beyond that impasse, and have the creative industries defined as those that are organized around "having a new idea" in any field from the arts and sciences to infrastructure and social policy. Howkins identifies the creative industries as those which use "brain work" to produce intellectual property. He then goes on to discuss the features of the creative economy, the distinctive management style common in predominantly creative enterprises, the crucial difference between innovation and creativity, and the need to "liberate IP" as well as to commercialize it. Throughout, Howkins is trying to clear the policy frame of legacy thinking and pragmatic fudges in order to get to the point where the fundamental historical challenge can be confronted: that the "Information Society" is or may be coming to an end. Instead, he argues, "we are moving rather hesitantly and by fits and starts into a world which puts the priority on ideas and personal expression."

## Creative Consumers

The general introduction discussed the privatization of public life and how citizen and consumer boundaries have become blurred. It is in this dynamic context that the notion of **creative identities** needs to be seen, and where it begins to connect with the creative industries. For in the turbulence and churn of identity formation in the commercialized public sphere there have clearly arisen business opportunities. They are most pronounced where personal and consumer tastes have led to new publics.

A prominent example of this is the popular music industry. The new social movements of the period following World War II, which flowered in the 1960s, were expressed first and foremost in music. Perhaps it all started with the blues, the form in which African American reaction to oppression started to be heard by wider communities and used for their own yearnings for freedom (and simultaneously, via mechanical and electronic recordings, to be consumed in the comfort of their own homes). Later, the anti-war sentiments of many Americans in the Vietnam era were organized via rock music, the record industry, and live concerts, that is to say, political protest conducted by means of personal leisure consumption within a taste culture. The baby-boomers began to have real effects on the traditional political domain. The year 1968 is often mentioned as a watershed in this context, where youth, music, and counter-cultural radicalism clashed with straight politics on the streets of Paris, at the Democratic Party convention in Chicago, and outside the American Embassy in Grosvenor Square in London. It seemed at the time that young people, idealism fired by the consumption of commercially produced pop songs, could change the world politically (see Gitlin 1993; Mercer 1992). In the Cold War "peace" was a political matter; after 1968 it was a personal greeting. But the aim was the same.

The era of the protest song was at hand. Gay rights were fought for in nightclubs and via the songs and activism of popular musicians. Generational politics were conducted through musical styles, from mod to punk, spilling beyond music to clothes, choice of road-vehicles, and entire taste cultures. The women's and environmental movements were by no means confined to music, nor did they originate in that context, but both encompassed musical expression in the politics of the personal, recruiting people and ideas in lyrics and on the dance-floor, and both attracted high-profile celebrity advocates from among the stars of the music industry. Nationalist activists were equally ready to take the chance to raise consciousness via music, through such hybrids as Celtic folk-rock (Welsh, Breton, Irish, and Scots) and the many national forms from across the continents, especially from Africa, the Caribbean, and Latin America, which eventually aggregated into World Music.

These new social movements were routinely ignored by mainstream politics and persecuted or prosecuted. They found expression exclusively in the private sphere of identity and self-formation, and they were popularized almost exclusively by commercial means. But they began to exert immense pressure on government and industry alike because these were the concerns of the economically decisive baby-boomer generation. What began as marginal, counter-cultural, radical, or just plain weird came eventually to express majority or at least mainstream views and tastes. What is more, as this generation matured, public policy and commercial enterprise were obliged to come with it, so that family-building and home-making began to reflect alternative identities, cultural values, and family models. Before too long, the new social movements had settled in the suburbs, where they paid the mortgage, loved the kids – and went to Stones concerts and anti-racism rallies. They turned into *The Osbournes*.

The new economy has seen private companies as well as individuals pursuing civic goals in contemporary media contexts, using the very formats of consumer commercialism to critique the political philosophies that underpin them. These include well-known international organizations like Greenpeace and Adbusters. On the web such initiatives have proliferated: see Danny Schecter "the news dissector" at Media Channel and associated Global Vision (<http://www.mediachannel.org/>; <http://www.globalvision.org/>), or the British-hosted OpenDemocracy.net (<http://www.opendemocracy.net/>), or Australians Against Racism (<http://www.australiansagainstracism.org/>). In Canada, where they do these things so well, there's even a group called "Creative Resistance" (<http://www.creativeresistance.ca/index.html>). Many sites used a combination of creativity, consumerism, and critique, often with wit and imagination: try <http://www.syntac.net/hoax/Hypno/index.php>. At time of writing there was no "critique.com" or "dissent.com" although there were variants of both (and a political magazine does exist with the title *Dissent*). But there was no doubt that dissent could be the surprise best-seller of the season (Chomsky 2001).

These ventures cross the public/private divide, using commercially disseminated "entertainment" media to pursue civic and political goals associated with new social movements, outside of the traditional political domain. In many cases they are founded on directly creative activities, such as music, TV or web design, as the attractant and glue that makes the entire project viable.

## Delia Smith Not Adam Smith: Charles Leadbeater

In this extract from his celebrated book *Living on Thin Air: The New Economy*, Charles Leadbeater makes a crucial distinction between two kinds of knowledge – tacit and explicit – in order to show how an economy based on knowledge and ideas actually works. Tacit knowledge – how to cook – has to be made explicit – a recipe – before it can be commercialized. In other words knowledge has to be commodified. But knowledge is not all like other sorts of commodity. As Leadbeater says, "Consumption is the pleasure of possessing something. Yet when we consume knowledge – a recipe for example – we do not possess it. The recipe remains Delia Smith's; indeed that is why we use it. . . . Consumption of the recipe is a joint activity. . . . The knowledge in the recipe is not extinguished when it is used; it is spread." (Leadbeater's argument about the recipe is very close to that of Nicholas Garnham about the "cultural commodity": see Garnham 1987.)

And so in a knowledge economy the role of the consumer can no longer be understood via the metaphors we've inherited from agriculture, where products are literally eaten up by consumers. Instead, "in a knowledge-driven economy, consuming will become more a relationship than an act; trade will be more like replication than exchange; consumption will often involve reproduction, with the consumer as the last worker on the production line; exchange will involve money, but knowledge and information will flow both ways as well. Successful companies will engage the intelligence of their consumers to improve their products."

Leadbeater notes in conclusion that the republic of knowledge knows no privilege: "In an economy which trades in know-how and ideas, everyone seems to have a chance to make it, working from a garage, their kitchen or their bedroom." But they need to combine their know-how with business skills to make any money, as Delia Smith has done with her cookbooks. Part of what makes them attractive to the Christmas shopper is her own personality, style, and individuality, which she has found a way to package. In other words, her own personality is part of the product, which isn't complete until consumers have had a go at the recipe for themselves. Creating knowledge is "a human process, not a technological one," and that's the basis of the creative industries.

## DIY Citizens

In commercial democracies, long-term trends have encouraged citizenship itself to become a creative act. People are making themselves up as they go along. They create their own identities, both individually and inside various groups, from taste cultures to youth subcultures. They combine elements of private (personal) with public (political) identity, and these with consumer goods and services (clothes, travel, and household products), using technologies of interactive mediation (entertainment media and products, games, and the internet).

These selves express social, cultural, and creative values that link their authors to some groups and distinguish them from others on an affinity-based, voluntarist principle, not from the necessity of proximity (territory) and propinquity (blood). Such affinities may be based on living in the same neighborhood, city, or region, but many are virtual communities that connect with each other only in media representations and mediated interactions.

I have called this phase of modern identity formation "DIY citizenship" (Hartley 1999). The idea of DIY ("do-it-yourself") citizenship owes something to the idea of DIY culture (see McKay 1998), which was an activist phase of youth culture in the 1990s, characterized by the newly emergent rave scene, 'zines, the open source movement, eco-warriors ("Swampy" became a national celebrity in the UK; McDonald's-trashing French farmer José Bové became a globalized icon of anti-globalization), ecstasy, backpacking across the world, the Glastonbury music festival, and "ethnic" bands. The role of creativity in producing both senses-of-self and products-and-services is obvious enough without having to wander through the hippy stalls at a music festival.

DIY citizenship harvests the same fields as DIY culture, but is not confined to spectacular subcultures or youth activism. It's just as likely to occur among – for instance – suburban women who have leisure to stay at home and browse the internet and who, it transpires, are busy inventing senses of themselves via genealogical and family research (see <http://www.genuki.org.uk/>, <http://www.cyndislist.com/>, <http://www.rootsweb.com/>, or the wonderfully named Sydney Dead Persons Society – find it on Google). Or it occurs among people who seek a voice and form through which to narrate their lives, as creative non-fiction or digital storytelling (see <http://www.bbc.co.uk/wales/capturewales/>). Or those who identify with fan or taste cultures, where affinity may be more impassioned when it is organized around an aspect of identity politics such as sexuality (e.g. slash fiction – see <http://www.geocities.com/TelevisionCity/4580/links.html>).

DIY citizenship is itself a new entertainment format, for it is what "reality TV" is really all about: people making themselves up as they go along *on television*. In the USA "reality" kicks in at an early age. A late extension of the format is mediated creative self-formation for kids, e.g. Fox TV's *American Juniors*, a talent quest for 6- to 13-year-olds (<http://www.americanjuniors.com/showinfo/>). From *Big Brother* and *Popstars* to *American Idol*, the quest is for selfhood, and celebrity (or at least fame) is its public currency. As *Australian Idol*'s slogan has it, the dream is to go from "Zero to hero."

There is thus some sort of relationship, real and imagined, between the lives of citizens in commercial democracies and the "reality" formats that form such a prominent part of large-scale entertainment. People are performing themselves ever more self-consciously and professionally. They are creating identities, and along the way they're choosing to watch and interact with entertainments that teach the ups and downs of that process.

---

### The Experiential Life: Richard Florida

"This much is certain: Experiences are replacing goods and services because they stimulate our creative faculties and enhance our creative capacities." So says Richard Florida, who argues that experience is a key stimulus to the creative economy. He argues that there's a two-way street between the consumer and entrepreneur: "Because we relate to the economy through our creativity and thus identify ourselves as "creative beings," we pursue pastimes and cultural forms that express and nurture our creativity."

Fitness, exercising, and displaying the body, talking and people-watching within the life of the street; all of these ordinary experiential activities are stimuli to creative production for producers and consumers alike – indeed for Florida's idea of a Creative Class that distinction

---

holds little meaning. Florida suggests in fact that creativity itself is a kind of *redaction* (see below): "in order to create and synthesize, we need stimuli – bits and pieces to put together in unfamiliar ways."

The only fly in the ointment for Florida is that marketization of experience can render experience inauthentic and turn people into trendy sheep. But he is persuaded that his catalog of American leisure pursuits amounts to more than "a pastiche of recreational fads and marketing gimmicks" because "the more people earn their keep by creating, the more these aspects of experience are likely to be highly valued and just plain necessary."

# Performing Choice

The "use value" of freedom and comfort (see the general introduction for a discussion of these terms), for those who have achieved a modicum of both, is choice. The more affluent the society, the more individuated the choice. Since time immemorial, the fortunate few who had the means have systematically chosen personal independence over having to rely on institutional or structural position (class or marital status). But until the present period, it has been difficult even to imagine how the institutional or structural components of society might deal with affluent and individuated levels of choice for *everyone* and not just for elites. This is the compelling question that reality TV shows grapple with. *Big Brother* in particular is a creative enactment of the problem that besets societies that have evolved beyond mass (organized) to individual (customized) forms: how to construct one's self in freedom and comfort but in circumstances that can't be controlled, and where customary structural roles do not exert much influence over behavior or interpersonal relations.

Contemporary subjectivity is a matter of choice. But that choice is not exercised by a "knowing subject" alone – it's exercised by all such subjects, interactively and competitively. *Big Brother* externalizes that troubling truth by means of the *plebiscite*. Not only do housemates have to "make themselves up as they go along" in plain and competitive sight of each other, they have to submit the results of that process to the popular vote. So you can't just put on a persona and blow your own trumpet; you are measured by the applause, which itself may be motivated by stratagems designed to undermine your performance. For TV audiences, *Big Brother* literally represents the tensions between public and private, citizen and consumer. It offers practical mechanisms for the regulation (by self, housemate, and stranger) of "creative identities" in societies characterized by what can be experienced at the individual level as infinitely large scale and choice. As you vote against that devious, scheming individual (or the irritatingly charming one), you are personalizing some very abstract tensions (see Hartley 2004 for a fuller discussion).

Like light, choices travel in all directions at once. How to represent them? Here the media of commercial entertainment are well ahead of the technologies of representative democracy. The machine-age technologies of politics are not up to the job (as the 2000 presidential election in the USA made clear). *Big Brother* is one innovative answer: people on the show play themselves; people watching the show make choices about the performance. The show responds to the choices of housemates and audiences. The winner is a joint achievement.

Stephen Coleman, Cisco Professor of e-Democracy at Oxford University, has argued in *A Tale of Two Houses* that representative democracy itself has much to learn from the voting practices and choice management techniques of *Big Brother* (Coleman 2003). Since audiences have shown little reluctance to participate in voting for and against their *semiotic* representatives, the housemates, then Houses of Commons or Representatives may well need to consider why young people especially are so resistant to voting for or against their *political* representatives, the politicians.

Another innovative approach to the same issue has been developed by an organization called Student Virtual Parliament. It is founded on the principle of the stock market – a reliable mechanism for establishing the value of shares (companies) by representing all of the choices being exercised by the market at a given moment. On that model, the website seeks to establish the value of ideas – in this case among school students – by subjecting them to a competitive plebiscite, live, online. As the site itself says, "It's like a free floating student 'opinion market' – transparent, continuous, live and competitive" (<http://www.studentparliament.net>).

## Creative Industries – Plebiscite and Redaction

The **creative industries** are enterprises that monetize (creative) ideas in a consumer economy. They are a product of the historical changes outlined above; beneficiaries of the drift from production to consumption, public to private, author to audience. They exploit the commercialization of identity and citizenship. They broker the convergence and integration of entertainment and politics (comfort and freedom). They represent a dispersed and unorganized but nevertheless coherent social effort to gear up individual talent to an industrial scale. They're the suppliers of goods and services *to* the "creative identities sector" of society, and the social organizers *of* creative identities. At the same time, they benefit *from* creative identities, using consumers as R&D innovators, learning from them what new opportunities will arise.

Many writers have glossed the creative industries as the **copyright** or **content** industries. This is a characterization based on analysts prioritizing production (copyright) and commodity (content). But they need to recognize these industries' dependence on consumers. The form consumers take in this context is *measurable scale*, and creative industries depend upon scaling up individual choices. In a word they are also the **plebiscitary industries**. They rely just as completely on the currency that measures and enumerates consumer choices as they do on copyright-content. Entertainment and service industries all require popularity as well as creativity to survive. Television cannot survive without ratings, newspapers without audited circulation figures, publishing without best-seller lists. Most such industries operate with a combination of audience measurement (to minimize risk by investing further in what's liked) and repertoire (offering choice to consumers whose preferences cannot be known for sure in advance). Lately, as the copyright and content industries have shifted from broadcast (mass, passive) to interactive (customized) forms, the plebiscite itself has become a feature of the entertainment package – it has shifted from industry tool to creative content.

Similarly, in line with longer-term changes, **content** itself has evolved. The drift from author or text as the source of meaning to readers and audiences has its equivalent in a drift beyond content based on authorial intent (art) or textual realism (the novel, the news) to content based on consumers themselves. Since consumers are too numerous to represent directly, their input has to be edited, giving rise to a new creative form that I've called **redaction**. Redaction – creative editing – is the production of new meanings from existing materials (Hartley 2003; see also part III). Creative industries are at the cutting edge of this process; finding ways to represent consumers' own input *as* creative content, for instance "reality" forms, interactive and plebiscitary elements in both journalism and entertainment. Customizing and re-versioning for local markets are also forms of redaction.

---

## Conclusion to *Global Hollywood*: Toby Miller, Nitin Govill, John McMurria, Richard Maxwell

Toby Miller and his colleagues take the themes elaborated so far and send them in a novel and challenging direction. Accepting that consumers, audiences and readers *work* to achieve the experiences they crave,

---

Miller et al. argue that a "labor theory of consumption" is needed. Consumption not production is the very place to elaborate a set of labor rights suited to the creative industries and the knowledge economy. They argue that consumption itself generates ownership in various ways, and that this ownership – of one's own labor of consumption – needs protection just as much as do other forms of property. Activism – and therefore citizenship – needs to regroup around consumer rights. Politics attends the reading of *Harry Potter*.

Policy needs to take seriously the consequences of redaction: "cultural policy must recognise that every act of consumption is an act of authorship," while "every act of authorship in any medium is more akin to translation and recombination than it is to a spurious originary act." Work that audiences and fans do, from reading to rewriting, adds value to the creative commodity. Furthermore, the very practices of the plebiscite render audiences themselves into IP – to be sold on to advertisers. Miller and his colleagues argue that these authorial practices of the consumer need to form the basis of new forms of cultural politics, policy and law.

## References

Chomsky, N. (2001) *9–11*. Seven Stories Press, New York.

Coleman, S. (2003) *A Tale of Two Houses: The House of Commons, the Big Brother House and the People at Home*. Hansard Society, London.

Garnham. N. (1987) "Concepts of Culture: Public Policy and the Cultural Industries." *Cultural Studies* 1(1), 23–37.

Gitlin, T. (1993, rev. edn) *The Sixties: Years of Hope, Days of Rage*. Bantam Books, New York.

Hartley, J. (1996) *Popular Reality: Journalism, Modernity, Popular Culture*. Arnold, London.

Hartley, J. (1999) *Uses of Television*. Routledge, London and New York.

Hartley, J. (2003) *A Short History of Cultural Studies*. Sage Publications, London.

Hartley, J. (2004) "Kiss Me Kate": Shakespeare, *Big Brother*, and the Taming of the Self." In S. Murray and L. Ouellette (eds.), *Reality TV: Re-making Television Culture*. NYU Press, New York.

McKay, G. (ed.) (1998) *DiY Culture, Party and Protest in Nineties Britain*. Verso, London.

Mercer, K. (1992) 1968: Periodizing Postmodern Politics and Identity. In L. Grossberg, C. Nelson, and P. Treichler (eds.), *Cultural Studies*. Routledge, New York.

# 5 *John Howkins*

# THE MAYOR'S COMMISSION ON THE CREATIVE INDUSTRIES

## Introduction

I want to start by making two fundamental suggestions. First, the information society that we've been speaking about and living in for 30–40 years, and which is symbolised by the boom in information technology, telecoms, media and financial services, is losing its grip on our imaginations and may, indeed, be coming to an end. I define an IS as a society characterised by people spending most of their time and making most of their money by handling information, usually by means of technology. If I was a bit of data I would be proud of living in an information society. But as a thinking, emotional, creative being – on a good day, anyway – I want something better.

Second – and these movements have a causal connection – we are moving rather hesitantly and by fits and starts into a world which puts the priority on ideas and personal expression. In the information world, we were dazzled by technology – usually technology developed by other people – and that's an important point. In the second, we have to grapple with the imagination – our own.

I am talking about a change of perspective, a shift of emphasis. Ideas and information are symbiotically intertwined. But when I say I have an idea I am expressing a more personal view, and making a different claim, from when I say I have some information.

Information is sufficient to execute logical steps in a series. But it cannot enable us to choose between steps that are equally logical. And having ideas – creativity – is seldom logical, except in hindsight. (This is why creativity and

"The Mayor's Commission on the Creative Industries" from John Howkins (2002), "Comments in Response to The Mayor's Commission on the Creative Industries, 12 December 2002", www.creativelondon. org.uk. Reprinted by permission of Creative London.

innovation are so very different.) We need information. But we also need to be active, clever, and persistent in challenging this information. We need to be original, sceptical, argumentative, often bloody-minded and occasionally downright negative – in one word, creative.

## Definitions

Let's start at the beginning. What is creativity? I believe it can be simply defined as 'having a new idea'. There are four criteria for a new idea – it must be personal, original, meaningful and useful (POMU). According to this, painting a canvas, inventing a new gadget, solving traffic congestion and enabling black and ethnic people to participate fully in an economy are – or can be – equally creative. Of course, this kind of creativity has no commercial value. That comes later if – and only if – the creative idea leads to or enhances a commercial output with a commercial value.

The definition of a creative industry is quite different. The concept of the creative industry emerged in Australia in the early 1990s. It was given a huge boost by Tony Blair and Chris Smith in the late 1990s when the UK Department for Culture, Media and Sport (DCMS) set up its Creative Industries Unit and Task Force. But, in the process, the DCMS moved the word 'creative' a long way from its common usage. The Unit's original brief was for all industries based on creativity that generated or dealt in intellectual property (IP); but it quickly narrowed the range to those industries that had an artistic or cultural bent, with a dash of computer electronics, and limited the IP to copyright, downplaying patents, trademarks and designs. (The reasons were obvious and transparent; DCMS is responsible for culture and media and wanted to highlight their economic contribution to the wider British economy.) The results are problematic. According to DCMS, science is not creative. Nor is marketing. Advertising is, but not marketing. Craft-making, which is an archetypal small-scale manufacturing industry, is categorised as a creative industry. This doubling up is acceptable only so long as we do not use the rise in creative industries as evidence of the decline of manufacturing.

Understandably, the industries involved have welcomed or ignored the term according to their own objectives. The term has been embraced by those wanting government attention and especially government subsidies (for example, community arts), but those which are well established and want to avoid government attention have been dismissive (e.g., newspaper publishing).

The government sometimes appears a bit confused. It is often difficult to disentangle the creative industries initiatives sponsored by DCMS and the enterprise and innovation initiatives coming out of DTI. In practice, it seems there isn't much difference – except that DCMS, through its remit for culture and the arts, has an awareness of and a greater responsibility for individuals and small companies (SMEs) and non-profit organisations. It is indeed one of the great strengths of creative work that it can be small-scale and non-profit (whereas you cannot start a small-scale, non-profit steel mill). But we must not get into the habit of thinking that the creative industries are primarily small and non-profit. This mixed childhood and continuing identity crisis is one reason why the phrase 'creative industry' has never really struck a chord with the public. It is jargon; it does not fit common sense.

In my view it is best to restrict the term 'creative industry' to an industry where brain work is preponderant and where the outcome is intellectual property. This definition does not pretend to include all industries where creativity takes place. Creativity can take place anywhere. But it does include industries where brain work is the determining motif. It seems more reasonable than including, say, copyright but not patents; or advertising but not marketing.

In this view, the other parameters that are characteristic of creative industries (such as a particular balance of large and small firms, a particular balance of public and private ownership, the relative amounts of single and collaborative work, the role of peer review, the role of public funding, the specific kind of IP usually generated, the business model, the centrality or art and culture and so on) are seen as not being endemic to all creative industries but only to some. They are not part of the definition of the genus, but do identify various species.

We are familiar with the creative industries' size. In brief, we know that they are small in economic terms but nonetheless significant. Global revenues in 2000 were about $2.2 trillion (about 7.5% of global GNP), with the UK responsible for about $157 billion. Overall, the industries have a higher than average growth rate compared to other industries though some are declining. The highest growth rate is in technology-based industries such as software programming and video games; the lowest is in music and film. Growth rates can vary widely between countries: while the US film industry is thriving Britain's film industry is in crisis, and the House of Commons Select Committee on Culture ended 2002 by asking, 'Is There a British Film Industry?' One hopes the answer is 'Yes'.

We also know that that data on the creative industries is not entirely robust. First, the data is scarce. There is a shortage of employer data and a shortage of full-time employee data. Data on freelance and self-employed working is notoriously unreliable. In financial terms, many companies earn revenues through licensing products and services over many years with one-off, complicated and essentially confidential payments. There is a severe lack of data on international trade (imports/exports), partly because of the high proportion of long-term licence deals. The Inland Revenue's rules on the amortisation of intangible assets do not reflect market reality and, as a result, neither allow analysts to collect accurate information nor investors to make sensible judgements.

Finally, aggregate data is often suspect. Each industry is idiosyncratic (what do TV and fashion really have in common?) Globally, the Standard Industry Classification (SIC) data are unsatisfactory, and America has recently persuaded the North American Free Trade Agreement (NAFTA) to go it alone. I will come back to some of these issues later.

## Four Factors

I now want to deal with four topics, four challenges.

- economics
- management
- innovation
- intellectual property

### Economics

I will start with economics. The growth of the creative economy is largely responsible for, a fundamental change in the nature of contemporary economics – especially the relationship between government and business. The working practices of idea-based businesses that sell their ideas globally (e.g., the media and entertainment industries) are leading this change.

Government's aim in Europe over the past 50 and even 100 years has been to have a balanced public–private economy with harmonised working conditions and, where possible, a high level of stable full-time employment and workplace welfare.

We are now seeing the emergence of what Phillip Bobbitt calls market states, as shown by the Reagan/Bush-led America and the Thatcher/Blair-led Britain. Market states aim to provide the minimum level of law and regulation to allow individuals (and indeed large corporations, which these governments regard as natural allies) to flourish in open markets. Starting with Reagan and Thatcher we can chart a move from government bodies to regulated monopolies to class licensing to open markets. This is sometimes called deregulation. There are countervailing trends – such as the increasing emphasis on health and safety, and consumer protection – but they are secondary. It is highly significant, in fact, that these countervailing rules apply to all companies, both national and foreign-owned (as indeed they have to, under World Trade Organisation agreements).

One thing I often emphasise is that creativity is not easy or routine. It is not fair. It is elitist and collaborative (think of a scientific R&D team or a film crew). It is not easily regulated. If the symbol of the old nation state was the unified work-force, all paid the same and under the same contract of employment, nationally negotiated, with government-licensed service providers and government-upheld tariffs on imports, the symbol of the new market state is the individual negotiating his or her own contract for services, in a liberalised trade world, ignoring industry classifications and national boundaries.

Creative businesses, as a whole, are the driver of this nomadic economy. But while some creative business welcome the change, many do not – especially those that depend on government protection or subsidy. For example, some British industries strongly welcome the WTO's current round of trade talks on the General Agreement on Trade in Services (GATS) such as the major music companies, but some are bitterly opposed, such as the TV and film industries. This debate is different from, and counter to, the anti-globalisation arguments of Naomi Klein. She wants to stop globalisation. Most creative artists, on the other hand, take the whole world as grist to their mill, and are more than happy to obtain from and distribute to all markets.

*Management*

The creative industries are notable for a distinctive management style. This is the result of a number of factors, including the economic changes already mentioned, but the prime cause is the nature of the (intangible) inputs and outputs. I have discussed these management factors elsewhere.

The most important can be headlined as:

- the role of the individual in relation to the organisation
- the 'Job of Thinker'
- the role of the producer
- the creative entrepreneur – especially the relationship between entrepreneurs and managers
- the 'Post-Employment Job'
- the 'Just-In-Time Person'
- finance

- the 'Temporary Company' and Joint Ventures
- the 'Network Office'
- deals and hits (portfolio management)

I want to comment on just three issues. First, finance. Creative people who want to make money out of their ideas need cheap and uncomplicated finance, supportive retail banking services, and appropriate accounting standards. By and large; we don't have them. There is no one single obstacle here; rather a historical, cultural vacuum, a lack of intelligent financial institutions, and a lack of qualified managers. We need new rules for financial reporting. Nobody in the creative industries is looking at this on a broad basis – nor is anyone in Whitehall. Is this a job for the Commission?

Second, I am often dismayed and saddened by the near invisibility and inaccessibility of Britain's university resources for everyone not on a full-time degree, compared to the vital and inclusive role played by universities in the US and the rest of Europe. This is a waste of a precious asset. We must do something about it, opening up education to the whole population

Third, many management resources and skills of the creative industries are now being picked up and exploited by people in the rest of the economy (which we could describe as the Ordinary Economy). The best-known examples are post-industrial jobs, expertise in IP, merchandising, the way to manage full-time thinkers, the ability to exploit clusters and domains and portfolio working. Creative people have been working in this way for centuries. Yet business schools and management experts can take a well-known technique (say, portfolio working) and announce it as 'new'.

I know the Commission's main focus is the creative industries themselves. I would urge you to also propose ways of transferring the creative industries' knowledge and skills to the rest of the economy. If the creative industry's skills remain within the creative industries, their effectiveness will be hobbled and curtailed, and London will be less competitive. The prize for leadership in this century will go to the city, the country, that uses its creative talents – and its management of creativity – throughout its entire economy, benefiting the wider society, the local community. That's the real challenge.

*Innovation*

My third point is innovation. The conventional thinking about innovation doesn't capture what actually happens in the creative industries. It doesn't capture what happens upstream in the minds of artists, writers, designers, etc., and any other full-time thinker, nor does it capture what happens downstream as their ideas are turned into products. For example, the DTI says the chief indicator of innovation is R&D with lesser roles being played by investments in capital equipment, skills, market development, new ways of working and other intangible assets. But take a writer – or take a massive corporation like the BBC. For both, the ideas, the words and the programmes are not something to be tacked on under 'other intangible assets' but the main work, the defining work, the core outcome. It's the business.

This matters. Calling James Tyson innovative is a compliment; but calling David Puttnam or Tom Cruise innovative misses the point – or is plain wrong. Mike Leigh's working methods are highly innovative. But his films succeed only if he and the actors are also creative. The success of (the non-innovative) Tom Cruise illustrates another point. Most creative industries – especially those in the entertainment business – thrive by being repetitive. They do produce new products (thereby satisfying the criterion of innovation used by the EU and the London Employer Survey). But should we really describe another rap album or another recording of a Beethoven symphony as being 'innovative'? To do so, seems to miss the point of innovation, and of music, too.

Creativity involves non-linear and often illogical personal expression. Innovation involves calculated novelty.

The problem is two-way. People who talk about innovation tend to ignore what happens in the creative industries; and the creative industries tend to downplay the benefits of innovation. I've yet to see a government inquiry that is big enough, brave enough, to deal with both creativity and innovation.

*Intellectual property*

The fourth topic, and a major challenge, is our attitude to intellectual property. IP is the *currency* of the creative economy. If someone says IP cannot be valued because it cannot be quantified, it means they are stuck in a world where everything has to be quantified. Where data is king. Where the update is always better. Those times have gone. Britain's current IP laws and practices are a time bomb at the heart of the creative economy, and of much the rest of the economy as well.

There is widespread awareness of particular problems – such as the cloning of Dolly, the mapping of the human genome and the publication of the mouse genome, the copyrighting of computer code, the uses of digital to copy sounds and images, the extension of patenting to business methods and even the recent battle between Mrs Beckham and Peterborough United Football Club over who is really posh.

What is not fully appreciated is how all these issues have a common root. They are the symptoms of a chronic, systemic failure in the law, regulation and judicial system of intellectual property. There is a massive failure to generate appropriate laws for the creative economy, with cumulative and harmful results. America bears the brunt of the blame, but the UK is not far behind.

Parliament has effectively handed oversight of IP law and regulation to the European Union and to the Patent Office. Parliament itself has not debated IP once since 1981 except to give formal approval to EU directives. As a result Britain has put too much emphasis on technical and bureaucratic issues, and gives hardly a mention of philosophy or morality, or the public interest.

The Patent Office's objective is to support innovation by encouraging people to apply for as much private IP as possible. It has been accused of lowering standards in order to satisfy its customers. Certainly, business corporations are successfully claiming property rights over many things that until recently were not patentable (I call this 'privatisation').

I see that one of the Commission's cross-cutting issues is 'commercialising IP'. I hope you will give equal attention to the opposite, to 'liberating' IP.

Not more attention, but equal. IP is a contract between creative people and the public. Someone needs to look at both sides. Creative people want both to access and use ideas, and to privatise ideas. Artists want both to appropriate other people's work, and to register their own. Their arguments are partly moral and partly economic.

There are too many special, vested interests. The property contract is becoming lopsided as the larger, richer and more powerful tilt the balance too far their way. It is claimed that IP is an incentive. The evidence is very slight. The voices of artists who want more freedom are scarcely heard.

We need to create new spaces for new information. For this, we need substantial public resources of ideas and intangible work – not public in the sense of being funded by the taxpayer but public in the sense of being free for all people to use – in the sense of the public domain, the public commons – whether the owner, the source, is private or public.

We need new, independent research into the property contract, into how far IP should be free and public and how far it should be private and commercial. There is some good work being done in America; but the UK should carry out its own work within its own cultural context.

Where there should be a great public debate there is a great silence. Who should champion a fair deal for IP? Who can look at this in terms of public policy and commercial common sense? Is there a role for the CIC?

# Conclusion: Points and Questions

1   Is it time to rethink the definition of a creative industry? The British definition excludes most of business creativity and almost all scientific creativity. What does this say for the future of Britain's business and science – and art? People will do whatever they want to do, but public policy-makers need to get it right, and for this they need to talk the same language as the public. So, how do we define creativity and creative industries? If we get this wrong, we will get everything else wrong, too.

2   It is time to take an inclusive, integrated approach to creativity and innovation. We need to be much more precise about both terms.

3   Intellectual property. Both actual and would-be rights-holders are complaining vigorously. There is deep-seated concern that IP is becoming too totalitarian. In the absence of effective parliamentary oversight, who should propose, evaluate and oversee the reforms? How can we ensure the public's voice is heard? What are the benchmarks for a national IP strategy? I suggest a role for the LDA, perhaps in providing something along the lines of my IP Project for a IP Advisory Centre.

4   We need integrated policies, embracing economics and tax, work, competition policy, education, diversity, employment and law. National government (Whitehall) is stuck with conventional departments whose rationale as independent units is hard to justify today – e.g., DCMS and DTI. How can the LDA exploit its ability to transcend these conventional demarcations?

5   The best way to encourage creativity (and much else) is to lead by example. How can the LDA – and other regional government development agencies – set a good example?

# 6    *Charles Leadbeater*

# DELIA SMITH NOT ADAM SMITH

Each year at Christmas, millions of people around the world give millions of other people cookery books, in the hope that those who receive the books will become better cooks in the following year. This exchange of gifts is an annual, global knowledge transfer on a vast scale. A few thousand cookery writers around the world distil their knowledge and deliver it to tens of millions of cooks. It is a world-wide upgrade of the software which runs our kitchens. The size and scale of this transfer of know-how is one mark of how much economic activity revolves around the production and distribution of knowledge. There is no better metaphor for the products of the knowledge economy than the recipe.

Our annual download of kitchen software exemplifies the value of different kinds of knowledge. A distinction that will recur in this book is between two kinds of knowledge: tacit and explicit. Tacit knowledge is not written down and is hard to articulate. It is often learned by osmosis, over long periods, in very particular contexts, by an apprentice learning at a craftsman's elbow, for example. Tacit knowledge is robust and often intuitive, habitual and reflexive. Most of us know how to ride a bike but could not write down in detail how to do it. It is knowledge best acquired by doing, and best communicated by example. Explicit knowledge is codified. It is articulated in writing and numbers, in books and reports. As a result, explicit knowledge can be taken from one context and transferred to another more easily than tacit knowledge. A manual that explains how a computer works can be used around the world. Explicit knowledge is more transferable than tacit knowledge, but less rich. Often tacit knowledge becomes valuable only when it can

"Delia Smith Not Adam Smith" from Charles Leadbeater (1999), *Living on Thin Air: The New Economy*. Viking, London, pp. 28–36. Reprinted by permission of Penguin Books Ltd and David Godwin Associates.

be communicated to a large audience. To make that possible it has to be conveyed in explicit, transferable form: an insight has to become an explanation, a rule of thumb a procedure. In the translation from tacit to explicit knowledge, many of the critical nuances may get left out. When people receive knowledge conveyed in explicit form, the process goes into reverse. Explicit knowledge, conveyed as information, has to be internalized to be brought back to life as personal knowledge. This internalization often makes knowledge tacit once more. A recipe is just information; to bring it to life, the cook has to interpret and internalize it by making his own judgements.

Knowledge is not just spread through this process; it is created. As an idea is transferred from setting to setting, person to person, kitchen to kitchen, it grows and develops. The original idea is modified and adapted; it is in perpetual motion. In traditional industries, dominated by craft skills, this motion is slow, constrained by tradition. In innovative, radical fields, ideas circulate at high velocity. Knowledge sharing and creation is at the heart of innovation in all fields – science, art and business – and innovation is the driving force for wealth creation. This is not an abstract process. It requires human initiative. Information can be transferred in great torrents, without any understanding or knowledge being generated. Knowledge cannot be transferred; it can only be enacted, through a process of understanding, through which people interpret information and make judgements on the basis of it. That is why so much of the hype about the information age leaves us cold. Great tides of information wash over us every day. We do not need more information; we need more understanding. Creating knowledge is a human process, not a technological one.

There is no better way of conveying the economic value of knowledge transformation than to think about the home economics of food. Think of the world as divided up into chocolate cakes and chocolate-cake recipes. A chocolate cake is what economists call a rival good: if I eat it, you cannot. A chocolate cake is like most products of the industrial economy: cars, houses, computers, personal stereos. A chocolate-cake recipe, by contrast, is what economists call a non-rival good. We can all use the same chocolate-cake recipe, at the same time, without anyone being worse off. It is quite unlike a piece of cake. The chocolate-cake recipe is like many of the products of the knowledge economy. Software, digital codes and genetic information are all like powerful recipes which control how hardware – computers and bodies – work. We are moving into an economy where the greatest value is in the recipes, rather than the cakes.

There are two different ways of distributing a recipe and the knowledge embedded within it. One is to spread tacit knowledge. This is how my mother learned how to cook beautiful chocolate cake: by watching her own mother. It's a time-consuming business, but it can produce lasting knowledge and very good results. The other distribution method is to put the know-how into an explicit form, by writing a cookery book, for example, or putting a recipe on the Internet. This kind of knowledge may be less nuanced than tacit knowledge, but it travels a lot further to a lot more people. Delia Smith, Britain's most successful cookery writer and a multi-millionaire, is really a knowledge entrepreneur. She makes money by selling her know-how. According to the *Sunday Times*, Delia is worth at least £24 million, all of it made from thin air, by understanding how to package recipes in an accessible, attractive form. Delia Smith and the stream of cooks who have followed in her wake, Rick Stein, Gary Rhodes, Nigel Slater and so on, have created a new market in cookery knowledge. In the process they have exemplified why transferring know-how that way is more socially and economically efficient.

Transferring knowledge through tacit means is inefficient. Tacit knowledge is limited by the context it is learned in. My mother's cookery knowledge was largely learned in Lancashire. My mother is a great cook but she could not teach me how to cook curry, pizza or sweet and sour pork. As our tastes have become more cosmopolitan so people have wanted to cook a much wider range of food. At bookshops we can buy in cookery know-how from Thailand, Korea, Tuscany and Australia. All the know-how which was locked into localized markets can be sold around the world. Tacit knowledge confines our range of recipes to those we learned from traditional, localized sources. The global market in cookery know-how provides us with a much wider range of expertise to draw upon. Globalization is good for our palates.

Learning how to cook at someone's elbow is inefficient. My mother studied in kitchens as a daughter and wife when she could have been studying for a degree or starting a business. The lengthy learning process that lies behind my mother's roast beef with crispy roast potatoes and Yorkshire pudding was made possible only by a social division of labour in which men went out to work and women stayed at home to rear children and cook the meals. That social division of labour was sustained by a relatively primitive knowledge economy: cooking based on transfers of tacit knowledge between women. The old knowledge economy has given way to a new economy in which knowledge is imparted through several different channels to men and women. The student cook has more choice about the speed at which they learn. I cannot sit in a kitchen watching Delia Smith to learn at first hand what makes her chicken in sherry wine vinegar quite so tasty. Instead I can read her recipe, over and over, and try it out, once (disastrously) and a second time more successfully. Learning becomes more efficient, less wasteful.

Knowledge about how to cook food, once a craft skill, has become a commodity. Instead of acquiring our own knowledge, we economize on learning by buying in the knowledge we need in standardized form from any number of fast-food restaurants or through cook chilled meals from Tesco and Marks & Spencer. I like Thai noodles but I do not know how to cook them. Learning the skill would require a lengthy investment of time replete with repeated failures and doubtful results. That is why I prefer to buy in the knowledge, when I need it, by going to a Thai restaurant.

Yet there is a crucial difference in the economics of recipes and the economics of food. Go back to the comparison between chocolate cakes and chocolate-cake recipes. Imagine for a moment that you had invented the perfect chocolate-cake recipe. You have two options to exploit this invention. One is to make chocolate cakes using the recipe and to sell the cakes. You would need to buy extra ingredients for each cake you made. You would need to install ovens and refrigerators. There would be a limit to the number of cakes that could be made and distributed efficiently. The second way to exploit the value of your creation is to turn it into a recipe. The fixed cost of developing a new recipe can be large: it takes repeated attempts and many failures to find just the right combination of ingredients, in the right proportions, cooked in the right way. Yet once the recipe is perfected and written up in an accessible, easy-to-understand form, with glossy pictures, it costs very little to reproduce it. The cost of producing another 100 or 10,000 versions of the same recipe is not that different from producing just one. That is why recipes are like software. It costs Bill Gates many hundreds of millions of dollars to develop a new generation of his Microsoft Windows software for personal computers. But once the software is perfected it costs him virtually nothing to reproduce it endlessly for a mass market.

The similarities between recipes and software do not end there. As with computer software, consumers are intimately involved in producing and reproducing the product. Cooks at home have to interpret the recipes to understand them. The transfer of knowledge is even more time-consuming than downloading a piece of software. A recipe has to be interrogated to be understood. This changes the character of consumption in a knowledge economy. We have been brought up with a physical, sensual notion of consumption inherited from agriculture and manufacturing. We are used to thinking that when we consume something it becomes ours, we take it into ourselves, we eat it up, like a piece of chocolate cake. Consumption is the pleasure of possessing something. Yet when we consume knowledge – a recipe for example – we do not possess it. The recipe remains Delia Smith's; indeed that is why we use it. By buying her book we have bought a right to use the recipes within it. Ownership of the recipe is in effect shared between

Delia and the millions of users. Consumption of the recipe is a joint activity. This is not consumption so much as reproduction or replication. The knowledge in the recipe is not extinguished when it is used; it is spread. The more knowledge-intensive products become, the more consumers will have to be involved in completing their production, to tailor the product to their needs. Consumption of knowledge-intensive products is not just joint and shared but additive as well: the consumers can add to the product's qualities. This is one of the most important ways that software producers learn about whether their products work: they give them to consumers to try them out and to develop them further. In a knowledge-driven economy, consuming will become more a relationship than an act; trade will be more like replication than exchange; consumption will often involve reproduction, with the consumer as the last worker on the production line; exchange will involve money, but knowledge and information will flow both ways as well. Successful companies will engage the intelligence of their consumers to improve their products.

As Britain's food economy has become more knowledge-intensive so it has become more efficient, choice has expanded and resources are being used more efficiently and creatively. Resources, mainly women's time, have been freed from the old, time-consuming way of learning. Women's opportunities for employment have expanded. An old, inefficient social division of labour which enshrined this tacit, traditional way of learning is being eroded. In cooking, as in so many other fields, we have made social and economic progress by replacing a relatively narrow, inefficient method of knowledge transmission with a far more effective range of mechanisms to spread know-how more widely, which is both more efficient and more fun.

An economy which becomes more knowledge-intensive has the potential to become more inclusive and meritocratic. Everyone with an education can have a go. That is what makes people like Delia Smith so intriguing. We all know people who are good cooks, and who might be able to come up with great recipes. Perhaps one day they could become famous for their cooking. In an economy which trades know-how and ideas, everyone seems to have a chance to make it, working from a garage, their kitchen or their bedroom. Twenty-five-year-old drop-outs can create best-selling computer games; a nerd fresh out of college can create the Internet's best browser; a boy with no formal education can become Europe's most precocious fashion designer. Knowledge empowers people to take charge of their lives. That is because knowledge can make a lasting impact on well-being: a recipe stays with you long after the cake has been eaten. The more an economy promotes the production and spread of knowledge, rather than just the exchange of goods and services, the better-off we become.

The rub, however, is that know-how on its own is never enough to make money. What stands out about Delia Smith is not just the quality of her recipes but how well she packages and communicates them. Delia Smith's skill is to combine her know-how with the complementary assets and skills – marketing, branding and publishing – which she needs to make money from her ideas. We do not buy Delia Smith's recipes; we buy her books. The tangible product – the book – is the way she makes money from the intangible content – the recipe – which is the true source of its value. It is because the recipes are packaged so attractively, in books which are marketed so skilfully, that we pay so much for them. Recipes may be used simultaneously by lots of people, but books cannot be. To make money from know-how, it is not enough to have good ideas; one has to be able to appropriate the value in them.

Recipes are the engines of economic growth: Paul Romer, Professor of Economics at Stanford University, in California, has formulated an economic theory based on the principle of the recipe. Romer argues that every economy is made up from three components: people; physical things, like raw materials and machines; and rules. Rules are recipes: different ways to combine people and things. As Romer put it in an article in *Worth* magazine:

> We used to use iron oxide to make cave paintings, and now we put it on floppy disks. The point is that the raw material we have to work with has been the same for all of human history. So when you think about economic growth, the only place it can come from is finding better recipes for rearranging the fixed amount of stuff we have around us.

The great advances in modern economies have come from the application of new recipes. A new recipe, invented by chance, created the modern chemical industry. Will Henry Perkin, a British inventor working in the mid-nineteenth century, came up with the first synthetic dye as a chance by-product of a failed attempt to make quinine. Working in a laboratory at home, Perkin obtained a precipitate from naphtha, called aniline black, from which he derived aniline blue. Perkin built a plant to manufacture the dye, which quickly led to an explosion of artificial colours: fuchsia, magenta, purples, pinks and oranges. Perkin's coal-tar industry eventually produced many other chemicals used in photography, medicine, fertilizers and plastics. Thanks to Perkin, Britain led the early chemical industry. Yet within a generation of Perkin's discovery most of the modern chemical industry had migrated to Germany. By 1881, Germany was making about half the world's artificial dyestuffs, and in 1900 between 80 and 90 per cent. British uniforms in the First World War were dyed with German dye. Germany left the rest of the world so far behind that when its major patents (recipes) were confiscated after that war, the best firms in the US could not make them work and had to hire German chemists to provide the tacit knowledge they needed.

The way Germany deposed Britain as the leader of the modern chemical industry marked a turning point in the role of knowledge in economic development. Before Perkin, technology had led science. Steam engines were invented and a few years later scientists explained how they worked. Inventions came from bright sparks on the shop-floor and heroic, amateur inventors in household laboratories. Inventions were the products of learning by doing. After the rise of the German chemical industry, swiftly followed by the electrical industry concentrated around Berlin, the roles of science and technology, explicit and tacit knowledge, were reversed. Science became the most important source of new technologies and products. Formal knowledge took precedence over hands-on experience. Institutions, such as universities and research laboratories, which produced and exploited formal knowledge, became more and more important to economic growth. Germany won leadership in the chemical industry because it had well-developed formal institutions of further education – which produced well-qualified technicians and scientists – and also the first global corporations – the German chemical giants, BASF, Bayer and Hoechst – which were organized to exploit this know-how to the full. Britain fell behind thanks to its reliance on pragmatic amateurism, learning by doing.

This transition marked the start of the rise of the modern knowledge economy. The Second Industrial Revolution in the second half of the nineteenth century was unleashed by complementary technical and organizational innovations – the rise of the joint-stock company and the internal-combustion engine, the university and the telephone. The power behind the Second Industrial Revolution was explicit knowledge, generated in institutions of learning and exploited by a new breed of company. Since then, knowledge, both tacit and explicit, codified and uncodified, formal and informal, has played a growing role in how our economies generate wealth and well-being and how companies compete with one another. At the end of the century, knowledge is not just one among many resources; it is becoming *the* critical factor in how modern economies compete and how they generate wealth and well-being.

# 7     *Richard Florida*

# THE EXPERIENTIAL LIFE

At the dawn of the millennium, on the morning of January 1, 2000, a new avatar of the New Economy made his debut. He was a twenty-six-year-old former systems analyst who had legally changed his name to DotComGuy. His website, DotComGuy.com, logged an astounding 10 million hits that New Year's Day. People around the world watched on their computer screens, via webcam, as the bland-looking young man moved into a bland suburban house in North Dallas, Texas. There he would remain for the rest of the year, living entirely on goods and services ordered over the Internet: groceries from Food.com, housecleaning by TheMaids.com, point-and-click pizza delivery and much more.

The secret of DotComGuy's appeal could not have been his daily routine, which often resembled that of an elderly shut-in waiting for Meals on Wheels. Nothing kinky here: no webcam sex or moody personal revelations. He spent much of his time playing with his dog, DotComDog, or watching TV, or surfing the web. Yet he drew a devoted on-line following, including a chat room frequented by young girls commenting on his cuteness. News reporters and eager visitors came to call. What made DotComGuy so fascinating was that he perfectly embodied all the myths of *homo new economicus* in the Internet age. Here was the quintessential maverick using the Internet to turn the system upside down. He was a free agent and entrepreneur, out on his own, doing it his way. He had lined up corporate sponsors to provide everything he needed free, in exchange for publicity and banner ads on his website. The sponsors included long-established firms like UPS; equipment and tech support for the website were donated by technology giants such as Gateway and 3Com. Rather than hold a faceless job in corporate America, DotComGuy had the big companies beating a path to *his* door. Rather than travel for what he wanted, he had the world brought to him. He was a virtual Horatio Alger, a house-bound king of infinite cyberspace.

DotComGuy's *über*-virtual lifestyle provoked two kinds of reactions. Some reveled in the prospect of the new world it represented. New Economy pundits had preached the virtues of business going virtual, and to true believers, much of life would be better that way as well: We would come together in on-line communities of like-minded individuals. New technologies and business models were converging to link everyone in a gigantic virtual global village, with virtual storefronts, virtual offices, virtual playgrounds and even virtual singles bars. When DotComGuy left his house at the end of the year 2000, he announced that he planned to marry a woman he had "met" in his website chat room.

Then there were the cynics. *Salon* called DotComGuy the "Poster Child for Internet Idiocy."[1] Other critics worried that the virtual lifestyle would tear apart an already fraying social fabric and bring an end to real community. In this dark view, we were becoming isolated and divided into a nation of lonesome cowboys, hunkered down with our PC screens.

Both perspectives miss the point. Virtual community is not replacing real community. Chat rooms have proliferated, but so have real coffee shops. And while DotComGuy's entrepreneurial spirit may be admired by many, his virtual lifestyle is not at all what vast and growing numbers of people want. Members of the Creative Class are not looking for a life delivered through a modem. They want one that is heart-throbbingly real.

## Creativity and Experience

On many fronts, the Creative Class lifestyle comes down to a passionate quest for experience. The ideal, as a number of my subjects succinctly put it, is to "live the life" – a creative life packed full of intense, high-quality, multidimensional experiences. And the *kinds* of experiences they crave reflect and reinforce their identities as creative people. My interviews and focus groups indicate that they favor active, participatory recreation over passive spectator sports. They like indigenous street-level culture – a teeming blend of cafés, sidewalk musicians, and small galleries and bistros, where it is hard to draw the line between participant and observer, or between creativity and its creators. They crave creative stimulation but not escape. As one young man told me, explaining why he and his friends favored nonalcoholic hangouts: "We can't afford the recovery time." Moreover, while many members of the Creative Class actively use computers, shop online, participate in chat rooms and even have virtual personas, I repeatedly find that the most computer-savvy people of all – high-technology professionals and computer-science-oriented students at schools like Carnegie Mellon – have interests extending well beyond the virtual. More than anything, they crave intense experiences in the real world.

In their insightful book *The Experience Economy*, Joseph Pine and James Gilmore observe that consumers are coming to favor the consumption of experiences over traditional goods and services.

> Experiences are a fourth economic offering, as distinct from services as services are from goods. . . . Experiences have always been around but consumers, businesses, and economists lumped them into the service sector along with such uneventful activities as dry cleaning, auto repair, wholesale distribution, and telephone access. When a person buys a service he purchases a set of intangible activities carried out on his behalf. But when he buys an experience, he pays to spend time enjoying a series of memorable events that a company stages – as in a theatrical play – to engage him in a personal way. . . .
>
> The newly identified offering of experiences occurs whenever a company intentionally uses services as the stage and goods as props to engage an individual. While commodities are fungible, goods tangible, and services intangible, experiences are *memorable*. Buyers of experiences – we'll follow Disney's lead and call them *guests* – value being engaged by what the company reveals over a duration of time. Just as people have cut back on goods to spend more money on services, now they also scrutinize the time and money they spend on services to make way for more memorable – and highly valued – experiences.[2]

But Pines and Gilmore are talking here mainly about pre-packaged experiences of the sort Disney provides. Members of the Creative Class prefer more active, authentic and participatory experiences, which they can have a hand in structuring. In practical everyday terms, this means running, rock climbing or cycling rather than watching a game on TV; it means travel to interesting locations that engage one physically or intellectually; it means the purchase of unique antique pieces or original "mid-century modern" furniture as opposed to just buying something to sit on.

The quest for experiences extends far beyond the point of purchase. Some commentators suggest that anticipation is more important than the actual consumption of experiences, dubbing this "imaginative hedonism."[3] Ben Malbon's book on the British club scene, *Clubbing*, highlights the role of such "experiential consuming." For the young people he studied, the actual visit to a dance club is only part of the scene, Malbon notes. He describes, in detail, the lengthy and intricate processes of clubbers debating where and when to go, laying out clothes for the event, and discussing and creating "histories" of their experiences afterward.[4] However one views it, this much is certain: Experiences are replacing goods and services because they stimulate our creative faculties and enhance our creative capacities. This active, experiential lifestyle is spreading and becoming more prevalent in society as the structures and institutions of the Creative Economy spread.

Writing in the 1950s, the psychologist Carl Rogers called attention to the relationship between creativity and experiences. At one point in his well-known book *On Becoming a Person* he criticized the overly rigid, bureaucratic society of his day for its stifling effect, arguing for the "desperate social need" for creativity.

> In our leisure time activities, passive entertainment and regimented group action are overwhelmingly predominant while creative activities are much less in evidence. . . . In individual and family life the same picture holds true. In the clothes we wear, the food we eat, and the ideas we hold, there is a strong tendency toward conformity, toward stereotypy. To be original, or different, is felt to be "dangerous."[5]

The creative or experiential lifestyle is a direct reaction to this predicament, as the economic need for creativity has grown. After outlining the dimensions of the creative process and offering his basic theory of creativity, Rogers went on to detail what he saw as the necessary connection between creativity and experiences.

> It has been found that when the individual is "open" to all his experience . . . then his behavior will be creative, and his creativity may be trusted to be essentially constructive. . . . In a person who is open to experience each stimulus is freely relayed . . . without being distorted by any process of defensiveness. Whether the stimulus originates in the environment, in the impact of form, color, or sound on the sensory nerves, or whether it originates in the viscera . . . it is available to awareness. . . . This last suggests another way of describing openness to experience. It means lack of rigidity and permeability of boundaries in concepts, beliefs, perceptions, and hypotheses. It means a tolerance for ambiguity where ambiguity exists. It means the ability to receive much conflicting information without forcing closure upon the situation. . . . This complete openness of awareness to what exists at this moment is, I believe, an important condition of constructive creativity.[6]

All of which brings us to the role that experiences play today in stimulating creativity. The old conformist lifestyle that Rogers disparaged has given way to a more creative one based on the eyes-wide-open pursuit of wide-ranging, highly engaging activities and stimuli.

Some might say the appeal of this lifestyle will necessarily diminish in the wake of the World Trade Center tragedy of September 11, 2001 – that these pursuits were the markers of a self-centered, fun-chasing and essentially aimless mindset, and that people are now becoming more serious and no longer so interested in such frivolities. I do not think that is the case. The new lifestyle is not mainly about "fun." Rather it complements the way members of the Creative Class work and is a fundamental part of the way they go about their lives.

Let me tell you a personal story that may help put this in perspective. The events of September 11 affected me powerfully. For two weeks I was unable to concentrate on my work or focus on my writing. I canceled a number of speaking engagements, because literally I could not speak. Like millions of Americans I sat in front of the television for hours on end watching news broadcasts. But there was one thing I wanted to do – that I was pulled to do. And that was to ride my bicycle. I am an avid road cyclist, and I took several hours each day to just go out and ride . . . and ride . . . and ride. It had little to do with my passion for cycling or an effort to stay fit. The pull toward my bike came from the release it afforded, the ability to stop thinking and let go, to stop my brain from turning, to do something physical, to just ride. And I suspect that much the same impulse drives the new lifestyle and the new leisure. As a way of both disconnecting and recharging, it is part of what we *need to do* as creative people.

Writing at the turn of the twentieth century, the iconoclastic economist Thorstein Veblen outlined his famous theory of the wealthy "leisure class."[7] Calling attention to the "conspicuous consumption" of the *nouveaux riche* capitalists and their families, Veblen found the new elite displaying their power and values through what their money bought. As the historian Gary Cross shows in his comprehensive review of consumption in the twentieth century, the consumption habits of this new elite revolved around giant mansions and estates, "vicarious consumption" through their wives' purchases of luxuries, and participation in "ostentatious time-killing activities" like golf.[8] Thus they were a leisure class indeed, flaunting not only their goods but their indolence.

The members of the Creative Class are less a leisure class in Veblen's sense of the term and more an "active class." Their consumption is not so crudely conspicuous and they certainly do not participate in time-killing activities of any sort, for they do not have the time to kill. Moreover, status and identity for these people come not so much from the goods they have, but from the experiences they have. As Julie Blick, a Wharton School graduate, retired Microsoft engineer and author of a 1995 book on her experiences, wrote: "Conspicuous consumption isn't the style. People don't have jets or huge vacation homes. They have a cabin in the woods furnished by Ikea."[9] There are good economic reasons for this shift. As economic historians have shown, average American living standards have risen to such an extent that material goods no longer confer the status they once did. In her detailed survey of American living standards in the twentieth century, the University of California–Berkeley labor economist Clair Brown wrote:

> By the late 1980s, daily material life had improved in ways that could not have been imagined in 1918. Working-class families had a richer material life in 1988 than the salaried class had in 1918. Their food, transportation, medical care, and home comforts provided a material quality of life that was not attainable even by the elite in any previous era. . . . [L]eisure time activities became an important part of life. Working-class families owned sports equipment and toys, attended sporting and cultural events, and even took vacation trips.[10]

The Nobel Prize-winning economic historian Robert Fogel sums up the situation this way: "Today, ordinary people wish to use their liberated time to buy those amenities of life that only the rich could afford in abundance a century ago. . . . The principal cost of these activities is not measured by cash outlays, but by outlays of time."[11] And with life itself having become the scarce and precious commodity, many increasingly define the quality of their lives by the quality of experiences they consume.

[ . . . ]

# The Hegemony of the Street

For more than a century, the mark of a cultured city in the United States has been to have a major art museum plus an "SOB" – the high-art triumvirate of a symphony orchestra, an opera company and a ballet company. In many cities recently, museums and the SOB have fallen on hard times. Attendance figures have declined and audiences are aging: too many gray heads, not enough purple ones. Consultants have descended to identify the problems and offer solutions. One problem is static repertoire. In a museum, for instance, the permanent collection is, well, permanent: It just hangs there. A typical solution is more packaged traveling exhibits, preferably interactive multimedia exhibits, with lots of bells and whistles. In the SOB, not a lot of new symphonies and operas are being written and fewer are performed, because staging them is expensive. One solution is to augment the experience. It's not just a night at the symphony; now it's Singles Night at the Symphony. At other times, orchestras bring in offbeat guest performers – a jazz or pop soloist, or a comedian for the kids. Or musicians are sent out to play in exotic locales – the symphony in the park, a chamber group at an art gallery, the symphony playing the *1812 Overture* at the Fourth of July fireworks. All this is reminiscent of the efforts of oldline churches to fill seats by augmenting the experience – how about a guitar and drumset with the organ? – or the efforts of many professional sports teams, with their mascots and exploding scoreboards.

Meanwhile, the Creative Class is drawn to more organic and indigenous street-level culture. This form is typically found not in large venues like New York's Lincoln Center or in designated "cultural districts" like the Washington, D.C., museum district, but in multiuse urban neighborhoods. The neighborhood can be upscale like D.C.'s Georgetown or Boston's Back Bay, or reviving-downscale like D.C.'s Adams Morgan, New York's East Village, or Pittsburgh's South Side. Either way, it grows organically from its surroundings, and a sizable number of the creators and patrons of the culture live close by. This is what makes it "indigenous." Much of it is native and of-the-moment, rather than art imported from another century for audiences imported from the suburbs. Certainly people may come from outside the neighborhood to partake of the culture, and certainly they will find things that are foreign in origin or influence, such as German films or Senegalese music. But they come with a sense that they are entering a cultural community, not just attending an event. I think this is a key part of the form's creative appeal. You may not paint, write or play music, yet if you are at an art-show opening or in a nightspot where you can mingle and talk with artists and aficionados, you might be more creatively stimulated than if you merely walked into a museum or concert hall, were handed a program, and proceeded to spectate. The people in my focus groups and interviews say they like street-level culture partly because it gives them a chance to experience the creators along with their creations.

The culture is "street-level" because it tends to cluster along certain streets lined with a multitude of small venues. These may include coffee shops, restaurants and bars, some of which offer performance or exhibits along with the food and drink; art galleries; bookstores and other stores; small to mid-sized theaters for film or live performance or both; and various hybrid spaces – like a bookstore/tearoom/little theater or gallery/studio/live music space – often in storefronts or old buildings converted from other purposes. The scene may spill out onto the sidewalks, with dining tables, musicians, vendors, panhandlers, performers and plenty of passersby at all hours of the day and night. Ben Malbon provides a vivid description of the late-night street scene in London's Soho drawn directly from his research diary:

> We stumble out of the club at around 3-ish – Soho is packed with people, crowding pavements and roads, looking and laughing – everyone appears happy. Some are in groups, bustling their way along noisily – others are alone, silent and walking purposefully on their way. . . . Cars crawl down narrow streets which are already impossibly full of cars, Vespas, people, thronging crowds. This wasn't "late night" for Soho – the night had hardly started.[12]

It is not just *a* scene but many: a music scene, an art scene, a film scene, outdoor recreation scene, nightlife scene, and so on – all reinforcing one another. I have visited such places in cities across the United States, and they are invariably full of Creative Class people.[13] My interview subjects tell me that this kind of "scene of scenes" provides another set of visual and aural cues they look for in a place to live and work. Many of them also visit the big-ticket, high-art cultural venues, at least occasionally, as well as consuming mass-market culture like Hollywood movies and rock or pop concerts. But for them, street-level culture is a must.

Consider just the practical reasons for this. Big-ticket, high-art events are strictly scheduled, often only on certain nights of the week, whereas the street-level scene is fluid and ongoing. As a large number of my interview subjects have told me, this is a big benefit for creative types who may work late and not be free until 9 or 10 p.m., or work through the weekend and want to go out Monday night. Moreover, creative workers with busy schedules want to use their cultural time "efficiently." Attending a large-venue event, be it a symphony concert or a professional basketball game, is a single, one-dimensional experience that consumes a lot of recreational resources: It is expensive and takes a big chunk of time. Visiting a street-level scene puts you in the middle of a smorgasbord; you can easily do several things in one excursion. The street scene also allows you to modulate the level and intensity of your experience. You can do active, high-energy things – immerse yourself in the bustle of the sidewalks or head into an energized club and dance until dawn – or find a quiet cozy spot to listen to jazz while sipping a brandy, or a coffee shop for some espresso, or retreat into a bookstore where it is quiet.

### Everything interesting happens at the margins

Consider, too, the nature of the offerings in the street-level smorgasbord. In culture as in business, the most radical and interesting stuff starts in garages and small rooms. And lots of this creativity stays in small rooms. Aside from Garrison Keillor and Spalding Gray, for instance, not many serious monologue artists have hit it big in the United States; you've got to go to the street-level venues to find them. These venues in Austin, Seattle and other cities offer a dense spectrum of musical genres from blues, R&B, country, rockabilly, world music and their various hybrids to newer forms of electronic music, from techno and deep house to trance and drum and bass. Nor is everything new. The street-level scene is often the best place to find seldom-performed or little-known works of the past. Recent offerings in Pittsburgh alone have included a small theater company staging Richard Brinsley Sheridan's eighteenth-century play *The Rivals*; a gallery specializing in historic photography; a local jazz-rock group performing old American political songs such as "For Jefferson and Liberty" and "The Farmer Is the Man Who Feeds Us All"; and a street musician who plays violin pieces you won't hear on the classical radio programs that endlessly recycle the equivalent of the symphonic "Top Forty."

The street scene is *eclectic*. This is another part of its appeal. Consider that eclecticism is also a strong theme within many of today's art forms. Think of DJs in Harlem nightclubs of the 1970s who started the technique known as "sampling" – frenetically mixing snatches of music from different records, on different turntables, for the crowd to dance to. Think of the proliferation of hyphenated music genres like Afro-Celt. Think of Warhol, Rauschenberg and a host of visual artists after them appropriating images from news photos, comic strips, food packages, wherever. Eclectic scavenging for creativity is not new. Picasso borrowed from African art as well as Greco-Roman classical forms; rock and roll pioneers melded blues and R&B; and one could argue that the literary DJ who really pioneered sampling was T. S. Eliot in *The Waste Land*, a poem built largely by stringing together, and playing upon, quotations and allusions from all corners of the world's literature. Today, however, eclecticism is rampant and spreading to a degree that seems unprecedented. It is a key element of street-level culture – and eclectic taste is a social marker that can usually be counted on to distinguish a Creative Class person. Eclecticism in the form of cultural intermixing, when done right, can be a powerful creative stimulus.

Furthermore, street-level culture involves more than taking in staged performances and looking at art. It is social and interactive. One can meet people, hang out and talk, or just sit back to watch tonight's episodes of the human comedy. To many the social milieu is indeed the street's main attraction. If that sounds a bit vapid and superficial, sometimes it is. This is not high art; it admits amateurs. Hanging in a sidewalk café does not deliver the exquisite and carefully crafted artistic intensity of Beethoven's *Ninth*. It is also true that for some people, hitting the street-level cultural scene devolves into little more than cruising the singles scene. And even when experiencing culture is truly the goal, if hanging out in nightspots frequented by artists and aficionados is how you choose to pick up your creative stimulation, you are going to pick up a lot of chaff along with it. You run the risk of becoming chaff yourself: a dilettante, a *poseur*, a gallery gadfly, a coffee-shop talker.

At the same time, let's not be too quick to belittle the social aspect of the street. Conversation, to begin with, is a valid art form. Dorothy Parker and Oscar Wilde are quoted more from their repartee than from their writing. Few people today read what Samuel Johnson wrote, but many have read Boswell's *Life* for its accounts of Dr. Johnson shooting the breeze with Oliver Goldsmith and Joshua Reynolds. All Socrates did was talk. I am not suggesting that you can routinely hear Socratic wisdom in a bar in Adams-Morgan at two o'clock in the morning. But though it may not produce deathless epigrams reliably, good conversation has creative possibilities. In my own work I often learn a great deal from talking with people in coffee shops and other such venues. I pick up observations and anecdotes from people who feel free to ramble. I listen to their ideas about work, leisure and community and this stimulates my own thinking. The creative faculties are fed by meeting and talking informally, by chance, with a diverse range of creative-minded others.

Just people-watching is arguably a valid form of cultural exchange. It is certainly one of my favorites, and as Andy Warhol noted, he didn't go to restaurants only to eat. Take the experience of strolling through a good street scene in, say, New York, or the city of your choice. The first thing that strikes you is the sheer visual variety of the people. Many ethnic groups are present, of course, in various ages, conditions and sizes, and this alone is thought-provoking. You may find yourself drawn to meditate on the history of our species – the many so-called races of humans, and how they came to grow apart as they spread across the globe, and how they endlessly intermix. You may find yourself meditating on your own history – how you were once as young as that one, and may someday be as old as that one, and are liable to look like that one if you don't mend your wicked ways. And then, if it is a proper street scene, there will be many people of exotic appearance: foreigners in long skirts and bright robes; young Americans with hair in colors and configurations that bend the laws of physics, at least Newtonian physics; people dressed as cowboys, Goths, Victorians, hippies – you get the picture. And for many people, the experience of this picture is exhilarating, liberating. It is similar to the thrill of a costume party, when people literally put on new identities – including masks that obliterate or alter the social "masks" they normally wear – and there is a delicious sense of adventure in the air. One has an awareness of the possibilities of life.

I would further argue, following Rogers and others, that this kind of experience is essential to the creative process. We humans are not godlike; we cannot create out of nothing. Creativity for us is an act of synthesis, and in order to create and synthesize, we need stimuli – bits and pieces to put together in new and unfamiliar ways, existing frameworks to deconstruct and transcend. I also feel it is inherent to the creative mindset to want to maximize choices and options, to always be looking for new ones, because in the game that Einstein called combinatory play, this increases your chances of coming up with novel combinations. And as more people earn their keep by creating, the more these aspects of experience are likely to be highly valued and just plain necessary.

## Pitfalls of the Experiential World

There is much that seems good about living a quest for experience. It seems an energetic and productive way to live. It can even be a more humane and benevolent way to live. The emphasis on active, participatory recreation seems healthy physically and psychologically, as well as more satisfying than the thin diet of the TV junkie. Done properly it should lead to good experiences all around. So where exactly does the insidiousness come in?

First with the fact that the packaging and selling of experience is often perceived to be – and often is – inauthentic. As Tom Frank and others have noted, the commercialization of experience can empty it of its original creative content.[14] Retailers from Banana Republic to Prada do this with clothes. They try to create brand recognition around experience, and in doing so sell you experience as brand: just wearing the clothes supposedly makes you cool and with-it. Or, to paraphrase what numerous Creative Class people have told me in my interviews: "You can't just enjoy a ballgame; you have to go to a 'state-of-the-art' $500 million stadium for a multimedia circus that distracts you from the very game you paid to see." Many Creative Class people are acutely aware of this pitfall. They thus tend to shun the heavily packaged commercial venues that they call "generica" – the chain restaurants and nightclubs, the stadiums with bells and whistles, and the like – or they patronize them with a conscious note of irony, as in the obligatory trip to a business conference in Las Vegas. They prefer more authentic, indigenous or organic venues that offer a wide range of options and where they can have a hand in creating the options.

Finding such venues can be an ongoing struggle, because generica has a way of creeping in everywhere. One of the last areas of social life where a modicum of authenticity can be found is the music scene. But today music clubs that used to be dynamic, street-level places to enjoy "real" music are being replaced by late-night versions of those multimedia circuses. Not only do you immerse yourself in booming music, but you get digital lighting, smoke machines, water sprinklers activated in concert with peaks in the music – everything you need to be hot and cool. Some such clubs have even become chains. What began as an organic development from the street has become a Disneyland facsimile of itself – safe, secure and predictable – trafficking not in a series of unique experiences of different styles of music and performance, but in the same generic experience night after night. There are deeper concerns as well. In his book *Clubbing*, Malbon focuses on the elaborate society that clubbers have woven for themselves. The book is a highly detailed study of the young people who frequent the club scene in Britain. (Malbon admits that he spent "150 nights out" researching the book, and as he puts it, "many of these were the best nights out I have had.") He notes that:

> Clubbers distinguish themselves from others through their tastes in clothing, music, dancing techniques, clubbing genre and so on. . . . These tastes are trained and refined, and constantly monitored not only in order to distinguish oneself from another, but also in identifying with those that share one's distinctive styles and preferences.[15]

In all of these ways they are, he says, constructing identities. Not to be too judgmental here: I did some of these things myself once upon a time and I still occasionally visit music venues and clubs. But one could well say that Malbon's clubbers sound like little more than trendy sheep. If the goal is to construct an identity or discover an identity, there are other, better ways to do it.

Marketplace attempts to satisfy the craving for experience can turn weirdly self-contradictory in many ways. The "fantasy kitchen" is a useful example. The showpiece of my eclectically decorated home is a kitchen full of everything a professional chef needs to make a meal – seldom used, of course. I sometimes refer to the stainless-steel All-Clad cookware hanging from a rack in my kitchen as my "giant charm bracelet." Kara Swisher, the *Wall Street Journal* columnist, wrote a column chronicling the renovation of her San Francisco home. Tallying the thousands of dollars she spent outfitting her fantasy kitchen, she concluded that she spent the equivalent of "about 1,000 takeout meals or at least 600 outings at pretty good restaurants."[16] The point is these are no longer appliances and cookware in the traditional utilitarian sense. They are part of the food *experience*. They are there to provide experiences – the visual experience of looking at them, the status experience of owning them, and the experience of cooking "like a professional" on those infrequent occasions when we actually do use them to whip up a dinner that mixes Pan-Asian, Italian and home-grown influences. A new experiential service, "Impromptu Gourmet," has taken the food experience to a new extreme. It allows you to purchase the ingredients for a meal from a roster of America's leading chefs. When the ingredients arrive in the mail, you can then have the experience of "cooking" this designer meal in your very own kitchen.

In short, if we crave experiences we will be sold experiences, and in the process we may find ourselves buying a bill of goods. The final pitfall is that even in the attempt to avoid packaged-and-sold experiences, we may pack our lives so full that we overdo it. While we scorn the couch potatoes hooked on TV, the desire for constant stimulation and experiences can itself come close to looking like addiction. But no way of life is perfect, and the trend is inexorable. The experiential life is more than a pastiche of recreational fads and marketing gimmicks. As I've shown, it is a product of the rising creative ethos – which is born from a deep new cultural fusion.

# Notes

1   Janelle Brown, "A Poster Child for Internet Idiocy." Salon.com, August 1, 2001: salon.com/tech/feature/2000/08/01/dotcomguy/print.html.
2   Joseph Pine III and James H. Gilmore, *The Experience Economy: Work Is Theatre and Every Business a Stage*. Boston: Harvard Business School Press, 1999, pp. 2, 11.
3   C. Campbell, *The Romantic Ethic and the Spirit of Modern Consumerism*. Oxford: Blackwell, 1987; and "The Sociology of Consumption," in D. Miller (ed.), *Acknowledging Consumption: A Review of New Studies*. London: Routledge, 1996, pp. 96–126.
4   Ben Malbon, *Clubbing: Dancing, Ecstasy, and Vitality*. London: Routledge, 1999, p. 33.
5   Carl Rogers, "Toward a Theory of Creativity," in *On Becoming a Person: A Therapist's View of Psychotherapy*. Boston: Houghton Mifflin, 1961, p. 348.
6   Ibid., pp. 352–4.
7   Thorstein Veblen, *The Theory of the Leisure Class*. New York: New American Library, 1959; orig. 1899.
8   Gary Cross, *The All-Consuming Century: Why Commercialism Won in Modern America*. New York: Columbia University Press, 2000.
9   As quoted in James Atlas, "Cashing Out Young." *Vanity Fair*, December 1999, p. 216.

10   Clair Brown, *American Standards of Living, 1918–1988*. Oxford: Blackwell Publishers, 1994, p. 3. [ . . . ]

11   Robert Fogel, *The Fourth Great Awakening and the Future of Egalitarianism*. Chicago: University of Chicago Press, 2000, p. 191. [ . . . ]

12   Malbon, *Clubbing*, p. 174.

13   This section draws heavily on interviews and focus groups conducted by the author between 1999 and 2001. [ . . . ]

14   See Tom Frank, *One Market Under God: Extreme Capitalism, Market Populism, and the End of Economic Development*. New York: Doubleday, 2001, and *The Conquest of Cool: Business Culture, Counterculture, and the Rise of Hip Consumerism*. Chicago: University of Chicago Press, 1997.

15   Malbon, *Clubbing*, p. 55.

16   Kara Swisher, "How Kitchen Fixes Can Add Up Fast." *Wall Street Journal*, August 7, 2001.

# 8  Toby Miller, Nitin Govil, John McMurria, and Richard Maxwell

# CONCLUSION TO *GLOBAL HOLLYWOOD*

[ . . . ] Audiences, too, are doing work. In contesting global Hollywood's command over the NICL, and with it the conditions and possibilities of cultural labour worldwide, we seek to articulate a materialist cultural policy on the same ground of supra-nationalism proposed by García-Canclini and Yúdice. Such a policy would extend to the consumer in order to comprehend the needs of any number of constituencies currently excluded or marginalised from formal discussions of cultural trade, labour and consumption. Our policy would thereby enact a different narrative of the filmgoing experience from the one that has closed around the narrow institutional identity disciplined by intellectual property, constituted in marketing narratives as an audience with tastes amenable to market criteria, and unaware of the surveillance that surrounds it.

Policy that disarticulates intellectual property (IP) from corporate interests removes the cornerstone of Hollywood's global control over the resources for making and watching movies. Such policy begins with the practical problems that already weaken the corporate enclosure around intellectual property: (1) the prioritisation of copyright law alone fails to insure monopoly rights because it neglects the shift towards trademark law embraced by licence-based industries (like television); (2) copyright is far too difficult to enforce in so-called emerging markets; and (3) copyright has trouble working in new distributional arenas without seriously compromising user privacy. Further weaknesses can be found in the liberal foundation that already

"Conclusion to *Global Hollywood*" from Toby Miller, Nitin Govil, John McMurria, and Richard Maxwell (2001), *Global Hollywood*. British Film Institute, London, pp. 202–10. Reprinted by permission of bfi publishing.

informs policy reform – whether to shore up progressive moral-rights provisions against corporate control or give corporations a human face. First, the issue of artistic livelihood is sustained only *accidentally* by copyright. More often than not, copyright involves the signing away of moral rights under work-for-hire doctrine. Second, copyright in its current evocation is tied to forms of legislation that grant legal personhood to corporations who become 'authors' in the act of contractual transfer. Finally, there is no equality in trade of IP because the slippery *Realpolitik* transfer of authorial moral-rights provisions privileges ownership-oriented regimes (which is what allowed the US, finally, to sign the Berne Convention). In sum, moral rights arguments work well within the narrow purview of tributary rights attached to the creative work (i.e., that it cannot be 'distorted' without approval from its author and that the authorship must always be attributed); however, by design, moral rights are incapable of negotiating the everyday ways in which IP relations are subject to the *commercial transfer* inherent in the 'right in the work'.

Perhaps what communications and cultural policy needs is a more nuanced approach to the issue of ownership. Rather than attend to issues of ownership at the level of production, why not begin with the act of *consumption*? Acts of consumption generate ownership in a myriad of ways. Taking advantage of limited rights attached to screen a copyrighted programme, you may screen Blockbuster videos within the confines of your own home, or in non-profit educational arenas. However, the rolling-back of first-sale rights creates digital property in the very act of consumption; this transitory act of ownership is used by the copyright industries as a warrant to install tracking technologies in your PC. Clearly, copyright cuts across the spatio-temporal parameters of ownership in specific ways.

Instead of endlessly recycling ownership ideals rooted in property, we suggest that cultural policy shift the debate to a recognition of bundles of consumer rights. Rather than protect sites of creation (rights to own) through the phantasmatic evocation of authorship under copyright law, policy might protect *rights to consume* (which are the key rights under fire in recent DMCA legislation). This would involve a thorough consideration of the public domain and fair use, not merely as byproducts designed in some way to compensate for the possible excesses of IP, but at a more fundamental level that ensures we have the rights to do things with texts, not simply the rights to sign them away in the act of creation (which is what common-law copyright does). A set of moral rights for the act of consumption (suggesting perhaps that we are libidinally connected to the acts of our consumption) rather than for the location of an originary act of creation might go a long way towards conceptualising the extension of fair use in the current informational environment. This re-tooling takes us away from fair use's traditional evocation as a form of subsidy given by copyright owners (see Ginsberg, 1997b), towards a form of subsidy to users, whose labour as audiences is exploited by market research that protects the results of their surveys – as IP, no less.

Since market research understands audiences as an untamed labour force that requires domestication, users might demand labour compensation in the form of an extension of fair use that keeps monopoly rights in check, rather than as simply an excuse for 'stealing'. In addition, user's rights would redeploy the public domain away from its conceptualisation as the maligned progeny of IP (Cain to the commercial imperative's Abel), which fences off discrete areas of knowledge from public use or serves as the public's toll for conferring private property rights in authorship. Instead, we might recognise that the public domain should be understood as 'a device that permits the rest of the system to work by leaving the raw materials of authorship available for others to use' (Litman, 1990: 968–9). In other words, the public domain must be the constitutive ground upon which creativity rests, rather than its remainder. This idea is at the heart of the open-source movement. To achieve this reorientation in US legal discourse, the Electronic Frontier Foundation (EFF) already funds ongoing legal challenges to the DMCA. By providing financial and strategic support to plaintiffs who deploy legal arguments based on the open-source movement in cases before the judicial court circuit, the EFF hope to counter the DMCA and other attempts to lock up intellectual property in corporate hands. One industry analyst worried that by 'forcing the government to defend the law over and over' the EFF poses a 'far more serious challenge in their battle to assert their intellectual property rights in cyberspace than a bunch of college kids swapping music via the Internet' (Sweeting, 2001).

Consider two further approaches to establish greater consumer control over copyright: usage as a speech act and as an act of labour. While 'US First Amendment jurisprudence has defined readers' rights only incidentally' (Cohen, 1996: 1003), there have been consistent claims for limiting copyright's power to interrupt the democratic imperatives of the public sphere through the constitutional guarantee of freedom of speech. Melvin Nimmer, for example, argued in 1970 that there existed a 'speech interest with respect to copyright', such that copyright would be subject to violation if the act of copying sustained a 'unique contribution to an enlightened public dialogue' (1193, 1197). While he had in mind a scenario where copyrighted photographs of the My Lai massacre might be withheld from a critical public, Paul Goldstein (1970) used Howard Hughes' attempt to stop Random House from publishing a biography (he created a corporate façade that bought the copyrights to articles written about him) to claim that copyright infringement should be excused when supporting the general public interest.

Media and legal theorists on the left often equate the copy-related rights of information creators with forms of speech (see, for example, Braman, 1998: 81) or maintain that copyright itself is a regulation of speech (Benkler, 1999: 446). Some suggest that copyright law pertain to acts of speech rather than property rights objectified in certain works (Rotstein, 1992: 739–42). Still others argue that the conflation of speech rights with property rights – even in its progressive modality – simply recapitulates the public/private and commons/commodity orthodoxies inscribed in IP law (Coombe, 1996: 239, 241, 247). What we are suggesting, however, is a reorientation of property rights (which undergird the NICL) towards labour rights. Such a fundamental move away from the politics of ownership to the politics of work recognises that, for fair use and the public domain to have any meaning, audience work will have to be recognised as a form of speech act. Julie Cohen (1996: 1038–9) notes that 'reading is intimately connected with speech', and is therefore amenable to constitutional protections. Hartley adds that reading as a form of media response is a practice akin to speech, in that it is 'a universal technology of communication, while not an already-existing attribute of persons' (1996: 119, 66). We suggest that, like speech, reading deserves protection.

The equation of basic human rights with reading rights is more than just rhetorical majesty. Under the strict schedules of harmonisation posed by the American and Western European powerhouses at the WTO, Venturelli warns,

> communications rights and human rights as expressed in communication policy and social policy can be contested on the grounds that they act to constrain trade through a set of non-commercial public interest requirements whether in infrastructure or content. (Venturelli, 1997: 63)

Following free-speech precepts, communications policy must think itself out of traditional forms of IP rights, in order to protect forms of creativity that stimulate the 'production of media content at the fringes of the range of preferences, thus promoting equal access to diverging preferences and opinions in society' (Van Cuilenburg, 1999: 204). But the DMCA curtails free-speech protection with anti-circumvention provisions that state consumers may not use devices or services designed to by-pass copyright management systems (such as watermarking). The only way in which corporate owners of copyrighted products can regulate such possible infringements is to monitor the entire terrain of media consumption; as such, the anti-circumvention policies pose a significant invasion of privacy as well as fair use. Cultural policy must deflate the widespread corporate acceptance of rights-management software that threatens significant sectors of use, and begin to 'contemplate built-in technological limits on copyright owners' monitoring capabilities' (Cohen, 1996: 988). In arguing for technologically guaranteeing the anonymity of media users in order to prevent a forced fixing of their audience practice within a prescribed form of affiliative politics, Cohen notes:

> Reading is an intellectual association, pure and simple. As such, it is profoundly constitutive of identity as direct interpersonal association. There are reasons for according even stronger protection to reading, moreover. Interpersonal association and group affiliation are, by definition, voluntary expressions of a common purpose or interest. (Cohen, 1996: 1014)

To modify the mostly individualist language of these rights, cultural policy might draw from the 1996 report by UNESCO and the UN's World Commission on Culture and Development. *Our Creative Diversity* notes that one of the challenges in the wake of the GATT is maintaining a 'balance between those countries that export copyright and those that import it' (Pérez de Cuéllar, 1996: 244). Defining an intermediary sphere of IP rights between individual authorial rights and the national/international public domain, *Our Creative Diversity* suggests that certain cultures deserve IP rights as *groups* (Pérez de Cuéllar, 1996). Not surprisingly, the protection of collective authorship (specifically with regards to folklore) was not raised at the January 1997 meeting of the WTO in Geneva, and when Third World countries supported such protection at a joint UNESCO/WIPO meeting later that year, the move was opposed by US and British delegates. As Kirster Malm writes,

> when the US delegate said that since most of the folklore that was commercially exploited was US folklore, Third World countries would have to pay a lot of money to the US if an international convention should come about. The Indian lawyer, Mr. Purim, answered that that was already the case with existing conventions and by the way all US folklore except the Amerindian one was imported to the US from Europe and Africa . . . . Thus the money should go to the original owners of that folklore. (Malm, quoted in Smiers, 2000: 397)

A current case involving the shutting down of a collective form of modern folklore illustrates the powerful correlation of consumption and speech act.

After the AOL-Time Warner aggression against fans and Website owners, the latter engaged in a war of position. The formation of such sites as www.potterwar.org.uk and the cleverly named www.harrypotter-warnercansuemyarse.co.uk was followed by the 'Defense Against the Dark Arts' (DADA) Project (www.dprophet.com/dada/), which urged a boycott of *Harry Potter* merchandise and the film (though, interestingly, *not* the books). DADA suggested that reparations be made to *Potter* fans by Warner Bros., 'whether this is in a substantial donation to UNICEF, or tickets to the premiere to the actual fans who were threatened themselves; we'd like to see Warner Brothers come up with a plan that shows how sorry they feel.' In rallying support for an upcoming constitutional battle, DADA put the corporate policing actions this way:

> There are dark forces afoot, darker even than He–Who–Must–Not–Be–Named, because these dark forces are daring to take away something so basic, so human, that it's close to murder. They are taking away our freedom of speech, our freedom to express our thoughts, feelings and ideas, and they are taking away the fun of a magical book.

Although AOL–Time Warner has stopped sending the cease–and–desist letters – no doubt swayed by the tremendous negative publicity their trademark protection generated – the *Potter* case is part of a long line of corporate policing efforts that stretch from *Star Wars* Websites to *The Simpsons, Star Trek* and the *X-Files* (see Tushnet, 1997). In connection with its licensing efforts, AOL–Time Warner is applying and registering 2,000 trademarks connected to *Harry Potter* (Demarco, 2001: 4). Clearly, the corralling of words associated with the novels has entailed a silencing of consumer speech.

In addition to the conceptualisation of consumption as a form of speech, which is protected under most forms of democratic constitutional provision, cultural policy must recognise that every act of consumption is an act of authorship, or rather an act that hybridises the traditional parameters of singular gatekeeping authority. In other words, every act of authorship 'in any medium is more akin to translation and recombination' than it is to a spurious originary act (Litman, 1990: 966). We have already shown how IP law fails to recognise collectively authored works like folklore, which are texts in constant states of flux, secured only through the contexts of their use and the forms of life constituted by their meanings. Ironically, we can use the restrictive language of corporate-friendly initiatives to substantiate our claim for the labour of consumption. [Earlier] we discussed the US negotiating team's position at the 1996 WIPO conference, which called for an inherent reproduction in every act of digital transmission. In effect, this makes *all* users of digital media *writers* – as Pool puts it, 'to read a text stored in electronic memory, one displays it on the screen: one writes to read it' (quoted in Van der Merwe, 1999: 311).

In many ways, the idea of the labour of consumption ironically redeploys Lockean labour theory (which traditionally underpins the romantic idea of authorship) towards a socialist vision of property rights gained through the act of adding one's labour (Boyle, 1996: 57). Although such conceptualisations of labour have supported worker exploitation, since wages transfer the property right of labour to the employer, they have also prioritised the forms of *creative* labour that make the author's work his or her own. Conceiving of a more open public use as a kind of *symbolic* wage for users is one way of working through the dilemma of monopoly rights, even though it recapitulates the foundation of property-exchange as the root of media transactions.

We might look further, then. Borrowing from studies of subcultural practices, Aoki refers to 'audience recoding rights'. He notes that focusing on the dynamic and fluid nature of textuality (with its audiences equal partners in the creative act) might 'dilute the property-ness of interests protected by copyright.' Such an approach, focused on 'texts-as-speech-events, would begin allowing space for a judicial consideration of "recoded" cultural productions and enhanced respect for free speech values' (Aoki, 1993: 826–7). While Aoki recognises that such a reconceptualisation might introduce commercial imperatives into the regulation of speech, understanding media consumption as a collaborative network of productive labour takes us part of the way towards a wider definition of 'fair use'.

Jane Ginsberg (1997a) has suggested that traditional forms of fair use privilege certain types of users and allow the redistribution of value enclosed by copyright to these users. Redirecting fair use towards *ordinary* users – who are otherwise 'paedocratised' as dopes by both academic and governmental cultures for supposedly being incapable of either 'critical distance, scepticism or reason, or with being able to integrate, compare or triangulate media discourses with other elaborated in different institutional sites' (Hartley, 1996: 59) – would entail a recognition of the transient nature of reading rather than the fixed site of authorship. Fair use, as Wendy Gordon (1982: 1653) notes, has not often been extended to 'ordinary users', since 'the public interest served by second authors [creators of derivative works or specialised users using the stuff of public domain] are likely to be stronger than the interests served by ordinary consumers'. This prejudice recapitulates copyright's espousal of the author as a functional exclusionary principle that impedes the free circulation and recomposition of cultural production. Authorship provides the common terrain for laws that claim that lists of telephone numbers are not copyrightable by phone directory publishers – because there is no proof of 'sweat of the brow' labour (see *Feist Publications Inc.* v. *Rural Telephone Service Co.*, 499 US (1991)), and statutory protections of market research firms' computer databases as copyrightable 'literary works', with all the ownership benefits of authorship.

As technology, such as the 'trusted systems' and 'rights management tracking software', begins to supplant copyright's traditional function (which includes a significant, if underdeveloped, evocation of fair use), legal manoeuvrability within the statutory sphere will become even more difficult: 'every single copy of a digital work would become its own tollbooth' (Benkler, 1999: 422). Of course, we will always have hackers, who will be the last guardians of an old system that recognises some forms of the public domain and private use.

'The tendency to undervalue the public domain,' writes Boyle, 'is a world-wide phenomenon' (1996: 130). Public policy designed to control knowledge capital by monopoly rents instead of a public archive-based consensual access to knowledge represents, as Frow (2000) notes, a 'major erosion of the public domain'. While the public domain has traditionally signified as the abject detritus of non-copyrightable materials, its roots in European feudalism (as the true public commons, scarce land reserved for public use) mask the fact that 'knowledge actually increases when it is shared' (Frow, 2000: 182). Yochai Benkler calls for two policy proposals alongside free and open source-software strategies that might meaningfully sustain the public domain and resist its enclosure: 'identifying and sustaining a series of commons in the resources necessary for the production and exchange of information', and a 'shift in distributive policies from low cost or free reception to ubiquitous access to the facilities necessary for production and dissemination of information' (2000: 576). The market model theorised by Napster suggests a group of peer users exchanging information, and Internet-based users rights might be conceived of along a service-based approach based on the shared-resource market network. Bundling users into groups that share resources, rather than individuated consumers who consume in private singular acts, clearly threatens both the existence of copyright as well as the corporate distributional middlepeople who have mediated between traditional artists and consumers.

With digital commerce changing the way we consume by compressing the traditional space and time of services interaction (the gap into which distributional middlemen have staked their claim), a cultural policy that privileges reception as an *act of creative labour* can help fracture the authorial underpinnings of copyright, while at the same time encouraging the proliferation of responses to new aesthetic forms. To use John Perry Barlow's (n. d.) words, a politics of labour (which prioritises *doing*) rather than of objects (which favours *owning*), reconceptualises media interaction as conduct 'in a world made more of verbs than nouns'.

Our call for a labour theory of consumption that inverts the negative liberties granted by the NICL is based, in part, on the acts of surveillance performed on media users. We have shown [in earlier chapters of the volume] how spectators are alienated from their labour as subjects of market research. The labour of audiences, owned by market research and protected by corporate IP laws, deny the research subjects access to the very speech acts that constitute the labour of reception. Like the broadcast media it supports, market research structures the diversity of user activity into suspected or probable sorts of 'audience,' wherein consumers *themselves* become the product.

# References

Aoki, Keith. (1993) 'Adrift in the Intertext: Authorship and Audience "Recoding" Rights: Comment on Robert H. Rotstein, "Beyond Metaphor: Copyright Infringement and the Fiction of the Work" '. *Chicago-Kent Law Review* 68.

Barlow, John Perry. 'The Economy of Mind on the Global Net'. (n.d.) www.eff. org/pub/Publications/John_Perry_Barlow/idea_economy.article.

Benkler, Yochai. (1999) 'Free as the Air to Common Use: First Amendment Constraints on Enclosure of the Public Domain'. *New York University Law Review* 74.

Boyle, James. (1996) *Shamans, Software, and Spleens: Law and the Construction of the Information Society*. Cambridge, MA: Harvard University Press.

Braman, Sandra. (1998) 'The Right to Create; Cultural Policy in the Fourth Stage of the Information Society'. *Gazette* 60, no. 1.

Cohen, Julie E. (1996) 'A Right to Read Anonymously: A Closer Look at "Copyright Management" in Cyberspace'. *Connecticut Law Review* 28.

Coombe, Rosemary. (1996) 'Innovation and the Information Environment: Left Out on the Information Highway'. *Oregon Law Review* 75.

Demarco, Peter. (2001) 'Legal Wizards Crack Whip at Harry Potter Fan Sites'. *Daily News*, 22 February.

Frow, John. (2000) 'Public Domain and the New World Order in Knowledge'. *Social Semiotics* 10, no. 2.

Ginsberg, Jane C. (1997a) 'Authors and Users in Copyright'. *Journal of the Copyright Society USA* 45.

Ginsberg, Jane C. (1997b) 'Copyright, Common Law, and *Sui Generis* Protection of Databases in the United States and Abroad'. *University of Cincinnati Law Review* 66.

Goldstein, Paul. (1970) 'Copyright and the First Amendment'. *Columbia Law Review* 70.

Gordon, Wendy. (1982) 'Fair Use as Market Failure: A Structural and Economic Analysis of the Betamax Case and its Predecessors'. *Columbia Law Review* 82.

MILLER, GOVIL, McMURRIA, AND MAXWELL

Hartley, John. (1996) *Popular Reality: Journalism, Modernity, Popular Culture*. London: Arnold.

Litman, Jessica. (1990) 'The Public Domain'. *Emory Law Journal* 39.

Nimmer, M. (1970) 'Does Copyright Abridge the First Amendment Guarantees of Free Speech and the Press?' *UCLA Law Review* 17.

Pérez de Cuéllar, J. (1996) *Our Creative Diversity: Report of the World Commission on Culture and Development*. Paris: UNESCO.

Rotstein, Robert H. (1992) 'Beyond Metaphor: Copyright Infringement and the Fiction of the Work'. *Chicago-Kent Law Review* 68.

Smiers, Joost. (2000) 'The Abolition of Copyright: Better for Artists, Third World Countries and the Public Domain'. *Gazette* 62, no. 5.

Sweeting, Paul. (2001) 'The Movie and Music Industries Have Good Reason to Feel Picked On'. *Video Business*, 12 March: 12.

Tushnet, Rebecca. (1997) 'Legal Fictions: Copyright, Fan Fiction and a New Common Law'. *Loyola of Los Angeles Entertainment Law Journal* 17.

Van Cuilenburg, Jan. (1999) 'On Competition, Access and Diversity in Media, Old and New: Some Remarks for Communications Policy in the Information Age'. *New Media and Society* 1, no. 2.

Van der Merwe, Dana. (1999) 'The Dematerialization of Print and the Fate of Copyright'. *International Review of Law Computers* 13, no. 3.

Venturelli, Shalini. (1997) 'Prospects for Human Rights in the Political and Regulatory Design of the Information Society'. *Media and Politics in Transition: Cultural Identity in the Age of Globalization*. Eds. Jan Servaes and Rico Lie. Leuven and Amersfoort: Acco.

# PART III
Creative Practices

*Brad Haseman*

# CREATIVE PRACTICES

## Creative Practices for the New Millennium

In the cultural domain we are witnessing a proliferation of forms, tastes, and patterns of creative production and consumption. An expanded and often extreme set of creative practices is subverting well-understood categories of the arts and culture, collapsing the borders between the traditional and the innovative, the polite and the rude, the everyday and the celebrity, the professional and the amateur. Performance merges with the theater of everyday life; shopping malls become stages or galleries. Celebrity and fame no longer necessarily follow from elite training and virtuosity but come as the prize at the end of the game show or video camera. Old formulations of art and culture no longer adequately describe creative practices in an environment where "competition is the main policy lever and consumer protection rather than cultural development is the social dividend" (Cunningham 2002: 5).

This introduction discusses the impact cultural, economic, and technological change is having on the creative practices of individuals and groups. The first part examines how traditional and widely held formulations of art and aesthetics are shifting within the creative industries to give rise to a new cultural ecology. It then considers the playful contingency and openness taken by the forms of these practices, together with the creative processes which shape them.

The term "creative practices" encompasses a wide range of activities that are encountered in a host of settings and for many different purposes. The second part of this introduction seeks to extract from this creative churn five specific characteristics which distinguish practice in the creative industries. In order to ground these characteristics in action, a case study of the creative practice of Robert Lepage follows. A Renaissance theater man, Lepage's work spans a wide range of forms – from the seven-hour epic *The Seven*

*Streams of the River Ota* to his one-person shows; from interpretations of the world's opera and theater classics to award-winning films and theatrical rock projects with Peter Gabriel. In addition, he has refined innovative work practices through his company Ex Machina at its multimedia center La Caserne Dalhousie in Quebec City, Canada. Lepage's work is an exemplar of creative practice for our time and references to it are woven through this introduction to illustrate its ideas in action.

## I.  Shifting Categories, Forms, and Processes of Creative Industries

John Hartley's general introduction to this volume presents a sweeping intellectual history of the creative arts and civic humanism through to the transformation of both in the creative industries formulations. Such a movement, from one paradigm to the next, is seldom painless. Nowhere is this more evident than when the arts become re-purposed within the creative industries. Here notions of individual genius give way to the collective creativity of collaborative teams, and priorities shift away from artists creating unique works of art toward the needs of creative producers developing content for the digital and networked infrastructure which covers much of the globe.

Many artists are unconvinced by one of the creative industries' core assumptions – that highly imaginative and groundbreaking content creation is all-important – that content is king. Instead they see "content" as merely a new name for the art that artists have been making proudly for centuries – these things known as plays and dances and symphonies and remixed tracks. Theater director Michael Kustow has the support of many in his scoff "now I am to be known as a content creator?" (Kustow 2001: 192).

This is coupled with a belief which values art over popular creative forms. Peter Hall, who directed the National Theatre in London from 1973 to 1988, is alarmed by government policy which he sees as being only interested in "the visible, the trendy – pop music, design, video, film, architecture" and destined to create "a land dominated by imported television, with art which is bland, unexceptional and multi-national" (Hall 1999: 26–7). Confronted by the torrent of digital content which demands our attention, many fear the arts are in danger of being corrupted – dumbed down and misused.

This view flows directly from beliefs about the value of the arts to society (see "Creative Industries"). Questions of aesthetics and a concern for the metaphysical and transcendent remain the preoccupation of many artists. The abiding task is to create symbolically dense forms. Even those who do not strive for the Kantian beautiful or sublime assert a desire to create significant work – perhaps even contribute to "the best that has been thought and said." Playwright David Mamet recently wrote:

> Theater exists to deal with problems of the soul, with the mysteries of human life, not with quotidian calamities. Eric Hoffer says there is art, for example *Waiting for Godot*. And there's popular entertainment – for example *Oklahoma*. And there's mass entertainment, like Disneyland. (Mamet 2001: 27)

There is a strong educational priority at play here, a civilizing agenda within a hierarchy of taste. Art leads the way to social enlightenment and personal fulfillment and stands at sharp odds with John Howkins's (2001) discussion of a hierarchy of desires best activated by "the entertainment gene."

The arts, it is argued, are of intrinsic public good and therefore demand financial support in the form of subsidy. As they eschew the popular and are seldom intended for mass appeal, the arts are unable to generate the sums of money that would allow them to be self-financing. When governments cut funding to the arts the cry is quickly heard: "Unless we understand the need for subsidy, our arts will not flourish. And if our arts diminish, our society will become dumber, more brutish, and less creative" (Hall 1999: 35).

Another related concern involves the re-evaluation of the place and importance of the live performer and the live event. The fear is that in the digital future the live stands to be devalued and marginalized, diminished because live events do not really constitute "an industry of multiples, but a vessel for memorable and transient one offs . . . [and] cannot be run off infinitely, as can a CD, a film print, a digital template" (Kustow 2001: 229). As Philip Auslander has written, we are witnessing an implosion of live and mediatized performance, resulting in a devaluing of that which is reproduced or technologically enhanced by those committed to the "natural" and "real":

> As the mediatized replaces the live within cultural economy, the live itself incorporates the mediatized, both technologically and epistemologically. The result of this implosion is that a seemingly secure opposition is now a site of anxiety, the anxiety that underlies many performance theorists' desire to reassert the integrity of the live and the corrupt, co-opted nature of the mediatized. (Auslander 1999: 39)

### Identifying the cultural ecology

These arguments are the result of a cultural landscape in which creative practices are understood and discussed through competing rationales. The creative arts, the cultural industries, and the creative industries all persist side by side as ways of describing creative production and meaning. But although critiques such as those rehearsed above express anxiety and opposition, the creative practices of others, such as Robert Lepage, seek to build a more inclusive, synoptic view of their cultural ecology.

An active and prolific creator, Robert Lepage works on many projects simultaneously. Some years this means developing eight productions across a range of forms, all at various stages of development. Not surprisingly, such diverse creative outputs are difficult to classify into tidy categories.

His work clearly belongs within the arts, embracing long-held aspirations of individual excellence and universal truth-telling. He maintains that "there is a sense of spirituality in theatre: it's a medium that you could use to talk about spirituality, about spiritual quests" (Delgado and Heritage 1996: 114). This call to the metaphysical has prompted the claim that Lepage is "one of the international theatre community's true creative geniuses" and his *The Seven Streams of the River Ota* is one of the "great art" works of the 1990s (e.g. Griffiths 1998).

However, unlike many who subscribe to idealist notions of art, Lepage does not separate his work's legitimacy from its material production and economic activity. While Ex Machina enjoys ongoing public support through subsidy and grants (these make up a diminishing component of their revenue − 12 percent in the late 1990s (Ouzounian 1997)), Lepage has directed his attention to the private market. The focus is not just on producing live performances but on how the media can be used to increase their distribution. Lepage has written and directed five films, collaborated with Peter Gabriel on such ventures as the *New Millennium Dome Experience* in London and sold sub-licensing rights to his productions. By turning artistic talent into creative goods and services, Robert Lepage and Ex Machina have built and used cultural markets and mass audiences as a substitute for patronage in all its forms.

While Lepage and his companies Robert Lepage Incorporated (1988) and Ex Machina (1994) and his film production company In Extremis Images Inc. (1995) can be understood as vibrant forces in the arts and the cultural industries, their creative practices place them also within the creative industries.

What is emerging is a relational and non-hierarchical habitat of symbolic activity in which the arts and the creative industries are realigned and sometimes merged under the influence of the analog and the digital, the commercial and the non-commercial. Lepage, like so many contemporary artists and workers, moves adeptly within this mixed ecology. Often "creatives" not only earn their living but use their experiences in one sector to challenge and enrich the other. One reason Lepage can move easily between sectors is his deep belief that "salvation is in not knowing what you are going to do" (Lepage in *Digging for Miracles*, 2000). Marie Gignac, an actor who has worked extensively with Ex Machina since its formation in 1994, likens the company's performance style to "playing" (from the French verb *jouer*) rather than "acting" in the theatrical sense. For her this is "like playing with a jigsaw puzzle." For Ex Machina, performance is "a game, it's play, just go and do it. It's very here and now. I don't know, you're like a football team. You are one of the players and you just have to throw the ball at the right time" (Gignac 1998).

"Throwing the ball at the right time" lies at the heart of openness, the formulation first identified by Eco over 40 years ago.

## Openness: the paradigmatic form of the creative industries

Any attempt to describe and identify common features of the forms most favored by the creative industries will almost certainly be incomplete. These forms, and the creative processes which give rise to them, are too mercurial, extend across too many disciplines, and have markedly different life spans and life cycles. However, as Umberto Eco asserts, "in every century, the way that artistic forms are structured reflects the way in which science and contemporary culture views reality." Does this mean that the forms of the creative industries reflect the science of uncertainty, relativity, and chaos (common descriptors of contemporary culture), where "everything is louder than everything else" (Meatloaf 1994)? In 1962 Eco's answer lay in recognizing "openness as *the* fundamental possibility of the contemporary artist or consumer," a proposition which stunningly prefigures emerging creative forms (see excerpt in this section). For Eco, openness sees creative producers making works that have been organized to multiply possibilities, both in their performance and reception.

In one sense these works appear to be "unfinished," with the composer handing them on to the performer "more or less like the components of a construction kit." Such uncertainty of form is a central characteristic of Eco's "open works," but this is an uncertainty that is to be celebrated rather than condemned. Such works, while being organically complete, maintain both a context and formal elements that are open to continuous revision and regeneration. Their internal mobility of form sets up the possibility of a dialog or interaction between author, performer, and audience. The works take on a dynamic openness, "a kaleidoscopic capacity to suggest themselves in constantly renewed aspects to the consumer."

## The Poetics of the Open Work: Umberto Eco

This reading is taken from the opening chapter of *The Open Work*, first published in Italian in 1962. Selling some tens of thousands of copies at the time, the book sets out a theoretical manifesto for avant-garde intellectuals and artists. Eco's identification and detailing of "open works" is a direct reaction against traditional notions of artistic form and aesthetic response.

Drawing on music to introduce his ideas, and considering the classics in the first instance, Eco proposes that "a classical composition . . . posits an assemblage of sound units which the composer arranged in a closed, well defined manner before presenting it to the listener. He converted his idea into conventional symbols which more or less oblige the eventual performer to reproduce the format devised by the composer himself" (Eco 1962/1989: 2–3). Such classic compositions were regarded by many to be the pinnacle of artistic achievement; excellence defined by linking artistic merit with closure and the artist's intentions.

Eco challenged this traditional view of controlled and closed order by taking the case of improvisatory jazz. When jazz musicians play together "The result is a 'creation' that is at once collective, simultaneous and extemporaneous, yet (at its best) perfectly organic" (p. 109). Jazz musicians not only interpret the composer's instructions, but they necessarily impose their judgments on the form of the piece in an act of improvised creation. Eco takes up the challenge posed by this more fluid work, acknowledging that it raised a different order of aesthetic questions to do with "the productive process and the personality of the author, the distinction between process and result, and the relationship between a finished work and its antecedents" (p. 109).

The key to understanding the difference between the two types of works lies in the concept of "openness."

It may seem that Eco's preoccupation with poetics reveals a rather abstract approach, far removed from the immediate concerns of grounded practice. Somewhat defensively he wrote that openness

can provide us with tools that are perfectly suited to experimental situations (whether in a lab or in the pages of a novel) but are not functional in everyday life. Which, of course, should not be taken to mean that they are not valid but that, on a daily basis (at least for the time being), more traditional parameters with a wider diffusion might be more effective. (Eco 1962/1989: 120–1)

Forty years after this was written, openness is now an important aspect of creative industries practice. Openness is seen in the poetics of interdisciplinary performance such as Dance/Theater or Music/Theater to the intertextuality of hyperfiction with links to other spaces, ideas, and works. Real-time composition and non-linear music blend improvisation with interactive electronics. Commentators note the emerging "loose" formats of reality TV (such as *Neighbours from Hell*) which diverge from the tightness of the *Big Brother* format (Sylvian 2002). The field of computer interaction design has bred its own species of open works, the technotext, defined by Hayles (2002) as works that investigate the material inscription technology that form the work. Networked online games now challenge their players to create scenarios and refinements which can then be incorporated into the game. By opening the architecture and the very form of the game in this way, players have the opportunity to become creative producers of the work as it grows (see JC Herz in part V below). These protean open forms can also be seen in emerging formats of cyberdrama.

## Digital TV and the Emerging Formats of Cyberdrama: Janet H. Murray

This reading is a speculation about the future written prior to the advent of digital television. Janet H. Murray imagines and explores the possibilities that new technologies present for artists and creative producers. Unlike those who remain deeply skeptical about the digital domain's capacity to produce works of substance Murray confidently asserts: "It seems to me quite possible that a future digital Homer will arise who combines literary ambition, a connection with a wide audience, and computational expertise" (Murray 1997: 231).

In this reading Murray makes four possible "guesses" at the future of cyberdrama – "the coming digital form." Of central importance to her argument is the multi-form story. Such stories reflect the non-linearity and fragmentation evident in many commonplace narratives and popping up in novels, films (*Run Lola Run*, *Adaptation*) and even cartoons.

Digital television and interactive media are now a reality. Some of Murray's guesses have been realized while others have been thwarted by policy or the market. However, Murray's "visions" remain an important exposition of the possibilities and challenges for creative practice arising out of new technologies and multi-platform distribution.

*Redactive creativity: the paradigmatic creative process of the creative industries*

In order to accommodate their distinctive work practices, Robert Lepage and Ex Machina opened a specially designed rehearsal and creation space called La Caserne Dalhousie in Quebec City. La Caserne operates as:

> an editing room floor – where a lot of ideas fall that are not part of shows or film any more. They can fall on the floor and other artists can come, pick them up and develop something elsewhere. It's a way of recuperating. (Delgado and Heritage 1996: 153)

In this playground-like environment Lepage is freely able to experiment, to revise, to edit at will. The center and its facilities operate as a physical manifestation of the computer's "delete" and "undo" buttons, enabling "accidents to happen but they must have the feel of truth. I only listen to coincidences" (Lepage 2001).

Similar creative processes can be seen across the creative industries as open works, with their internal mobility of form, are constructed by skillfully editing together a range of materials from diverse sources and contexts. For commentators like John Hartley this manipulation of unfinished parts into a whole is emblematic of contemporary society where:

> editorial practices determine what is understood to be true, and what policies and beliefs should flow from that . . . a period where it is not information, knowledge or culture as such that determine the age but how they are handled. (Hartley 2000: 44)

Hartley calls this editing process "redaction," and it is redactive creativity which expands possibilities for meaning through the use of fragmentation, appropriation and intertextuality.

*The aesthetics of "rip, mix and burn"*

Originally from an obscure branch of theology, "redaction criticism" was used to uncover the cultural presuppositions of the Gospel writers as they edited their texts. Today the *Oxford English Dictionary* notes "redaction" as "The action or process of preparing for publication; reduction to literary form; revision, rearrangement. . . . The action of bringing and putting into a definite form."

The process whereby creative producers bring information into a certain form, and combine diverse materials together into one body, is one of reduction, revision, and rearrangement. Redactive creativity guides creative producers as they revise, prepare, adapt, remotivate, recontextualize, abridge, and reduce materials to shape them "into a definite form."

Redactive creativity then can be seen as a paradigmatic creative process, reflected in the way leading contemporary artists approach their work. Robert Lepage describes his creations as "a tray filled with hors-d'oeuvres from which we choose what we wish" (quoted in Charest 1997: 166), and the international theater/opera director Robert Wilson likens his creations to "a game of baseball" (quoted in Kostelanetz 1994: 90).

However, redactive creativity is not only found in the work of the avant-garde. We are regularly reminded that brains and bodies aged around 10 to 16 years old seem most comfortable with the ever-changing possibilities for "editing" contemporary life. Perhaps it's their capacity for "a broader attention range and a shorter absorption time" (Rushkoff 1996: 51), perhaps it's their gymnastic minds shaped from by the filmic conventions of *Sesame Street* and MTV, but the ease and enthusiasm with which young people scavenge, take up, and discard symbolic materials from their (and other) cultures convincingly demonstrates that they are the true avant-garde in these matters.

Music provides a good example. The artistry of the DJ is found in the way they snatch and sample sounds, remixing to create music that is both fresh and familiar. A recent advertising campaign by Apple Computers describes the poetics of redactive creativity:

---

**Rip**.
The new iMac with iTunes lets you take all of your favorite songs,
**Mix**.
Organise them into an MP3 library, put them in any order you want
**Burn**.
And then burn your own custom CDs. After all, it's your music.

---

For many creative producers this process of selecting and editing, of "ripping, mixing, and burning," is pivotal as they embrace an open aesthetic which enables them to play with and remix the cultural materials they have at their disposal.

The power of editing to affect and alter meaning has long been recognized. Some time ago François Truffaut demonstrated in *Love on the Run* that editing could be used to offer multiple renditions of a single event. In connecting the proliferation of open works created through processes of redactive creativity with the current paradigm shift, the question must be asked: Why now? What makes these practices central to the creative industries? One answer lies in the ease with which openness and redaction can accommodate research and testing. These plastic forms and processes are ideal subjects for innovation, able to be formed, transformed, and reformed though innovative experimentation. The highly malleable predisposition of such practices is particularly suited to consumer-driven innovation which relies on users to refine and develop designs by customizing them. Creative practices which deploy "the user as researcher" are particularly appropriate in an age where the speed of innovation is seen as a key source of competitive advantage.

## II.   Creative Practices of Creative Industries

While openness and redactive creativity are recurring features of the creative industries, it is also possible to identify a cluster of five attributes which make these creative practices distinctive from the range of other activities which typically make up the creative arts and cultural industries. Although not every attribute can be seen in all creative practices, there is a recognizable inflection toward the following:

### 1.   Creative practices involve interactivity

Interactivity is a focus of study for those creative disciplines which seek to create live or digital environments for entertainment or education. New industries are appearing in the area of interaction design which "entails creating user experiences that enhance and extend the way that people work, communicate and interact" (Preece, Rogers, and Sharp 2002: v). Increasingly a concern for interactivity drives the creation and integration of content to develop sustainable, immersive, environments.

### 2.   Creative practices are intrinsically hybrid

Fundamentally a process of unification, hybridization is:

> the combination of materials, genres, period references to produce highly eclectic constructions, both in content and form. (Owens 1995: 120)

Throughout the twentieth century the impulse for avant-garde artists to collaborate and create hybrid works has been strong. In the fine and performing arts, a recent priority has been to create original multimedia works through the use of performance, installation, sound, and digital art.

The creative rub of such interdisciplinary possibilities now infuses all of the creative industries as producers design experiences that depart from singular disciplines and forms by pursuing what John Howkins calls "collaborative creativity." Fundamentally this involves "an open and free discussion around a common purpose, without stopping at fixed points to claim private property rights"(Howkins 2001: 184). Participating in such a way is essential, for in the "converged world" of the creative industries there is a pressing need for collaborative creativity in sectors "notoriously non-collaborative with each other, living within their separate smokestacks" (Malcolm Long in Cunningham 2002: 8).

## 3. Creative practices embrace new sites and forms of cultural production

The transformations brought by the new technologies give creative producers the opportunity to expand the forms and platforms at their disposal. At the center of these changes lies the critical capacity of the digital media – radio, mobile phones, movies, TV, email, games, websites – to receive and transmit content. Mobile phones, with their capacity to read and send text, sound and image, are among the newest platforms for creative work. Similarly the creative potential of the computer screen, the third screen after the large screen of the cinema and the small screen of television, holds rich promise especially when connected to the mobile phone and television. The recent popularity of "flash mobbing," where, by email or SMS instruction, people gather suddenly and then disappear, is a good example of a playful creative practice which depends upon the new communication technologies and physical site for its execution.

## 4. Creative practices are oriented toward multi-platform, cross-promotional means of distribution

Many artists focus their energy on artistic production – on the creation of work for their audiences. The creative industries framework challenges them to pay at least as much attention to the way their work will be distributed once it has been created. Increasingly innovative artists and producers are creating opportunities for multi-platform delivery and cross-promotion of their work.

Models of complex and innovative distribution systems are emerging. *Big Brother* was screened on free-to-air TV but was enriched by an interactive website with discussion forums, live streaming via the internet, a host of unofficial sites, radio grabs throughout Australia, SMS updates, and telephone voting.

---

## Performing the "Real" 24/7: Jane Roscoe

The *Big Brother* phenomenon has surprised many. As we have seen, it is generally disliked and dismissed by older viewers. Viewers in France went so far as to storm the "house" to liberate the inhabitants and invade the TV network offices to express their feelings. For some the show represented "rampant fascism," others worried about the contestants' rights to privacy, still others argued "When people agree to take part in such a humiliation, it's a little bit of each of us who feels humiliated" (Johnson-Woods 2002: 10).

The success of *Big Brother* cannot be explained by the format alone. What has worked so well is the multi-platform and cross-promotional means of distribution Endemol has put in place around the TV product. In this reading Jane Roscoe describes how the viewing experience has been expanded across a number of media platforms including on-site visits and weekly evictions which played on the performativity of fans.

---

*5.   Creative practices are not approached as if they are commercially irrelevant*

The final characteristic of the practices of the creative industries is the belief that cultural production will not operate apart from commercial realities. Patronage, subsidy, and sponsorship are all means of funding work, but cultural entrepreneurs, in the vanguard of the new economy, look for new ways to grow their businesses.

It must be remembered that government support for highly commercial ventures is still occurring within in the cultural ecology. In Australia over $700,000 was paid to the producers of *Big Brother* in payroll tax concessions and employment rebates and a $2.5 million loan made at a discounted interest rate (Odgers 2003).

Within the creative industries, some activities have always existed as commercial operations. While creativity is central and protected, so too is the system of production and distribution. Fashion is one such discipline with a tradition which goes back to the 1850s, when Charles Worth "invented the system which is the basis of modern fashion." In recent years, however, we have seen the emergence of networked enterprise models of clothing design, production and selling. Zara, the Spanish clothing company, has reduced its design/production/distribution cycle to two weeks, a far cry from Worth's original practice, which was to allow "a new fashion style a life of five years before making major changes" (Healey 1993: 20). The Zara example shows that the speed of contemporary forms of cultural production demands that creative producers adopt innovative production tools and processes in order to establish and maintain commercial security.

---

### Connecting Creativity: Luigi Maramotti

This article connects creativity with the other design and production processes of a fashion business. This reading is by Luigi Maramotti, the chairman of the highly successful Max Mara fashion group. Maramotti is from a dressmaking family which goes back to the 1850s, and today his group has an annual turnover of £600m and over 1,000 stores worldwide. Here we find an industry leader discussing "forced innovation" and the need for all members of the organization, not just those in the design team, to have a creative attitude.

What emerges is an account of the importance of creativity and the way it is stimulated at all levels of the organization. But creativity and love of experimentation cannot reign unchecked in a global business setting, and Maramotti describes the accompanying range of stages and processes which check and support the creative practices of all workers to achieve the best outcomes.

---

The five attributes identified above enable us to understand what is distinctive about current practices across the creative industries. They suggest also how creative practices may evolve as each of these attributes is transformed in the light of developments in taste and technology.

*Case study: the creative practices of Robert Lepage*

All of these five attributes can be identified in the practices of Robert Lepage and Ex Machina. The first, "interactivity," is demanded by contemporary audiences and consumers. Lepage acknowledges that they have:

> a very modern way of connecting things; they watch TV, they know what a flash-back is, they understand the codes of a flash forward, they know what a jump cut is. And if you don't use that, you don't trigger that, of course

they're bored. They have gymnastic minds now and a gymnastic understanding of things. (Robert Lepage in Delgado and Heritage 1996: 148)

To cater for these gymnastic minds Lepage has sought to build a sense of agency for the audience, a sense that as individuals they "have to feel that they are changing the event, even if they're just asked to be quiet and not to laugh when the actress is trying to cry her heart out. They have to feel that their presence is changing the course of things" (p. 147).

In his earlier works, this sense of agency was built through openness of form and improvisation. Now Lepage is moving to connect this underlying notion of improvised playing with digital communication technologies which promise greater interactivity and audience participation.

This push toward interactivity is bringing together artistic, design, and production talent with the reach of information technology. Together they have the potential to transform current understandings of live and digital entertainment spaces. For Tobie Horswill, a technical designer with Ex Machina, one frontier lies in resolving the technical questions involved with 3D projection. The goal ultimately is to create a 3D character and then have it interact meaningfully with live actors.

3D tracking is a tool and at the moment it is not part of any show and we cannot really think how we'll use it. But we see computer generated characters as promising. The attraction is these characters can adapt quickly – can change shape, colour – and we need this new modeling with its flexibility to follow Robert. (Horswill 2003)

This intense interest in interactivity by contemporary artists such as Lepage is extending beyond the borders of live art and into the creative industries generally, as the design, writing, and production disciplines seek to build immersive, digital environments which draw from information technology, media, entertainment, and education.

The second attribute of creative practice, convergence and hybridity, is seen in the organizational design of Ex Machina and the company's efforts to extend the range of media forms deployed through its performances. Ex Machina was set up from the very beginning to encourage "exchanges between disciplines and crossing boundaries between them" (Bernatchez 2003). Frequently these hybrid collaborations produce an amalgam of dance and movement, music, multi-media, installation, performance, video, and design – hybrids which have become known as the "slash arts" music/theater, dance/theater, and so on.

This hybridity is closely tied to the third attribute of creative practice – experimentation and the use of new sites and forms of cultural production. Robert Lepage has always been willing to turn existing and frontier technologies to the service of his design, and sometimes this has resulted in accusations of technological "trickery" with barbs like "Nice picture, glib evasion" (e.g. Taylor 1994). Despite this, Lepage remains committed to developing new sites and forms of performance. His most recent work, *Zulu Time*, which opened in Montreal in 2002, is the first of a new species of work – a technological cabaret. The set is an abstract mechanical structure constantly shifting and morphing its shape and use, and though even the eight huge venetian blinds are motorized there is an organic feel to this obviously mechanical structure. The actors who inhabit this set do not talk; they sing and dance upside down on the ceiling and perform like contortionists.

Lepage's hope for *Zulu Time* is that it will harness the capacities of the digital network enabling Mpeg streaming and remote control of the show's fully mechanized set from La Caserne. It is hoped that live actors at La Caserne will be projected into a remote *Zulu Time* set.

For the moment, network linkages are too slow and expensive for these ideas to be realized, but Michel Bernatchez believes these distributed performances will be important in the future. With just a hint of frustration he explains:

> We have developed tools that are not yet used. As to what influence it will have? Of the pieces distributed through networks, we have yet to see how the network shapes their content, how they are edited through the network. (Bernatchez 2003)

Bernatchez is wrestling with Lepage's most recent request, a show on string theory in physics, requiring projected 3D images where the audience would wear 3D glasses and virtual performers will interact through avatars. The enabling technology is likely to come from advanced computer game software, "certainly there will be parts of shows from video game culture but how it extends to interaction we just don't know yet" (Bernatchez 2003).

The guiding idea for the whole of the creative industries is that action created for one context can be re-purposed for another. This multi-platform or cross-promotional distribution (the fourth attribute of creative practice) is seen in the connections between Lepage's stage and screen works. As Lepage moves from project to project he reapplies those good ideas which finally were not used in his earlier show. "It may be a clever device which never fitted in – I'll start from that." The real benefit of working this way is that it is "an opportunity to empty out what has not been said from earlier shows" (Lepage 2001). For example in 1998 one whole section from *The Seven*

*Streams of the River Ota* served as the basis for the film *Nô*. Similarly in early 2003 Lepage adapted and filmed a version of *The Far Side of the Moon*, a one-person theater piece he devised and toured internationally during 2001 and 2002. The original work can be seen as the root property, to be re-versioned for different audiences and different media. In this way the play becomes the film, which becomes the themed ride, which becomes the game. The enabling technologies of a digital environment are used to connect with larger and technically savvy audiences everywhere.

The fifth and final attribute is easily demonstrated. It is clear that commercial realities have shaped the creative practices instituted by Lepage and Ex Machina. Although significant government funds assisted in establishing the multimedia production facility at La Caserne Dalhousie, Lepage also needed to personally invest in the vision. However, Lepage has a range of commercial strategies to ensure the health of his operations. As demand for Ex Machina content remains high, the company has remounted major and established works (*The Dragon's Trilogy* returned to the repertoire in 2003 after a 15-year break) and has sold sub-rights to stage *The Seven Streams of the River Ota* in Brazil.

A commercial research and development imperative also underpins this. Many of the technical innovations which surface in Lepage's work are devised specifically by a team of in-house technical designers who have become expert in solving the problems which arise when live works incorporate new media forms such as animation and projection. Consequently, a spin-off commercial enterprise is planned to market technical solutions and purpose-built devices to the theater and entertainment industry. Marketing these products which have been developed through practice-led research is another way to guarantee financial security and independence. Products in development range from indexable dousers for LCD projectors to wireless-controlled and wearable lighting sources embedded in clothes.

## Creative Practices Beyond the Creative Industries

Before closing this discussion of creative practices it is important to remember that, in the creative industries, creative practices are seen as not just intrinsically valuable for their own sake, but as potent inputs to other industries. This accords with critiques of many European theories of art which have been informed by Enlightenment consciousness and discussions of beauty and "feeling form." Creative practices in non–Western societies such as Asia or Africa are often more about social, political, or religious expression than they are about the "artistic." While Clifford Geertz (1973) writes a metasocial commentary on the Balinese cockfight to show how it is a form of cultural affirmation for the Balinese, Schechner concludes that such practices "effect and cause life, not reflect or express it" (1993: 21).

These observations demand an expanded understanding of the aesthetic, one which considers the aesthetics of culturally bound objects and practices which occur in everyday life. Although this has been addressed in sociology and cultural studies (Featherstone, Willis, de Certeau), the creative industries set a new relationship between aesthetics and industry. On the one hand they acknowledge the importance of the culturalization of everyday life by identifying the experience economy which creates income by explicitly engaging customers in a personal and memorable ways – though experiential "shoppertainment" or "entertailing" (Pine and Gilmore 1999). On the other hand, and more significantly, the practices of the creative industries are being applied to what are traditionally thought of as non-creative industries. Howkins explains:

> Perhaps the greatest impact of the creative economy is not only within the traditional creative industries but in the way their skills and business models are being used to create value in other areas of life. (Howkins 2001: xvi–xvii)

Consequently, creative practices which are at home in the creative industries find application in surprising and new settings. Performance artists shape innovative corporate training programs, choreographers work with pyrotechnicians to choreograph fireworks in the black space of the night sky, and interactive web designers work with city councils to create the virtual heritage of their community.

Above all else is the recognition that creativity has a privileged place in teaching and learning. Many education systems are now struggling to shape a creative society and workforce adroit enough to exploit the opportunities of a new economy where innovation is seen as paramount. Creativity is seen as an innate human capacity able to be developed in all members of society, breaking with the belief that creativity is only possessed by the gifted and talented few.

### Balancing the Books: Ken Robinson

Traditional notions of education are being unsettled by the paradigm shift shaping the current age. The pressures for change require educators to imagine afresh what it is to teach and to learn in this culture and economy and the challenges are considerable. The human race faces an exponential growth in knowledge and information, an explosion which is certainly unprecedented and, until only a few years ago, unimaginable. In this environment are teachers destined to become expensive search engines pointing students toward "important" materials and discourses (with an increasingly short shelf life)? What is it to teach, when, for the first time in human history, the entire content of adult life is available to our children?

In this reading Ken Robinson faces this crisis with creativity in education. He supports the case for creativity by calling for a rebalancing of education so that teaching does not stifle creativity, even though much of the prescribed curriculum is focused heavily on content rather than on the creative application of knowledge. For Robinson this is the fundamental challenge which must be overcome if we are to recognize and value the talents of all humans. Educators must learn to care for the ecology of human resources and correct our current "partial form of education" which has "wasted or destroyed a great deal of what people had to offer because we couldn't see the value of it."

## References

Auslander, P. (1999) *Liveness: Performance in a Mediatized Culture*. Routledge, London.

Bernatchez, M. (2003) Interview with the author, July 16.

Charest, R. (1997) *Robert Lepage: Connecting Flights/interviews with Remy Charest*, tr. Wanda Romer Taylor. Methuen, London.

Cunningham, Stuart (2002) Culture, Services, Knowledge *or* Is Content King, or Are We Just Drama Queens? Communications Research Forum, October 2–3, 2002, see <http://www.dcita.gov.au/crf/papers02/cunningham.pdf>.

Delgado, M. M., and P. Heritage (1996) *In Contact with the Gods*. Manchester University Press, Manchester.

*Digging for Miracles* (2000) documentary film. Director David Clermont-Beique. In Extremis Images.

Eco, U. (1962/1989) *The Open Work*, tr. Anna Cancogni. Hutchinson Radius, UK.

Geertz, C. (1973) *The Interpretation of Cultures*. Basic Books, New York.

Gignac M. (1998) speaking at the Adelaide Festival Forum, March 6.

Griffiths, G. (1998) Seven Hours of Great Reward. *The Australian*, February 16, 13.

Hall, P. (1999) *The Necessary Theatre*. Nick Hern Books, London.

Hartley, J. (2000) Communicative Democracy in a Redactional Society: The Future of Journalism Studies. *Journalism Studies* 1(1), 39–47.

Hayles, N. K. (2002) *Writing Machines*. MIT Press, Cambridge, Mass.

Healey, R (1993). *Worth to Dior*. National Gallery of Victoria, Melbourne.

Horswill, T. (2003) Interview with the author, July 16.

Howkins, J. (2001) *The Creative Economy*. Allen Lane, London.

Kostelanetz, R. (1994). *On Innovative Performance(s): Three Decades of Recollections on Alternative Theater*. McFarland & Co, Jefferson, NC.

Johnson-Woods, T. (2002) *Big Bother: Why Did That Reality-TV Show Become Such a Phenomenon?* University of Queensland Press, Brisbane.

Kustow, M. (2001) *Theatre@risk*. Methuen, London.

Lepage, R. (2001) speaking at the Sydney Opera House, January 14.

Mamet D. (2001) *Three Uses of the Knife*. Vintage Books, New York.

Meatloaf (1994), *Bat Out of Hell* (audio recording).

Murray, J. H. (1997) *Hamlet on the Holodeck: The Future of Narrative in Cyberspace*. Free Press, New York.

Odgers, R. (2003), Taxpayers Pour $700,000 into Big Brother's Kitty. *Courier Mail*, Brisbane, July 18.

Ouzounian, R. (1997) Lepage's Struggle to Stay Free. *The Globe and Mail*, August 12.

Owens, C. (1995) Beyond Recognition: Representation, Power, and Culture. In N. Wheale (ed.), *Postmodern Arts*. Routledge, London.

Pine, B. Joseph II, and J. H. Gilmore (1999) *The Experience Economy: Work Is Theatre & Every Business a Stage*. Harvard Business School Press, Harvard.

Preece, J., Y. Rogers, and H. Sharp (2002) *Interaction Design: Beyond Human–Computer Interaction*. Wiley & Sons, New York.

Rushkoff, D. (1996) *Playing the Future*. HarperCollins, New York.

Schechner, R. (1993) *The Future of Ritual*. Routledge, London.

Sylvian, M. (2002) *Formats: The Next Generation*. Realscreen.

Taylor, P. (1994) Review of *Seven Streams of the River Ota* for the *Independent* newspaper. In *Edinburgh Supplement to Theatre Record*, issue 19, pp. 6–7.

# 9    *Umberto Eco*

# THE POETICS OF THE OPEN WORK

[ . . . ] To avoid any confusion in terminology, it is important to specify that here the definition of the "open work," despite its relevance in formulating a fresh dialectics between the work of art and its performer, still requires to be separated from other conventional applications of this term. Aesthetic theorists, for example, often have recourse to the notions of "completeness" and "openness" in connection with a given work of art. These two expressions refer to a standard situation of which we are all aware in our reception of a work of art: we see it as the end product of an author's effort to arrange a sequence of communicative effects in such a way that each individual addressee can refashion the original composition devised by the author. The addressee is bound to enter into an interplay of stimulus and response which depends on his unique capacity for sensitive reception of the piece. In this sense the author presents a finished product with the intention that this particular composition should be appreciated and received in the same form as he devised it. As he reacts to the play of stimuli and his own response to their patterning, the individual addressee is bound to supply his own existential credentials, the sense conditioning which is peculiarly his own, a defined culture, a set of tastes, personal inclinations, and prejudices. Thus, his comprehension of the original artifact is always modified by his particular and individual perspective. In fact, the form of the work of art gains its aesthetic validity precisely in proportion to the number of different perspectives from which it can be viewed and understood. These give it a wealth of different resonances and echoes without impairing its original essence; a road traffic sign, on the other hand, can be viewed in only one sense, and, if it is transfigured into some fantastic meaning by an imaginative driver, it merely

"The Poetics of the Open Work" from Umberto Eco (1989 [1962]), *The Open Work*, tr. Anna Cancogni. Hutchinson Radius, UK, pp. 3–4, 4–5, 13–19, 20–3, 251–2.

ceases to be *that* particular traffic sign with that particular meaning. A work of art, therefore, is a complete and *closed* form in its uniqueness as a balanced organic whole, while at the same time constituting an *open* product on account of its susceptibility to countless different interpretations which do not impinge on its unadulterable specificity. Hence, every reception of a work of art is both an *interpretation* and a *performance* of it, because in every reception the work takes on a fresh perspective for itself.

[ . . . ]

Pousseur has observed that the poetics of the "open" work tends to encourage "acts of conscious freedom" on the part of the performer and place him at the focal point of a network of limitless interrelations, among which he chooses to set up his own form without being influenced by an external *necessity* which definitively prescribes the organization of the work in hand.[1] At this point one could object (with reference to the wider meaning of "openness" already introduced in this essay) that any work of art, even if it is not passed on to the addressee in an unfinished state, demands a free, inventive response, if only because it cannot really be appreciated unless the performer somehow reinvents it in psychological collaboration with the author himself. Yet this remark represents the theoretical perception of contemporary aesthetics, achieved only after painstaking consideration of the function of artistic performance; certainly an artist of a few centuries ago was far from being aware of these issues. Instead nowadays it is primarily the artist who is aware of its implications. In fact, rather than submit to the "openness" as an inescapable element of artistic interpretation, he subsumes it into a positive aspect of his production, recasting the work so as to expose it to the maximum possible "opening."

The force of the subjective element in the interpretation of a work of art (any interpretation implies an interplay between the addressee and the work as an objective fact) was noticed by classical writers, especially when they set themselves to consider the figurative arts. In the *Sophist* Plato observes that painters suggest proportions not by following some objective canon but by judging them in relation to the angle from which they are seen by the observer. Vitruvius makes a distinction between "symmetry" and "eurhythmy," meaning by this latter term an adjustment of objective proportions to the requirements of a subjective vision. The scientific and practical development of the technique of perspective bears witness to the gradual maturation of this awareness of an interpretative subjectivity pitted against the work of art. Yet it is equally certain that this awareness has led to a tendency to operate against the "openness" of the work, to favor its "closing out." The various devices of perspective were just so many different concessions to the actual location of the observer in order to ensure that he looked at the figure in *the only possible right way* — that is, the way the author of the work had prescribed, by providing various visual devices for the observer's attention to focus on.

[ . . . ]

In every century, the way that artistic forms are structured reflects the way in which science or contemporary culture views reality. The closed, single conception in a work by a medieval artist reflected the conception of the cosmos as a hierarchy of fixed, preordained orders. The work as a pedagogical vehicle, as a monocentric and necessary apparatus (incorporating a rigid internal pattern of meter and rhymes) simply reflects the syllogistic system, a logic of necessity, a deductive consciousness by means of which reality could be made manifest step by step without unforeseen interruptions, moving forward in a single direction, proceeding from first principles of science which were seen as one and the same with the first principles of reality. The openness and dynamism of the Baroque mark, in fact, the advent of a new scientific awareness: the *tactile* is replaced by the *visual* (meaning that the subjective element comes to prevail) and attention is shifted from the *essence* to the *appearance* of architectural and pictorial products. It reflects the rising interest in a psychology of impression and sensation — in short, an empiricism which converts the Aristotelian concept of real substance into a series of subjective perceptions by the viewer. On the other hand, by giving up the essential focus of the composition and the prescribed point of view for its viewer, aesthetic innovations were in fact mirroring the Copernican vision of the universe. This definitively eliminated the notion of geocentricity and its allied metaphysical constructs. In the modern scientific universe, as in architecture and in Baroque pictorial production, the various component parts are all endowed with equal value and dignity, and the whole construct expands toward a totality which is close to the infinite. It refuses to be hemmed in by any ideal normative conception of the world. It shares in a general urge toward discovery and constantly renewed contact with reality.

In its own way, the "openness" that we meet in the decadent strain of Symbolism reflects a cultural striving to unfold new vistas. For example, one of Mallarmé's projects for a multidimensional, deconstructible book envisaged the breaking down of the initial unit into sections which could be reformulated and which could express new perspectives by being deconstructed into correspondingly smaller units which were also mobile and reducible. This project obviously suggests the universe as it is conceived by modern, non-Euclidean geometries.

Hence, it is not overambitious to detect in the poetics of the "open" work – and even less so in the "work in movement" – more or less specific overtones of trends in contemporary scientific thought. For example, it is a critical commonplace to refer to the spatiotemporal continuum in order to account for the structure of the universe in Joyce's works. Pousseur has offered a tentative definition of his musical work which involves the term "field of possibilities." In fact, this shows that he is prepared to borrow two extremely revealing technical terms from contemporary culture. The notion of "field" is provided by physics and implies a revised vision of the classic relationship posited between cause and effect as a rigid, one-directional system: now a complex interplay of motive forces is envisaged, a configuration of possible events, a complete dynamism of structure. The notion of "possibility" is a philosophical canon which reflects a widespread tendency in contemporary science; the discarding of a static, syllogistic view of order, and a corresponding devolution of intellectual authority to personal decision, choice, and social context.

If a musical pattern no longer necessarily determines the immediately following one, if there is no tonal basis which allows the listener to infer the next steps in the arrangement of the musical discourse from what has physically preceded them, this is just part of a general breakdown in the concept of causation. The two-value truth logic which follows the classical *aut-aut*, the disjunctive dilemma between *true* and *false*, a fact and its contradictory, is no longer the only instrument of philosophical experiment. Multi-value logics are now gaining currency, and these are quite capable of incorporating *indeterminacy* as a valid stepping-stone in the cognitive process. In this general intellectual atmosphere, the poetics of the open work is peculiarly relevant: it posits the work of art stripped of necessary and foreseeable conclusions, works in which the performer's freedom functions as part of the *discontinuity* which contemporary physics recognizes, not as an element of disorientation, but as an essential stage in all scientific verification procedures and also as the verifiable pattern of events in the subatomic world.

From Mallarmé's *Livre* to the musical compositions which we have considered, there is a tendency to see every execution of the work of art as divorced from its ultimate definition. Every performance *explains* the composition but does not *exhaust* it. Every performance makes the work an actuality, but is itself only complementary to all possible other performances of the work. In short, we can say that every performance offers us a complete and satisfying version of the work, but at the same time makes it incomplete for us, because it cannot simultaneously give all the other artistic solutions which the work may admit.

Perhaps it is no accident that these poetic systems emerge at the same period as the physicists' principle of *complementarity*, which rules that it is not possible to indicate the different behavior patterns of an elementary particle simultaneously. To describe these different behavior patterns, different *models*, which Heisenberg has defined as adequate when properly utilized, are put to use, but, since they contradict one another, they are therefore also complementary.[2] Perhaps we are in a position to state that for these works of art an incomplete knowledge of the system is in fact an essential feature in its formulation. Hence one could argue, with Bohr, that the data collected in the course of experimental situations cannot be gathered in one image but should be considered as complementary, since only the sum of all the phenomena could exhaust the possibilities of information.[3]

Above I discussed the principle of ambiguity as moral disposition and problematic construct. Again, modern psychology and phenomenology use the term "perceptive ambiguities," which indicates the availability of new cognitive positions that fall short of conventional epistemological stances and that allow the observer to conceive the world in a fresh dynamics of potentiality before the fixative process of habit and familiarity comes into play. Husserl observed that

> each state of consciousness implies the existence of a horizon which varies with the modification of its connections together with other states, and also with its own phases of duration . . . In each external perception, for instance, the sides of the objects which are *actually perceived* suggest to the viewer's attention the unperceived sides which, at the present, are viewed only in a nonintuitive manner and are expected to become elements of the succeeding perception. This process is similar to a continuous *projection* which takes on a new meaning with each phase of the perceptive process. Moreover, perception itself includes horizons which encompass other perceptive possibilities, such as a person might experience by changing deliberately the direction of his perception, by turning his eyes one way instead of another, or by taking a step forward or sideways, and so forth.[4]

Sartre notes that the existent object can never be reduced to a given series of manifestations, because each of these is bound to stand in relationship with a continuously altering subject. Not only does an object present different *Abschattungen* (or profiles), but also different points of view are available by way of the same *Abschattung*. In order to be defined, the object must be related back to the total series of which, by virtue of being one possible apparition, it is a member. In this way the traditional dualism between being and appearance is replaced by a straight polarity of finite and infinite, which locates the infinite at the very core of the finite. This sort of "openness" is at the heart of every act of perception. It characterizes every moment of our cognitive experience. It means that each phenomenon seems to be "inhabited" by a certain *power* – in other words, "the ability to manifest itself by a series of real or likely manifestations." The problem of the relationship of a phenomenon to its ontological basis is altered by the perspective of perceptive "openness" to the problem of its relationship to the multiplicity of different-order perceptions which we can derive from it.[5]

This intellectual position is further accentuated in Merleau-Ponty:

> How can anything ever *present itself* truly to us since its synthesis is never completed? How could I gain the experience of the world, as I would of an individual actuating his own existence, since none of the views or perceptions I have of it can exhaust it and the horizons remain forever *open*? . . . The belief in things and in the world can only express the assumption of a complete synthesis. Its completion, however, is made impossible by the very nature of the perspectives to be connected, since each of them sends back to other perspectives through its own horizons . . . The contradiction which we feel exists between the world's reality and its incompleteness is identical to the one that exists between the ubiquity of consciousness and its commitment to a field of presence. This ambiguousness does not represent an imperfection in the nature of existence or in that of consciousness; it is its very definition . . . Consciousness, which is commonly taken as an extremely enlightened region, is, on the contrary, the very region of indetermination.[6]

These are the sorts of problems which phenomenology picks out at the very heart of our existential situation. It proposes to the artist, as well as to the philosopher and the psychologist, a series of declarations which are bound to act as a stimulus to his creative activity in the world of forms: "It is therefore essential for an object and also for the world to present themselves to us as 'open' . . . and as always promising future perceptions."[7]

It would be quite natural for us to think that this flight away from the old, solid concept of necessity and the tendency toward the ambiguous and the indeterminate reflect a crisis of contemporary civilization. On the other hand, we might see these poetical systems, in harmony with modern science, as expressing the positive possibility of thought and action made available to an individual who is open to the continuous renewal of his life patterns and cognitive processes. Such an individual is productively committed to the development of his own mental faculties and experiential horizons. This contrast is too facile and Manichaean. Our main intent has been to pick out a number of analogies which reveal a reciprocal play of problems in the most disparate areas of contemporary culture and which point to the common elements in a new way of looking at the world.

What is at stake is a convergence of new canons and requirements which the forms of art reflect by way of what we could term *structural homologies*. This need not commit us to assembling a rigorous parallelism – it is simply a case of phenomena like the "work in movement" simultaneously reflecting mutually contrasted epistemological situations, as yet contradictory and not satisfactorily reconciled. Thus, the concepts of "openness" and dynamism may recall the terminology of quantum physics: indeterminacy and discontinuity. But at the same time they also exemplify a number of situations in Einsteinian physics.

The multiple polarity of a serial composition in music, where the listener is not faced by an absolute conditioning center of reference, requires him to constitute his own system of auditory relationships.[8] He must allow such a center to emerge from the sound continuum. Here are no privileged points of view, and all available perspectives are equally valid and rich in potential. Now, this multiple polarity is extremely close to the spatiotemporal conception of the universe which we owe to Einstein. The thing which distinguishes the Einsteinian concept of the universe from quantum epistemology is precisely this faith in the totality of the universe, a universe in which discontinuity and indeterminacy can admittedly upset us with their surprise apparitions, but in fact, to use Einstein's words, presuppose not a God playing random games with dice but the Divinity of Spinoza, who rules the world according to perfectly regulated laws. In this kind of universe, relativity means the infinite variability of experience as well as the infinite multiplication of possible ways of measuring things and viewing their position. But the objective side of the whole system can be found in the invariance of the simple formal descriptions (of the differential equations) which establish once and for all the relativity of empirical measurement.

★ ★ ★

This is not the place to pass judgment on the scientific validity of the metaphysical construct implied by Einstein's system. But there is a striking analogy between his universe and the universe of the work in movement. The God in Spinoza, who is made into an untestable hypothesis by Einsteinian metaphysics, becomes a cogent reality for the work of art and matches the organizing impulse of its creator.

The *possibilities* which the work's openness makes available always work within a given *field of relations*. As in the Einsteinian universe, in the "work in movement" we may well deny that there is a single prescribed point of view. But this does not mean complete chaos in its internal relations. What it does imply is an organizing rule which governs these relations. Therefore, to sum up, we can say that the "work in movement" is the possibility of numerous different personal interventions, but it is not an amorphous invitation to indiscriminate participation. The invitation offers the performer the opportunity for an oriented insertion into something which always remains the world intended by the author.

In other words, the author offers the interpreter, the performer, the addressee a work *to be completed*. He does not know the exact fashion in which his work will be concluded, but he is aware that once completed the work in question will still be his own. It will not be a different work, and, at the end of the interpretative dialogue, a form which is *his* form will have been organized, even though it may have been assembled by an outside party in a particular way that he could not have foreseen. The author is the one who proposed a number of possibilities which had already been rationally organized, oriented, and endowed with specifications for proper development.

[ . . . ]

Now, a dictionary clearly presents us with thousands upon thousands of words which we could freely use to compose poetry, essays on physics, anonymous letters, or grocery lists. In this sense the dictionary is clearly open to the reconstitution of its raw material in any way that the manipulator wishes. But this does not make it a "work." The "openness" and dynamism of an artistic work consist in factors which make it susceptible to a whole range of integrations. They provide it with organic complements which they graft into the structural vitality which the work already possesses, even if it is incomplete. This structural vitality is still seen as a positive property of the work, even though it admits of all kinds of different conclusions and solutions for it.

The preceding observations are necessary because, when we speak of a work of art, our Western aesthetic tradition forces us to take "work" in the sense of a personal production which may well vary in the ways it can be received but which always maintains a coherent identity of its own and which displays the personal imprint that makes it a specific, vital, and significant act of communication. Aesthetic theory is quite content to conceive of a variety of different poetics, but ultimately it aspires to general definitions, not necessarily dogmatic or *sub specie aeternitatis*, which are capable of applying the category of the "work of art" broadly speaking to a whole variety of experiences, which can range from the *Divine Comedy* to, say, electronic composition based on the different permutations of sonic components.

We have, therefore, seen that (1) "open" works, insofar as they are *in movement*, are characterized by the invitation to *make the work* together with the author and that (2) on a wider level (as a sub*genus* in the *species* "work in movement") there exist works which, though organically completed, are "open" to a continuous generation of internal relations which the addressee must uncover and select in his act of perceiving the totality of incoming stimuli. (3) *Every* work of art, even though it is produced by following an explicit or implicit poetics of necessity, is effectively open to a virtually unlimited range of possible readings, each of which causes the work to acquire new vitality in terms of one particular taste, or perspective, or personal *performance*.

Contemporary aesthetics has frequently pointed out this last characteristic of *every* work of art. According to Luigi Pareyson:

> The work of art . . . is a form, namely of movement, that has been concluded; or we can see it as an infinite contained within finiteness . . . The work therefore has infinite aspects, which are not just "parts" or fragments of it, because each of them contains the totality of the work, and reveals it according to a given perspective. So the variety of performances is founded both in the complex factor of the performer's individuality and in that of the work to be performed . . . The infinite points of view of the performers and the infinite aspects of the work interact with each other, come into juxtaposition and clarify each other by a reciprocal process, in such a way that a given point of view is capable of revealing the whole work only if it grasps it in the relevant, highly personalized aspect. Analogously, a single aspect of the work can only reveal the totality of the work in a new light if it is prepared to wait for the right point of view capable of grasping and proposing the work in all its vitality.

The foregoing allows Pareyson to move on to the assertion that

> all performances are definitive in the sense that each one is for the performer, tantamount to the work itself; equally, all performances are bound to be provisional in the sense that each performer knows that he must always try to deepen his own interpretation of the work. Insofar as they are definitive, these interpretations are parallel, and each of them is such as to exclude the others without in any way negating them.[9]

This doctrine can be applied to all artistic phenomena and to artworks throughout the ages. But it is useful to have underlined that now is the period when aesthetics has paid especial attention to the whole notion of "openness" and sought to expand it. In a sense these requirements, which aesthetics has referred widely to every type of artistic production, are the same as those posed by the poetics of the "open work" in a more decisive and explicit fashion. Yet this does not mean that the existence of "open" works and of "works in movement" adds absolutely nothing to our experience because everything in the world is already implied and subsumed by everything else, from the beginning of time, in the same way that it now appears that every discovery has already been made by the Chinese. Here we have to distinguish between the theoretical level of aesthetics as a philosophical discipline which attempts to formulate definitions and the practical level of poetics as programmatic projects for creation. While aesthetics brings to light one of the fundamental demands of contemporary culture, it also reveals the latent possibilities of a certain type of experience in every artistic product, independently of the operative criteria which presided over its moment of inception.

The poetic theory or practice of the "work in movement" senses this possibility as a specific vocation. It allies itself openly and self-consciously to current trends in scientific method and puts into action and tangible form the very trend which aesthetics has already acknowledged as the general background to performance. These poetic systems recognize "openness" as *the* fundamental possibility of the contemporary artist or consumer. The aesthetic theoretician, in his turn, will see a confirmation of his own intuitions in these practical manifestations: they constitute the ultimate realization of a receptive mode which can function at many different levels of intensity.

Certainly this new receptive mode vis-à-vis the work of art opens up a much vaster phase in culture and in this sense is not intellectually confined to the problems of aesthetics. The poetics of the "work in movement" (and partly that of the "open" work) sets in motion a new cycle of relations between the artist and his audience, a new mechanics of aesthetic perception, a different status for the artistic product in contemporary society. It opens a new page in sociology and in pedagogy, as well as a new chapter in the history of art. It poses new practical problems by organizing new communicative situations. In short, it installs a new relationship between the *contemplation* and the *utilization* of a work of art.

Seen in these terms and against the background of historical influences and cultural interplay which links art by analogy to widely diversified aspects of the contemporary worldview, the situation of art has now become a situation in the process of development. Far from being fully accounted for and catalogued, it deploys and poses problems in several dimensions. In short, it is an "open" situation, *in movement*. A work in progress.

## Notes

1 Henri Pousseur, "La nuova sensibilità musicale," *Incontri musicali* 2 (May 1958), 25.
2 Werner Heisenberg, *Physics and Philosophy* (London: Allen & Unwin, 1959), ch. 3.
3 Niels Bohr, in his epistemological debate with Einstein; see P. A. Schlipp, ed., *Albert Einstein: Philosopher-Scientist* (Evanston, Ill.: Library of Living Philosophers, 1949). [ . . . ]
4 Edmund Husserl, *Méditations cartésiennes*, Med. 2, par. 19 (Paris: Vrin, 1953), p. 39. The translation of this passage is by Anne Fabre-Luce.
5 Jean-Paul Sartre, *L'être et le néant* (Paris: Gallimard, 1943), ch. 1.
6 M. Merleau-Ponty, *Phénoménologie de la perception* (Paris: Gallimard, 1945), pp. 381–3.
7 Ibid., p. 384.
8 On this "éclatement multidirectionnel des structures," see A. Boucourechliev, "Problèmes de la musique moderne," *Nouvelle revue française* (December–January, 1960–1).
9 Luigi Pareyson, *Estetica: Teoria della formatività*, 2nd edn. (Bologna: Zanichelli, 1960), pp. 194 ff, and in general the whole of chapter 8, "Lettura, interpretazione e critica."

# 10 Janet H. Murray

# DIGITAL TV AND THE EMERGING FORMATS OF CYBERDRAMA

I have referred to these various new kinds of narrative under the single umbrella term of *cyberdrama* because the coming digital story form (whatever we come to call it), like the novel or the movie, will encompass many different formats and styles but will essentially be a single distinctive entity. It will not be an interactive this or that, however much it may draw upon tradition, but a reinvention of storytelling itself for the new digital medium. At first the most strongly participatory cyberdrama formats may be the domain of children and adolescents, who will eagerly move from shooting games to assuming personas within dense fictional worlds, but it would be wrong to think that the format itself is merely childish. As a new generation grows up, it will take participatory form for granted and will look for ways to participate in ever more subtle and expressive stories.

Of course, the story forms described here are guesses, dependent on market forces as well as audience tastes. The term *cyberdrama* is only a placeholder for whatever is around the corner. The human urge for representation, for storytelling, and for the transformational use of the imagination is an immutable part of our makeup, and the narrative potential of the new digital medium is dazzling. As the virtual world takes on increasing expressiveness, we will slowly get used to living in a fantasy environment that now strikes us as frighteningly real. But at some point we will find ourselves looking through the medium instead of at it. Then we will no longer be interested in whether the characters we are interacting with are scripted actors, fellow improvisers, or computer-based chatterbots, nor will we continue to think about whether the place we are occupying exists as a photograph of a theatrical set or as a computer-generated graphic, or about whether it is delivered to us by radio waves or telephone wires. At that point, when the medium itself melts away into transparency, we will be lost in the make-believe and care only about the story.

[ . . . ]

## The Hyperserial: TV Meets the Internet

One of the clearest trends determining the immediate future of digital narrative is the marriage between the television set and the computer. The technical merger is already under way. Personal computers marketed to college students allow them to switch off the central processing unit and tune in to the latest episode of *Friends* on the same screen they use for word processing. The most computer-phobic couch potatoes can now buy a "Web TV" that will allow them to point and click their way across the Internet and even to send and receive e-mail, using an ordinary phone line. American television is rapidly moving toward a high-definition digital standard, which will turn the broadcast TV signal into just another form of computer data. Meanwhile, the Internet is beginning to function as an alternate broadcasting system; already it offers a wide assortment of live programming, including on-line typed interviews, digital radio programs, and even live video coverage of rock music concerts, club openings, and performance art. As television channels and the World Wide Web come closer together, the telephone, computer, and cable industries are racing to deliver the new digital content to the end user faster and in greater quantities. The merger that Nicholas Negroponte has long been predicting is upon us: the computer, television, and telephone are becoming a single home appliance.[1]

From the consumer's point of view, the activities of watching television and surfing the Internet are also merging, thus driving the marketplace to create new frameworks of participation. Television viewers populate hundreds of computer chat rooms and newsgroups, often logging on to these collective environments while watching the shows in order to share their responses with fellow audience members. Broadcasters have experimented with displaying some of these comments in real time, as subtitles beneath the images of an entertainment program, as questions for interviewees, or as quotations at the beginning and end of news segments. The network formed by the cooperative venture between Microsoft and NBC exists as both a Web site and a cable television station; these two separate venues are so intertwined and mutually referencing that it would be hard to say which one is "the" MS/NBC. They are one entity, even though they now appear on two separate screens. Viewer digital participation is moving from sequential activities (watch, then interact), to simultaneous but separate activities (interact while watching), to a merged experience (watch and interact in the same environment). Although we cannot yet predict the economics of the television–Internet merger, these increasing levels of participatory viewership are preparing us for a near-future medium in which we will be able to point and click through different branches of a single TV program as easily as we now use the remote to surf from one channel to another.

The more closely the new home digital medium is wedded to television, the more likely it will be that its major form of storytelling will be the serial drama. As we have already seen, the daytime soap opera has already been translated into the more participatory Web soap now popular on the Internet. Adding motion video to the format will increase demand for the dramatic immediacy and more tightly plotted action that we expect on TV. It will be hard for the chattily written Web soaps – which are based on a scrapbook metaphor – to compete in the same environment as television serials once the novelty of Web surfing has passed. At the same time, linear television will seem too passive once it is presented in a digital medium, where viewers expect to be able to move around at will.

Probably the first steps toward a new *hyperserial* format will be the close integration of a digital archive, such as a Web site, with a broadcast television program. Unlike the Web sites currently associated with conventional television programs, which are merely fancy publicity releases, an integrated digital archive would present virtual artifacts from the fictional world of the series, including not only diaries, photo albums, and telephone messages but also documents like birth certificates, legal briefs, or divorce papers. Such artifacts appear in the best of the current Web soaps but do not sustain our interest without the motivation of a central dramatic action.

The compelling spatial reality of the computer will also lead to virtual environments that are extensions of the fictional world. For instance, the admitting station seen in every episode of *ER* could be presented as a virtual space, allowing viewers to explore it and discover phone messages, patient files, and medical test results, all of which could be used to extend the current story line or provide hints of future developments. The doctors' lounge area could contain discarded newspapers with circled advertisements, indicating, for example, that Dr. Lewis is looking for an apartment in another state or that Dr. Benton is shopping for an engagement ring. An on-line, serially updated virtual environment would open up a broadcast story in the same way a film expands a story told in a stage play, by providing additional locations for dramatic action or wider coverage of the characters or events merely referred to in the broadcast series. We might see more of the home life of the *ER* doctors, perhaps noticing that Mark Green keeps a photo of the absent Susan Lewis next to a picture of his daughter or that Doug Ross has held on to the medical ID bracelet of a woman who died partly as a result of his out-of-control sexual life. Like the set design in a movie, a virtual set design would be an extension of the dialogue and dramatic action, deepening the immersive illusion of the story world.

All of these digital artifacts would be available on demand, in between episodes, so that viewers could experience a continuous sense of ongoing lives. A hyperserial might include daily postings of events in the major story line – another fight between feuding characters or a set of phone messages between separated lovers – that would be alluded to in the broadcast segments but detailed only in the on-line material. The Web-based material might also contain more substantial development of minor characters and story lines. Maybe Shep, whom Carol broke up with last year, is sending her letters telling her how he is dealing with the stresses of his job as an emergency medical worker, or perhaps the ex-prostitute with AIDS is in danger of losing her apartment. By filling out the holes in the dramatic narrative, holes that prevent viewers from fully believing in the characters, and by presenting situations that do not resolve themselves within the rhythms of series television, the hyperserial archive could extend the melodramatic broadcast drama into a more complex narrative world.

Putting broadcast television into digital form would also allow producers to make previously aired episodes available on demand. A hyperserial site would offer a complete digital library of the series, and these episodes, unlike the same content stored on a VCR tape, would be searchable by content. Viewers could call up individual segments of past episodes (the diner scene in which Mark finalizes his divorce agreement) or view a single continuous story thread (the deterioration of Mark's marriage) that was originally woven into several episodes. Such an encyclopedic representation of the complete series would offer television writers the larger, more novelistic canvas that serial drama has been moving toward for the last two decades. Writers could think of a hyperserial as a coherent, unfolding story whose viewers are able to keep track of longer plot arcs and a greater number of interconnected story threads. Compared to today's television writer, the cyberdramatist could explore the consequences of actions over longer periods of time and could create richer dramatic parallels, knowing that viewers would be likely to juxtapose events told months or even years apart.

[ . . . ] In a well-conceived hyperserial, all the minor characters would be potential protagonists of their own stories, thus providing alternate threads within the enlarged story web. The viewer would take pleasure in the ongoing juxtapositions, the intersection of many different lives, and the presentation of the same event from multiple sensibilities and perspectives. The ending of a hyperserial would not be a single note, as in a standard adventure drama, but a resolving chord, the sensation of several overlapping viewpoints coming into focus.

## Mobile Viewer Movies

The hyperserial model of cyberdrama described above is based on a transitional situation in which viewers are alternately watching television broadcasts and navigating a Web-like environment accessible from the same screen. But as digital television evolves as a delivery medium, viewers may find themselves unable to sit still for a conventionally told two-hour story. Just as the movie camera made the stage box seem too confining, so may the computer mouse make the director's camera seem too confining. Interactor/viewers may want to follow the actors out of frame, to look at things from multiple vantage points. We can already see evidence of such viewer restlessness in the hyperactive camera style of the most filmic television series (*Homicide, NYPD Blue*), in which the noncontinuous cuts and rapid circling movements of the often handheld cameras reflect the audience's own desire to roam around the space, to experience the action in three dimensions, and to jump forward to the next interesting moment as quickly as possible. Although critics who are strongly attached to older forms of presentation might see such restlessness as evidence of a shortened attention span or an increased need for stimulation, it can also be seen as the expression of a more active curiosity or eagerness to look around for oneself and make one's own discoveries.

[ . . . ]

Moviegoers of the future may watch a single visual presentation but be offered multiple sound tracks. Everything that is said aloud in the scene might be on one track, available to everyone, but the private thoughts of various characters would be on their own tracks. A movie of a poker game or a sting operation might keep the motives of the protagonists secret from one another; since viewers could choose which character to align with, different members of the audience would watch the same scene with very different information. Moviegoers might be lured back to see such a movie again from a different point of view or to gain access to the thoughts of a character whose motivations were hidden from them the first time. Viewers in a 3-D theater watching a scene of an exotic café might hear all of the conversations spoken normally by people at their own table but would also be able to eavesdrop on whispered conversations or on people at adjoining tables by leaning their heads toward the speaker. This multidirectional audio, an enhancement of existing sound technology, would serve to make the perception of three-dimensional space much more concrete. Since these possibilities would lead to multiple viewings of the same film, and would therefore yield greater revenue for movie production companies without requiring the creation of additional footage, they seem likely to be attempted.

The mobile viewer approach could also be combined with the hyperserial. Perhaps a future *ER* will offer us a choice of trauma rooms in which to locate ourselves, or a future *Homicide* might offer us a choice of murder investigations to follow. Viewers who did not indicate explicit choices or who were watching with conventional television sets would see a continuous drama made up of default scenes, just as viewers with black-and-white sets were unable to take full advantage of the first color programs. But those with interactive access could choose to see more of some plotlines than others and could follow certain characters more closely. All of the dramas would end appropriately at the same time, and mobile viewers would also have a sense of having chosen from among several sequences to pursue the action or situation most dramatically intriguing to them.

This mobile viewer format would be very well suited to the current television genre of the problem drama, which addresses a socially charged issue, like racism or abortion, on which viewers hold very different views. A mobile viewer cyberdrama could be presented in such a way that viewers' choice of point of view would influence the kind of information they receive. Choosing to see the story in a particular way would therefore be a self-revealing act that might leave the viewer questioning his or her values.

The cyberdramatist would have the task of constantly arousing the mobile viewer's curiosity, fears, and sympathies, since every choice made by the mobile viewer should be expressive of a particular moment of imaginative engagement. Such choices, which would not correspond to a simple right – wrong dichotomy, should be interestingly different from one another and even more revealing when juxtaposed.

[ . . . ]

Mobile viewer audiences might then be offered the opportunity to converse with one another in chat rooms that are configured as sites within the universe of the program (i.e., sites such as cafés or squad rooms or school cafeterias). The treatment of controversial subjects in divergent narratives and the subsequent public on-line discussion would be a particularly appropriate format for television, which serves as a medium for what David Thorburn has called "consensus narrative," that is, for stories that define the concerns of the society and present the received wisdom about these concerns.[2] This format would provide a less voyeuristic way of engaging people in discussions about the kinds of disturbing behaviors upon which sensational talk programs focus. Issues of gender identity, sexual behavior, child rearing norms, or domestic violence could be framed by compelling stories that would then provoke discussion.

[ . . . ]

# Virtual Places and Fictional Neighborhoods

Currently the most inhabited fictional spaces – the MUDs – are made of words alone, but as the Internet becomes faster and more capacious, as the conventions of three-dimensional environments become standardized, and as graphical authoring tools become more functional and user-friendly, there will be an explosion of virtual architecture that will make the public digital environment look less like a billboard-strewn highway and more like a populated landscape. In the next decade, as the dungeons and forests of the MUDs are translated from words into three-dimensional images, more and more users may find themselves residing in such shared fantasy kingdoms.

Perhaps the first steps in this direction will be in the form of immersive visits to pleasurably explorable 3-D dreamscapes. The videogame manufacturers are already moving in this direction by offering worlds so well realized that the moat at the front portcullis is as appealing as the adventure within the castle. As joysticks and VR gear allow us greater mobility (not just up, down, left, and right but also in and out of a 3-D space) with more power of observation (i.e., with the ability to switch position as if we were operating a camera focused on the dramatic action) and with less physical encumbrance or need for manual dexterity, interactors will be lured into worlds where they float, tumble, and arc through thrillingly colored spaces, fly through imaginary clouds, and swim lazily across welcoming mountain ponds. The nightmare landscape of the fighting maze, in which we feel perpetually imperiled, may give way to enchanting worlds of increasingly refined visual delight that are populated by evocative fairy-tale creatures.

A visit to such a space will combine the rhythmic kinetic pleasures of dancing with the visual pleasures of sculpture and film; the space itself will be expressive, as our movement through it will be, and the landscape will be filled with objects of desire and enchantment. We will go out over digital networks to experience the thrill of entering previously inaccessible environments: an erupting volcano, a primeval rain forest, a distant planet; we will walk across the parted Red Sea with Moses or sit down to a performance in a virtual Elizabethan theater. These compelling immersive landscapes might constitute a new kind of pastoral art, an artificial re-creation of nostalgically fantasized natural or historical environments. Just as ancient Greek city dwellers enjoyed reciting verses about frolicking shepherds, so too will twenty-first-century citizens of the information age enjoy transmuting their data-laden screens into elfin groves, Victorian parks, or galactic fireworks displays.

## Role-Playing in an Authored World

The kinds of virtual worlds I am imagining would combine the immersive pull of an authored story, like an ongoing television serial, with the open-ended agency of the MUDs. They would relieve the interactors of the responsibility for inventing the fictional world on their own.

Multiuser worlds without such external authoring run into trouble in establishing the boundaries of the illusion. For instance, one of the first experiments with a graphics-based virtual world, called Habitat, found itself immediately divided between interactors who wanted to shoot and kill one another and those who wanted to form a shared community. The organizers of the project negotiated a compromise by creating a wilderness land in which violence was routine and a town where it was outlawed. Soon the members of the town founded a church and elected a sheriff – they had essentially re-created the popular fantasy of the pioneer American West – and they immediately began quarreling over whether the townspeople could outlaw violence altogether.

The role of a central author (or team of authors) in such an environment might be to negotiate such boundary issues, for example, by insisting that the improvisational elements remain consistent with a general story line. This need not mean censoring the interactors' imagination. Moreover, the author should be able to improvise along with the interactors and to take advantage of spontaneous actions to create dramatic events appropriate to the fictional world. For instance, the Habitat world was disrupted whenever a player gained possession of the villain Death's deadly virtual gun, designed for use by the wizards of the system only. One wizard handled this situation by threatening to throw the player off the system unless he returned the gun, but a more imaginative genie faced with the same situation staged an elaborate ransoming ritual, which became a spectacle for the whole community.[3]

If participatory environments merge with authored environments, as I think they will, tensions between the author and the participants may increase. There will always be a trade-off between a world that is more given (more authored from the outside and therefore imbued with the magic of externalized fantasy) and a world that is more improvised (and therefore closer to individual fantasies). The area of immersive enchantment lies in the overlap between these two domains. If the borders are constantly under negotiation, they will be too porous to sustain the immersive trance.

A cyberdrama that combines a strong central story with active role-playing would need clear conventions to separate the area in which the interactors are free to invent their own actions from areas over which they cannot expect to have control.

[ ... ]

The participation of thousands, or perhaps even millions, of interactors in a centrally controlled story world would only be possible by limiting the kinds of roles they could play and the kinds of actions they could take.

[ ... ]

It will probably take a large, hierarchically organized writing team, comparable to the groups of writers who work on daytime television series, to generate enough plot material to maintain the interest of participants and to make sure that events in one part of the story do not anticipate or obstruct events in another. It will also take carefully ritualized patterns of participation, so that the interactors know what to expect of one another and of the authors controlling the virtual world. Most challengingly, it will take programmed occurrences that make the story world eventful and unpredictable for all of the interactors without limiting their freedom or intruding on their improvisational pleasure.

## Notes

1   For the best statement of Negroponte's vision of a world in which much that is now done by "atoms" (or separate physical objects) is transferred to "bits" or electronic representations, see *Being Digital*. Negroponte's work with what we now think of as interactive multimedia dates to the late 1960s in the Architecture Machine Group, which became the foundation of the current MIT Media Lab, founded in 1985.
2   David Thorburn, "Television as an Aesthetic Medium." *Critical Studies in Mass Communication* 4 (1987): 161–73.
3   For the story of Habitat, see Chip Morningstar and F. Randall Farmer. "The Lessons of Lucasfilm's Habitat." In *Cyberspace: First Steps*, edited by Michael Benedikt. Cambridge, MA: MIT Press, 1992.

# 11    *Ken Robinson*

# BALANCING THE BOOKS

## Creativity in Crisis

Like all countries, the United States is facing a future of rapid social and technological change in which many of the old skills and attitudes will be redundant. At the same time, there is a crisis of creativity, a war for talent, which is as acute as in Europe and in other parts of the world. In 1996 a national symposium was held in the United States entitled *American Creativity at Risk*. The symposium brought together artists, scientists and others to discuss the conditions under which the creative resources of the United States could be best realised. The symposium was set against a mounting concern in many areas of education, the economy and the professions that national policies were deepening the crisis. The symposium confirmed the core principles I have set out here.

- A remarkably powerful creative synergy arises when people of different professional backgrounds and skills work together. This creative synergy has led to successful problem-solving, revolutionary ways of seeing, thinking and approaching the conflicts of our daily human lives, in both the arts and sciences, time and time again.
- Creative environments give people time to experiment, to fail, to try again, to ask questions, to discover, to play, to make connections among the seemingly disparate elements. This experimentation or research may not lead to an artistic product or scientific application for many years, as all original ideas and products spring from an initial period of experimentation

"Balancing the Books" from Ken Robinson (2001), *Out of Our Minds: Learning to Be Creative.* Capstone, Oxford, pp. 194–203, 211. Reprinted by permission of John Wiley & Sons Ltd.

or fooling around. This may sometimes seem purposeless but it is the essence of the creative process.

- Creativity is a basic human attribute that must be nurtured among all people, not just artists and scientists. The freedom to learn, to create, to take risks, to fail or ask questions, to strive, to grow; this is the ethic upon which the US was founded. Promoting creativity among all people of all occupations, economic classes and ethnic backgrounds is essential to the common good.

The symposium concluded that universities and school programmes are now being run more like businesses, with an attention to the bottom line that it is often detrimental to the quality of education they provide. Investment in basic science, which in the past has led to applications we now take for granted, such as computers and laser technology, is decreasing dramatically. This is because the gap between basic research and application can be years or even decades, too long for the short-term economic gain our society now demands. This perception is by no means unique to the United States. There are similar pressures affecting organisations in the public and private sectors throughout the world. Their consequences are particularly serious in education.

I began this book by arguing that companies are trying to address a downstream problem. In order to revive and promote creative abilities, they need to remedy the narrowness of conventional academic education. There is a great deal that organisations can do immediately to apply the ideas and principles I've outlined. But the longer-term solution does lie upstream. Education systems must change too to meet the radically new circumstances in which they are now operating. The economic and intellectual assumptions on which our national systems of education have been built originated in another time and for other purposes.

## The Challenge for Education

Education must be rebalanced to conform to three principles:

- balance across the curriculum;
- balance within the teaching of disciplines; and
- balance between education and the wider world.

### Frameworks and cages

In many school systems throughout the world, there is an imbalance in the curriculum. The emphasis is on science, technology, mathematics and language teaching at the expense of the arts, humanities and physical education. It is essential that there is an equal balance between these areas of the curriculum. This is necessary because each of these broad groupings of disciplines reflects major areas of cultural knowledge and experience to which all young people should have equal access. Second, each addresses a different mode of intelligence and creative development. The strengths of any individual may be in one or more of them. A narrow, unbalanced curriculum will lead to a narrow, unbalanced education for some if not all young people.

The UK system, like many systems in Europe, starts from the premise that there are ten subjects in the world and we devise a system of education to teach them. Why do educational institutions have a curriculum in the first place? There are two reasons. The first is *epistemological*; it is to do with the organisation of knowledge. A curriculum suggests that there are distinctive domains of knowledge, understanding and skills that provide a framework for teaching and learning. The categories into which we divide our experiences are very important. Beyond education, beyond institutions, people work quite comfortably without these sorts of categories. We all have categories for different purposes, but education divides the world into lumps of knowledge so that we can teach children the material, ideas, knowledge and skills that we deem to be important. There are many things that are not taught in schools. Witchcraft and necromancy are not taught in most schools. One of the functions of education is to identify the legitimate areas of cultural knowledge and experience, to put a stamp of approval on certain sorts of knowledge and experience and by implication to suggest that others are not so worthwhile. Education distinguishes between the spheres of 'orthodox and heretical culture'.[1]

When the structure of the National Curriculum in England was first announced in 1986, I went with a group of others to see the then Secretary of State for Education. We asked him what the provision would be for the arts. He told us that art and music would be the foundation subjects. 'What about dance and drama', I asked. 'Well drama, of course, is part of English', he said, 'and dance is part of physical education'. Well, of course, they are not. This is a very common mistake. Because dramatic texts are written down, they are commonly treated as literature to be read, rather than actions to be performed. Drama is an active art form not a literary one. The fact that it can be written down does not make it a textual form any more than the existence of musical notation should suggest that music is a form of Morse code. Similarly, it is a mistake to group dance with track and field events.

Physical education is primarily associated with competitive sports and with games and exercises in the gymnasium. These are extremely important. But there are important differences between athletics and dance: winning, for example. On the whole we do not come out of a performance of Swan Lake asking who won. I am a board member of the Birmingham Royal Ballet. We did not send a team to the Sydney Olympics. We are not funded by the Sports Council. These are small indications of functional differences between sport and dance. Saying that dance is part of PE is like saying that history is really part of English because we write essays in English and in history. We use our bodies in dance and in physical education but this does not mean they are the same thing.

Dance is slotted into PE only if the starting point is that there are ten subjects in the world and everything has to be part of one of them. If so you may as well put dance with PE because it's convenient, and you're changed anyway. Outside education, these categories don't help very much. If you go to an opera performance, what is that? Is it drama? Is it music? Is it visual art? A dance performance is a physical experience for the dancers but it's a visual and musical experience for the audience. What is theatre? The best we can do is to describe these as integrated art forms. But they are not. They are only integrated in the sense that education has disintegrated them in the first place so that they can be taught.

The first function of a curriculum is epistemological. But a curriculum has a second function; this is *managerial*. Educational institutions need a curriculum so that they can organise themselves, know how many teachers to hire, what resources are needed, how to arrange the day, whom to put where, at what time and for how long. A curriculum is a management tool. What tends to happen is that the managerial functions of the curriculum eventually overtake the epistemological functions. One reason that dance is part of PE is that the UK government couldn't afford to have dance as a compulsory part of everybody's education. There weren't the teachers around to do it. If they were to commit themselves to dance as a central part of education, as they've done with science, it would have involved a massive reorganisation of teacher education and funding. But there was another reason. They saw no need to make this provision in the first place. In most education systems, the arts are not seen as sufficiently important to be at the heart of education, and it is simply taken for granted that this is the way things should be.

A distinction is commonly made between academic and non-academic subjects in schools. So pupils who are not very good at academic subjects might be encouraged to concentrate on less academic ones. Alternatively, academic subjects might be balanced in some way with non-academic subjects. Usually, for example, science or history or mathematics are seen as academic subjects and art, music or drama as non-academic. This is a basic misconception. It reinforces two assumptions, which must be rethought. The first is the very idea of subjects. This idea suggests that different areas of the curriculum are defined by their content or subject matter. Science is different from art because it deals with different subject matter.

[ . . . ]

The second assumption is that some subjects are academic and some are not. This is not true. All issues and questions can be considered from an academic point of view and from others too. They can be investigated in the deductive mode or in other modes. Schools and universities teach many subjects but one dominant way of thinking – the verbal, mathematical, deductive and propositional. These processes can be applied to any phenomena: plants, weather, poetry, music, social systems. On this basis, the person who writes about the arts may be thought to be intellectually superior to the person who produces the work. A Picasso scholar – but not Picasso himself – may be given a PhD. Doing the arts should be recognised as being as legitimate an intellectual process as critical inquiries about the arts. The heart of this argument is that knowledge can be generated in many ways other than in words and numbers. Not all that we know can be put into words and numbers, nor is what can be put into words and numbers all that we do know.

## The balance of teaching

[Elsewhere, I have] distinguished between the two traditions of individualism, the *rational* and the *natural*. To some extent these have been associated with different styles of teaching. Facilitating creative development requires the teaching of knowledge and skills, together with opportunities to speculate and experiment. This is a sophisticated process that combines elements of what are thought of as traditional and progressive education. So-called traditional methods are usually associated with formal instruction to the whole class and with rote learning; progressive methods with children working individually or in groups and exploring their own interests and opinions. Real life in education is not normally as neat as this. Some teachers favour particular methods: many use a mixture. Nor is there a neat distinction in relation to my argument here. Traditional methods are associated with conventional academic standards. The apparent decline in the use of these methods is often seen as a root cause of the apparent decline in these standards.

I am not arguing against academic standards in themselves nor would I celebrate a decline in them. My concern is with the preoccupation with these standards to the exclusion of everything else. I am not arguing against formal instruction. I am not appealing for a wider use of so-called progressive teaching methods. Both have an important place in teaching. Some of these methods do put a strong emphasis on creativity: some do not. Some of this work is excellent: some is not. A common failing is the tendency to misunderstand the nature of creative activity not only in education but more generally. Too often what passes for creativity has been an undisciplined and undemanding process.

The emphasis in schools on academic learning has tended to value only one mode of knowing and, in so doing, has displaced others. This has been to the detriment of all of them. Creativity depends on interactions between feeling and thinking, and across different disciplinary boundaries and fields of ideas. New curricula must be evolved which are more permeable and which encourage a better balance between generative thinking and critical thinking in all modes of understanding.

Our systems of education are based on the view that intelligence is a linear process of rational thought. From this we have derived economic models of education which are equally linear. The reason that all countries are taking these issues so seriously now is the recognition that these old assumptions won't do any more. The economic circumstances in which we all live, and in which our children will have to make their way, are utterly different from those of 20 or even 10 years ago. For these we need different styles of education and different priorities. We are generating cultural and social circumstances within which the old processes of rationalism in themselves are increasingly inadequate. We need a new Renaissance that moves beyond these old categories and develops the relationships between different processes rather than emphasising their differences. We need to re-evaluate the relationships of areas of educational experience that are now separated. We need new structures of learning for a different type of future. We cannot meet the challenges of the 21st century with the educational ideologies of the 19th.

Education policies for the future must learn from the past but must not be dictated by it. We cannot approach the future looking backwards. We now have a school curriculum that teaches ten subjects but only limited ways of thinking. We need an education that values different modes of intelligence and sees relationships between disciplines. To achieve this, there must be a different balance of priorities between the arts, sciences and humanities in education and in the forms of thinking they promote. They should be taught in ways that reflect their intimate connections in the world beyond education. Achieving this is not easy but the benefits of success are substantial and the price of failure is high.

## The Ecology of Human Resources

[ . . . ] Ironically, some people resist new approaches to education precisely because they are concerned about helping people to be employable.

They seem to think that arguing for more creative approaches to education and developing human resources are luxuries that are out of step with the hard-headed realities of finding work. They are not. One of Europe's leading employment agencies is Reed Executive plc. The company was founded in 1960 by Alec (now Sir Alec) Reed with an initial investment of £75, and specialised in temporary secretarial appointments. It was capitalised in 2000 at approximately £114 million and now covers an enormous range of employment opportunities in many different fields. Its development over 40 years has coincided with the profound changes in labour and employment that I have outlined here. It is now growing at a faster pace than ever and has introduced an entirely new structure and strategy to face the new realities of the world of work. The present chief executive James Reed sees the development of creative abilities as fundamental to the future success of companies and individuals alike – in all areas of employment.

'In our world that is changing so quickly and becoming so much more complex, the opportunities that are offered by new technologies and by new ways of doing business are clearly immense. We must seize these opportunities. But if we are to do so successfully, we must be creative, we must cherish the individual and we must be courageous enough to meet ever greater challenges head on. We must routinely do what has never been done before and must be obsessed with improving what we do already. In this new world the winners will be those who attract the best talent, who have the best insights and transform the way they do business to bring real and enduring value to customers.

'For certain the winners of the future will be focused and they will be fast. To this end, over the last six months we have put a new strategy and structure in place that has speed, simplicity and service at its core. At a time when our Group is larger than it has ever been, our absolute priority is to reorganise into smaller more customer focused and more commercially agile business units. We call this our Starburst strategy. At the very heart of the strategy is the belief that we will deliver much more to clients, candidates and co-members (or stars) if we create room for individual expression and for the development of distinctive client focused strategies in the different arenas in which we operate . . . Our new structure with a very small central team together with the Starburst strategy means that we now look more like a venture capitalist company than a traditional business. This is deliberate, but we could choose to describe ourselves as a "Venture Peoplists". The focus of our future activities and future investment will be people first and foremost. In the new creative economy, more than ever before, it will be people and not capital that make the difference. Our philosophy has always been that been people make the difference and our future investment strategy will reflect this.'

At the heart of the new strategies that are needed for business and for education there must be a new conception of human resources. This is where the ideas about intelligence and creativity that I have developed [ . . . ] are pointing. It is fundamentally a question of ecology. The idea of ecology has had a major impact on our thinking about the natural resources of the earth. We now recognise that during the Industrial Revolution, we made very partial use of the earth's resources. We wasted or destroyed a great deal of what it had to offer because we couldn't see the value of it. Along the way we have jeopardised the balance of nature by not recognising how different elements of the environment sustain each other. Although the dangers persist, they are now understood. There is a similar calamity in our use of human resources that has not been recognised.

In the interests of the industrial economy and of academic achievement, we have subjected ourselves to a partial form of education. We have wasted or destroyed a great deal of what people had to offer because we couldn't see the value of it. Along the way we have jeopardised the balance of human nature by not recognising how different elements of our abilities sustain and enrich each other. The dangers persist, and they are not yet widely understood. Education and training are the key to the future, but a key can be turned in two directions. Turn it one way and you lock resources away, even from those they belong to. Turn it the other way and you release resources and give people back to themselves. The companies, communities and nations that succeed in future will balance their books only by solving the complex equation of human resources. Our own times are being swept along on an avalanche of innovations in science, technology, and social thought. To keep pace with these changes, or to get ahead of them, we will need all our wits about us – literally. We must learn to be creative.

# Notes

1  P. Bourdieu, 'Systems of Education and Systems of Thought', in M. F. D. Young (ed.), *Knowledge and Control*, Collier Macmillan, London, 1971.

# 12    *Luigi Maramotti*

# CONNECTING CREATIVITY

[ . . . ]

It is widely agreed that clothing is a language, but a very ambiguous one. Its vocabulary changes or evolves, and can express different meanings at different times according to the wearer and the observer.[1] We might say that clothing is a dynamic language open to endless resetting. Some adhere to the view that fashion follows a 'trickle down process'[2] whereby innovative ideas are transmitted from the elite top layers of the social pyramid to the bottom. Others consider it mainly a matter of points of view, where each style creates an anti-style that defines it, and stimulates further change.[3] In reality, it is difficult to frame the rules by which creative thought gives a shape to fashion and its changes, although it appears that a good many can be linked in some way to technological innovations in textiles, and there seem to be recurrent patterns such as the relaunch of historic items in different contexts.

For as long as it has existed, fashion, being a language, has always been used as a means of communication. This very peculiar kind of communication takes place on two levels: an open one, and a hidden one. There is in fact an underlying reading we might call a creative value left to each individual, which allows the transmission of ambiguous and equivocal messages; think of the eroticism of neglected lace, the hardness of riding boots or the provocativeness of some metal details.

If we agree that fashion is a language we should emphasize that it is a very sophisticated one and in a way complementary, a tool for articulating and supporting words rather than substituting them. And if we agree that fashion is distinct from style, we must admit that its acknowledged codes are variable.

"Connecting Creativity" from Luigi Maramotti (2000), "Connecting Creativity". In Nicola White and Ian Griffiths (eds.), *The Fashion Business: Theory, Practice, Image*. Berg, Oxford, pp. 3–102. Reprinted by permission of Berg Publishers.

These changes can occur at different levels mainly, but not only, visually, often revamping outdated meanings. The system of constantly shifting meanings, codes and values is in fact fundamental to fashion as we understand it in our culture. Designers know this well and they are the first to perceive signs of instability, the trends pervading society. The instabilities, ambiguities and ambivalences, described by Fred Davis in his excellent book on the subject drive creativity to and fro between opposites such as young/old, male/female, work/play, simplicity/complexity, revelation/concealment, freedom/constraint, conformism/rebellion, eroticism/chastity, discretion/overstatement and so on.[4] The field where the game of change is played is framed within couples of constantly recurring antithetic meanings. Fashion delights us by playing on the tensions between these couples – we derive a frisson from the contradictions they suggest. We may tire of a look but whenever one of these themes returns, its freshness is restored; our fascination with them seems endless. James Carse, a professor of philosophy at New York University, and a friend of mine, in one of his books divides the world of human relations into 'finite and infinite games'.[5] What is the difference? In the former case the goal of the game is to select a winner, in the latter it is to play the game forever. Incidentally, the latter is typical of the games of children, which were in fact the author's chief source of inspiration. Without doubt, fashion is an infinite game, since nobody is interested in starting the ultimate trend, the final one.

Though changes in fashion correspond to macrochanges in cultures or societies, they nevertheless require human action, the work of creative people, of industry and the complicity of consumers. Fashion, after all, does not happen by accident.

The fashion industry purposefully identifies garments and accessories as indicators of social status. Historians have suggested that this has been so since the fourteenth century.[6] Nowadays, this identification has become a carefully planned and greatly accelerated activity. In the eternal ping-pong game between antithetical meanings, the motivating force for creativity within fashion is nearly always, or often, cultural. When Chanel urged her wealthy clients to dress like their maids,[7] she was playing on dialectics between rich and poor, high and low status, snobbery and inverted snobbery, but the reason for her attraction to these particular themes, and the reason for the fashion's success, was her ability to intuit the predominant social tensions of the moment (in this case ideas the uncertainties of wealth and power initiated by the economic unrest of the 1930s).

The potential of cultural models to drive creativity cannot be overemphasized. Successful designers refer to as wide a variety as possible, drawing from history and going beyond it, they focus on conceived models of an ideal future life. No matter how successful though, designers cannot create the desire to possess or acquire a particular product, but they can create products which satisfy or arouse incipient or otherwise undetected desire. This, in my opinion, is usually achieved by the 'lifestyle' associations a product has for the consumer; designers and companies like ours devote themselves increasingly to formulating our identities from visions of an ideal existence.

The stimuli for creative ideas in fashion have always originated from the widest variety of sources. Even in the last few years, we have seen influences exerted by exhibitions, films, writers, geographical areas, traditional cultures and metropolitan phenomena. It seems that fashion can appropriate practically anything and turn it into a 'look', the success of the look depending of course on its resonance with the cultural/social concerns of the day. Many enjoy the challenge of 'unpicking' fashion to reveal the influences which shaped it, but to me, what really matters is not to identify fashion's sources, but to examine how they generate innovative product ideas, the design process and the marketing of the product.

I have compared fashion to a language, and to a game, and there are sufficient similarities to justify both analogies. But where fashion differs is in its scant regard for rules. In a field which prioritizes innovation and change, practices are swept aside before they become established. Rules have a very short life indeed, and this is what I appreciate most about my work. Successful strategies inevitably become harder and harder to forecast, since the elements to be considered, from the creative and marketing point of view, have multiplied, and everything is subject to change. And yet we must attempt to devise strategies for innovation, since the successful inauguration of new fashions is increasingly likely to be the result of such planned approaches and less the result of the almost accidental fashionableness that was the case with the mini skirt in the 1960s, or Timberland shoes. In noting the necessity for a strategic approach I refute the widely held view that fashion is 'change for change's sake'; Craik has described how the current fashion acts as a determinant for the future one.[8] We who work in the industry are acutely aware that not everything is possible, and have learned by experience that new ideas must usually relate to what already exists if they are to succeed. At the same time we are conscious that the evolution of fashion is punctuated by spasmodic flashes of revolutionary genius, such as Chanel's, which radically change its course before it becomes too predictable. If we are to be successful, therefore, we must keep an ear to the ground ready to detect the first signs of such.

A company producing fashion is the utmost example of forced innovation. It is absolutely necessary to relaunch, recreate, rethink and to discuss things over and over again. Despite what one might think, this does not only apply to the design team, but the whole organization. To be successful, each element in the process of developing and marketing the product must be innovative and everybody should have a creative attitude. I must emphasize that I consider a designed garment 'fashion' only when it is marketed and worn by someone. I have a high opinion of the 'idea' but I believe we should consider it developed and embodied only when it has passed through some kind of process and become a 'product', no matter how small the market. Original ideas are only the first step of a long journey towards a desired success.

Before examining how the creative process develops in a company I should observe that companies, being human organizations, have many similarities with living organisms. Each possesses its own original 'genetic code' which is normally connected to the figure of its founder, but during its life its character may evolve in consequence of the external stimuli it is subjected to. A company possesses its own culture, which will become stronger over the years, transmitting itself through the inevitable conditioning of the individuals entering its ranks. But company culture is not necessarily positive, in fact, it is sometimes so deeply rooted that it hinders that renewal which is so critical to its survival. Company culture is like an enormous database from which can be read the company's life, experience, skills, individuals' contributions over the years but also its limitations and handicaps.

If we consider the product as being at the core of a manufacturing company's culture, and all the related activities of development, production, marketing and promotion arranged around it, we can appreciate how the company's internal activities, through reciprocal flows, engender a distinctive texture in the image of the product itself. Connecting creativity means, to me, positive interaction between different functions. The designer's creativity must be linked to a project; the company itself cannot exist without one. A well-delineated project multiplies the opportunities for the application of creative ideas, just as the artists and craftspeople who symbolized creativity in the past worked freely, yet to precise briefs. At the same time, we must recognize that creativity cannot be strictly planned, and especially in such a complex organization as ours, we must be flexible and ready to modify, at least partially, our project. A simple but frequent example of that need for flexibility is evident in the process of selecting materials. We may happen, in the course of our work, to discover fabrics and colours we find interesting, and wish to include them in a project, where they had not been foreseen. This might appear straightforward but the introduction of something new in to a collection can have enormous implications for supply, production, workability and quality control. Even the smallest of variations can cause a chain reaction, which must be assimilated. The potential dangers of creativity are undoubtedly a factor in industry's ambivalence towards it, yet to cut it out of the company culture is to risk stagnation and decline.

How, then, does MaxMara handle creativity? Our firm has a singular history. It was founded by my father, Achille Maramotti, more than fifty years ago and its roots are to be found in the tradition linking my family to dressmaking on one side and to education on the other. My great-great-grandmother was the head of a well-known local couturier in the middle of the last century, whilst my grandmother was a true pedagogue. Experimental by nature, she not only taught the techniques of design, pattern cutting and sewing, she also invented new methods, offering at the same time moral and practical guidance to the girls attending the 'Scuole Maramotti' which she established in the 1930s.

There is no doubt that this history has greatly spurred love of experimentation and innovation at every level in our company. But as I have argued, creativity is of little purpose unchecked or unsupported. We have over the years established a sequence of critical mechanisms by which creative energy is directed to the most effective ends. These are outlined in the paragraphs that follow.

## Market Research

Despite the importance of market information, I happily confess that our group has no dedicated research department, and rarely uses the services of research consultants. We have discovered that the most effective strategy is to conduct this kind of research through those members of the group who are operative (namely the design, sales and marketing areas). We base our work on a very simple method: observation. Those who are involved with the development and marketing of the product know it well enough, and are sufficiently armed with the history of the company to know where to look for the most relevant material, and how to interpret information.

The fashion market is so segmented that it is not uncommon for a manufacturer to obtain results quite different from the ones foreseen by the macro-trend. In 1996, for instance, the sales of our coats increased by 15 per cent yet this outcome contradicted the general survey of the market that had predicted a negative trend for this item. Trends in spending, social behaviour and lifestyle gained through macroanalysis therefore must be regarded as background information.

It is of course essential that the company applies its creativity to developing the right products for real market needs. With awareness of our capabilities, our potential and our position in the market we must be alert to new opportunities. Again, we at MaxMara believe that the most attentive and intuitive lookouts are likely to be those that work within the company. Nobody from outside, however well qualified, could produce a piece of market research which says that if you product jacket x in cloth y and at z price you will sell 10,000 of them, but with a healthy company culture we can expect our project to evolve and develop along the right lines.

## Data Processing

This kind of work is concerned less with broad intuition and more with minutely detailed knowledge. We are in a position to check daily precisely how the market is reacting to our products with reference to style, size and colour. This can be done thanks to a data-processing system we developed independently, to our specific requirements many years ago. Our sales information is supplemented by interviews with the managers of our stores, who can give us reasons for the success or failure of a particular model.

The importance of change in the fashion industry might tempt us to conclude that we should not be too greatly influenced by information on the market's reaction to a particular product; after all the market is bound to change and the product will be superseded. I have found that designers especially are sometimes particularly reluctant to confront this kind of information; it is unnerving to discover that the market does not affirm one's convictions. But a cumulative knowledge of how our customers' taste develops and what influences their choice, besides being deeply interesting, is an invaluable tool in predicting the chances of success for the next season's product, and in forming future strategies.

## Technological and Technical Innovation

I have acknowledged the role of textile developments in launching new fashions. Fabric research is of fundamental importance to MaxMara. Innovative textiles, offering for instance enhanced comfort, practicality, fluidity, lightness, stability, or which allow new techniques of construction, for example the new generation of 'double face' fabric, or can engender new modes of dressing, for example the recent 'urban sportswear' phenomenon based on luxurious interpretations of high-performance fabrics. Innovative solutions can and should extend to the entire process of the development and even the marketing of a product, and we should consider this a critical aspect of research. Innovation can be the primary reason for a product's success.

## Design

The market research, retail, information, fabric and technical research, the social tensions, ambivalences and ambiguities, the projections of future life, all that I have mentioned in this essay are transformed first into a drawing, then a form. This is the core of our work, and it has for me a magic and mysterious appeal. The sketches, patterns, prototypes, the styling and accessories are all equally important steps which require great investment. It is in the transition from bidimensional to tridimensional that we encounter the crucial artisanal aspect of our business. There is no substitute for the accumulated experience and craftsmanship of those pattern cutters and technicians in achieving the delicate balance that validates, authenticates or qualifies a designed garment. The designer must have an eye for these subtleties, and an appreciation of the crafts that enables his/her ideas to come into being.

## Cost Analysis

If a seam in the back of a jacket can save 20 per cent in the fabric lay, is it worth doing? Questions of this type represent the difficult but necessary mediation between the defining characteristics of the original idea and the demands of reality. Cost analysis is a challenge to the designer since it requires him/her to devise ingenious solutions and should be regarded as a spur to the creative process, not an impediment.

## Production Opportunities

Although most of our products are manufactured in Italy, we are conscious that in the future there will be a proliferation of opportunities for high-quality production in other parts of the world. Information on new manufacturing and finishing techniques and special processes is part of the research described above, and can stimulate new products, but we must be circumspect regarding, for example potential bottlenecks and other damaging production problems. When we embark on new projects in production, we must verify our willingness and ability to train, and the investment which that entails.

## Marketing

Creating for sale is different from creating for creation's sake. At MaxMara, the product is rigorously defined in relation to the retail concept. There are over 600 MaxMara stores and our organization regards the selling phase as integral to the project. The visual merchandizing and display of proposed products, their coordination and communication are a vital part of the design activity.

## Advertising

The importance of creating in this field is obvious, but more than anywhere else it must be exercised with a view to consistency since our objective is that the product should be immediately recognizable and associated with an absolute, possibly unique, identity. In my experience, the most successful advertising campaigns are those resulting from a very close collaboration between designers, photographers, and those such as stylists who, from an external perspective, can add to this a story, an element of conceived reality. Advertising in the fashion field is, in my opinion, more conventional than in others. Whilst we require it to be new and innovative, conveying an important element of fantasy, imagination and feeling, fashion advertising must also be relatively representative and explicative. To the question 'do advertised garments sell better?' I simply answer: Yes, but mainly if they are original and unusual.

## Promotion

In the field of fashion, promotion means documentation, through the press in general and through the branch of the press that serves it specifically. I recently debated with some American journalists the ideal contents of a fashion publication. Their opinions were, predictably, very different and our discussion returned to the familiar dilemma between dream and reality, between the desire to report extreme and fascinating trends and the need to give useful advice and information to the readership. Everyone agreed on one point: the apparently 'objective' documentation of a product acts as a kind of endorsement or legislation which augments its chances of commercial success. It is therefore critical that an organization such as ours invests in effective communication with the media.

When these elements are synchronized, a circle is completed where creativity can flow freely. Since the creative thought represented by Archimedes' light bulb has always fascinated me, it has been a pleasure to have worked in a field where one can experiment with its deployment. Where these experiments are successful, the results are tangible and I attribute our company's success, in no small part, to the way in which creativity is embedded at the heart of its culture. Further satisfaction is to be gained from the certainty that our experiments will never reach a conclusion. The game will last for ever.

## Notes

1   F. Jullien, *Procès ou création: Un Introduction à la Pensée des lettres chinois*, Paris: Editions du Seuil, 1989.
2   After T. Veblen, *The Theory of the Leisure Class: An Economic Study of Institutions*, London: Allen & Unwin, 1970.
3   A. Hollander, *Sex and Suits*, New York: Alfred A. Knopf, 1994.
4   F. Davis, *Fashion, Culture and Identity*, Chicago: Chicago University Press, 1992.
5   J. Carse, *Giochi finiti e infiniti*, Milan: Arnoldo Mondadore Editore, 1986.
6   C. Breward, *The Culture of Fashion*, Manchester and New York: Manchester University Press, 1995, pp. 22–9.
7   E. Charlie-Roux, *Chanel*, trans N. Amphoux, London: The Harrill Press, 1995.
8   J. Craik, *Cultural Studies in Fashion*, London: Routledge, 1994, p. 60.

# 13    *Jane Roscoe*

# PERFORMING THE "REAL" 24/7

## All About Performance (and Being Famous) ————

> All life is but a rehearsal for television.
> (Quentin Crisp, quoted in Kilborn, 2000: 118)

*Big Brother* is a show that is constructed around performance. With 25 cameras and 36 microphones there is literally nowhere to hide. Those who go into the house know that they are there to perform – for each other, and for the audience watching at home either on the internet or television. There are clearly different levels of performance, as participants are playing a number of different and often contradictory roles. Within the house each has to play the role of 'housemate' which requires them to be a team player and to bond with the group. Housemates have to be liked by the group to enhance their chances of avoiding being nominated for eviction. At the same time, they have to play as a gameshow contestant; after all, there is a prize and there can only be one winner. While the housemates tend to play down this aspect of the show, it is still a key part of the experience. Gameshow contestants are expected to do anything to win, which might include cheating, lying and other deceptions. While the cameras might pick up such activities, each housemate has to keep such activities hidden from the other houseguests. However, as well as managing their images within the house, the housemates also have to perform for the audience who can, potentially, see everything they do.

"Performing the 'Real' 24/7" from Jane Roscoe (2001), "*Big Brother* Australia: Performing the 'Real' Twenty-Four-Seven." *International Journal of Cultural Studies* 4(4), pp. 482–5, 486–7. Reprinted by permission of Sage Publications Ltd. © 2001 by Sage Publications.

There are a number of different levels of performance taking place, not just in terms of individuals, but across the formats of the different shows. The weekday evening shows tend to foreground what might be called the performance of the everyday. Here, we as viewers join in the game of normality – the narratives are constructed around the simulation of the everyday: mealtimes, washing, general emotional ups and downs, deciding on the shopping list and so forth. Here, we might also begin to glimpse some of those contradictions in the roles played by each participant. For example, quite early on in the series, it became clear that Johnny was seen to be the caring and sharing type by the housemates themselves. However, viewers who knew who he had voted for and what he said in the diary room perceived him to be more of an 'operator' – more of a contestant – than the other participants.

*Big Brother* is also about being famous. For some of the houseguests it is a motive for their participation: Andy said she wanted 'money and fame' out of her *Big Brother* experience. For others, fame comes with the experience. As Jemma arrived at the house to be greeted by hundreds of onlookers all screaming and waving, she shouted that she 'felt like a rock star'. As the show progressed there were a number of discussions amongst the housemates about how they imagine their lives will have been changed by the experience of being on the show.

## Developing a Fan Base

*Big Brother* has created an active fan base as well as an audience for the show. The show has rated well with Channel Ten's target audience; in the first five weeks they have managed to secure (and retain) over 50 percent of the 19–39 year olds. However, it is not just that people are watching, but they are participating in a number of ways across the various media platforms.

There are three important ways in which *Big Brother* has allowed for participation on behalf of the audience: through the site at Dreamworld, through Big Brother Online, and through telephone voting. These activities and sites are central to the creation of a fan base. Here I am drawing on the work of Jenkins (1992) and Abercrombie and Longhurst (1998), who see fans as active in their appropriation of texts, critical in their understandings of them, and, importantly, also as a producer rather than a consumer of texts.

The location of the house, production facilities and the studio at Dreamworld allows for a number of different spin-off events and experiences. It brings together entertainment and education, via the location set within the theme park, and is certainly unique in terms of the worldwide *Big Brother* productions. For the fan of the show there are opportunities to go behind the scenes and find out more about how the show is put together. Visitors to the *Big Brother* exhibit are able to view the control room, although they cannot look into the actual house. They can visit a mock-up diary room and have their photograph taken, and share a confession or two (which may be used in a future Saturday or Sunday show) as well as watching live feeds from the house on the giant screens in the auditorium. For the fan visitor it is a chance to engage in what Couldry (2000: 69) calls a 'shared fiction', that is the shared experience of being there. Couldry suggests that this experience is not always about memories or nostalgia, but is an 'anticipated act of commemoration' (2000: 77), an experience to be remembered in the future when watching the show.

Being on-site can enhance the viewing experience and enjoyment of the show because it allows access to the production processes that are so often hidden. Seeing the banks of TV screens in the control room gives a sense of how much material there is, and how little makes the 7pm show. It erodes the usual distinction between viewer and producer by allowing the visitor access to knowledges that are specialized and usually reserved for those working in the industry.

In every *Big Brother* there is always a crowd to greet the week's evictees, but in Australia, the crowd is managed and regulated in quite a specific way. One of the reasons why locating the house at Dreamworld was so attractive was the possibility of using the large auditorium to turn the eviction show into a live event. It has proved to be popular, with the A$20 tickets selling fast each week. The eviction show has evolved into a forum in which a whole range of fan activities can be performed. The live audience are there to be seen, both by the evictee on arrival in the auditorium, but also by the audience at home. They are encouraged to dress-up as their favourite house-mate, conscious that a prize of a A$20,000 entertainment package awaits the best-dressed fan of the series. Sarah-Marie's fans dress in her trademark paja-mas with bunny ears (and often false breasts!) and perform the 'bum-dance' on request from the host, Gretel. Christina's fans often turn up in tutus with signs saying 'Christina Ballerina'. By the time the evictee has reached the auditorium at the end of the show, the crowd has been primed to roar with excitement. For the evictee, it is the first time they will experience 'fame', and their arrival on stage is not unlike the appearance of a pop star at a concert. The fans cheer, the evictee waves and thanks them for being there. What the show does very successfully is to turn the experience of being an audience into an active participation, where the viewer is as much a producer of the text as a consumer of it. This is continued with the use of the website.

The website is a central component of the event that is *Big Brother* and it provides the audience with a range of activities that allow them to construct different relationships with the text and other viewers. 'We never intended to be just a support site for the TV show. It's actually about something extra. . . . More depth is what we like to think. Also, it's a direct interface to viewers and users'.[1] The *Big Brother* website is extensive with activities ranging from the live streams (four cameras and one audio track), through to daily updates on the activities in the house, an archive of all previous stories, chat rooms, open forums, an uncut section, background information on all of the participants, the house and show as well as various shopping sites. You can also vote online (as well as download the theme tune for your mobile phone). Traditional notions of authorship and audience fail to convey the new and diverse ways in which users interact with this material, both consuming and producing these texts.

This highlights an aspect of the programme which is often missed by the media commentators, the kind of literacies it takes for granted. As a media event, *Big Brother* assumes its audience to be highly media-literate. It is assumed that viewers know the show is constructed for television, that they are able to engage with it as a hybrid format, and that they are able to acknowledge it as a performance of the real. There are many moments of self-reflexivity built into the event, from the behind the scenes studio tours, through to the insider gossip on the Saturday show, and the on-screen discussions between the housemates about their experiences of being in front of the cameras 24 hours a day. There has even been a task in which the housemates have had to make a short film. There has been an increasing amount of discussion in the house about how they imagine they are being represented, and some understanding of the processes through which they have become the driving force of the constructed narratives. When housemates leave the house they are often asked to reflect on the experience of being part of a TV show, and to reveal the perceived gap between their 'real' selves and their representations. On balance, they seem better informed than most experimental subjects.

## Big Brother: The Future of Television?

*Big Brother* in Australia is an example of the new fact–fiction hybrid formats that are changing the face of contemporary television. It owes as much to drama (especially soap opera) as it does to the fly-on-the-wall observational documentary, and the gameshow. It treats its audience as knowing, and gives them a central role in the construction of the narrative of the house. It problematizes boundaries between public and private, and between notions of consumers and producers. As a media event it has successfully developed across various media platforms, and through its association with a theme park has created a new forum for audiences. In this way, it must be seen as a precursor to fully interactive TV and a prototype for future media events, as well as both a symptom of, and a response to, changes in fictional and factual programming in global TV. These changes are not unique to Australia, but detailed analysis of the local can help us to understand the broader significance of such forms. In doing so, we open up the debate about popular factual entertainment programming to move beyond the simplistic political commentary that currently pervades the public sphere.

## References

Abercrombie, N. and B. Longhurst (1998) *Audiences*. London: Sage.
Couldry, N. (2000) *The Place of Media Power*. London: Routledge.
Jenkins, H. (1992) *Textual Poachers: Television Fans and Participatory Culture*. London: Routledge.
Kilborn, R. (2000) 'The Docusoap: A Critical Reassessment', in J. Izod, R. Kilborn and M. Hibberd (eds.), *From Grierson to the Docusoap: Breaking the Boundaries*, pp. 111–20. Luton: Luton University Press.

## Notes

1  Interview with Louise O'Donnell, Executive Producer of BBOnline, 22 May 2001.

# PART IV
## Creative Cities

*Jinna Tay*

# CREATIVE CITIES

Creative cities are spaces you want to be in, places to be seen. Their work-shops, restaurants, and bars are both the "most superficial manifestations of a creative environment" (Leadbeater and Oakley 1999: 31) and the signposts of a dynamic and vibrant lifestyle. Beyond their "scenes," creative cities also possess various characteristics: the existence of a vibrant arts and cultural sector; capacity to generate employment and output in the service and cul-ture industries (Sassen 1995); and policy initiatives concerned with the distri-bution of resources between global and local demands (Leadbeater and Oakley 1999). Broadly, "creative cities" is about how local urban spaces can be reimagined, rejuvenated and re-purposed within a competitive global framework (Crewe and Beaverstock 1998; Abbas 2000).

The city has traditionally been studied from within the disciplines of archi-tecture, sociology, and urban planning, both within the academy and in policy reform units. Each carries its own set of historical and ideological concerns, which influence how the city is conceived. Where they meet is in a common development ambition, articulated through policy initiatives aimed at bringing the city to greater regional or global prominence. Concern over how the new economy may impact on the local has also played a part in directing attention toward the city as a possible site for social and eco-nomic renewal (Brown et al. 2000; King 1996; Kong and Law 2002; Pratt 2000; Zukin 1995). Creative city policies therefore need to be understood as filtered through national (or sub-national) continua of social, political, and economic objectives. The establishment of a creative milieu (networks, en-terprises, and entrepreneurs) is frequently identified as the means of meeting development outcomes – a means to prosperity.

Within the literature on cities, much attention has been focused on the dynamic between local and global forces and how international flows in trade, goods, information, and culture are impacting upon local spaces (private and public). In this introduction, I will discuss some of the implications of this dynamic, including the tensions arising between cultural and national identities, formalized citizenship and creative freedom, policy directives and naturally evolving creative quarters. The first thing to recognize is that cities are sites where shifts in social and economic processes (such as reflexive consumption), developmental strategies (clusters and networks), and emerging spaces (in cities and urban sectors) can be observed. Therefore, while the concept of the creative city was intended as a template for urban renewal and budding cosmopolitanism, it also provides a language through which to speak of such transitions and their opportunities. Furthermore, creative cities highlight the significance of consumption-led economics, cultural production and what it means to design urban space. In many respects, the city has been viewed as a signifier of change and progress at key junctures throughout history. Reading the city in this way is not new, even if the idea of a creative city is a relatively recent project.

## A Short Detour through the City

In 1851 and 1855 World "Expo" Fairs were held in London and Paris respectively, signaling important transformations for both cities. People traveled to the Expo from surrounding areas to marvel at and be entertained by the latest in trade, as well as scientific and technological innovation (transportation, textiles, imported goods). The Expo succeeded in drawing people to these wares as never before, contributing to the development of mercantile capitalism, nineteenth-century modernity, and a shift in the way the public itself was understood. Through the Expo, the "populace" became "consumers" (Bowlby 1985). It was a historical juncture in the structural development of urban spaces, growth in trade, consumption, and innovation.

Around this time, private commerce and political change (such as citizenship rights) were shaping cities from the ground level up. Improvements ranged from architectural design to better transport and communication systems. As a result of these changes, entrepreneurial innovation, consumption, and a new level of accessibility became the defining features of the modern metropolis. For instance, innovations in glass, electric lighting and building technologies meant that London became taller and better lit (Bowlby 1985). Old boundaries and gateways were demolished, paving the way for a "faster," "more uniform," "improved" London (interconnected by the world's first underground railway). The changes were implemented for the purposes of commerce and wealth-creation, but, as Peter Ackroyd (2001) points out in his biography of London, they also made London an accessible and "public city."

Improving the physical spaces, designs, and structures of the city further induced development across different sectors of the urban economy. Francis Place, an early nineteenth-century London radical and democratic reformer, observed that "progress made in refinement of manners and morals seems to have gone on simultaneously with the improvement in arts, manufactures and commerce" (Ackroyd 2001: 522). While there are no clear measurements of these historical transformations, Victorian London seemed "less gross and brutal" than its preceding era with "an abatement of observable vice and squalor" (see Ackroyd 2001: 522–3). It is entirely possible that the vice, squalor, and poverty had merely been moved "behind the scenes" (Ackroyd 2001: 523). However, this does not preclude the fact that the aesthetic manifestation of change was important in preparing imperial London for its advancement toward modernity, adding to its status as the world's first "great metropolis."

## Cities as Anchors

This historical detour signals some key aspects of the current interest in creative cities:

- locations (cities) retain their significance in economic and creative development;
- consumption and innovation are implicated in strategies for social, economic, and political revitalization;
- people need face to face interaction, socialization, and networks to create synergies.

All three points can be identified among the articles in this section, revolving around the idea that geographical location remains relevant in the new knowledge economy (Gilbert 2000; Porter 1998; Pratt 2000). This idea is at odds with the early popular assumption that technological advancement in communications, e-commerce, and electronic solutions would make geographical limits redundant. Urban geographer Andy Pratt (2000) suggests that on the whole, "none . . . seem to be able to sustain the popular argument that geography, or specifically place and distance, no longer matters" (Pratt 2000: 425). Pratt's work examines the importance of social networks among new media developers in Silicon Alley. Louise Crewe and Jonathan Beaverstock (1998) argue that the night-time economy at the Nottingham Lace Market is underpinned by social and business networks embedded within cultural production. In both cases, the city is the site for local agency. The concept of "creative cities" thus refutes the death-of-distance thesis whereby everyone everywhere will have equal access to economic opportunities.

Michael Porter (2000) writes that places where creative clusters and networks are found are gaining competitive success overall. This is in spite of the fact that business inputs (resources, capital, and technology) can now be provided by global markets, and that businesses and individuals are presented with opportunities to bypass local economies. The "clusters" concept is realized often through the rejuvenation of old industrial quarters in cities such as Dublin, Sheffield, Newcastle, Austin, Tijuana, Mexico, Helsinki, and Antwerp. Existing features such as manufacturing infrastructure (warehouses and tailoring) and past-time music collections become new inputs (loft spaces, fashion and design skills, music archives) for the redevelopment of industry through culture (Leadbeater and Oakley 1999; Sassen 1995). In this way, creative city policies can provide opportunities for regional and old industrial cities to connect with the new economy; to regenerate their industries or create new ones.

Charles Leadbeater and Kate Oakley, in *The Independents* (1999), list possibilities for policy formation that not only generate creative sectors but, more importantly, cultivate and sustain them (see "Innovative Cities"). They recognize that "investment in cultural industries is a cumulative process which requires policy makers to be flexible rather than . . . fixed plan" (Leadbeater and Oakley 1999: 37). This means utilizing strategies such as clusters and networks theory within larger policy contexts. The creative milieu, defined as "a shared space and tradition in which people can learn, compare compete and collaborate and through which ideas can be proposed, developed, disseminated and rejected" (Leadbeater and Oakley 1999: 31), is critical to the building of networks and creative clusters. Beyond the business-related aspects, the networks within a milieu are a way to "embed in people the distinctive, shared, tacit knowledge that make up a distinctive style, sound or look for which a city can become known: the Mersey sound, Manchester, Britart in Hoxton" (Leadbeater and Oakley 1999: 14). Creative milieux involve the formation of social and informal networks that enable know-how, relationship reciprocity, and the use of middlemen to facilitate ideas. Through this, the uniqueness of local cultural products can be recognized and distributed.

## Local Clusters in a Global Economy: Michael Porter

A dimension of this development is the cluster theory – a central element of geographically based innovation that was refined by Michael Porter of the Harvard Business School. Porter (2000) defines clusters as "geographic concentrations of interconnected companies, specialized suppliers, service providers, firms in related industries, and associated institutions (e.g. universities, standards agencies, trade associations) in a particular field that compete but also cooperate" (Porter 2000: 15). Porter sees the competitive advantages that accrue from successful cluster development as being threefold:

- they increase the productivity of firms within the cluster through access to specialist inputs, labor, knowledge, and technology;
- they promote innovation by making all firms more quickly aware of new opportunities and enhance the capacity for rapid and flexible responses to those opportunities;
- they promote new business formation in related sectors through access to the necessary labor, skills, knowledge, technology, and capital.

An issue raised but not resolved by Porter's work on cluster development is the relationship between creativity and innovation in the development of economically dynamic cities and regions. Put differently, is there a relationship between the cultural vibrancy of cites and regions and their economic dynamism? And if so, what are the best ways for governments to combine industrial and cultural development?

Creative cities policy has also been significant in conceptualizing frameworks and driving ideas for promotion and publicity. Policy consultancy work such as Leadbeater and Oakley's *The Independents*, Charles Landry's *The Creative City*, and Richard Florida's *The Rise of the Creative Class* have served to foster and embed notions of innovation and creative milieux. However, the formulation of creative policy strategies offers no miracle cure. Policy intervention needs to be balanced by knowledge of the particular cultural sector and the operative processes of the creative grassroots.

One not-so-successful example of this difficult task was seen in Britain in the 1990s. Pinning economic recovery and revitalization on its growing creative industries, which are clustered disproportionately in London, the "New Labour" government of Tony Blair was moved in 1997 to imagine a

"Cool Britannia" that would "brand" British-made culture in order to make an impact on the global market (McRobbie 2000: 253). But the move was rejected by many working within the creative industries. As *Vogue* put it at the time: "the prodigious wealth of talent and all that is excellent in this country needs no fanfare. We know we're cool" (Brampton 1998: 137).

However, the Singapore government, always quick to note global trends, was not far behind the UK. By 1999 it announced its Renaissance City Report, noting that, "to ensure sustained growth in the long run, Singapore must forge an environment that is conducive to innovations, new discoveries and the creation of new knowledge" (<http://www.mita.gov.sg/renaissance/ES.htm>). Goh Chok-Tong, prime minister of Singapore, argued that "a culturally vibrant city attracts global creative talent" which is needed in the building of a knowledge-based economy. Seemingly, both the British and Singapore governments viewed the creative industries as a means to invigorate growth and to stimulate local economies. However, while the British attempt to promote local cultural commodities (music, media, publishing, fashion, software, design, lifestyle) met with mixed feelings from its own cultural commentators, the Singapore strategy is showing signs of being a cultural watershed. By focusing on its emergent arts and culture scene, the Singapore government hopes to expand local creativity in addition to attracting global creative personnel and retaining entrepreneurs in an effort to create a more cosmopolitan city-state (Goh, National Day Rally, 2002).

Although the creative city template can be replicated, its success will largely depend on how it deals with long-standing development questions, such as economic and social sustainability, gentrification and local displacement, exclusionary practices, and local identities. It is clear that an amount of dexterity in policy formulation is required. In Asia, a recurring question is how to deal with democratic practices. Creative expression may come up against conservative systems or ideological cultural bias, which may act to smother the natural diversity of creativity.

## London as a Creative City: Charles Landry

Charles Landry delivered this paper at a conference organized by Hong Kong's Central Policy Unit in 2001. It demonstrates the creative cities agenda at work, using the London experience to outline the benefits and issues for creative development. Although London has been a creative center for centuries, creative industries policy represents the first attempt to treat the seemingly disparate sector as a coherent and

powerful force. Landry provides a useful overview of the creative industries sector in London and the "cool factor" that has made the city a
destination for both creative workers and tourists.

One of the more significant problems facing creative industries
development in London is the availability of affordable housing
and workspaces. The city has already witnessed the gentrification of
creative hubs. Local authorities are faced with a situation where they
must devise methods for ensuring that creative activity remains part
of the mix.

## Local Cities, Global Spaces

Cities operate as nodes in a global network with the potential to direct the
flow of international and local traffic in commodities, ideas, and services.
Saskia Sassen stresses that cities today are playing an increasingly important
role in "linking national economies with global circuits" (Sassen 2002: 2). In
this scenario, the global is privileged at the expense of the national. New
global economics such as banking and services replace the typically older
nationalized manufacturing core, reinforcing global cities as "key sites for the
production of services for firms" (Sassen 1998: 65). Sassen is concerned that
global capital and cultures reproduce "existing forms of inequalities" as well
as dissonance within local cityscapes. For example, governments introduce
new legal structures to attract global capital to cities. This contests the rights,
entitlements, and membership of the nation's citizens.

It is important to take into account these broader shifts in geographic
centrality and marginality. Such a critique raises complex needs within urban
redistribution strategies. However, it is also necessary to understand the full
value chain of consumption practices. A specific study from the other end –
consumption – which looks at the local uses made of city spaces and creative
practices can yield other alternative and active forms of resistance and
expression.

Changing patterns of consumption, shaped by and contributing to globalization, are reinventing the systemic practice of business and its attendant;
production processes (see Hartley's introduction to part II of this volume).
Consumption-led economic strategies are altering conventional business
practices. Crewe and Beaverstock (1998) argue that, "Increasingly, what distinguishes places from one another is the strength of their 'consumptional
identities' . . . as places are reconstructed and sold not as centers of production
but of consumption" (p. 289). It is consumption – symbolic, innovative, and

self-directed – that dictates the success and allure of creative places. Concentrating on the Nottingham Lace Market, they highlight the creative strategies of the old industrial quarter and how policy strategies are mediating the ground-level-up synergies of local firms, creative entrepreneurs, and networks. Crewe and Beaverstock argue that it is in these unique and creative locales that local "taste constellations" are being formed and becoming embedded within a system of cultural consumption and production:

> Consumption spaces are fascinating precisely because they reflect cultural as well as economic processes, and the constant shifts in the meanings and practice of particular places reminds us that "the building and revolutionizing of an urban landscape is never just physical and economic; it is also social, cultural and political" ... (p. 290)

In other words, consumption, which has always straddled the spaces of economic practices and cultural reflexivity, has been further incorporated into social spaces where sites of identity formation, social memberships and subcultural affiliations are found.

## Cities and Networks

Holston and Appadurai (1996) argue that, "In some places, the nation itself is no longer a successful arbiter of citizenship ... the project of a national society of citizens, especially liberalism's ... appears increasingly exhausted and discredited" (p. 188). Into this fragmented spatial structure enter competing identity formation processes – some global and cosmopolitan, others differentiated and niche – but becoming more relevant and accessible at a community level.

This renewed focus on social identities also manifests in lifestyle and service consumption practices – cafés, restaurants, bars, tourism, the night-time economy. Cities that offer lifestyle and a creative sector but which "still have affordable loft spaces and cheap beer" (Ward 2002) will attract a greater number of creative workers and diverse communities. As an article in the British *Guardian* newspaper pointed out, "A city with artists, a nightlife, diversity will also draw entrepreneurs, academics, tech geeks – those able to drive economic growth in the new age" (Ward 2002). This social aspect of the creative industries links the cultural network to economic and creative production.

These networks are forms of "social capital" (Brown et al. 2000: 446). Brown, O'Connor, and Cohen have pointed out that cheap rents and proximity to the city center, key venues, and services are reasons why creative clusters are emerging in places such as Mexico City, Austin, Newcastle, Dublin, and Cape Town, allowing them to compete for creative city status. Although such conditions set the tone for experimentation and innovation, creative cities also require a cohesive policy framework set within the cultural context to allow fruition of creativity.

In a study of the Cultural Industries Quarter (CIQ) in Sheffield and the Northern Quarter (NQ) in Manchester, Brown et al. (2000) discuss the application of the creative city template to old industrial "smoke-stack" cities. Networks and clusters, both socially and commercially, are vital to the growth of local industry. These networks provide socially embedded knowledge, information, and experiences which are often collaborative yet competitive. For instance, they argue that "networks are about how the sector interacts... knowledge is passed around... ideas, sounds, 'product' are tested, validated, given credibility" (p. 445).

They warn that policy interventions often ignore the complex networks within cultural scenes, which, they argue, are more vital to the embedding of creativity than "hard" infrastructures such as facilities. Cultural policies need to focus on the local, place-based networks that encourage integral synergies. These are the "soft" infrastructure – people, social networks, and business skills. It is these informal yet important links that span both social and business relationships which are capable of embedding a culture of innovation in the local context. A further drawback for locals is the prospect of gentrification and soaring property prices, with newcomers outbidding and alienating the original inhabitants (also discussed by Sassen 1995; Zukin 1995).

## Cities, Culture and Transitional Economies: Developing Cultural Industries in St. Petersburg: Justin O'Connor

In this reading, Justin O'Connor reflects upon a creative industries partnership project between Manchester (UK) and St. Petersburg (Russia). His account highlights the interventional aspects of creative cities policy, showing how creativity can be mobilized for economic growth by local government initiatives and intermediaries. This is not always a straightforward process.

Creative industries' ambitions can be at odds with existing cultural frameworks and assumptions. St. Petersburg experienced an abrupt introduction to the global economy after the collapse of communism and, as a result, does not possess the strong civil society structures and networks that characterize markets and creative enterprise in western Europe. Although Russia is no longer a communist state, the legacy of earlier power structures can be seen in the lack of intermediaries between the state and the people and a general distrust for those that do exist. Added to this is a long-standing anti-commercial approach to culture, seen in both the dominant elite arts and counter-culture. O'Connor describes this as an implicit dimension of the cultural "narratives" of St. Petersburg. The city is known for its world-famous institutions and architecture, a place where people can "pursue cultural interests for their own sake." The state has historically demonstrated paternalistic support for high culture which has become embedded in the city's identity, not just as national identity but as a sphere where transcendence of state ideology was permissible. As a result, the arts have been important in the creation of St. Petersburg's identity and, for its people, a reassurance in hard times. The European separation of "culture" and "entertainment" (see "Creative Industries") is therefore pronounced in Russia – a significant hurdle for creative industries.

## Emerging Creative Cities

Even as regional cities are discarding their old industrial image, previously self-contained economies are emerging as local contenders for global status. Shanghai opened up to the world after almost 40 years of relative isolation. It aims to reclaim its former status as the "Pearl of the Orient" – a global, cosmopolitan city. The city is attempting to strategically build a future that taps into the economics of global cities and their attendant functions, employing aspects of the creative industries template. Shanghai is located in the mid-range of the global hierarchy, which allows us "to capture a dynamic in formation, unlike what is the case with global cities already well established" (Sassen 2002: 3). This is demonstrated in Shanghai by the spate of rapid urban development. The architectural ethos of Shanghai, which began in the early 1990s, is a planned attempt to build a "faster," "more uniform," and improved city. It was certainly fast: in 2001, a quarter of the world's cranes were located in Shanghai, where over 1,000 buildings of greater than 20 stories were completed within one year – a rate of four new skyscrapers a day.

## Cosmopolitan De-scriptions: Shanghai and Hong Kong: Ackbar Abbas

In his analysis of Shanghai, Ackbar Abbas uses a comparative, historical approach of extraterritorial legality in order to explore the underlying tensions between Shanghai and Hong Kong. In the past, cosmopolitanism was displayed through the negotiation of colonial powers residing in Shanghai. Interestingly, the notion of "cosmopolitan" has re-emerged as a gauge of success. His account of the processes of change in Hong Kong and Shanghai retreats from policy analysis and toward discourses of everyday lived spaces. As Holston and Appadurai (1996: 189) maintain, these are "the lived spaces not only of its uncertainties but also of its emergent forms."

This is captured by Abbas in various snapshots of the reconstructive process. He substantiates the idea that cities have always been "stages for politics of a different sort than their hinterlands" (Holston and Appadurai 1996: 189) or nation. He shows what is at stake in the effort to be both cosmopolitan and to maintain a local identity – from the tensions surrounding the role of the nation-state to the looming question of Hong Kong's global and financial viability as Shanghai rises. Long-standing issues of marginality in city spaces – where squalor contrasts with splendor (the dominance of wealth and power) – are now revealed within the context of a local/global divide, through space and identities.

Abbas uses Lee Ou-Fan's historical reinterpretations of the 1930s Shanghai cosmopolitanism where the locals were, in a sense, cultural bricoleurs who took advantage of the colonial extraterritoriality system to create distinct and hybridized cultures for themselves. The cosmopolitan experience in early Shanghai is inconsistent with the dominant radical accounts of a subjugated community. As Abbas argues, "cosmopolitanism in Shanghai could be understood, *not* as the cultural domination by the foreign but as the appropriation by the local of elements of foreign culture to enrich a new national culture" (Abbas 2000: 775). Within a cosmopolitan culture, he portrays citizens as being active participants in self-creation, consciously aware of how to make their own meanings and identities, resisting generalized accounts of locals as victims. Historical reinterpretations such as Abbas's substantially shift our perception of the past.

Historical preservation of Shanghai's past glory thus takes a significant place in its present constructions. As a city undergoing rapid development, heritage preservation is given priority. Abbas argues that

Shanghai's interest in preservation shows a link between the geographical-spatial dimensions of the city and its aspirational desires. He describes how the new Shanghai Museum is dramatically different visually from its surroundings, demonstrating the global and local divide. Shanghai strives to become part of "a virtual global cultural network" (p. 782), showing itself off to the world through its museum. Local citizens, however, may be alienated from this space, leading him to argue that the rapidity of globalization in emerging cities may create "transnationalism without a corresponding transnational subject" (p. 783). For Abbas, this raises concerns over how local citizens might renegotiate these global spaces while attempting to make sense of their culture and identity.

The articles in this section show that the path to prosperity is complex for global, regional, and emerging cities. In some respects, the realization of the creative city and the identities it seeks to cultivate must already be present in the existing local context. However, it is in the development of flexible cultural policy the recognition of new economic "actors" (such as cultural production and consumption, networks, reflexive identities) that the city can be successfully, and creatively, reimagined.

## References

Abbas, A. (2000) Cosmopolitan De-scriptions: Shanghai and Hong Kong. *Public Culture* 12(3), 769–86.

Ackroyd, P. (2001) *London: the Biography*. Vintage, London.

Bowlby, R. (1985) *Just Looking: Consumer Cultural in Dreiser, Gissing and Zola*. Methuen, New York.

Brampton, S. (1998) There Is No British Style. *Vogue* 2399/164 (June), 137.

Brown, A., J. O'Connor, and S. Cohen (2000) Local Music Policies within a Global Music Industry: Cultural Quarters in Manchester and Sheffield. *Geoforum* 31, 437–51.

Chrisafis, A. (2001) Manchester Rises from the Ashes. *Guardian*, Friday, January 5.

Coyle, D. (1997) *The Weightless World: Strategies for Managing the Digital Economy*. Capstone, Oxford.

Crewe, L. and J. Beaverstock (1998) Fashioning the City: Cultures of Consumption in Contemporary Urban Spaces. *Geoforum* 29(3) [Elsevier Science], 287–308.

*Economist* (1998) Britain: In London's Shadow. *The Economist*, August 1, 48–50.

Florida, R. (2002) *The Rise of the Creative Class and How It's Transforming Work, Leisure, Community and Everyday Life*. Basic Books, New York.

Gilbert, D. (2000) Urban Outfitting: The City and the Spaces of Fashion Culture. In S. Bruzzi and P. C. Gibson (eds.), *Fashion Cultures: Theories, Explorations and Analysis.* Routledge, London, 7–24.

Goh, C. T. (2000) Remaking Singapore – Changing Mindsets. National Day Rally Address, Singapore Government Press Release, MITA University Cultural Centre, NUS, August 18, 2002.

Holston, J. and A. Appadurai (1996) Cities and Citizenship. *Public Culture* 8(2), 187–204.

King, A. D. (ed.) (1996) *Representing the City: Ethnicity, Capital and Culture in the Twenty-First Century Metropolis.* Macmillan, London.

Kong, L., and L. Law (2002) Introduction: Contested Landscapes Asian Cities. *Urban Studies* 39(9), 1503–12.

Landry, C. (2000) *The Creative City: A Toolkit for Urban Innovators.* Comedia, London

Landry, C. (2001) London as a Creative City. Paper presented at *Cultures of World Cities,* Central Policy Unit, Hong Kong, July 31, 2001, <www.info.gov.hk/cpu/english/culcities.htm> (accessed February 19, 2004).

Leadbeater, C. and K. Oakley (1999) *The Independents: Britain's New Cultural Entrepreneurs.* Demos/Institute of Contemporary Arts, London.

McRobbie, A. (2000) Fashion as a Culture Industry. In S. Bruzzi and P. C. Gibson (eds.), *Fashion Cultures: Theories, Explorations and Analysis.* Routledge, London, 253–63.

O'Connor, J. (2004) Cities, Culture and Transitional Economies: Developing Cultural Industries in St. Petersburg. In D. Power and A. J. Scott (eds.), *Cultural Industries and the Production of Culture.* Routledge, London.

Porter, M. (1998) Clusters and the New Economics of Competition. *Harvard Business Review* 76(6), 77–91.

Porter, M. (2000) Location, Competition, and Economic Development: Local Clusters in a Global Economy. *Economic Development Quarterly,* 14(1), 15–34.

Pratt, A. C. (2000) New Media, the New Economy and New Spaces. *Geoforum* 31, 425–36.

Sassen, S. (1995) On Concentration and Centrality in the Global City. In P. L. Knox and P. J. Taylor (eds.), *World Cities in a World-System.* Cambridge University Press, Cambridge, 63–78.

Sassen, S. (1998) Introduction: Whose City Is It? Globalisation and the Formation of New Claims. In *Globalization and its Discontents.* The New Press, New York, pp. xix–xxxvi.

Sassen, S. (ed.) (2002) Introduction: Location Cities on Global Circuits. In *Global Networks, Linked Cities.* Routledge, New York, 1–38.

Singapore Ministry of Information the Arts (MITA). Renaissance City report, Executive Summary, <http://www.mita.gov.sg/renaissance/ES.htm> (accessed July 31, 2003).

Ward, D. (2002) Forget Paris and London, Newcastle Is a Creative City to Match Kabul and Tijuana. *Guardian,* Monday, September 2 (accessed August 9, 2003).

Zukin, S. (1995) *The Cultures of Cities.* Blackwell, Oxford.

# 14  *Charles Landry*

# LONDON AS A CREATIVE CITY

## Creative Cities Overview: Twin Tracks, Same Destination

The London creative city agenda is involved with two of the most complicated words in the English language – culture and creativity. Creativity is an overused concept difficult to define or grasp and often only associated with the arts. Briefly, genuine creativity involves the capacity to think problems afresh or from first principles; to discover common threads amidst the seemingly chaotic and disparate; to experiment; to dare to be original; the capacity to rewrite rules; to visualize future scenarios; and perhaps most importantly "to work at the edge of one's competences rather than the centre of them."

These ways of thinking encourage urban innovations and generate new possibilities. Differing types of creativity are needed to develop and address the complexities of a world city, which continuously needs to deal with conflicting interests and objectives. This might be the creativity of scientists to solve problems related to pollution or that of planners to generate new urban policy; that of engineers to solve technical problems concerned say with transport; that of artists to help reinforce the identity of a place or spur the imagination; that of business people to generate new products or services that enhance wealth-creation possibilities; as well as those working in the

"London as a Creative City" by Charles Landry. Paper presented at *Cultures of World Cities*, Central Policy Unit, Hong Kong, July 31, 2001, <www.info.gov.hk/cpu/english/culcities.htm> (accessed February 19, 2004). Reprinted by permission of Charles Landry.

Charles Landry is the author of *The Creative City: A Toolkit for Urban Innovators* (Earthscan, London, 2000); *Riding the Rapids: Urban Dynamics in an Age of Complexity* (CABE/RIBA, London 2004); and, with Marc Pachter, *Culture @ the Crossroads: Culture and Cultural Institutions at the Beginning of the 21st Century* (Comedia, Bournes Green, 2001).

social domain in order to develop social innovations that might help with issues such as social fragmentation.

Thus creative solutions can come from any source, whether from within the worlds of the public, private, or voluntary sectors or from individuals operating on their own behalf. The key issue is for a city to provide the conditions within which creativity can flourish.

The term culture is even more elusive because it has multiple meanings. On the one hand there is the notion of "culture and development" and on the other "cultural development." The first is about beliefs, traditions, and ways of living and how these affect behavior and the things people do. So when we talk of "culture and urban development in London or Hong Kong" we are discussing the relationship between cultural factors and their development and how these influence each other. For example, if Hong Kong were to have low self-esteem and confidence this would be a cultural factor determining how it develops. Equally if being imaginative is not legitimized, or alternatively if a technocratic mindset is allowed to dominate, these would be cultural factors shaping London's or Hong Kong's future.

Thus all development is cultural as it reflects the way people perceive their problems and opportunities. Culture is central, because it "is the sum total of original solutions a group of human beings invent to adapt to their . . . environment and circumstances."

For cities, especially global cities, to thrive in the twenty-first century, there is a need for a culture of creativity – the capacity to think afresh when your world seems to be undergoing a paradigm shift, high ambition, entrepreneurship and opportunity, beauty and acute sensitivity to high-quality urban design, all of which shape their physical and social environment.

This implies thinking through social, political, and cultural as well as economic and technological creativity. It means power-holders need to devolve power and to trade it for creative influence within a framework of guiding strategic principles within which it is possible to be tactically flexible. It thus affects a city's organizational culture. This cultural capital represents the raw materials and scope within which the creativity of people in, say, London or Hong Kong can operate.

Typically, creative cities have a number of characteristics which frame the possibilities for the arts more narrowly defined. They include:

- developing a clarity of purpose and ambition
- fostering visionary individuals and organizations
- being open-minded and willing to take risks
- being strategically principled and tactically flexible

- being determined in planning rather than deterministic, thus being antici-
  patory
- being willing to recognize and work with local cultural resources and
  local distinctiveness
- ensuring that leadership is widespread
- moving from a high-blame culture to a low-blame one.

On the other hand there is "cultural development" in its humanistic and
artistic dimension, including the arts as an empowering, self-expressive activity, the arts as helping provide meaning, purpose, and direction, the arts as
fostering aesthetic appreciation, or the arts as creative industries. Today these
elements are intimately connected to the objectives above. Firstly because the
arts encourage a particular form of critical imagination and innovation, which
needs to be embedded more deeply into city's culture if it wants to become a
"learning city" that develops on from past mistakes. Secondly, the arts are
concerned with quality, attractiveness, performance, and beauty and the design of our environment and how it is animated. Thirdly, the arts and creative industries play a role both as economic engines of growth and in terms
of their social impacts. As a consequence the arts and culture in this narrower
sense affect as well as draw on the work of other fields, from economic
development to health and planning.

## London as a Creative City

An array of studies on London have shown that London is a city of world
status in cultural terms. It has a diversified, sophisticated, and internationally
oriented cultural industries structure that nurtures and supports a wealth of
local and international artistic activity – commercial, subsidized, and voluntary. Importantly this hive of activity creates the buzz, vibrancy, and sub-
cultures that make London attractive and contribute to its standing as a
world city economically, socially, and culturally.

In London 680,000 people work in the creative industries, representing 15
percent of the London economy and nearly 20 percent of the workforce and
a turnover of between £25 billion and £29 billion. It has 12 percent of the
UK's population but 40 percent of its arts infrastructure, 70 percent of its
music recording studios, and 90 percent of music business activity, 70 percent
of the UK's film and television production, 46 percent of advertising, 85
percent of fashion designers, and 27 percent of architectural practices.

The occupations with the greatest increases over the last decade have been
"clothing designers," up 88 percent over the period; "artists, commercial

artists and graphic designers," up 71 percent; "actors, entertainers, stage managers, producers and directors," up 47 percent; and "authors, writers, and journalists," up 43 percent. To this must be added the massively increased number of people working in multimedia, an industry that hardly existed in 1991, the date of the last census. There was also a particularly marked increase among the self-employed, up 81 percent.

Overseas earnings are estimated at £3,852 million against imports of £2,522, leaving a net balance £1,300 million. There are believed to be around 11,700 cultural industry companies and groups in London, in addition to around 25,700 self-employed people.

London has been a creative center for several centuries, its store of talent continually replenished through domestic and foreign immigration in order to feed this machine. It thus vacuums up global and domestic talent with ever-shifting artistic quarters rising and falling, but over time these quarters are being pushed to the periphery.

London's cosmopolitan richness – from Jews to Indians to the new knowledge workers to asylum-seekers – has helped develop and sustain its role as a creative world city. Indeed, Greater London residents speak over 300 languages with nearly 50 communities of over 10,000.

Throughout London evidence of this contribution is visible in historic buildings, older craft forms, food, traditions, and cultural expressions such as the Notting Hill Carnival, the jewelers in Hatton Garden, Little Italy in Clerkenwell, Fournier Street in Spitalfields, the furniture-makers in Shoreditch, and pottery in Southwark.

Equally important is how the creation of the City of London's financial and banking power was supported by immigrant groups, as well as how new trades, skills, and products have helped underpin London's economic strength. Today this process continues, though the technologies are different. Multimedia, film, and music talent is both home-grown as well as drawing in outsiders to London.

At the same time London has the most unequal distribution of wealth of any city in the UK, 13 of the 20 most deprived districts in the UK, 64 percent of the most deprived housing estates, the highest level of homelessness, and 40 percent of urban crime.

A mass of investments, some undertaken in the last century within an ethos of public provision for self-improvement, as well as in the more recent decades and latterly through the National Lottery – approaching £1 billion over seven years – has given London a wealth of museums and galleries, internationally renowned theater, opera, and ballet companies, a number of major symphony orchestras, and an unsurpassed concentration of live theater in and around the West End as well as a world-respected training infrastructure for the arts.

The National Lottery has been a crucial element in reviving London's subsidized cultural infrastructure. The new Tate Modern, the courtyard at the British Museum, the wing at the Science Museum, Somerset House and the Gilbert Collection, the refurbished National Portrait Gallery, Sadler's Wells ballet, Covent Garden opera house, and Shakespeare's Globe are just some institutions which have benefited from its largesse. These are the more traditional building-based institutions, and a debate is currently underway to support more radical, innovative art projects and activities. For example only 1.2 percent of lottery funding since its inception in 1993 has gone to ethnic minority groups in London, although they represent 30 percent of the population. However the current allocation for this year is set to rise to 20 percent.

Importantly London is also internationally recognized for its popular culture and its sub-cultures, often cosmopolitan in nature, especially in music, comedy, alternative theater, design, and fashion. London's cultural creativity is not only concentrated in the center, but also in most inner suburbs such as Hackney, Islington, Camden Town, Brixton, and Hammersmith and more recently south of the Thames to Southwark and Deptford. Indeed London's center has largely become a focus for consuming rather than making culture and in some senses is completely uncreative, with the productively creative hubs spread across the inner ring abutting the center. Yet even here a major crisis looms as property prices have increased, causing severe problems for artists or incubating firms that essentially anchor London's contemporary creativity.

Although the idea that London is the "coolest capital in the world" (*Newsweek*) is overblown, as it is subject to fashion (for example on the DJ scene Paris is now setting the pace), it has an element of truth. It is the "cool factor," the young innovators who need those cheaper places to operate from, who form a significant part of the image a city exudes.

This wealth of provision offers not only residents opportunities for participation and spectating, but also is a major attractor for tourists.

London has strengths in all the industrial areas which sell reproducible products, such as records, television programs, or corporate videos. The music business, largely based in London, is one of Britain's largest export industries; London is Europe's center for the commercial audio-visual and the corporate communications area; and its design consultancies and advertising agencies which operate on a world-wide basis include some of the world's largest companies. However, London is relatively weak in film production and in picking up on the new multi-media opportunities that are emerging based on computer developments where the US may be developing a stranglehold.

A major problem for the creative cultural industries, and a problem for London too, is that until recently the sector was rarely viewed as an integrated one in policy-making terms. Theater, the visual arts, music, filmmaking, or design and fashion are seen as separate sectors without recognition of the interconnections between them. Creative artists often work across different cultural fields. A musician, for example, may perform at a live orchestral concert at one moment, then as a recording studio musician in record production, and later as a musician involved in a film score. A graphic artist may produce advertising copy, then pictures for individual sale, acting in this sense as a "pure" artist, and then produce covers for records or film publicity. The creative products themselves are now usually not confined to one medium. Most are cross-media products: the book of the play, the film of the book, the record of the film, and so on. Underpinning this convergence and cross-media recycling is the way the cultural industries themselves are being linked to and shaped by the development of the communication, computing, and "knowledge" industries. It is increasingly frequent for creative people to work in teams across disciplines and move between them, as has traditionally happened between, for example, actors in the theater, radio, and television. Looked at in isolation each sector may seem relatively small, but looked at as a group they are powerful. Compared to the situation in other world cities, London's cultural economy is in second position after New York. Its particular strengths are in the performing arts and music, and, increasingly, the visual arts. At the moment London is certainly seen as the world leader in street fashion and pop culture.

## Why are the Cultural Industries and Cultural Activities Now Seen as Important?

Four years ago the government acknowledged the central role of the sector for the future of the UK economy by setting up a Creative Industries Task Force. This has attempted to track activity on a consistent basis and to develop policy accordingly in areas such as dedicated financial support, rethinking legal requirements, intellectual property law, and the regulatory and incentives regime in general.

A decade of lobbying and the provision of evidence by the cultural sector has brought into focus the reasons why the creative and cultural industries have crucial characteristics that explain their importance to the development and maintenance of global cities like London and the boroughs within them.

For this reason London policy-makers even outside the cultural field are recognizing the centrality of culture as a driving force for development. They include physical planning, social services, economic development, and leisure.

Taking a broad view of cultural activities, they have recognized that the arts are more than purely an aesthetic experience, so expanding their possible contribution to urban regeneration and visioning. This involves recognizing the multi-faceted nature of what arts and culture can offer.

Cultural activity can weave its way like a thread through endeavors of all kinds, adding value, meaning, local distinctiveness, and impact as it proceeds. Making a successful partnership between the arts, culture, and urban regeneration thus requires a more imaginative understanding of arts and culture, and the way they work. Policy-makers have begun to appreciate that "high" art, "low" art, popular art, or "community" art all have something to offer London. The arguments policy-makers use include:

- Cultural activities, both traditional and new, create "meaning" and thus are concerned with and embody the identity and values of London, both in terms of what it was and what it is becoming – here the intercultural and social inclusion agenda is moving to the fore. These activities express local distinctiveness – ever more important in a world where places increasingly look and feel the same. Heritage, especially local heritage and stories, is seen as inspiring to residents and visitors alike, perhaps because in the headlong rush to develop economically people find solace and inspiration in buildings, artifacts, and skills of the past, and because in a globalized world they seek local roots: connection to their histories and their collective memories anchors their sense of being. The wealth of culture is linked in policy-makers' minds with engendering civic pride. This pride in turn, they argue, can give confidence, can inspire and provide the energy to face seemingly insurmountable tasks that may have nothing to do with culture.

The difficulty for London is that it is a city of multiple identities. Whose should be cherished and whose are being left out? Should it be forward-looking or nostalgic? Should it be locally, nationally, or internationally focused? Simultaneously the drivers of commercial culture are seen to be wrapping up "real" experience and throwing it back to Londoners in a disembodied form as they attempt to create urban entertainment districts made up of well-known brand names that have nothing to do with London.

- Cultural activities are inextricably linked to innovation and creativity, and historically this has been the lifeblood of cities as a means of unleashing their capacity to survive and adapt. Creativity is, of course, legitimized in the arts, and increasingly is also seen by business as the key attribute to look for in employees. In many emerging business fields well beyond multi-media, it is people with arts training who are in particular demand.

A key aspect that is neglected is that, in encouraging deeper-seated creativity, institutional inertia needs to be tackled, as do support mechanisms that tend to favor the tried and tested rather than the radical.

- In a world dominated by images the cultural sector is inextricably linked to the image of a place, and a strong culture is believed to create positive images. Culture is associated with a high quality of life. For this reason city marketing strategies the world over tend increasingly to focus on their cultural offer, the presence of arts institutions, artists, and creative people and cultural industries in general. Culture is thus seen as a means of attracting international companies and their mobile workforces, who seek a vibrant cultural life. Thus by helping to create positive images the cultural sector has a direct impact on inward investment.

The key dilemma, though, is whose images are legitimized. In an "experience economy" world corporate cultural offers are blandifying cultural inventiveness, smoothing any radical edges, and creating merely "sanitized razzmatazz" that feels safe for consumption.

- Culture's role in tourism is key: it is the primary reason a visitor comes to an area in the first place. And tourism might be the first step that allows someone to explore and know a place and later perhaps invest in it. Tourism offers are largely focused on cultural activities, be they the national collecting institutions like museums or galleries which exude presence and power, or live activities like theater, clubs, festivals, or locally distinct rituals.

Again the danger is that London's heritage culture is forefronted. An intensive debate is underway on how to project both tradition and innovation simultaneously. The ill-fated "cool Britannia" notion emerged from this debate.

- The recognition of the cultural industries as an economic sector has become an anchor in the debate about the future of culture, in particular their role as a platform to provide content for the IT-driven knowledge-based economy. Here the catalytic role of higher education institutions such as the four colleges of the London Institute or the Royal College of Arts in replenishing content is seen as key. Their capacity to attract the best students world-wide through their global scanning activities is seen as significant. The dynamic links between the subsidized and commercial sectors are increasingly acknowledged. For example, actors working in subsidized theaters often end up working for the BBC, whose research and development have then effectively been supported. Thus the decline in arts funding throughout the Thatcher era and beyond has been reversed.

In spite of an encouraging recognition in policy terms, little action has hit the ground. There is, for example, much discussion of dedicated venture capital funds, yet the only one in Britain to have emerged so far is Creative Advantage West Midlands around Birmingham.

- The social inclusion agenda has been central to government policy since 1997 and this has been reflected in the government's Department of Culture, Media and Sports' thinking in relation to those, mainly national, institutions it supports directly. The same applies to the London Arts Board – a regional offshoot of the national Arts Council. Funding is largely shaped by the extent to which these funded entities incorporate social inclusion objectives within their programming and outreach work. Much of this policy direction was based on research that assessed the social impact of culture. It has been argued that cultural activities help engender the development of social and human capital and transform the organizational capacity to handle and respond to change: that they can strengthen social cohesion; assist in personal development, increase personal confidence, and improve life skills; create common ground between people of different ages; improve people's mental and physical well-being; strengthen people's ability to act as democratic citizens; and develop new training and employment routes.

The overriding issue for culture in London is property prices, which are driving locational choices and thus the feel of various parts of London. Where high added value can be created, the West End remains crucial as the headquarters center, but design consultants, suppliers to the film industry, artists, or music-recording businesses are largely locating to inner urban rings or outside the city in a telecommuting mode.

A good way of viewing London is as a series of concentric circles. These circles are largely determined by property prices. This logic is well known and applies to places as diverse as New York, Berlin, Sydney, or Madrid.

At the hub are the high-value-added services – finance and business services, retail, activities such as advertising or estate agency, and high-profile cultural institutions or the headquarters of cultural industry organizations. Surrounding this core is an inner urban ring which provides supply services to this hub – be that printers, couriers, or catering. It is also usually the home of the less well established creative industries that provide the innovative and buzzy atmosphere on which cities thrive, such as design companies, young multi-media entrepreneurs, even artists. It is they who tend to experiment with new products and services. London's city fringe is a typical area of this kind. This fringe is currently expanding to south London – Greenwich and Southwark generating what is called the South London Phenomenon.

The jump occurred once the Tate Modern was built in Southwark and the ill-fated Dome in Greenwich was supported by new transport nodes – the Jubilee Line – which focused on high-class architecture. The new Laban Centre in Lewisham, to be completed in 2002, will reinforce this drive.

As is known, "cultural types" tend to provide the clientele for the interesting restaurants, to which ultimately the more "staid" people from the hub want to go to. The buildings in London's inner urban rings are usually a mix of old warehousing, small industrial buildings, and older housing with a large element of mixed uses. They have a more higgledy-piggledy feel.

The strategic struggle local authorities are facing is whether to allow change of use to housing where they can sell sites, if owned by the public sector, for considerably more than for cultural incubators and the like. For example Lewisham in south London has just announced a "creative business enterprise zone" and has sold sites at below market value to ensure cultural activities remain part of the mix. A few developers are forgoing larger profits by anchoring developments around contemporary and radical cultural facilities rather than a mainstream store, so as to let "the soul" of culture infuse developments. One example, undertaken by Urban Catalyst, has raised City of London funds to put an ethnic arts organization, Innova, at the core of a development in a deprived area – Peckham.

The danger is that over time some of these inner areas themselves become gentrified, as Sharon Zukin exemplified over 20 years ago, and that in turn pushes out low-value users such as artists or local shopkeepers who cannot afford the new higher rents. The artists then in turn look for another low-value area . . . and so the cycle moves on.

As incubating companies grow and become more profitable they either then move into the hub or gentrify their inner area, as has already happened in Camden, Chiswick, and Islington. This inner urban ring has historically proved vital for London as it provides the breathing space and experimentation zone – it is the incubator unit for London – as well as a buffer between the richer core and housing developments beyond. This fringe is now filling up, and the pressure is to move further out, yet the housing estates and suburbanized areas have few buildings of interest, and planning authorities are beginning to take a more imaginative look at how this more outer rim can be allowed to develop.

The transition zone between London's hub and the inner urban ring is where London's biggest urban renewal battles have taken place, because the inner ring community usually seeks to resist the encroachments of higher-value uses such as office buildings; this is happening, for example, in Spitalfields where the economic dynamic and the property profits to be made are pushing the hub to expand beyond its natural location. If the City of London is allowed to expand into Spitalfields the charm, distinctiveness, and uniqueness of Spitalfields will have gone.

# 15    *Justin O'Connor*

# CITIES, CULTURE AND "TRANSITIONAL ECONOMIES": DEVELOPING CULTURAL INDUSTRIES IN ST. PETERSBURG

This chapter looks at some issues around the transfer of cultural industry policy between two very different national contexts, the UK and Russia. Specifically it draws on a partnership project between Manchester and St. Petersburg[1] financed by the European Union as part of a program to promote economic development through knowledge transfer between Europe and the countries of the former Soviet Union. This specific project attempted to place the cultural industries squarely within the dimension of economic development, and drew on the expertise of Manchester's Creative Industries Development Service (CIDS) and other partners to effect this policy transfer.[2]

## St. Petersburg: City of Culture

St. Petersburg is Russia's second city, with a population of nearly 5 million. Founded in 1703 by Peter the Great as the capital of a new, modernizing Russia, it acts as a powerful and complex symbol of the country's relationship to the West. Moscow, the medieval capital, which regained this status in 1918 during the revolutionary civil war, is by far the biggest city in Russia, with over 10 million people. It is the economic powerhouse – almost an economic region unto itself – as well as being the center of political power.

"Cities, Culture and Transitional Economies: Developing Cultural Industries in St. Petersburg" by Justin O'Connor (2004). In D. Power and A. J. Scott, *Cultural Industries and the Production of Culture*. Routledge, London. Reprinted by permission of Thomson Publishing Services on behalf of Routledge.

It is also the largest center for the big cultural industries – broadcasting, newspapers and magazines, film, music recording, fashion, and design. However, St. Petersburg retains its symbolic role as the city of culture. This relates to its undisputed pre-eminence in the field of classical culture, with over 3,000 historic buildings in its central area and a range of world-famous institutions including the Hermitage, the Maryinsky Theatre, and the Russian State Museum.

This classical heritage is one dimension of the Petersburg "mythos"; that of "victim city" is another (Volkov 1995). The shift of power to Moscow, and the devastation of the city in the revolutionary civil war (1918–21), were often portrayed as a form of punishment. The notion of imperial hubris visiting disaster on its inhabitants was embedded in the Petersburg mythos by Pushkin's famous poem of *The Bronze Horseman*, which evokes the suffering inflicted by the building of the city and, by implication, the forced modernization of the country. Added to this was a sense of the city paying for its decadent sins in the poetry of Akhmatova, and indeed in the pronouncement of the communist leaders in Moscow who associated the city with tsarism and dangerous Western ideas. The "Great Purge" of 1937 began in the city and focused on its intelligentsia; the catastrophe of the 900-day siege by the Nazis did not stop subsequent purges and attacks on the city by Stalin (Berman 1984; Clark 1995; Figes 2002; Volkov 1995).

The "victim city" thus had long historical roots, although there was also a more mundane "second city" syndrome involving – in common with many other cities proud of a distinct heritage – a resentment at the dominance and perceived self-aggrandizement of a larger, more powerful capital city. Moscow – "Mother Moscow" – had always been set against the willful, artificial, un-Russian Petersburg; Moscow was the spiritual home abandoned by Peter in his pursuit of Western knowledge and values. In the early twentieth century St. Petersburg (or Leningrad, as it had become in 1924) became associated with the preservation of the spiritual values of European culture in the face of Moscow's "Asiatic" barbarism. In more recent times this shifted again, with Moscow now being characterized as a city given to the dirty business of money and politics, home to the brash *novye russkie*, the new Russians, spending without taste or culture. St. Petersburg became the city of culture; charged with defending the values of this culture against the plutocracy of the new Moscow, preserving a unique classical heritage in the face of budget cuts and mass culture (and in some iterations representing a "time capsule" or "ark" which European culture itself had long forgotten).[3] A less bombastic version of this saw the city as a place where people could pursue cultural interests for their own sake, having a more laid-back, bohemian lifestyle and attitude, and a more cynical, pessimistic face to present to the shallow optimism of Moscow (Nicolson 1994; Volkov 1995).

It would be unwise to underestimate the power of this mythos of St. Petersburg; such narratives show up in the talk of people from well outside the social and cultural elites. However, the 1990s witnessed a severe economic crisis which dominated the political horizon. Like most Russian cities its situation in the 1990s was dire. In particular its main industries, based on military production, collapsed as a result of demobilization after 1991. Unemployment, industrial decline, a massive implosion of self-identity – these were all worse than anything suffered in the rust bowls of Europe and North America. Petersburg had the same infrastructure problems as other Russian cities – roads, housing, transport, water and sewerage, etc. – but it also had a unique collection of historic buildings, over 40 percent of which were in need of urgent repair (Leontief Centre 1999; Danks 2001). These buildings had been chronically starved of funding at least since the 1970s, with most of the hard currency earned by Intourist, the state-owned travel agency, being retained by central government in Moscow.

The global distinctiveness of these buildings and the cultural heritage they represented were mobilized very effectively in the "rebranding" of the city by the mayor, Anatoly Sobchak, who steered through the renaming of the city in 1991 and embarked on a goodwill tour around various European cities (Causey 2002). Sobchak attempted to use St. Petersburg's cultural profile to present a modern, dynamic, and democratic image for the city, much in the same way as Pasqual Maragall had done for Barcelona at the end of the 1980s. However, under trumped-up accusations of corruption Sobchak was voted out of power in 1996, and the city administration became dominated by corrupt and inefficient ex-apparatchik personnel as in many other Russian post-socialist cities (Andrusz et al. 1996; Mellor 1999). The city became one of the worst places in the country for violent – often gang-related – crime and failed to tackle its basic physical, social, and economic infrastructure problems. It was Moscow which got the charismatic mayor in the form of Yuri Luzhkov.

Some improvements were to be found as St. Petersburg began to develop new service-sector businesses – which now represents 60 percent of the city's GDP – and tried to bring investment into the city center (Leontief Centre 1999). But the recent tercentenary was generally perceived to be a huge wasted opportunity, failing to deliver the improvement in tourist infrastructure (transport, information, affordable hotels, visa restrictions, etc.) or to pass on benefits to the cultural infrastructure outside those of the big global brands. The fact that President Putin was deputy mayor to Sobchak, and that many of his close advisors are drawn from his former St. Petersburg administration (as well as the city's FSB – the successor to the KGB), has certainly meant that St. Petersburg now feels more investment and attention may come its way. The election of Putin's protégé as new governor (the title changed from mayor in 1996), with a brief to end corruption and improve efficiency in the administration, is also something that points this way.

## Cultural Policy in St. Petersburg

The first half of the 1990s saw attempts to place cultural institutions on a more "normal" footing – formalizing their property ownership, removing perks and privileges, detaching them from the leisure and welfare structures of the cultural unions. But from 1996 the main problem facing cultural policy in St. Petersburg was the rapid reduction in state funding for culture, which fell 40 percent between 1991 and 2001. Less than 1 percent of a (until recently) shrinking or static GNP was now spent on culture (Belova et al. 2002). In 1996 and 1998 this had fallen to 0.29 percent and 0.32 percent respectively. Wages were hardly paid, and if so in arrears; buildings and collections were in serious danger. Faced with sheer necessity, managers of cultural institutions had to find new sources of funding; if this was sometimes portrayed as market forces unlocking new resources it was mostly felt for what it was – a chaotic scramble (Causey 2002). In this process the city administration provided barely minimal leadership and strategic framework. Foundations began to provide new sources of funding – the Open Society Institute (Soros Foundation), the Ford, Eurasia, and Getty Foundations, and other smaller funders – but found it extremely difficult to work in this context, and looked to promote arts administration and marketing skills within the cultural sector as well as trying get the city administration to think more strategically. In this they worked closely with a growing number of educational and training organizations from North America and western Europe, and, closely linked to these, cultural policy professionals who aimed to intermediate between Western know-how and the realities of the Russian situation.

As well as supplying training programs, these organizations and intermediaries also pushed for the commercialization of activities such as cafés, merchandizing, the loan of artifacts, the renting of space, associated publishing, etc. In the process they identified the following problems:

1   a lack of arts administration and marketing skills;
2   legal, bureaucratic, fiscal, and cultural constraints on entrepreneurial activities;

3   lack of flexible human resources management powers (difficult to get rid of or financially reward staff);
4   a tendency for the large institutions to be self-contained and remote from other locally based cultural institutions;
5   the continued existence of many financially unviable small state institutions, over-manned, lacking basic skills, and contributing little to the overall cultural life of the city.

While the lack of professional managerial skills and the limited flexibility of human resources were important, it was the local city administration which also proved an obstacle. The problems here were:

1   the city's lack of a clearly outlined unified cultural and tourism strategy;
2   the opacity and clientele basis of its cultural funding system;
3   the wider lack of understanding of the economic dimensions and potential of the cultural sector;
4   the city's organizational confusion with regard to tourism, culture, and small business development responsibilities (Belova et al. 2002).

Part of the task of the foreign foundations, organizations, and consultants was to argue the case for the enhanced role of culture in the economic regeneration of the city – something Sobchak was clear about but which subsequent administrations have found difficult. The promotion of culture as a regeneration tool necessarily touches on wider policy domains which have rarely had to conceive of any systematic relationship to culture. For Russians culture was important, it was something precious that should have money spent on it – but as a gift to the patrimony, *not* as an economic investment.

The arguments for the economic role of culture, made by foreign policy intermediaries but also by local reformers,[4] inevitably centered on developing the city's huge tourism potential and on the related search for new ways of attracting investment into the historic center. They looked to examples of Western cities which had somehow used culture to transform their image and regenerate the physical infrastructure of the city center. It was in this context that arguments about cultural industries appeared – as a contribution to debates over the cultural tourist "offer" and related investment in the historic center. Previous work (Causey 2002; Landry 1997) had established that St. Petersburg's tourist appeal was severely limited – its over-reliance on the huge, prestigious institutions masked a lack of smaller, more innovative cultural activities which make up the ecosystem of a major destination city (St. Petersburg has its own *Rough Guide* and *Lonely Planet*!).

Cultural industries were thus introduced not in terms of large-scale global businesses but of supporting small, independent cultural producers who could somehow add to the overall cultural offer of St. Petersburg; and maybe even provide new funding possibilities for state-supported culture. Further, the exclusive appeal to classical culture meant the image of the city completely lacked a contemporary profile. The absence of a small cultural producer sector also meant that the animation and retail/leisure occupation of the city center either failed to appear or was completely inappropriate; newly refurbished areas lay empty, historic buildings were surrounded by shops selling things no "cultural tourist" would wish to buy. At root was the failure of small, independent cultural producers to make any major impact on the landscape of the city – physical or imaginary. And behind this, it was argued, was the lack of any infrastructure or support for the development of cultural SMEs.

## Culture and "Transitional" Economics

A fundamental debate rages about the role of culture in post-Soviet Russia. In the 1990s, during years of economic collapse and chaos, the question arose as to what was the basis of state funding. What should it fund and how should it do so? Was it to remain in the framework of patrimony to be promoted and sustained by the state apparatus, as it had been up to 1989, or was it to find its way in the market place, somehow linked to the new consumption preferences of the population? At certain levels the state was not going to let go – it continued to have a central role in print and broadcast media regulation, and its control here has recently got tighter (Danks 2001; Freeland 2003). The issue of defending a national patrimony looms large, especially when linked to the nationality questions in the regions, where discussions are dominated by questions of the different rights of state, ethnicity, and minority groups to preserve and promote their cultural heritage (O'Connor 2003). This is not a debate restricted to policy elites – "high culture" has a widespread role in civil society and is seen as a crucial part of identity-making, not only in giving a sense of national identity but also of personal survival in hard times (Causey 2002).

This current project to promote cultural industries was set within a fairly clear narrative of Russia as a "transitional economy" where "expertise transfer" from the West would expedite the country's move from a command to a modern democratic and market society. In cultural policy terms what happened in the West in the 1970s and 1980s – cuts in straight subsidy, professionalization, commercialization, diversification of markets and constituencies, deregulation and pluralism, etc. – was seen to be what would happen in Russia, albeit in a telescoped, maybe chaotic, manner. In terms of cultural industries this was also linked to the emergence of a small business economy which was a key target of the World Bank and other development agencies (Leontief Centre 1999).

However, it was quite clear that such a narrative was fiercely resisted in Russia, and especially so in the realm of culture. The schizophrenic history of Russian attitudes of "catching up with the West" or "finding a unique path" is too long to go into here, but these certainly continue to play a key role (Figes 2002). The "shock therapy" administered to the Russian economy in the early 1990s produced a wave of disenchantment about the nature of transition. Many believed that the West would not let Russia catch up and would simply assign it a peripheral role in the new world order. Thus market reforms were simply a means by which (mainly) US capital would penetrate and dominate the assets and the markets of Russia. A more sweeping debate returns to the notion of Russia as not being part of "the West," but a different culture entirely. Politically this also looks to a strong nation-state as a defense against globalization. The openness and freedom which the West saw as crucial to modernization were, for these, signs not of backwardness but of difference; and just as Western agencies got increasingly annoyed at the persistence of such attitudes many Russians embraced these as part of a national culture (Danks 2001; Pilkington and Bliudina 2002).

For those not concerned with cultural geopolitics there was still a burning awareness of the collapse of Russia's Great Power status, followed by loss of health care, education, and science "as well as outward opulence against a background of growing poverty and moral degradation" (Pilkington and Bliudina 2002: 8). The transition was frequently experienced as shame, disorientation, anger, and despair. In this context culture was a key site of conflict – in which some national tradition or national soul was at stake. At the level of cultural policy, the cut in jobs, pay, and security, the fear of selling (out) a treasured heritage, and the all-pervasive penetration of Western cultural goods also meant that, after early enthusiasm, the transfer of "expertise" could not be seen as merely technical but was hedged by ambiguity, cynicism, and resentment.

St. Petersburg, of course, was always presented locally as "the most European city," the "window on the West," so, while not free from the narratives of Russia's European-Asiatic uniqueness, it was much more used to, and welcoming of, Westernizing narratives. However, as we have seen, its self-image was closely associated with a classical European heritage; many saw the association with commerce and culture as something suspicious. This was never more clearly so than in the notion of "cultural industries." This opposition came not only from the administration and the large cultural institutions – who could afford to stress non-commercial idealism – but from those in the sector which the project had specifically set out to target – the independent cultural producers.

## Independent Cultural Producers in St. Petersburg

This project first targeted the city administration, addressing workshops and seminars to key individuals and departments, as is the practice in the UK. It became very apparent early on that the administration was not buying into this argumentation; it did not see culture as an issue other than to attract external funding – which it frequently siphoned off elsewhere; its various departments had little success in coordinating its own activities, let alone cross-connecting to others on a "cultural" theme, and its hierarchical structures and frequent changes of personnel meant that it became impervious to external argumentation and rigidly frozen in fixed attitudes. Many international funding agencies had indeed tried to stress culture as a key factor of its economic future but became increasingly frustrated by its inflexibility, its incompetence, and its corruption.[5]

It had also become apparent that any initiative led by the city administration would automatically be received with cold cynicism by those in the cultural sector. For the above reasons of incompetence and corruption certainly, but compounded by the experiences of the previous 80 years. Authorities were to be avoided, distrusted, lied to – sometimes ethically shunned. In such a context "partnership" was not an immediate option. In which situation the best solution seemed to be to work directly with the cultural producers themselves – in order to raise awareness of their potential role and indeed existence as a "sector," and to get them to take active ownership of any subsequent initiative. But in so approaching the sector – through research interviews, workshops, seminars, and away days, along with many informal activities – it demanded a clarification of what exactly was intended by "cultural industries."

The terminology was a clear problem – as noted above, a direct translation of the term evokes a factory, and not in any Warholian ironic terms either. Most of those interviewed initially rejected the term, until it was explained. But even when translated into "cultural business" it ran into a lot of problems, especially in a context where "businessman" could act as slang for "criminal" (often with reason, see Freeland 2000). But the deeper territory of resistance was that of the boundaries between culture and commerce. This has a number of dimensions.

Initially it relates to the separation of subsidized culture ("art") and commercial culture ("entertainment") which was general in European cultural policy fields at least until the changes occurring there in the 1970s. This separation was firmly rooted in the cultural policy of the Soviet Union (Clark 1995; Figes 2002). However, this has a specific Russian dimension relating to the politicized role of "high culture" in the Soviet Union – when it was both a vehicle for political ideology but also a site for the transcendence of that ideology. The state tightly controlled cultural production for ideological purposes, but within a framework of respect for (usually pre-twentieth-century European bourgeois) "high culture." Soviet culture was of course defiantly non-commercial (i.e. non-capitalist). On the other hand, oppositional, "alternative" culture was by necessity non-commercial also, both in the sense that it did not generate income and in that it rejected immediate acceptance/popularity, envisaging for itself an ideal audience of the future (sometimes beyond the existing regime, or some more general "judgment of history," or a mixture of both). There was also a sense of an "international cultural mainstream" – which both officials and dissidents saw in terms of non-commercial "high culture." The former would produce artists of all kinds to compete in the mainstream to the glory of the nation; the latter would also look to this as some transcendent court of appeal, beyond the horizon of the nation. Unlike official culture, of course, the opposition espoused modernism – but imagined in a cultural context very different from its actuality in the West.

Oppositional culture had a sacred apartness; it was less about an Adorno-esque transcendence through the difficult and opaque work of art structured by a painful negativity, more about the way Shostakovich and Akhmatova spoke a secret coded critique, a message of hope for those who could listen, keeping open the image of the artist in communication with the people which had long atrophied in the West. It was this that was threatened by Western commercial culture. The commercialization of culture was seen by oppositional culture as a degradation of culture; production for the market was as much (maybe more?) anathema for these as it was for official culture. The shocked encounter between a preserved (through political opposition) notion of "high art" and the reality of commercial culture industries in the West was prefigured in the reactions of exiled oppositionists (one thinks of Solzhenitsyn and Sakharov). It can be seen today in the cynicism of writers such as Victor Pelevin (Pelevin 1999).

At a more basic level, as we have seen, the impact of the rapid market reforms in Russia was very hard on the cultural sector. Not only were the institutions and jobs of official subsidized culture under severe threat but the complex ecosystem which had sustained oppositional culture (and the liminal areas which of course linked the two) – in the form of university jobs, commissions from larger institutions, state grants, more private unofficial commissions, etc. – suffered severely, with the result that there was frequently as much antagonism and anxiety about the collapse of state funding for culture on the oppositional side as there was on the official side, at least for an older generation.

Cultural business, many said, equals cuts in subsidy to both institutions (and institutional jobs) and to individual artists; policies to develop the creative industries mean the sustainability of culture relying increasingly on the market. Culture produced for the market, it was said, means pleasing the lowest common denominator, creation of easy "entertainment," and the courting of immediate (and thus transitory) popularity. In this way, many people saw the autonomy of the artist – which should be at the heart of authentic cultural production – being betrayed "for thirty pieces of silver."

It was impossible for the project team to dismiss these fears as unfounded: pressures on state budgets, the power of the market, the globalization of the large cultural industries have set the context for cultural producers and policy-makers in the West for two decades. As we have seen, the simple idea of telescoped transition is frequently rejected as an impossible "catch up" and seen as partly futile, partly a screen for Western penetration. In response we could only argue the following, taken from the project document:

> Like all changes, they present both dangers and opportunities.
>
> This is the situation of risk facing St. Petersburg culture today, whose addressing can be postponed, but not avoided. "Globalization" has involved accelerated flows of money, information, goods and people passing through cities. These flows include ideas, signs and symbols, the whole range of cultural products, information and ideas which make up the complex global cultural circuit of the contemporary world; and driven by publishing, satellite, internet, the internationalization of production and distribution etc. which have transformed the immediate day-to-day context and wider significance of local cultures.
>
> Inevitably both local cultural production and cultural consumption now take place in a much wider context – culturally, economically and organizationally. All cities need to be much more reflexive and responsive to the changes – cultural policy therefore now looks to the preservation and promotion of local, place-based cultures through active engagement with these wider contexts. (Belova et al. 2002)

The project thus initially presented itself to cultural producers in terms of the positive defense of a local culture in the face of a global economic and cultural threat. The direction offered was to engage with the economic dimension of culture through the promotion of independent cultural producers, now conceived not as artists but as freelancers and SMEs. In pursuing this line we hoped to establish a new set of understandings on behalf of both producers and policy-makers for the development of support structures necessary for such a cultural ecosystem. SME policy was a key platform here – education and training; tax and business legislation; the opening up of premises through managed workspace or incubation schemes, as well as managed "gentrification"; small loan programs; and network development (Belova et al. 2002).

The case for these policy tools, however, needed to be linked to an explicit cultural politics in order to avoid straight identification with a simple transition thesis. There was certainly an emphasis on the tourism, urban regeneration, employment, and image benefits to the city – but these economic benefits were attached to a narrative of a "cultural renewal" of the city. The "cultural renewal" was about reinventing St. Petersburg as the city of culture in a new century – a complex process but one that pointed to the wider development of a functioning civil society. This "modernization" could also be interpreted in terms of simple transition – where a market economy of small businesses and autonomous risk-taking symbolic professionals becomes the hallmark of a healthy emergent creative economy (Wang 2004). A cultural politics in this context attempts the difficult task of making "modernization" work at the local (Petersburgian, Russian) level, and most especially if it is a narrative aimed at cultural producers whose sense of personal and professional identity is rooted in this context.

In short, the cultural industries argument needed to mobilize cultural and economic arguments in the context of a city culture. The linkage of this argument to the renewed infrastructure, image, and identity of the St. Petersburg reminds us that cities are divisions of labor but they are also an imaginative work (Blum 2003). The cultural ecosystem is a key generator of economic value, but also of the imaginative work that is the city. Neither can thrive in a restricted civil society. The circulation of money, people, ideas, desires, and things that is the city demands the spaces and places necessary to their flowing. This, at the present juncture, implies markets; not The Market, but multiple sites for a series of exchanges which are economic but also social and cultural.

Highlighting the absence of an SME support structure in St. Petersburg is one way of saying this; and the failures of this support structure are predicated on a wider failure of civil society. The catastrophe of "shock therapy" underlined the absence of any social and civil underpinnings of a market in Russia – and their absence precisely reveals these underpinnings. Similarly long-standing, culturally embedded structures of power continue play a role. Danks, for example, highlights the notion of the "hour glass society"

(Danks 2001: 193). In this notion, networking at the bottom and the top of the social structure are identified as extensive but horizontal – the elites effectively floating clear of civil society constraints and where legal and institutional support is barely trusted by those below, who rely on strong personal networks of trust. Both of these are destructive of the civil society context – the actions of the oligarchs speak for themselves, but networks based on personal trust quickly become restrictive, cliquey, and indeed corrupt. The sort of fluid, open trust networks found in cultural ecosystems in the West are noticeably absent from St. Petersburg (O'Connor 1999a, 2000), where distrust of representatives, lead bodies, support agencies, intermediaries, etc. was a key finding of our research (CISR 2003). People work with those they know and are wary of others.

The St. Petersburg project is in its second phase, which involves the establishment of a lead partnership agency and the placing of the cultural industry issue on the administration's agenda. But in trying to make these arguments, the "expert," as a suspect figure, has to find ways of gaining trust. Only to some extent can this be on technical terms, as some intrinsically valuable "know-how." If the cultural industries argument looks to an embodied performative shift or new habitus, then this not only takes time, but it is also done in a distinctly local context. Negus (2002), for example, characterizes intermediaries in the music industry in London as "public schoolboys"; in Manchester they have been seen as "Thatcher's children," the unemployed and disaffected. It involves the adoption of a "lifestyle," or more fundamentally a "habitus" in which the local cultural context is crucial. Thus despite the seemingly easy acceptance of Western cultural exports and models amongst the younger generation in Russia – and these are very much more open to the arguments around cultural industries – the selectivity of these has been strongly underlined by research (Pilkington and Bliudina 2002). In this context it is quite likely that, if the expertise is to be in any way effective, it must engage on this local cultural terrain, which at once puts limits on the role of "expert" and opens up a new role of transnational cultural intermediary, who has to have an explicit cultural politics.

# References

Adorno, T. and M. Horkheimer (1997/1944) The Culture Industry as Mass Deception. In J. Curran, M. Gurevitch, and J. Wollacott (eds.), *Mass Communication and Society.* Edward Arnold, London.

Andrusz, G., M. Harloe, and I. Szelenyi (1996) *Cities After Socialism: Urban and Regional Change and Conflict in Post-Socialist Societies.* Blackwell, Oxford.

Belova, E., T. Cantell, S. Causey, E. Korf, and J. O'Connor (2002) *Creative Industries in the Modern City: Encouraging Enterprise and Creativity in St. Petersburg.* TACIS-funded publication, St. Petersburg.

Berman, M. (1984) *All That is Solid Melts Into Air: The Experience of Modernity.* Verso, London.

Blum, A. (2003) *The Imaginative Structure of the City.* McGill-Queens University Press, Montreal.

Bourdieu, P. (1986) *Distinction: A Social Critique of the Judgement of Taste.* Routledge, London.

Causey, S. (2002) Cultural Institutions in Transition: Issues and Initiatives in Russia's Cultural Sector. Unpublished paper presented at the International Museum Association Conference, Salzburg, May.

Caves, R. (2000) *Creative Industries: Contracts Between Art and Commerce.* Cambridge, Mass.: Harvard University Press.

CISR (Centre for Independent Social Research) (2003) Feasibility Study for Cultural Industries Agency St. Petersburg: Unpublished research.

Clark, K. (1995) *Petersburg: Crucible of a Cultural Revolution.* Harvard University Press, Cambridge, Mass.

Danks, C. (2001) *Russian Society and Politics: An Introduction.* Longman, London.

Department of Culture, Media and Sport (1998) *Creative Industry Mapping Document.* DCMS, London.

du Gay, P. and M. Pryke (2002) *Cultural Economy.* Sage, London.

Featherstone, M. (1990) *Consumer Culture and Postmodernism.* Sage, London.

Figes, O. (2002) *Natasha's Dance: A Cultural History of Russia.* Allen Lane: Penguin, London.

Florida, R. (2002) *The Rise of the Creative Class: And How It's Transforming Work, Leisure, Community and Everyday Life.* Basic Books, New York.

Freeland, C. (2000) *Sale of the Century: Russia's Wild Ride from Communism to Capitalism.* Times Books, New York.

Freeland, C. (2003) Falling Tsar. *Financial Times Weekend,* November 1/2, pp. 1–2.

Hall, S. and M. Jacques (1989) *New Times.* Lawrence and Wishart, London.

Harris, J. (2003) *The Last Party: Britpop, Blairism and the Demise of English Pop.* Fourth Estate, London.

Hesmondhalgh, D. (2002) *The Cultural Industries.* Sage, London.

Landry, C. (with M. Gnedovsky) (1997) Strategy for Survival: Can Culture Be an Engine for St. Petersburg's Revitalisation? Unpublished discussion paper, St. Petersburg.

Leadbeater, C. and K. Oakley (1999) *The Independents: Britain's New Cultural Entrepreneurs.* Demos, London.

Leontief Centre (1999) *Rehabilitation of the Centre of St. Petersburg: Investment Strategy.* Leontief Centre, St. Petersburg.

Mellor, R. (1999) The Russian City on the Edge of Collapse. *New Left Review* 236, 53–76.

Negus, K. (2002) The Work of Cultural Intermediaries and the Enduring Distance between Production and Consumption. *Cultural Studies* 16(4), 501–15.

Nicolson, J. (1994) *The Other St. Petersburg*, St. Petersburg [no publisher details].

O'Connor, J. (1999a) *Cultural Production in Manchester: Mapping and Strategy*. Manchester Institute for Popular Culture, Manchester Metropolitan University. <www.mmu.ac.uk/h-ss/mipc/iciss>.

O'Connor, J. (1999b) *ICISS Transnational Research Report*, Manchester Institute for Popular Culture, Manchester Metropolitan University. .

O'Connor, J. (2000) Cultural Industries. *European Journal of Arts Education* 2(3), 15–27.

O'Connor, J. (2003) Cultural Diversity, Development and Globalization. In *Cultural Diversity, Development and Globalization*. Russian Institute for Cultural Research, Moscow.

O'Connor, J., M. Banks, A. Lovatt, and C. Raffo (1997) Modernist Education in a Postmodern World: Critical Evidence of Business Education and Business Practice in the Cultural Industries. *British Journal of Education and Work* 9(3), February, 19–34.

O'Connor, J., M. Banks, A. Lovatt, and C. Raffo (2000a) Risk and Trust in the Cultural Industries. *Geoforum* 31(4), 453–64.

O'Connor, J., M. Banks, A. Lovatt, and C. Raffo (2000b) Attitudes to Formal Business Training and Learning amongst Entrepreneurs in the Cultural Industries: Situated Business Learning through "Doing with Others." *British Journal of Education and Work* 13(2), 215–30.

O'Connor, J. and D. Wynne (1998) Consumption and the Postmodern City. *Urban Studies* 35(5–6), 841–64.

Pelevin, V. (1999) *Babylon*, tr. A. Bromfield. Faber & Faber, London.

Pilkington, H. and U. Bliudina (2002) Cultural Globalisation: A Peripheral Perspective. In H. Pilkington, E. Omel'chenko, M. Flynn, U. Bliudina, and E. Starkova, *Looking West? Cultural Globalization and Russian Youth Culture*. Pennsylvania University Press, Pennsylvania.

Volkov, S. (1995) *St. Petersburg: A Cultural History*. The Free Press, New York.

Wang, Jing (2004) The Global Reach of a New Discourse: How Far Can "Creative Industries" Travel? *International Journal of Cultural Studies* 7(1).

## Notes

1  The City of Helsinki (Urban Facts) were involved in the first phase of the partnership project and remain informally connected.
2  There were two phases to the project. First, an 18-month project (February 2001–July 2002) financed by the European Union's TACIS Cross Border Co-operation Programme, aimed at research and policy development for the cultural industry sector in St. Petersburg – conceived predominantly as SMEs and free-lancers – as well as promoting entrepreneurialism amongst state- and city-funded

cultural institutions. This was a formal three-way partnership between the city administrations of St. Petersburg, Helsinki, and Manchester, though it was led and managed by Timo Cantel (Helsinki Urban Facts), Sue Causey (Prince of Wales Business Leaders Forum), Elena Belova (Leontief Centre), and myself at Manchester Institute for Popular Culture. The second (January 2003–June 2004) was a continuation of this, within the TACIS Institution Building Partnership Programme (IBPP), under the specific line "Support to Civil Society and Local Initiatives." This second program is a partnership between two independent not-for-profit agencies – the Creative Industries Development Service, Manchester, and a similar emergent organization in St. Petersburg. The intention is to establish this latter as a lead agency in promoting cultural industries in St. Petersburg, within a local policy context made more amenable to such initiatives.

3   See the film by Alexander Sokurov *Russian Ark* (Hermitage Bridge Studio, 2001) – where the Hermitage becomes, by a historical paradox, the Ark where European culture preserved itself against the floods of ignorance and mass culture. Sokurov: "We are much closer to our past than Englishmen are to Victorian times. Our past hasn't become past yet – the main problem of this country is that we don't know when it will become past." *Guardian*, March 28, 2003

4   Such as Leonid Romankov, until last year the main cultural spokesperson for the city's Legislative Assembly; the Leontief Centre, the city's economic research agency; or Alexander Kobak, ex-head of the Soros Foundation and now head of the Likhachev Foundation, under whose aegis Charles Landry of Comedia, a leading international cultural consultancy, wrote the first cultural document pointing to the economic role of culture in the city (Landry 1997).

5   Private conversation with the manager of an international fund agency in St. Petersburg.

# 16    *Michael E. Porter*

# LOCAL CLUSTERS IN A GLOBAL ECONOMY

Economic geography in an era of global competition involves a paradox. It is widely recognized that changes in technology and competition have diminished many of the traditional roles of location. Resources, capital, technology, and other inputs can be efficiently sourced in global markets. Firms can access immobile inputs via corporate networks. It no longer is necessary to locate near large markets to serve them. Governments are widely seen as losing their influence over competition to global forces. It is easy to conclude, then, that location is diminishing in importance.[1]

This perspective, although widespread, is hard to reconcile with competitive reality. In *The Competitive Advantage of Nations* (Porter, 1990), I put forward a microeconomically based theory of national, state, and local competitiveness in the global economy. In this theory, clusters have a prominent role. Clusters are geographic concentrations of interconnected companies, specialized suppliers, service providers, firms in related industries, and associated institutions (e.g., universities, standards agencies, trade associations) in a particular field that compete but also cooperate. Clusters, or critical masses of unusual competitive success in particular business areas, are a striking feature of virtually every national, regional, state, and even metropolitan economy, especially in more advanced nations.

Although the phenomenon of clusters in one form or another has been recognized and explored in a range of literatures, clusters cannot be understood independent of a broader theory of competition and competitive strategy in a global economy. The prevalence of clusters reveals important insights about the microeconomics of competition and the role of location in

"Local Clusters in a Global Economy" from Michael E. Porter (2000), "Location, Competition, and Economic Development: Local Clusters in a Global Economy." *Economic Development Quarterly* 14(1), pp 15–21, 33–4. Reprinted by permission of Sage Publications, Inc.

competitive advantage. Even as old reasons for clustering have diminished in importance with globalization, new influences of clusters on competition have taken on growing importance in an increasingly complex, knowledge-based, and dynamic economy.

Clusters represent a new way of thinking about national, state, and local economies, and they necessitate new roles for companies, for various levels of government, and for other institutions in enhancing competitiveness. For companies, thinking about competition and strategy has been dominated by what goes on inside the organization. Clusters suggest that a good deal of competitive advantage lies *outside* companies and even outside their industries, residing instead in the locations at which their business units are based. This creates important new agendas for management that rarely are recognized. For example, clusters represent a new unit of competitive analysis along with the firm and industry. Cluster thinking suggests that companies have a tangible and important stake in the business environments where they are located in ways that go far beyond taxes, electricity costs, and wage rates. The health of the cluster is important to the health of the company. Companies might actually benefit from having more local competitors. Trade associations can be competitive assets, not merely lobbying and social organizations.

For governments, thinking about the competitiveness of nations and states has focused on the overall economy, with national-level policy as the dominant influence. The importance of clusters suggests new roles for government at the federal, state, and local levels. In the global economy, sound macro-economic policies are necessary but not sufficient. Government's more decisive and inevitable influences are at the microeconomic level. Among them, removing obstacles to the growth and upgrading of existing and emerging clusters takes on a priority. Clusters are a driving force in increasing exports and are magnets for attracting foreign investment. Clusters also represent an important forum in which new types of dialogue can and must take place among companies, government agencies, and institutions such as schools, universities, and public utilities.

Knowledge about cluster theory has advanced, and the publication of *The Competitive Advantage of Nations* (Porter, 1990) helped trigger a large and growing number of formal cluster initiatives in countries, states, cities, and even entire regions such as Central America. [ . . . ]

## What is a Cluster?

Clusters have long been part of the economic landscape, with geographic concentrations of trades and companies in particular industries dating back for centuries. The intellectual antecedents of clusters date back at least to Marshall (1890/1920), who included a fascinating chapter on the externalities of specialized industrial locations in his *Principles of Economics*.[2]

A cluster is a geographically proximate group of interconnected companies and associated institutions in a particular field, linked by commonalities and complementarities. The geographic scope of clusters ranges from a region, a state, or even a single city to span nearby or neighboring countries (e.g., southern Germany and German-speaking Switzerland).[3] The geographic scope of a cluster relates to the distance over which informational, transactional, incentive, and other efficiencies occur.

More than single industries, clusters encompass an array of linked industries and other entities important to competition. They include, for example, suppliers of specialized inputs such as components, machinery, and services as well as providers of specialized infrastructure. Clusters also often extend downstream to channels or customers and laterally to manufacturers of complementary products or companies related by skills, technologies, or common inputs. Many clusters include governmental and other institutions (e.g., universities, think tanks, vocational training providers, standards-setting agencies, trade associations) that provide specialized training, education, information, research, and technical support. Many clusters include trade associations and other collective bodies involving cluster members. Finally, foreign firms can be and are part of clusters, but only if they make permanent investments in a significant local presence.

[ . . . ]

Drawing cluster boundaries often is a matter of degree and involves a creative process informed by understanding the linkages and complementarities across industries and institutions that are most important to competition in a particular field. The strength of these "spillovers" and their importance to productivity and innovation often are the ultimate boundary-determining factors.

Clusters are defined too broadly if they are aggregates such as manufacturing, services, consumer goods, or "high tech." Here, the connections among included industries are weak at best, and discussion about cluster constraints and potential bottlenecks will tend to gravitate to generalities. Conversely, equating a cluster with a single industry misses the crucial interconnections with other industries and institutions that strongly affect competitiveness.

Clusters occur in many types of industries, in smaller fields, and even in some local industries such as restaurants, car dealers, and antique shops. They are present in large and small economies, in rural and urban areas, and at several geographic levels (e.g., nations, states, metropolitan regions, cities).

MICHAEL E. PORTER

Clusters occur in both advanced and developing economies, although clusters in advanced economies tend to be far more developed (Porter, 1998b).

Cluster boundaries rarely conform to standard industrial classification systems, which fail to capture many important actors in competition and linkages across industries. Because parts of a cluster often are put into different traditional industrial or service categories, significant clusters might be obscured or even unrecognized. In Massachusetts, for example, there proved to be more than 400 companies connected in some way to medical devices, representing at least 39,000 high-paying jobs. The cluster was all but invisible, buried in several larger and overlapping industry categories such as electronic equipment and plastic products.

The appropriate definition of a cluster can differ in different locations, depending on the segments in which the member companies compete and the strategies they employ. The lower Manhattan multimedia cluster, for example, consists primarily of content providers and firms in related industries such as publishing, broadcast media, and graphic and visual arts. The San Francisco Bay area multimedia cluster, by contrast, contains many hardware and software industries that provide enabling technology. Clusters also can be examined at various levels of aggregation (e.g., agriculture cluster, wine cluster), thereby exposing different issues.

The boundaries of clusters continually evolve as new firms and industries emerge, established industries shrink or decline, and local institutions develop and change. Technological and market developments give rise to new industries, create new linkages, or alter served markets. Regulatory changes also contribute to shifting boundaries, for example, as they have in telecommunications and transport.

Why view economies using the lens of clusters instead of, or in addition to, more traditional groupings such as companies, industries, SIC codes, and sectors (e.g., manufacturing, services)? The most important reason is that the cluster as a unit of analysis is better aligned with the nature of competition and appropriate roles of government. Clusters, broader than traditional industry categorizations, capture important linkages, complementarities, and spillovers in terms of technology, skills, information, marketing, and customer needs that cut across firms and industries. These externalities create a possible rationale for collective action and a role for government.

[ . . . ] [S]uch connections across firms and industries are fundamental to competition, to productivity, and (especially) to the direction and pace of new business formation and innovation. Most cluster participants are not direct competitors but rather serve different segments of industries. Yet they share many common needs, opportunities, constraints, and obstacles to productivity. The cluster provides a constructive and efficient forum for dialogue among related companies, their suppliers, government, and other institutions. Because of externalities, public and private investments to improve cluster circumstances benefit many firms. Seeing a group of companies and institutions as a cluster also highlights opportunities for coordination and mutual improvement in areas of common concern with less of a risk of distorting competition or limiting the intensity of rivalry.

Viewing the world in terms of narrower industries or sectors, conversely, often degenerates to lobbying over subsidies and tax breaks. Resulting public investments involve fewer spillover benefits across firms and industries and, therefore, are prone to distort markets. Because large proportions of participants in such narrow groupings often are direct competitors, there is a very real threat that rivalry will be diminished. Companies also often are hesitant about participating for fear of aiding direct competitors. An industry or narrow sectoral perspective tends to result in distorting competition (anti-competitive rent-seeking behavior), then, whereas a cluster perspective focuses on enhancing competition (pro-competitive). The presence of customers, suppliers, and firms from related industries in the dialogue helps to police proposals that will limit competition. I return to these issues when I explore the implications of clusters for government policy.

## Location and Competition

During recent decades, thinking about the influence of location on competition has been based on relatively simple views of how companies compete. These see competition as largely static and resting on cost minimization in a relatively closed economy. Here comparative advantage in factors of production is decisive. In more recent thinking, increasing returns to scale play a central role.

Yet actual competition is far different. Competition is dynamic and rests on innovation and the search for strategic differences. Close linkages with buyers, suppliers, and other institutions are important, not only to efficiency but also to the rate of improvement and innovation. Location affects competitive advantage through its influence on *productivity* and especially on *productivity growth*. Generic factor inputs themselves usually are abundant and readily accessed. Prosperity depends on the productivity with which factors are used and upgraded in a particular location.

Economic development seeks to achieve long-term sustainable development in a nation's standard of living, adjusted for purchasing power parity. Standard of living is determined by the productivity of a nation's economy, which is measured by the value of the goods and services (products) produced per unit of the nation's human, capital, and physical resources. Productivity, then, defines competitiveness. The concept of productivity must encompass both the value (prices) that a nation's products command in the marketplace and the efficiency with which standard units are produced.

The productivity and prosperity of a location rest not on the industries in which its firms compete but rather on how they compete. Firms can be more productive in any industry if they employ sophisticated methods, use advanced technology, and offer unique products and services, whether the industry is shoes, agriculture, or semiconductors. All industries can employ "high technology," and all industries can be "knowledge intensive." Thus, the term *high tech*, which normally is used to refer to fields such as information technology and biotechnology, is of questionable relevance. A better term might be *enabling* technology to signify that these fields provide tools that can enhance technology in many other industries.

Conversely, the mere presence in any industry does not by itself guarantee prosperity if firms there are unproductive. Traditional distinctions between high tech and low tech, manufacturing and services, resource based and knowledge based, and others have little relevance per se. Improving the productivity of all industries enhances prosperity, both directly and through the influence one industry has on the productivity of others.

National productivity ultimately is set by the sophistication (e.g., technology, skill) with which companies compete. Unless companies become more productive, an economy cannot become more productive. The sophistication of companies' approaches to competing determines the prices that their products and services can command and the efficiency with which they produce.

Company sophistication in competing can be thought of in two parts. The first and most basic is what I term *operational effectiveness*, or the extent to which companies in a nation approach *best practice* in areas such as production processes, technologies, and management techniques (Porter, 1996). The second aspect of company sophistication relates to the types of strategies companies employ such as the ability to compete on differentiation and not just cost, the array of services that can be provided, and the approaches used in selling internationally.

Yet the sophistication of how companies compete in a location is strongly influenced by the *quality of the microeconomic business environment*. Some aspects of the business environment (e.g., the road system, corporate tax rates, the legal system) cut across all industries. These economy-wide (or "horizontal") areas are important and often represent the binding constraints to competitiveness in developing economies. In more advanced economies and increasingly elsewhere, however, the more decisive aspects of the business environment for competitiveness often are cluster specific (e.g., the presence of particular types of suppliers, skills, or university departments).

Capturing the business environment in a location is challenging given the myriad of locational influences on productivity and productivity growth. In *The Competitive Advantage of Nations* (Porter, 1990), I model the effect of location on competition through four interrelated influences, graphically depicted in a diamond; the diamond metaphor has become common in referring to the theory (Figure 1).[4] In a recent two-part article, I explore and statistically test the sequential process by which the diamond must upgrade if an economy is to advance (Porter, 1998b). Parallel improvements in the sophistication of company operations and strategies and the quality of the diamond provide the microeconomic foundations of economic development.

A few elements of this framework deserve highlighting because they are important to understanding the role of clusters in competition. Factor inputs range from tangible assets such as physical infrastructure to information, the legal system, and university research institutes that all firms draw on in competition. To increase productivity, factor inputs must improve in efficiency,

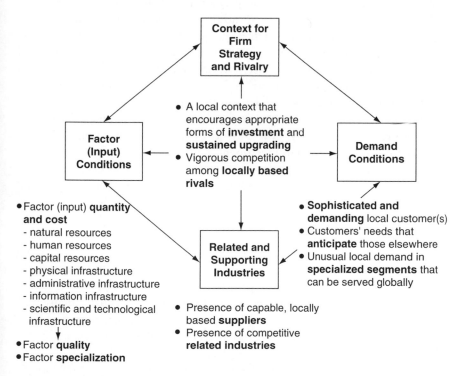

**Figure 1.** Sources of locational competitive advantage

quality, and (ultimately) specialization to particular cluster areas. Specialized factors, especially those integral to innovation and upgrading (e.g., a specialized university research institute), not only are necessary to attain high levels of productivity but also tend to be less tradable or available from elsewhere.

The context for firm strategy and rivalry refers to the rules, incentives, and norms governing the type and intensity of local rivalry. Economies with low productivity are characterized by little local rivalry. Most competition, if present at all, comes from imports. Local rivalry, if occurring at all, involves imitation. Price is the sole competitive variable, and firms hold down wages to compete in local and foreign markets. Competition involves minimal investment.

Moving to an advanced economy requires that vigorous local rivalry develop. Rivalry must shift from low wages to low total cost, and this requires upgrading the efficiency of manufacturing and service delivery. Ultimately, rivalry also must evolve from cost to include differentiation. Competition must shift from imitation to innovation and from low investment to high investment in not only physical assets but also intangibles (e.g., skills, technology). Clusters, as will be evident, play an integral role in these transitions.

The character of rivalry in a location is strongly influenced by many aspects of the business environment (e.g., the available factors, local demand conditions). Yet the investment climate and policies toward competition set the context. Things such as the macroeconomic and political stability, the tax system, labor market policies affecting the incentives for workforce development, and intellectual property rules and their enforcement contribute to the willingness of companies to invest in upgrading capital equipment, skills, and technology. Antitrust policy; government ownership and licensing rules; and policies toward trade, foreign investment, and corruption have a vital role in setting the intensity of local rivalry.

Demand conditions at home have much to do with whether firms can and will move from imitative, low-quality products and services to competing on differentiation. In low-productivity economies, the focus is heavily on foreign markets. Advancement requires the development of more demanding local markets. The presence or emergence of sophisticated and demanding home customers presses firms to improve and provides insights into existing and future needs that are hard to gain in foreign markets. Local demand also can reveal segments of the market where firms can differentiate themselves. In a global economy, the quality of local demand matters far more than does its size. Clusters of linked industries play a central role in giving rise to demand-side advantages.

A cluster is the manifestation of the diamond at work. Proximity, arising from the co-location of companies, customers, suppliers, and other institutions, amplifies all of the pressures to innovate and upgrade. In the *Global Competitiveness Report 1998* article (Porter, 1998b), I find evidence of the role of clusters in economic development. I test statistically across a broad sample of countries and find empirical support for the overall theory about the relationship between the microeconomic business environment and the prosperity of national economies and, in particular, for the impact of local clusters on economic development. The presence of a well-developed cluster provides powerful benefits to productivity and the capacity to innovate that are hard to match by firms based elsewhere.

# References

Cairncross, F. (1997). *The Death of Distance: How the Communications Revolution Will Change our Lives*. Boston: Harvard Business School.

Enright, M. (1993). The Geographic Scope of Competitive Advantage. In E. Dirven, J. Groenewegen, and S. van Hoof (eds.), *Stuck in the Region? Changing Scales of Regional Identity* (pp. 87–102). Utrecht: Netherlands Geographical Studies.

Marshall, A. (1890/1920). *Principles of Economics* (8th edn). London: Macmillan.

Porter, M. (1990). *The Competitive Advantage of Nations*. New York: Free Press.

Porter, M. (1996). What Is Strategy? *Harvard Business Review*, 74(6), 61–78.

Porter, M. (1998a). Clusters and Competition: New Agendas for Companies, Governments, and Institutions. In M. Porter, *On Competition* (pp. 197–287). Boston: Harvard Business School Press.

Porter, M. (1998b). The Microeconomic Foundations of Economic Development [Parts I and II]. In *The Global Competitiveness Report 1998* (pp. 38–63). Geneva: World Economic Forum.

# Notes

1  For a recent example, see Cairncross (1997).
2  Readers can find a full treatment of the intellectual roots of cluster thinking in Porter (1998a).
3  Enright (1993) illustrates the varying geographic scope of clusters.
4  See Porter (1990), especially chapters 3 and 4.

# 17    *Ackbar Abbas*

# COSMOPOLITAN DE-SCRIPTIONS: SHANGHAI AND HONG KONG

[ . . . ] Cities have historically been the privileged, if not necessarily exclusive, sites for the emergence of the form of life that we call the cosmopolitan. In Shanghai and Hong Kong, in particular, some form of the cosmopolitan did indeed emerge under colonial conditions, and some other form of cosmopolitanism may be developing today. Nevertheless, the description of Shanghai and Hong Kong I give here is not intended to be a straightforward empirical account of what kind of cosmopolitan city each became under colonial rule or what crucial changes each is undergoing as communist China today reasserts itself as a global power. Rather, I direct attention to a certain elusive quality of both cities and to the fact that the most familiar images of these cities do not necessarily describe them best. To put this another way: cosmopolitanism must take place somewhere, in specific sites and situations – even if these places are more and more beginning to resemble those "non-places" that French anthropologist Marc Augé has argued characterise the contemporary city. In a non-place, "one is neither *chez soi* nor *chez les autres*."[1] Like the city, Augé's non-place must be understood not literally, but as paradox: a non-place is far from being nonexistent. Rather, it is a result of excess and overcomplexity, of a limit having been exceeded. Beyond a certain point, there is a blurring and scrambling of signs and an overlapping of spatial and temporal grids, all of which make urban signs and images difficult to read. The overcomplex space of non-places means, among other things, that even the *anomalous* detail may no longer be recognisable as such because it coexists with a swarm of other such details. This means the anomalous is in danger of turning *nondescript*, in much the same way that the more complex the city today, the more it becomes a city without qualities. The cosmopolitan as urban phenomenon is inevitably inscribed in such non-places and paradoxes, raising the question we will have to address at some later point of how it might survive there.

To grapple with the anomalous/nondescript nature of overcomplex spaces, I draw on what Ludwig Wittgenstein called "description" and appropriate it for the analysis of cities.[2] On the one hand, when Wittgenstein writes that "we must do away with all *explanation*, and description alone must take its place," description can be understood as a kind of *de-scription*. This means that it is concerned not with knitting together explanations that make smooth connections between disparate series; rather, it welcomes friction – that is, disjuncture – and the mobile, fugitive, fragmentary detail. Wittgenstein writes: "We want to walk: so we need *friction*. Back to the rough ground!" On the other hand, Wittgenstein also insists that what concerns description is "of course, not empirical problems": "And this description gets its light, that is to say its purpose, from the philosophical problems. These are, of course, not empirical problems; they are solved, rather, by looking into the workings of our language, and that in such a way as to make us recognize those workings: in despite of an urge to misunderstand them." For our purposes, what might correspond to "language" is space. As philosophical issues are resolved by looking into the workings of language, so urban issues like cosmopolitanism might be clarified through a critique of space. Like language, space produces "an urge to misunderstand" its workings, an urge that needs to be resisted through de-scription.

What follows, then, is neither a theoretical nor an empirical account, but a de-scription of the cosmopolitan in relation to the spatial history of Shanghai and Hong Kong.

★ ★ ★

Shanghai and Hong Kong have always had a special relation to each other, if only through their relationship to the rest of the world. The historical facts about them are well known. Both cities were essentially created by Western colonialism in the aftermath of the Opium Wars: Shanghai as a lucrative treaty port and Hong Kong as a British colony and staging post for trade with China. For better or for worse, the two cities seemed to have been linked at birth, which makes it possible sometimes to read what is tacit in the history of one city in the history of the other. Each developed a form of cosmopolitanism under colonialism. From the outset, Shanghai generated a set of images about itself that contributed to its mystique but that we some-times think of as merely outlandish or bizarre. Nevertheless, it is these often conflicting and contradictory images that we will need to interrogate. It may be that every city gives itself away in the self-images that it produces; some-what like dream images that lead us to another history, or like cinema where, as Gilles Deleuze has argued, it is the filmic image that underlies the film narrative and not the other way around.[3]

We can begin with Shanghai, which was historically the senior city. Consider the political anomaly of extraterritoriality. In Shanghai, within the space of a hundred years, the extraterritorial presence of foreigners – British, American, and French, and after 1895, Japanese (to name only the most obvious) – turned the city into the Shanghai of legend, into what J. G. Ballard called "this electric and lurid city more exciting than any other in the world."[4] The existence of the different concessions, each with its own set of extraterritorial laws, meant that internal control of the city always had to be negotiated, often with the triad underworld operating as unofficial arbiters. However, this created less an anarchic city than a polycentric, decen-tered city controlled by many different hands. For example, the French Set-tlement used a 110-volt electric system, while the International Settlement used 220 volts! But far from being lawless, the space of Shanghai was subject to constant negotiations, and every initiative was observed from multiple perspectives. It was the existence of such a negotiated space that helped Shanghai in the 1920s and 1930s develop its own special brand of cosmopoli-tan urban culture: what we might call a cosmopolitanism of extraterritoriality.

The most visible signature of extraterritoriality was in the city's built space, with its proliferation of different styles of architecture, by turns elegant and kitschy. There were Tudor-style villas, Spanish-style townhouses, Russian-style churches, and German-style mansions, along with the internationalism of the buildings on the Bund and, of course, the Shanghainese lanehouses or Li Long housing complexes, these last also built by foreign architects with their preconceptions of what vernacular housing should look like. It was all a question of style imported from elsewhere – a shallow kind of cosmopolitan-ism, a dream image of Europe more glamorous even than Europe itself at the time; the whole testifying, it seems, to the domination of the foreign, espe-cially if we remember the decrepitude of the Chinese section of the city. But, at least in part, this was a deceptive testimony because within this setting something contrary was also happening. It could be argued, as Leo Ou-fan Lee has done in "Shanghai Modern," that the foreign presence produced not only new kinds of public and social spaces (such as cinemas, department stores, coffeehouses, dance halls, parks, and racecourses), but also spaces that could be *appropriated* by the Chinese themselves and used to construct a

Chinese version of modern cosmopolitan culture. From this point of view, cosmopolitanism in Shanghai could be understood not as the cultural domination by the foreign but as the appropriation by the local of "elements of foreign culture to enrich a new national culture."[5] Lee's persuasive account, rich in fascinating details, is interesting, too, for its attempt to steer the argument away from too facile "political critiques" of the cosmopolitan as cultural imperialism, towards a more nuanced reading of cultural history.

Still, foreign domination and local appropriation are not necessarily mutually exclusive. For example, it should not be forgotten that Shanghai's strength as a cosmopolitan city was always based on China's weakness as a nation. As such, there was always an underlying tension between national culture on the one hand, which could only be constructed as anticolonial resistance, and Shanghai cosmopolitanism on the other. Shanghai was always a subtly nonviable city, where splendour and squalor existed side by side. It was precisely the city's characteristic multivalence – its capacity to be all at once a space of negotiation, domination, and appropriation – that generated yet another image, perhaps the most telling of all: the grotesque. This grotesque nature of the city is captured best in a scene in Ballard's semiautobiographical novel, *Empire of the Sun*, documenting the last days of old Shanghai. The scene is set outside the Cathay Theater, at the time the largest cinema in the world. For its showing of *The Hunchback of Notre Dame*, the management recruited two hundred real-life hunchbacks from the back streets of Shanghai to form an "honour guard" for the glitterati attending the show! A *grand guignol* quality was never far behind the cosmopolitanism of Shanghai.

This grotesque element hints at something quite significant about Shanghai's cosmopolitanism, which could be extended even to the cosmopolitanism of other cities. It suggests that the cosmopolitan "attitude" in this case consists not in the toleration of difference but in the necessary cultivation of *indifference*: the hunchbacks were hired not in the spirit of equal opportunity employment but to create a gross sensation. Furthermore, to some extent the colonial experience had shattered the innocence of difference. The end result of having to negotiate a multivalent space that makes so many contrary demands on the individual was the cultivation of indifference and insensitivity to others. Even scandal and outrage could be openly accepted. Indeed, in its time old Shanghai had the reputation of being the most "open" city in the world. It was the one place in China that was free from the control of a debilitated and bureaucratic state apparatus, giving it an air of freedom that drew in both political reformers and intellectuals, both prostitutes and adventurers. The other side of this freedom and openness, however, was a certain isolation – a linkage to the world that went together with a delinkage from the rest of China. There was always something very fragile about Shanghai cosmopolitanism. After 1949, Chinese communism, born in Shanghai, quickly made Shanghai's urban culture no more than a memory.

[ . . . ]

For a long time, Hong Kong did not develop the kind of cosmopolitan culture that Shanghai exhibited in the 1920s and 1930s, a cosmopolitanism that emerged from the anomalous space of extraterritoriality. Dependency meant that for most of its history, Hong Kong, culturally speaking, was caught in the double bind of divided loyalties. It was politically ambivalent about both Britain and China; ambivalent about what language, English or Chinese, it should master; and confident only about capital. The one moment when it began to rival the cultural vibrancy of Shanghai in the 1930s was during the 1980s and 1990s, after the Joint Declaration announcing the return of Hong Kong to China in 1997: that is, at precisely the moment when Hong Kong felt most vulnerable and dependent. This was the period when more and more people discovered, invented, and rallied behind what they called "Hong Kong culture." This Hong Kong culture was a hothouse plant that appeared at the moment when something was disappearing: a case of love at last sight, a culture of disappearance. In contrast to Shanghai in the 1930s, nationalism was a negative stimulus: one major anxiety was that the internationalism of the port city would be submerged and smothered by its reinscription into the nation. But the anxiety was tempered by a tacit hope that Hong Kong might indeed be a special case. This was what redirected attention back to the city's local peculiarities, in an attempt to reinvent it one last time even as it disappeared. This sense of disappearance as the experience of living through the best and the worst of times was the seminal theme of the New Hong Kong Cinema. If filmmakers like Wong Kar-wai, Stanley Kwan, Ann Hui, and Tsui Hark managed to convey in their films a cosmopolitan sensibility, it was partly by focusing on local issues and settings, but in such a way that the local was dislocated: through the construction of innovative film images and narratives and, above all, through the introduction of the disappearing city as a major protagonist in their films.[6] Hong Kong cosmopolitanism was stimulated then not so much by a space of multivalence – which was the case in 1930s Shanghai – as by a space of disappearance, one effect of which was the transformation of the local into the *translocal* as a result of historical exigencies.

★ ★ ★

To recapitulate: in Shanghai in the 1920s and 1930s we found a cosmopolitanism of extraterritoriality, and in Hong Kong from the 1980s onward, a cosmopolitanism of dependency, with its thematic of the disappearing city.

But what of today and tomorrow? Two events in the 1990s can be considered symptoms that the cultural space these two cities seem destined to cohabit is once again changing. The 1990s saw not only the return of Hong Kong to China as an SAR (Special Administrative Region) but also the economic and cultural reappearance of Shanghai after more than four decades in the political cold. To consider if a new kind of cosmopolitanism is emerging today in Shanghai and Hong Kong, we will first have to consider the changing historical space of these two cities.

Now that Hong Kong is part of China again, there is a lot of speculation about whether Shanghai will replace it as the country's main economic and financial center once the Chinese yuan becomes fully convertible. The mayor of Shanghai, Xu Kuangdi, in a Hong Kong newspaper interview, addressed the issue of Shanghai and Hong Kong as follows: "You don't have to worry about Shanghai replacing Hong Kong; or that because of Hong Kong, Shanghai is not going to become a financial centre. They play different roles. . . . In the future, their relationship will be like two good forwards on a football team. They will pass the ball to each other and both will do their best to score more goals. But they are on the same team – China's national team." In the same interview, he conceded that Hong Kong "is more international than Shanghai. It is a financial centre for Southeast Asia. Not only does it link China with the world, it also serves as a trading market for Southeast Asian countries. Shanghai primarily serves as a link between the mainland and the rest of the world."[7]

Xu's homely image of Shanghai and Hong Kong as two good forwards on the national team is reassuring because as a public statement it understandably minimises whatever tensions might exist between the city, the nation, and the transnational or global. But such tensions do exist. In Hong Kong, for example, these tensions produced a skewing of cultural and political space that could be read in the city's cultural forms, such as its architecture and new cinema. The return of Hong Kong to China threatened to make the former disappear in the sense that the transnational status it had established for itself might be merged and submerged into the national. In Shanghai, because of the different relation of the city to the nation, it is not a question of the city's disappearance but of its reappearance, a reappearance coinciding with China's reinscription, after decades of closure, into the global economy. But Shanghai's "reappearance" is as complexly situated as Hong Kong's culture of disappearance in a space of tensions and skewed images. For example, since the early 1990s Shanghai has been obsessed with a mania for building and urban development, but accompanying it like a shadow is something that at first sight seems rather puzzling: the state's interest in preservation projects. It is within the problematic of tensions between the city, the nation, and the transnational that comparisons between "reappearance" in Shanghai and "disappearance" in Hong Kong can be made and the question of cosmopolitanism can be posed.

Let's take the Shanghai case. Before the early 1990s, there was very little interest among the Shanghainese in the buildings they lived and worked in. If a large part of old Shanghai was preserved, it was by default, because the city had too few resources to embark on major programs of urban restructuring. As late as the early 1990s, visitors to Shanghai often remarked how little Shanghai had changed visually from its pre-1949 days, except to note that a large part of the glitter had gone. However, after Deng Xiaoping's 1992 visit, and within the space of a few years, the Pudong area of Shanghai across the Huangpu River from the Bund has developed into a mini-Manhattan, following Deng's agenda for it: "A new look each year, a transformation in three years." Today, even Hong Kong visitors, blasé about new buildings, are amazed by Shanghai. In a few short years, Shanghai saw the construction of over a thousand skyscrapers, a subway line, a highway overpass ringing the city, another bridge and tunnel across the Huangpu to Pudong, and the urbanization of Pudong itself, now coming into being before our eyes like the speeded-up image of time-lapse film. Interestingly enough, together with this frenzy of building and development – subsidised by the sale of land leases and joint venture capital – the city has shown an interest in preservation, something not specifically recommended by Deng. So far, around 250 buildings have been registered as municipal listed buildings, with another 200 more being considered. This is remarkable enough for us to ask, What, in fact, is happening?

Let me offer the following hypothesis: Preservation in Shanghai is motivated by something quite different from the usual pieties about "cultural heritage," which, given the city's colonial past, can only be ambiguous. It is motivated more by anticipations of a new Shanghai to rival the old than simply by nostalgia for the past. In other words, preservation is something more complex than just a question of the past remembered: in Shanghai, the past allows the present to pursue the future; hence "memory" itself is select and fissured, sometimes indistinguishable from amnesia. This paradox of the past as the future's future also throws a particular light on Shanghai's urban development, which, like preservation, takes on a special quality: Shanghai today is not just a city on the make with the new and brash everywhere – as might be said more aptly of Shenzhen, for example. It is also something more subtle and historically elusive: *the city as remake*, a shot-by-shot reworking of a classic, with the latest technology, a different cast, and a new audience. Not "Back to the Future" but "Forward to the Past." The minor story of preservation in Shanghai gives an important *gloss* – in both senses of the word – to the major story of urban development.

In rapidly developing cities, urban preservation as a rule is either ignored or merely paid lip service. Take the case of Hong Kong, in many ways a role model for Shanghai and other Chinese cities. Yet Hong Kong offers a comparatively straightforward example of the relationship between development and preservation. Though it is true that there are some preserved buildings in this former British colony – the best known being the clock tower of the demolished Hong Kong–Canton Railway Station, now a part of the Hong Kong Cultural Centre Complex; the old Supreme Court building; Western Market; and Flagstaff House, formerly British military headquarters and now a tea museum – on the whole, preservation happens ad hoc, with no systematic plan for municipal preservation comparable to Shanghai's. An interest in Hong Kong and its history, moreover, and hence in preservation, is only a recent phenomenon with origins tied to 1997 and an anxiety that Hong Kong as we knew it might come to an end with the handover. However, such an interest in preservation never proved strong enough to prevent hardnosed development decisions from being made in the market economy of a so-called noninterventionist state, and this circumstance has changed little since Hong Kong became an SAR. By contrast, the twist that Shanghai provides is in opting to develop and, at the same time, preserve at least part of the city, as if deliberately giving the lie to the notion that development and preservation are incompatible. This presents us with enough of an anomaly to prompt the question: Precisely what role is preservation meant to play in Shanghai's impending transformation?

To begin with the obvious, the economic importance of preservation cannot be underestimated. Invoking a continuity with a legendary past – no matter how ambiguous that past may have been – enhances the city's attractiveness, gives it historical cachet, and hence equips it to compete for foreign investment and the tourist trade on more favourable terms. The past is a kind of symbolic capital. At the same time, preservation often accompanies the revitalization and gentrification of decaying areas of the city and contributes to urban renewal. But preservation has a third feature peculiar to Shanghai itself: namely, the way the economic role of preservation maps onto the tensions inherent in China's "socialist market economy." Since late 1978, this economy has created a private sector within a socialist state; that is, it has allowed the global into the national. Moreover, the new private sector has consistently outperformed the state in the marketplace, raising questions of to what degree the state is in touch with the new market conditions. Mao had succeeded in curtailing capitalism by establishing the socialist state, just as Europe had ameliorated capitalism's effects through the welfare-democratic state. But that was a bygone capitalism. The new capitalism, global capital, is freshly able to act, constantly outpacing the interventions of the nation-state and making it look heavy-footed.[8]

In this context, the state's interest in preservation, via municipal policy, makes a lot of sense. Not only is preservation well within the competence of the state; it is also a way by which the state can enter the global market through promoting the city's past – that is, through the heritage industry. It is an implicit assertion of the state's involvement in and contribution to the future development of Shanghai – a way of mediating the need of the state for legitimacy and the demand of the private sector for profitability. By a strange twist, the state's interest in preservation is an assertion that it is still a player in the new global game. Hence, the entirely different relation to preservation in Hong Kong and Shanghai: in the one, ad hoc and linked to anxieties about the city's disappearance; in the other, state-planned and related to the city's reappearance as a soi-disant "City of Culture."

★ ★ ★

The working together of development and preservation in Shanghai suggests that a new problematic is emerging. Something peculiar must be happening if preservation produces not a sense of history but the virtuality of a present that has erased the distinction between old and new – or where local history is another gambit in the game of global capital. Perhaps virtual cities can only look like what Shanghai today looks like, with old and new compressed together in an apocalyptic now. The listed buildings on the Bund and the chaos of skyscrapers in Pudong do not so much confront as complement each other on either side of the Huangpu River; in a sense, both old and new are simply steps in the remake of Shanghai as a City of Culture in the new global space. In such a space, heritage issues can be fused and confused with political and economic interests. And precisely because of this, urban preservation in the global era cannot be seen in isolation from other urban and social phenomena. Links begin to emerge between what at first sight seem to be unrelated social spaces – between, for example, the municipal *preservational* projects such as the old buildings around Yu Yuen Garden, in the old "Chinese city," now turned into a kind of vernacular mall, and the city's much more publicized *developmental* projects of cultural modernization, such as the new Shanghai Museum and the Grand Theater, both in an already modernized Renmin Square. We can see hints of a similar logic of globalism operative in each.

Take the new Shanghai Museum, which was opened in 1996. It is designed to resemble a giant *ting*, an antique Chinese bronze vessel. The obvious visual message here is that in the city's pursuit of modernity, Chinese tradition is not forgotten. But there is also something else. Consider the experience of entering the museum. In the exhibition halls, we find the rare artworks that the museum is famous for expertly displayed: the ancient bronzes, the Sung and Yuan paintings. But what also catches the attention is how ostentatiously *clean* the museum is, not a common experience in Shanghai. There always seem to be some workers polishing the brass on the railings or the marble on the floor. Even the toilets are kept meticulously clean. The dirtier the streets around it, the cleaner the museum. And suddenly you realize that the museum does not think of itself as being part of a local space at all, but as part of a virtual global cultural network. The Shanghai Museum is not just where artworks are being shown in Shanghai; it is also where Shanghai *shows itself off* in its museum, with its image cleaned up and in hopes that the world is looking.

But "globalism" is not without its own aporias and anomalies. For example, something of the tensions in Shanghai's new social space can be felt in one admittedly minor but symptomatic example: the etiquette of mobile phones. For the newly affluent entrepreneurial class, these phones are as much functional tools as symbols of the culture of globalism. It is also this class that, along with foreign visitors, can patronize the expensive and elegant restaurants that are reappearing in Shanghai. One of the most expensive of these is the Continental Room at the Garden Hotel, whose standards of elegance require guests to switch off their mobile phones out of consideration for fellow diners. What seems an unobjectionable policy from one point of view has produced many a contretemps. For these new entrepreneurs, dining at the Garden Hotel and using mobile phones go together. There is no conception that these electronic devices can be in certain social situations sources of irritation for oneself or others. What we find here is an example of transnationalism without a corresponding transnational subject. These new kinds of social embarrassment may not be insignificant in that they are symptoms of how the speeded-up nature of social and cultural life inevitably results in the production of multiple, sometimes conflicting, paradigms confusing for the person who needs to negotiate them.

Of course, it is true that social life since the modern era has always been marked by change and confusion. Cosmopolitanism has been seen as an ability to acquit oneself, to behave well, under difficult cultural situations by juggling with multiple perspectives – even when these perspectives were forced upon us or adopted in indifference. The question is: Are the kinds of changes taking place in Asian cities and elsewhere today forcing upon us situations in which we cannot behave well, because these changes are threatening to destroy the space of cities as we know them and creating cities we do not know? From this point of view, the apparently slight example of the use of mobile phones in "inappropriate" situations now takes on greater weight. Their indiscriminate use in the present case is neither an example of boorishness nor a lack of consideration for others, nor even a transgression of the boundaries of social etiquette. It is, rather, a genuine confusion about where the boundaries are, making both "transgression" and "behaving well" equally problematic.

★ ★ ★

If the speed of change is creating spaces we do not understand, then one strategy might be to slow things down – to preserve some almost erased concept of civility and respect for otherness in the midst of chaos. This was what the older cosmopolitanisms had strived for. But, it seems to me, such a *conservative* strategy has little space for manoeuvre. One of the most interesting things we can learn from the example of urban preservation in Shanghai today is how it, too, is infused with the spirit of globalism. "Preservation" and "heritage" do not act as brakes against development; in some strange way, they further a developmental agenda. The problem of cosmopolitanism today still remains how we are to negotiate the transnational space that global capital produces.

[ . . . ]

Clearly, cosmopolitanism can no longer be simply a matter of behaving well or even of an openness to otherness. Otherness lost its innocence as a result of the colonial experience. Even less attractive is the alternative of a brutal embrace of ethnocentric vision, an anticosmopolitanism made more extreme because it exists in the new and charged situation of information and speed. Information does not only dispel bigotry but also disseminates it. Can there be a cosmopolitanism for the global age, and what would it be like?

We might look for an answer in the analysis of the nature of cities today, particularly an analysis of their linkage to the transnational more so than to the national. As the fashion designer Yohji Yamamoto said in Wim Wenders's 1989 film *Notebook on Cities and Clothes*, "I like all big cities. More than Japanese, I feel I'm from Tokyo. . . . Tokyo has no nationality." Large nation-states like the previous Soviet Union have been breaking up, but this is not because some kind of transnational state is coming into being, only a transnational or global space where nation-states are still located. And cities are the locales or nodal points of this transnational space, which exists not in some abstract dimension but in the very specific sites and problem areas of the city. It exists, for example, in the problematic details of heritage and preservation in present-day Shanghai, in the non-places that Augé has pointed to, or in new kinds of social embarrassment that are the result of quickly shifting cultural paradigms. Whether a cosmopolitanism for the global age will emerge depends on our ability to grasp a space, that of the global city, that is always concrete even in its elusiveness. And this involves not so much imagining a transnational state as reimagining the city.

## Notes

1   Marc Augé, *A Sense for the Other*, trans. Amy Jacobs (Stanford, Calif.: Stanford University Press, 1998), 106.
2   All quotations are from paragraphs 107 and 109 of Ludwig Wittgenstein, *Philosophical Investigations*, trans. G. E. M. Anscombe (Oxford: Basil Blackwell, 1974), 46–7.
3   See Gilles Deleuze, *Cinema*, 2 vols., trans. Hugh Tomlinson and Barbara Habberjam (Minneapolis: University of Minnesota Press, 1986–9).
4   J. G. Ballard, *Empire of the Sun* (London: Grafton Books, 1985), 17.
5   Leo Ou–fan Lee, "Shanghai Modern: Reflections on Urban Culture in China in the 1930s," *Public Culture* 11 (1999), 104.
6   See Abbas, "The Erotics of Disappointment," in *Wong Kar-wai*, ed. Jean-Marc Lalanne, David Martinez, Ackbar Abbas, and Jimmy Ngai (Paris: Editions Dis Voir, 1997), 39–81.
7   Xu Kuangdi, interview by Matthew Miller and Foo Choy Peng, *South China Morning Post* (Hong Kong), China Business Review section, 9 July 1998, 8.
8   On these issues, see Ulrich Beck, *What Is Globalization?* (Cambridge: Polity Press, 2000).

# PART V
## Creative Enterprises

*Stuart Cunningham*

# CREATIVE ENTERPRISES

It follows from the ambitiousness and scope of understandings of the nature of creative industries that there is a corresponding diversity in the nature of creative enterprises. If garage rock bands and weekend craft stalls through to some of the world's biggest "content" multinationals – AOL TimeWarner, News Limited, Bertelsmann, Vivendi and the rest – equally fit the "creative enterprise" bill, any examination of the way their modes of activity and enterprise work is bound by necessity to be nimble, while needing at the same time to set out the ranges and types of enterprise across the sector.

This section's approach to the field is not principally through organizational studies of different types of business (for which see Hesmondhalgh 2002: ch. 5; and see part VI in this volume). Instead it looks at how creative enterprise has been and might be viewed through a policy and industry development perspective. Taking both a descriptive and analytic approach, it divides the policy and industry development perspective into "culture," "services," and "knowledge." These approaches are beginning to serve as possible rationales for state support of the creative industries, as well as the sector's own understandings of its nature and role.

Creative enterprises benefited from a cultural industries and policy "heyday" around the 1980s and 1990s, as the domain of culture expanded. But this moment is being transformed by the combined effects of the "big three" – convergence, globalization, and digitization – which underpin a services industries model of industry development and global regulation. This model, despite dangers, carries advantages in that it can mainstream the creative industries as economic actors and lead to possible rejuvenation of hitherto marginalized types of content production.

But new developments around the knowledge-based economy point to the limitations for wealth-creation of efficiency gains and liberalization strategies that operate only at the micro-economic level; the classic services industries strategies. Recognizing that such strategies won't undergird innovative, knowledge-based industries, governments are now accepting a renewed intervention role for the state in setting twenty-first-century industry policies. Creative enterprises are beginning to be seen, and to see themselves, in the light of these new frameworks for innovation and knowledge-based industries, which may be the most likely to advance the sustainability and positioning of the cutting-edge end of the creative industries into the future.

This section therefore includes both a descriptive account of the diverse nature of creative enterprises, seeking to create a useful taxonomy of their activity, and also a normative argument about policy frameworks and strategies that are or could be used to advance the viability and growth of creative enterprises.

Table 1 outlines some typical characteristics of these approaches to understanding creative enterprise.

**Table 1**. Characteristics of creative enterprises

| Culture | Services | Knowledge |
| --- | --- | --- |
| Micro and SMEs | Medium to large firms | Small and large |
| Production | Distribution/aggregation | Innovation |
| Cultural, often not-for-profit, steady-state | Mature businesses/industry sectors | Emergent/recent but rapid growth sector |
| Creativity at the margins: the mothership–flotilla model | Organized creativity | Intense creativity and big aggregators |
| Culturally specific | Both culturally specific and generically creative | Generically creative |
| Cultural and creative industries | Service industries model (including telcos, health, education, government services, etc.) | Creative industries and inputs into wider service industries |
| Wide range of content, but generally cultural in intent and markets culturally specific | Large established content and service enterprises | Digital content and applications |
| Cultural policies | Industry and regulatory policies | Innovation and R&D policies |

## Culture: Not Just a Business, or Just Not a Business? –

The general introduction outlined the long history of the movement from arts and culture to creative industries. Despite the predilection for commentators to continue to treat many of these terms as interchangeable or treat differences of terminology as superficial, from an enterprise perspective, there is purchase in differentiating them.

We have had policies on arts, media, and new media for some time. There are also the various terms "cultural" industries, "content" industries, "copyright" industries, "entertainment" industries, and more in this terminological mishmash. Why is the term "creative industries" useful?

- It mainstreams the economic value of the arts and media. It does this through recognizing that creativity is a critical input into the newly developing sections of the economy – the so-called "new economy."
- It brings together in a provisional convergence a range of sectors which have not typically been linked with each other.
- The sectors within creative industries – the established visual and performing arts, dance, theater, etc.; the established media of broadcasting, film, TV, radio, music; and new media, including software, games, e-commerce and e-content – move from the resolutely non-commercial to the high-tech and commercial. This continuum moves from the culturally specific non-commercial to the globalized and commercial, where *generically creative*, rather than *culturally specific*, content drives advances.

This continuum is less coherent than the neat definitions for the arts, media, and cultural industries, but more dynamic, ambitious, and policy-relevant. One of the reasons the idea of creative industries has been taken up so widely is that it connects two key contemporary policy clusters:

- *production in the new economy*: high-growth ICT and R&D-based sectors;
- *consumption in the new economy*: the "experience" economy with cultural identity and social empowerment.

The term "cultural industries" was invented to embrace the commercial industry sectors – principally film, broadcasting, advertising, publishing, and music – which also delivered popular culture to a national population. This led to a cultural industries policy heyday around the 1980s and 1990s, as the domain of culture expanded. In some places it is still expanding, but is not carrying much heft in the way of public dollars with it, and this expansion has elements trending towards the – perfectly reasonable – social policy end of the policy space, with its emphasis on culture for community development ends.

Meanwhile, cultural policy fundamentals are being squeezed. They are nation-state specific in a time of globalization and power of the World Trade Organization. Cultural nationalism is no longer in the ascendancy socially and culturally. Policy rationales for the defense of national culture are less effective in the convergence space of new media. Marion Jacka (2001) shows that broadband content needs industry development strategies rather than cultural strategies as broadband content is not the sort of high-end content that has typically attracted regulatory or subsidy support. The sheer size of the content industries and the relatively minute size, economically speaking, of the arts *per se* within them, underline the need for clarity about the strategic direction of cultural policy. John Howkins (2001) estimates the "creative economy" total at $US2.2 trillion in 1999, with the arts at 2 percent of this (although controversially he includes science R&D as "creative," thus marginalizing the arts in a major way). Perhaps most interestingly and ironically, cultural industries policy was a "victim of its own success": cultural industry arguments have indeed been taken seriously, often leading to the agenda being taken over by other, more powerful, industry, economic development, and innovation departments (see O'Regan 2001; Cunningham 2002).

Having put the case for moving from the arts, media, and cultural industries to a notion of the creative industries, it must also be acknowledged that these are unusual "industries." The professional interest group Focus on Creative Industries (FOCI) in the UK captures its distinctiveness well:

> Whilst FOCI welcomes the recognition of the strong economic contribution made by the creative industries in terms of wealth creation and employment,

**Table 2.** Cultural industries compared to creative industries

| Cultural industries model | Creative industries model |
| --- | --- |
| Nation-state | Global/local |
| Analog | Digital |
| Neoclassical economics applied to the arts | "New economy" economics |
| Rebadging large established popular industries as "cultural" | SMEs in flotilla–mothership formation |
| Established sectors | Emergent sectors and inputs into wider service economy |

we would also keenly stress that this sector is very different from traditional industries. They deal in value and values, signs and symbols; they are multi-skilled and fluid; they move between niches and create hybrids; they are multi-national and they thrive on the margins of economic activity; they mix up making money and making meaning. The challenge of the creative industries is the challenge of a new form of economic understanding – they are not "catching up" with serious, mainstream industries, they are setting the templates which these industries will follow. <http://www.mmu.ac.uk/h-ss/mipc/foci/mission.htm>

In his wide-ranging study of the economics of the creative industries, Richard Caves (2000: 2–10) has identified seven distinctive characteristics of these industries:

- Considerable uncertainty about the likely demand for creative product, because creative products are "experience goods" where buyers lack information prior to consumption, and where the satisfaction derived is largely subjective and intangible.
- The ways in which creative producers derive non-economic forms of satisfaction from their work and creative activity, but are reliant upon the performance of more "humdrum" activities (for example, basic accounting and product marketing) in order for such activities to be economically viable.
- The frequently collective nature of creative production, and the need to develop and maintain creative teams that have diverse skills, and who often also possess diverse interests and expectations about the final product.
- The almost infinite variety of creative products available, both within particular formats (for example videos at a rental store), and between formats.
- Vertically differentiated skills, or what Caves terms the "A list"/"B list" phenomenon, and the ways in which producers or other content aggregators rank and assess creative personnel.
- The need to coordinate diverse creative activities within a relatively short and often finite time frame.
- The durability of many cultural products, and the capacity of their producers to continue to extract economic rents (for example copyright payments) long after the period of production.

This makes for unusual organizational forms and a viral form of growth and activity that is often hard for industrial-age statistics and strategies to grasp and respond to. A study of the shape and trends in European businesses in

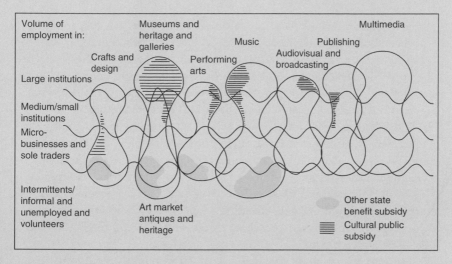

**Figure 1**. The 'hourglass' diagram from *Banking on Culture*
*Source*: Hackett et al. 2000

the sector points to high levels of employment volatility apart from the echelon of senior executives and managers, concentration of power amongst a small number of large multinational companies at the distribution and aggregation end of the value chain, and an "hourglass effect" (see figure 1) in the distribution of employment, with much smaller employment in medium-sized businesses than normal for industry sectors in general, which exhibit a pyramid rather than hourglass shape (Hackett et al. 2000). "The difference between the cultural sector and other industries is the result of public support inflating the number of larger organizations and the difficulty and lack of propensity of small scale enterprises to grow into medium sized ones" (p. 10).

## Why Cultural Entrepreneurs Matter: Charles Leadbeater and Kate Oakley

Charles Leadbeater and Kate Oakley have been influential as consultants and analysts of creativity and the new economy in Blair's Britain. *The Independents: Britain's New Cultural Entrepreneurs* is an early staking out of what was then rather new conceptual territory. This small report, which was jointly funded by industry and government, points to a "missing middle" in policy-making at both national and local levels in respect of creative industries enterprises and entrepreneurs:

how they work, where they come from, their distinctive needs, and how government at all levels might interact with them. This "missing middle" also refers to a necessary culture change amongst many in the creative sector. The challenge for emerging creatives is to grasp opportunity and to fashion themselves towards the new economy, and to adopt a more entrepreneurial and business-like approach to creative production.

Published in 1999 but researched on the cusp of the DCMS task force's work, it performs for creative enterprises what Garnham (1987) did previously for the cultural industries argument – put it on the agenda with an astute mixture of new theory, empirics, and policy nous. Leadbeater and Oakley steer mid way between what Angela McRobbie would call "cheerleading" (see part VI) and critique – the voice is constructive but conscious of the volatility and fragility of the small creative enterprise.

How to take some of the changes forced through the economy and public institutions during the long reign of Thatcher (and her "enterprise culture") and make them over for more inclusive and social democratic ends? This had particular importance for production outsourcing policies of the public broadcasters, including the BBC, ITV, and Channel 4. How to deal with the dominance of London - one of the embedded themes of cultural life in the UK – by taking a strategic regionalist perspective that takes up the insights offered by economic and cultural geography (which has gone on to exert a powerful influence on the creative industries field)? How to show that the flotilla–mothership model of connecting widely dispersed SMEs and large electronic and other aggregators might work?

Many of the key themes of subsequent creative industry debates are touched on in *The Independents*: strategic regionalism, informed by cultural geography and notions of the cluster; a thoroughly mixed economy approach, connecting the non-commercial with the commercial; the centrality of the creative entrepreneur and a small business approach; an awareness of consumption driving the creative industries as significantly as production.

## Cultural Services and the "Culturization" of Services

Howkins points out that it is "indeed one of the great strengths of creative work that it can be small-scale and non-profit (whereas you cannot start a small-scale, non-profit steel mill). But we must not get into the habit of thinking that the creative industries are primarily small and non-profit" (Howkins, 2001: 2, see part II). This takes us on to a consideration of large service industries, which include the big creative industries such as publishing, broadcasting, games, and music companies.

But the broader service industries, such as health, telecommunications, finance, education, and government services, also need more creativity through increased intermediate inputs, and it is here that much of the growth opportunity for creative enterprises is occurring. Just as it has been received wisdom for two decades that society and economy are becoming more information-intensive through ICT uptake and embedding, so it is now increasingly clear that the trend is toward "creativity-intensive" enterprise. This is what Lash and Urry (1994) refer to as the "culturalization of everyday life" and why Venturelli calls for "moving culture to the center of international public policy" (see part VI).

It is not surprising that this is where the growth opportunities are, as all OECD countries display service sectors which are by far the biggest of their respective economies (the services sector is in the 60+ − 70+ percent range for total businesses; total gross value added; and employment across all OECD economies), and that relative size has generally been growing steadily for decades.

We can begin to see how this "services" conception of creative enterprises might work by considering **television**, a *big creative industry* that can also be seen as a *central service industry*. Much convergence talk has it that a potent but as yet unknown combination of digital television and broadband will become a − if not *the* − prime vehicle for the delivery or carriage of services. Education, banking, home management, e-commerce, and medical services are some of the everyday services which types of interactive television and broadband might deliver.

But for television to be considered a central service industry takes the convergence tendency to a new level. For most of its history, media content, and the conditions under which it is produced and disseminated, have typically been treated as issues for cultural and social policy in a predominantly nation-building policy framework. They have been treated as "not just another business" in terms of their carriage of content critical to citizenship, the information base necessary for a functioning democracy, and as the primary vehicles for cultural expression within the nation.

In the emerging services industries policy and regulatory model, which has also been called the "new" public interest, media content could be treated less as an exception ("not just another business") but as a fundamental, yet everyday, part of the social fabric. Rather than television's traditional bedfellows of cinema, the performing arts, literature and multimedia, it is seen as more related to telecommunications, e-commerce, banking and financial services, and education.

John Hartley's *Uses of Television* (1999) provides a sophisticated theoretical support for this services industries model of media content. For Hartley, the media, but especially television, have a "permanent" and "general," rather specific and formal, educational role in the manners, attitudes, and assumptions necessary for citizenly participation in communities (1999: 140). "Contemporary popular media as guides to choice, or guides to the attitudes that inform choices" (p. 143) underpin Hartley's allied claim for the media's role in promoting DIY or "do-it-yourself" citizenship.

The model carries dangers. As the concerns about the WTO expressed through the Alliance for Cultural Diversity show, it subjects all television systems to a normative, globalizing perspective and thus weakens the specifics of a cultural case for national regulation and financial support. Its widespread adoption would see the triumph of what might be called the US regulatory model, where competition is the main policy lever and consumer protection rather than cultural development is the social dividend. The application of this model across the board is not a universal panacea for all industry regulatory problems, as most mid-level and smaller countries need to, or do, acknowledge.

However, there are also possible advantages. Hitherto marginal programming could be significantly upgraded in a services industries model. Programming produced for and by regional interests might be regarded as fundamental as the guarantee of a basic telephone connection to all, regardless of location. The need for programming inclusive of demographics such as young people and children might be as crucial as free and compulsory schooling. Moves in various jurisdictions, including the EU and Canada, to give greater weighting to regional, infotainment, youth and children's programming, signal a shift in priority of content regulation to include these alongside a continuing emphasis on drama and social documentary (see Goldsmith et al. 2002). While the latter advance core cultural objectives such as quality, innovation, and cultural expression, the former warrant greater consideration in a services industries model of media content regulation in terms of their contribution to diversity, representation, access, and equity.

What of "creativity-intensive" service industries? Taking one central example, **design** is one of the most dynamic and diverse of the creative industries, and in 1999 was worth globally $US140 billion, according to John Howkins (2001: 96), of which the US, Japan, and Germany produced 60 percent. There is huge growth – the average annual growth in design jobs over 1995–2000 was 21 percent. Design is also a fundamental input into most products and services in the new economy; it is one of the key instances of creativity-as-enabler of the service economy.

The World Economic Forum's Global Competitiveness Report 2001–2 shows that there is a distinct correlation between design intensity in enterprise activity and product development, and broad economic competitiveness. This is borne out at the headline level by the observation that the countries identified as most competitive each have developed product brands that are world-leading (table 3).

PriceWaterhouseCooper's research demonstrates that design "is seen as a strategic asset by the highest performing enterprises, while less successful businesses give design a lower level of importance" (cited in Design Taskforce 2003: 25). One of the key issues that design raises for the contemporary service enterprise is a demand- rather than supply-driven focus. Chairman of web services business LookSmart Evan Thornley (2003) points out that an exclusively production-centered focus is a legacy of a commodity-driven economy, and a really competitive environment with a central export focus will bring customer research, branding, and distribution to the fore. For high-growth creative and service industries, innovation is as much a customer-driven as a technology-driven process (see part II).

In the telecommunications market, much growth occurs at the retail end through the huge uptake of PDAs, mobile/cellphones and the use of new networks (3G) and network features (audiovisual data exchange). Whereas a great deal of business practice remains production-centric – with the matter of design inputs often relegated to marketing and commercialization strategies – the strong players in the retail phone market regard design-for-branding as their core business.

The headline case of Nokia illustrates this well, as described by Kotro and Pantzar (2002, to whom the following paragraphs are indebted). When Nokia first took on the dominant phone-making company in the US market, Motorola, it had a brand recognition deficit of 10 percent to 63 percent. In a matter of a decade or less to 2000, Nokia was rated among the five most valuable brands in the world. Nokia's success in the global phone market is a good example of players other than the dominant US, UK, Japanese, and western European players gaining a competitive (rather than comparative) advantage in the new economy. Companies from Finland, Sweden, the Netherlands, New Zealand, and South Korea are examples of this.

Nokia's history is one of a Finnish equivalent of a Korean *chaebol* – a conglomerate in many incommensurate markets – that turned in the early 1990s from this failing strategy to focus on wireless telephony. It started to distance itself from "the dominance of technical issues and the image of a sophisticated, and thus 'demanding,' technology" (Kotro and Pantzar 2002:

STUART CUNNINGHAM

34). It was arguably the first phone company to sense the fundamental shift from mobile telephony for business only to daily life and "lifestyle," and fashioned a strategy around that shift. Its focus on branding, the design thinking that linked Nokia phones to fashion shows and to advertising in fashion scenes, product placement in key movies like *The Matrix*, and physical design improvements like different-color skins for the phone led Nokia to think of itself not as a telecommunications product retailer but as a "design house for mobile communication" (Kotro and Pantzar 2002: 36).

## Value-Added, Knowledge-Based Enterprises

Creative enterprises should increasingly be seen as an integral element of high-value-added, knowledge-based emergent industries. This is the least developed of the triad of positions outlined here, but it is the one most likely to advance new positioning of the high-growth cutting edge of the creative industries into the future.

To make this argument, it is necessary to consider how and why – and which – creative enterprises might qualify as high-value-added, knowledge-based industry sectors. From where has this new macro-focus emerged? In part, it has been around for some time, with notional sub-divisions of the service or tertiary industry sector into quaternary and quinary sectors based on information management (fourth sector) and knowledge generation (fifth sector). But the shorter-term influence is traceable to new growth theory in economics which has pointed to the limitations for wealth creation of only micro-economic efficiency gains and liberalization strategies (Arthur 1997; Romer 1994, 1995). These have been the classic services industries strategies.

Governments are now attempting to advance knowledge-based economy models, which imply a renewed interventionary role for the state in setting twenty-first-century industry policies, the prioritization of innovation and

**Table 3**   Leading world brands, by country

| Country | Branded product or service |
| --- | --- |
| Finland | Nokia, Fiskars, Suunto |
| United States | Google.com, Apple, Coca Cola |
| Netherlands | Shell, Philips, Heineken |
| Germany | BMW, Volkswagen, Adidas |
| Switzerland | Nestlé, Bodum, Swatch |
| Denmark | Carlsberg, Lego, Bang & Olufsen |

*Source*: Design Taskforce 2003: 24.

R&D-driven industries, the intensive reskilling and education of the population, and a focus on universalizing the benefits of connectivity through mass ICT literacy upgrades. Every OECD economy, large or small, or even emerging economies (e.g. Malaysia) can try to play this game, because a knowledge-based economy is not based on old-style comparative factor advantages, but on competitive advantage, namely what can be constructed out of an integrated labor force, education, technology and investment strategies.

The creative industries *don't as a rule figure* in R&D and innovation strategies. But they should. Creative production and cultural consumption are an integral part of most contemporary economies, and the structure of those economies is being challenged by new paradigms that creativity and culture bring to them.

Worldwide, the creative industries sector has been among the fastest-growing sectors of the global economy, with growth rates better than twice those of advanced economies as a whole. Entertainment has displaced defense in the US as the driver of new technology take-up, and has overtaken defense and aerospace as the biggest sector of the southern Californian economy (Rifkin 2000: 161). Rifkin (2000: 167) claims that cultural production will ascend to the first tier of economic life, with information and services moving to the second tier, manufacturing to the third tier, and agriculture to the fourth tier.

Most R&D priorities reflect a science and technology-led agenda at the expense of new economy imperatives for R&D in the content industries, broadly defined. But the broad content industries sector – derived from the applied social and creative disciplines (business, education, leisure and entertainment, media and communications) – represents 25 percent of the US economy, whilst the new science sector (agricultural biotech, fiber, construction materials, energy, and pharmaceuticals), for example, accounts for only 15 percent of the economy (Rifkin 2000: 52).

In fact all modern economies are consumption-driven, and the social technologies that manage consumption all derive from the social and creative disciplines. We can no longer afford to understand the social and creative disciplines as commercially irrelevant, merely "civilizing" activities. Instead they must be recognized as one of the vanguards of the new economy. R&D strategies must work to catch the emerging wave of innovation needed to meet demand for content creation in entertainment, education, and health information, and to build and exploit universal networked broadband architectures in strategic partnerships with industry.

Political economy or critical cultural studies (see e.g. *IJCS* 2004) might view these kinds of claims for creativity in the new economy as reductionist economism, and a "cheerleading" boosterism fatally deflated by the dot.com bust. However, I would argue that the creative and informational economy poses a serious challenge to traditional "scale and scarcity" economic orthodoxy as well as heritage notions of culture, and also that the trends toward the "culturization" of the economy are more long-term than the hothouse events of the late 1990s and early 2000s. As Venturelli argues: "the environmental conditions most conducive to originality and synthesis as well as the breadth of participation in forming new ideas comprise the true tests of cultural vigor and the only valid basis for public policy" (2002: 10). There is enough in new growth theory, and evolutionary and institutional economics, to suggest progressive new takes on traditional political economy. Creativity, once considered marginal, has had to be brought toward the heartland of economic thought, and with it its values. What was once considered the only model for innovation (science and technology) has had to make some way for creative content and process.

Despite the difficulties in shoehorning creative enterprises into innovation frameworks, designed as they are for the manufacturing sector, it is nevertheless beginning to occur as innovation and R&D policies evolve. Some talk of "third-generation" innovation policy, while others contemplate five generations of innovation. The trend is the same, however. Earlier models were based on the idea of a linear process for the development of innovation. This process began with basic knowledge breakthrough courtesy of laboratory science and public funding of pure/basic research and moves through successive stages – seeding, pre-commercial, testing, prototyping – till the new knowledge was built into commercial applications that diffused through widespread consumer and business adoption. Contemporary models take account of the complex, iterative, and often non-linear nature of innovation, with many feedback loops, and seek to bolster the process by emphasizing the importance of the systems and infrastructures that support innovation.

What, then, is R&D in creative enterprises? Major international content growth areas, such as online education, interactive television, multi-platform entertainment, multiplayer online games, web design for business-to-consumer applications, and virtual tourism and heritage, need *research* that seeks to understand how complex systems involving entertainment, information, education, technological literacy, integrated marketing, lifestyle and aspirational psychographics and cultural capital interrelate. They also need *development* through trialing and prototyping supported by test beds and infrastructure provision in R&D-style laboratories. They need these in the context of ever-shortening innovation cycles and greater competition in rapidly expanding global markets.

## Games, the New Lively Art: Henry Jenkins

The pieces by Henry Jenkins and JC Herz on the games industry may be treated as making a cogent case for games as an innovation sector from two sides of the same creative enterprises coin: Jenkins on cultural innovation and Herz on R&D as innovation. Consider, in the light of the R&D needs of the sector above, this description of latest or "fifth-generation" innovation framework:

> Systems integration and networking model: Fully integrated parallel development. Use of expert systems and simulation modelling in R&D. Strong linkages with leading edge customers ("customer focus" at the forefront of strategy). Strategic integration with primary suppliers including co-development of new products and linked information and design systems. Horizontal linkages: joint ventures; collaborative research groupings; collaborative marketing arrangements, etc. Emphasis on corporate flexibility and speed of development (time-based strategy). Increased focus on quality and other non-price factors. (Rothwell 1994)

Although based on manufacturing, it describes strongly what Jenkins and Herz are getting at in their accounts of the games industry. There is the tacit agreement that games are the quintessential high-end creative industry: globalized; fully digitized; highly networked (such as massive multiplayer online gaming); technologies driven by content innovation, not the other way around; and a sector that through convergence confounds old-style distinctions between broad- and narrow-band media (a major popular form that is highly interactive and "mass customized" through value-added use).

Jenkins continues in this piece his ongoing exploration of the cultural ecologies of game-playing and development. His address could be as much to gamers and developers as it is to the academic and student communities (who of course may be both). Taking the long view of how new media forms are routinely misconstrued as the part standing for the whole – as social problem, technological challenge, and economic force, but also as an art form demanding serious aesthetic evaluation – Jenkins shows that R&D is happening in the realm of the aesthetic: "art exists . . . on the cutting edge and that is where games had remained for most of their history." Games are being created without the "safety net" that "inherited modernist rhetoric" provides for established art forms.

## Harnessing the Hive: JC Herz

> For Herz, R&D becomes an explicit and central feature of games –
> there is "distributed innovation beyond the developer's walls" during
> which 10,000 people might be engaged in research and development.
> She is clear that the intense innovation, or value-adding, that is occur-
> ring is because of anthropology rather than code: content (and creative
> interaction) is king; and innovation occurs through collective (or rather
> networked) interactions. This echoes Leadbeater and Oakley's (2001)
> arguments against the "Eureka" individualist model of innovation and
> entrepreneurship in creative enterprises. Herz's analysis is allied to that
> of Lessig and arguments for a "creative commons" (see part I); indeed
> they are at the leading edge of that position, given Sony's predilection
> for control and litigation rather than partnering with their legions of
> value-adding users of the massive multi-player online success story
> *Everquest*.

National innovation frameworks are beginning to contemplate this shift to
include content creation. The US government's R&D effort continues to be
dominated by science-engineering-technology (SET) and particularly
defense-industry SET – the kinds of creative enterprise innovation discussed
here occur largely outside of governmental regulation or funding. Nevertheless, arguments are being advanced by policy "influencers" to shape national
thinking. Venturelli's arguments for "moving culture to the center of international public policy" (see part VI), and probes such as the National Academy of Sciences' "Beyond Productivity" (a good example of searching for
purchase for an investment strategy for the digital arts and design based on
innovation (Mitchell et al. 2003)), demonstrate that the terms of engagement
have been broached.

In Europe, while innovation and R&D policy, for the most part, remain
focused on big science and technology, the exception is probably digital
content creation, which is beginning to slip in as part of "technology," both
at an EU and a member state level (see www.cordis.lu). This is not happening at this stage through processes of explicit policy reconsideration, and
there are very few high-level policy documents, either in R&D or on innovation more broadly, which explicitly mention R&D for the creative industries. While there is the usual range of industry development support for
creative industries (soft loans, grants, development of networks), recognition
of the more particular R&D claims of creative skills and services more
broadly as intermediate input into a wider range of activities, while supported
in rhetoric, is not yet showing up in policy. There are also intriguing developments in other parts of the world.

The reason that these contemporary attempts to fit creative industries into an innovation policy framework are interesting is that they must deal with the quite unusual nature of the creative enterprise. While many if not most creative enterprises are intensely innovative (remember the almost infinite variety of creative products that Caves speaks about), innovation often occurs within the embrace of large, thoroughly commercial, enterprises which don't need to describe such and such a process as innovation in order to qualify for government support. Also, innovation can occur at almost any point in the "value chain" that a creative enterprise is involved in. This doesn't obey the linear logic of traditional policy frameworks which work to support the "pre-commercial" beginnings of the innovation process. The creative enterprise will continue to pose challenges to innovation frameworks because of its peculiarities, but also because of its increasing centrality to the shape of twenty-first-century economy and society.

# References

Arthur, B. (1997) Increasing Returns and the New World of Business. In J. S. Brown (ed.), *Seeing Differently: Insights on Innovation*. Harvard Business Review Books, Boston, 3–18.

Caves, Richard (2000) *Creative Industries: Contracts between Art and Commerce*. Harvard University Press, Cambridge, Mass.

Cunningham, S. (2002) From Cultural to Creative Industries: Theory, Industry, and Policy Implications. *Culturelink* 19–32.

Design Taskforce (2003) *Success by Design NZ: A Report and Strategic Plan*, Design Taskforce/New Zealand Government (GIF), May.

Garnham. N. (1987) Concepts of Culture: Public Policy and the Cultural Industries. *Cultural Studies* 1(1), 23–37.

Goldsmith, B., J. Thomas, T. O'Regan, and S. Cunningham (2002) Asserting Cultural and Social Regulatory Principles in Converging Media Systems. In Marc Raboy (ed.), *Global Media Policy in the New Millennium*. University of Luzon Press, Luzon.

Hackett, K., P. Ramsden, D. Sattar, and C. Guene (2000) *Banking on Culture: New Financial Instruments for Expanding the Cultural Sector in Europe*. Final report, September.

Hartley, J. (1999) *Uses of Television*. Routledge, London.

Hesmondhalgh, D. (2002) *The Cultural Industries*. Sage Publications, London.

Howkins, J. (2001) *The Creative Economy: How People Make Money from Ideas*. Allen Lane, London.

*IJCS* (2004) The New Economy, Creativity and Consumption. Special issue of the *International Journal of Cultural Studies* 7(1), Sage Publications, London.

Jacka, M. (2001) *Broadband Media in Australia: Tales from the Frontier.* Australian Film Commission, Sydney.

Kotro, T. and M. Pantzar (2002) Product Development and Changing Cultural Landscapes – Is our Future in "Snowboarding"? *Design Issues* 18(2), 30–45.

Lash, S., and J. Urry (1994) *Economies of Signs and Space.* Sage Publications, London.

Leadbeater, C. and K. Oakley (2001) *Surfing the Long Wave: Knowledge Entrepreneurship in Britain.* Demos, London.

Mitchell, W., A. Inouye, and M. Blumenthal (eds.) (2003) *Beyond Productivity: Information Technology, Innovation and Creativity,* National Academies Press, Washington.

O'Regan, T. (2001) *Cultural Policy: Rejuvenate or Wither?* Griffith University <http://www.gu.edu.au/centre/cmp/mcr1publications.html#tom>.

Rifkin, Jeremy (2000) *The Age of Access: How the Shift from Ownership to Access is Transforming Modern Life.* Penguin, London.

Romer, P. (1994) The Origins of Endogenous Growth. *Journal of Economic Perspectives* 8(1), 3–22.

Romer, P. (1995) Interview with Peter Robinson. *Forbes* 155(12), 66–70.

Rothwell, R. (1994) Towards the Fifth-Generation Innovation Process. *International Marketing Review* 11(1), 7–31.

Thornley, E. (2003) The Money or the Box. Warren Centre, <http://www.warren.usyd.edu.au/warren/2003 percent20Innovation percent20Lecture.pdf>.

Venturelli, Shalini (2002) *From the Information Economy to the Creative Economy: Moving Culture to the Center of International Public Policy.* Center for Arts and Culture, Washington.

*Charles Leadbeater and Kate Oakley*

# WHY CULTURAL ENTREPRENEURS MATTER

[ . . . ] A growing share of the employment and output of some of the fastest growing sectors of the British economy is accounted for by this new breed of Independents. The government's Creative Industries Task Force estimated that the cultural industries generate revenues of £50 billion a year, employ 982,000 and generate value-added of about £25 billion (4 per cent of gross domestic product) and had export earnings of £6.9 billion. These industries are growing at almost twice the rate of the economy as a whole, driven by powerful forces: cheaper and more powerful communications and computing, the spread of the Internet and growth in digital networks, which are opening up new distribution channels for small producers to serve global markets. As incomes and literacy levels rise around the world, so does the audience for English language services and content.

The Independents [ . . . ] are a driving force of this growth. A large and growing share of employment in these industries is accounted for by the self-employed, freelancers and micro-businesses. These new Independents are often producers, designers, retailers and promoters all at the same time. They do not fit into neat categories. The Independents thrive on informal networks through which they organise work, often employing friends and former classmates. Although some are ambitious entrepreneurs, many want their businesses to stay small because they want to retain their independence and their focus on their creativity. Yet that does not mean they see themselves as artists who deserve public subsidy. They want to make their own way in the market. They have few tangible assets other than a couple of computers. They usually work from home or from nondescript and often run-down

"Why Cultural Entrepreneurs Matter" from Charles Leadbeater and Kate Oakley (1999), *The Independents: Britain's New Cultural Entrepreneurs*. Demos, London, pp. 10–12, 13–19, 24–5, 26–7, 29–30, 75. Reprinted by permission of Demos, www.demos.co.uk.

workshops. Their main assets are their creativity, skill, ingenuity and imagination. Across Britain there are thousands of young Independents working from bedrooms and garages, workshops and run-down offices, hoping that they will come up with the next Hotmail or Netscape, the next Lara Croft or Diddy Kong, the next Wallace and Gromit or *Notting Hill*.

Yet alongside the growth of this thriving ecology of small Independents, two other trends are reshaping these cultural industries. One is the rapid pace of technological change, particularly digitalisation and the Internet, which is fundamentally altering how television, film software and entertainment will be distributed, stored and viewed. Another is the growing role of large companies, with global brands and reach, that increasingly dominate the distribution and publishing of commercial culture: Microsoft and Sony, Dreamworks and Disney, Time Warner and QVC. One of the aims of this report is to show how policy-makers can respond to give these young, often fragile companies a better chance of surviving amidst the swirl of these much larger forces. The capacity for the cultural industries, which are big exporters, to generate growth in jobs will in large part depend on whether this emerging base can be developed and strengthened to withstand the turbulence of the global markets upon which their output will increasingly depend.

One of the main findings of this research is that there is a large 'missing middle' in public policy at a national level and also, critically, at the regional and local level, where it most counts. Policy-makers know little about this new generation of entrepreneurs – how they work, where they come from, what makes them tick, their distinctive needs – nor how to interact with them. One of the chief aims of this report is to close that gap.

It is all too easy to dismiss cultural entrepreneurs as marginal, fashion conscious and ephemeral: a distraction from the real business of manufacturing or financial services. The new Independents matter not just because they will be a source of jobs and growth in the future but also because they provide one model of how work and production is likely to change in the future in other sectors. Our research shows that cultural entrepreneurs matter for six main reasons, as set out below.

## Jobs and Growth

Cultural industries are increasingly important to the generation of new jobs and economic growth.[1] Even on modest assumptions of 4 to 5 per cent growth in these industries, twice the rate of the economy as a whole, they could employ 1.5 million and generate revenues of £80 billion, worth 6 per cent of gross domestic product, by the end of the next decade. These estimates from the Creative Industries Task Force report are confirmed by our findings. The cultural industries employ between 2 and 8 per cent of the workforce in most British cities, rising to perhaps 10 per cent in London. To take Manchester as an example, a detailed analysis by the Manchester Institute of Popular Culture[2] found that 6 per cent of the Manchester workforce were employed in cultural industries, more than in construction and close to the scale of the long-established transport and communications sectors. The Independents account for perhaps two-thirds of the output of the faster growing sectors within the cultural economy.

## Local Economic Growth

Cultural industries can create local sustainable jobs, which are less prey to the ups and downs of the global economy than, for example, jobs in branch offices and factories of large multinational companies.

Cultural industries are people intensive rather than capital intensive. They raise few of the environmental concerns that surround large industrial developments. Cultural entrepreneurs within a city or region tend to be densely interconnected. They trade with one another: pop bands need videos made, video makers need graphic designers. This high level of internal trade within the cultural industries means that an extra £100 of spending on the output of these industries will tend to generate more local jobs than £100 spent on tradable commodities.

Cultural entrepreneurs, who often work within networks of collaborators within cities, are a good example of the economics of proximity. They thrive on easy access to local, tacit know-how – a style, a look, a sound – which is not accessible globally. Thus the cultural industries based on local know-how and skills show how cities can negotiate a new accommodation with the global market, in which cultural producers sell into much larger markets but rely upon a distinctive and defensible local base.

## A New Model of Work

The Independents represent a vision of the future of work with new technology that is especially appealing to the young and could influence the development of other service industries in which self-employment and micro-businesses are growing.

In the 1980s it was commonplace to argue that new technology was creating a future in which capital would do without workers: workerless factories and paperless offices would usher in 'the end of work'. The Independents represent a quite different vision of the future of work: workers who want to do without capital.[3]

The Independents of the 1990s have emerged from a convergence of three forces:

*Technology.* This is the first generation that grew up with computers and that understands how to reap the benefits of modern computing power and communications. In earlier decades, increased computer power primarily benefited large organisations. The Independents feel enabled, not threatened, by new technology.

*Values.* The Independents were brought up by parents who were teenagers in the 1950s and 1960s, and they themselves became teenagers under Mrs Thatcher. They are anti-establishment, anti-traditionalist and in respects highly individualistic: they prize freedom, autonomy and choice. These values predispose them to pursue self-employment and entrepreneurship in a spirit of self-exploration and self-fulfilment.

*Economics.* The Independents came into the workforce in the late 1980s and 1990s as public subsidies to the arts were under pressure and many large commercial organisations were in the midst of downsizing. Careers in large organisations became more risky and uncertain: self-employment and entrepreneurship became a more realistic option.

These three factors – technology, values and economics – have converged to make self-employment and entrepreneurship a natural choice for young people in these industries. The risks that would have put off their parents do not daunt them. Their values encourage them towards entrepreneurship. The falling price of technology makes self-employment a real possibility. The crisis of employment in large organisations makes it a more attractive option.

Life as an Independent is not nirvana, nor even necessarily a recipe for making money. It can provide choice, autonomy and satisfaction but it also involves constant uncertainty, insecurity and change. Many young people find this trade-off of autonomy against insecurity more attractive than working for a large, impersonal organisation. The Independents have an approach to developing a career as a portfolio of projects, contacts and skills that may become increasingly important in other sectors of the economy.

## A Model of Creative Production

The Independents are developing a highly collaborative, creative and networked model of production, which shows how other industries could be organised in future. These businesses are built on *the commercial application of creativity*. That is why they may have much to teach companies in other industries, from retailing and consumer goods to software and biotechnology, in which competition is increasingly driven by innovation. The way cultural entrepreneurs organise their creativity carries lessons for other businesses. Independents have individualistic values but highly collaborative working practices. Their collaborative networks provide lessons for other sectors that are developing more networked forms of organisation, with more people working at home or as self-employed 'e-lancers'. The cultural industries are home to frequent job-hopping. Partnerships, bands and teams are formed and reformed. In the process ideas and skills get spread. The predominance of team-based project work means people have to learn how to trust one another very speedily. Other industries, in which large companies have predominated, may well have to come to learn these skills which seem intuitive to the Independents.

## The Future of Cities

Cultural industries and entrepreneurs will play a critical role in reviving large cities that have suffered economic decline and dislocation over the past two decades. Culture is not just a source of jobs and income but also a sense of confidence and belonging. Cities that have invested successfully in cultural renewal do so to generate not just economic growth but also a renewed sense of civic pride and purpose.

Modern cities are nothing if they are not creative. They are centres for the largest and most diverse audiences for the consumption of culture and, as a result, cities are also home to the most productive clusters of cultural businesses. Cities attract newcomers and outsiders; they are places where people and ideas mix and mingle. They are places where knowledge and ideas are created, tested, shared, adapted and disseminated.[4] Policy towards the cultural industries is largely for and about cities. Cultural entrepreneurs will play two main roles in the regeneration of our larger cities.

Firstly, cultural entrepreneurs often take over offices, warehouses and factories left behind by the demise of older city-based industries. Employment in the cultural industries is primarily metropolitan: about 65 per cent of original production in cultural industries takes place in cities.[5] These industries thrive on a milieu that is itself creative and lively. Thus although the cultural industries do not, strictly speaking, include retailing, restaurants, hotels, bars and cafes, they can often create jobs in these sectors.

Secondly, cities that once based their identities around manufacture and trade are increasingly turning to sport and culture as a source of civic pride. Culture is increasingly central to how cities 'brand' themselves to attract students, inward investment and tourists. One of the most outstanding recent examples of this strategy is the transformation of Bilbao's international reputation with the building of Frank Gehry's Guggenheim Museum. Cultural entrepreneurship at the civic level will be critical to instil a renewed a sense of purpose, especially in cities that have been hollowed out by job losses and economic decline. To be effective, however, this demand-side approach to 'rebranding' a city with a new cultural image has to be matched by investment in indigenous production and business creation.

## Social Cohesion

Cultural entrepreneurs can play a critical role in promoting social cohesion and a sense of belonging. That is because art, culture and sport create meeting places for people in an increasingly diversified, fragmented and unequal society. Once these meeting places might have been provided by work, religion or trade unions.

Art and culture play a central role in some of the most impressive examples of social entrepreneurship, such as the Bromley-by-Bow project in the London's East End. Culture provided a central focus for the debate over Scottish identity in the run up to devolution, for example, through the opening of the National Museum of Scotland. Culture is often consumed publicly and jointly, it helps to provide a flow of shared experiences, language and images. For example, much modern pop music, and the fashion, language and style which goes with it, would be inconceivable without the influence of black music from which it sprang. Black people have probably had more influence on the dominant culture in Britain through pop music than any other channel.

Yet the growth of the cultural industries also poses some significant challenges in terms of social cohesion. Graduates make up a higher proportion of people in the youngest and fastest growing sectors than in other parts of the economy. Relatively few cultural entrepreneurs are from ethnic minority backgrounds. There is also a pronounced regional split in the distribution of jobs within these industries: London takes a far larger share of jobs in these industries than it does in other industries.

So although cultural consumption is critical to social cohesion, these cultural industries are less socially inclusive in terms of employment than other industries.

## Conclusion: Unrealised Potential

The rise of the cultural entrepreneurs has exposed a serious shortfall in public policy. This is a classic example of how the speed of change in society – in technology, values, consumer habits and business organisation – frequently outpaces the capacity of public policy to learn, adapt and respond. Public policy is lagging behind for numerous reasons:

- Traditional arts and culture policy has focused on grant-giving to subsidised institutions for visual and performance arts. Traditional 'public' arts bodies know relatively little about commercial, cultural entrepreneurs, who are often suspicious of public subsidies. They want to prove themselves in the commercial market.

- Policy-making within local and national government is often split between 'culture' and 'economic development' departments that have different agendas.

- Policy-makers in economic development agencies – the Welsh Development Agency and the Scottish Development Agency, for example – are used to dealing with large inward investment projects that bring hundreds of jobs. They lack the knowledge, time and tools to help develop a cluster of hundreds of independent micro-businesses.

- Cultural entrepreneurs need to develop a mix of creative and business skills often at different stages of their careers. Education institutions are often too inflexible to deliver these skills as and when the entrepreneurs need them. The skills of cultural entrepreneurship, managing a rock band for example, can be learned but usually from experience and peers rather than in a classroom.

- Business advice and finance, for example through the Business Links scheme or via the banks, is tailored to the needs of mainstream businesses. Cultural entrepreneurs recognise they need business advice but they want it from peers with whom they can identify rather than from 'men in suits' with little knowledge of these new industries.

- Finance is often unavailable at the time and of the scale these entrepreneurs want. Often at the outset when they are developing their ideas they need very small sums of money: a few thousand pounds to buy some computers. That micro-credit is often hard to come by. Later when they are hoping to develop their own products they need a form of venture capital. Although venture capital has become easier to access, many of these businesses find it hard to raise.

This shortfall in the capacity of public policy is part of the 'missing middle' – the institutions and policies that should stand between these small businesses and the global companies they are often supplying. Partly – but only partly – as a result of this shortfall, many cultural entrepreneurs run fragile, low-growth companies in industries that have low barriers to entry and a high turnover of talent and ideas. Their businesses are often under-capitalised and lack the management skills and bargaining power to deal with national and international publishers and distributors. As a result many of these businesses do not realise their full potential for growth.

[ . . . ]

Cultural entrepreneurs opt for independence because it allows them to work in the way they want, which they would find hard to justify within a larger organisation. This mode of work is central to the way they generate and apply their creativity to commercial ends. The Independents are generally highly motivated and have a strong work ethic, although they do follow a traditional workday or week. They accept their work will be judged on performance, in competition with their peers. People are usually only as good as their last project. They work in a highly competitive environment, in which fashions and technologies can change very rapidly. Their approach to work is based on four ingredients.

- *They blur the demarcation line between consumption and production.* Creativity is only rarely a flash of brilliance that revolutionises an industry or a discipline. Creativity is more usually an incremental development that modifies and adapts what has gone before. That means a creative producer has to learn from a stream of complementary and competing products, which might provide ideas for their own work. Creativity in these industries is a constant process of borrowing and mixing. To be a creative producer it helps to be an avid consumer.
- *They blur the demarcation line between work and non-work.* As consumption and leisure are inputs into the creation of cultural products, the corollary is that periods not at work – leisure, relaxation, entertainment – can be as important as periods at work hunched over a computer terminal. Both contribute to delivering a creative product. Many of these independents say their best ideas come to them when they are not at work. Finding and justifying this 'downtime' is critical to any creative business. This

carries lessons for larger businesses that pride themselves on punishing work schedules for executives that leave little room for thinking and creating new ideas.

- *They combine individualistic values with collaborative working.* Cultural producers generally have a core discipline, for example, as a designer, director, camera operator or animator. These skills are their central contribution to the creative process. However they recognise their particular skill is next to useless unless it can be combined with the skills of others: producers, set designers, actors, musicians. Although there are plenty of prima donnas, these Independents accept collaborative team-working as the norm. They expect to work in teams; they collaborate to compete.

- *They are members of a wider creative community.* Creative communities can provide ideas, contacts, complementary skills, venues and access to the market. They induce a process of intense rivalry and competition as well as promoting cooperation and collaboration. These creative communities are invariably formed within cities, often around hubs: universities, arts centres, managed workspaces or broadcasters.

## The Independent Business

[ . . . ]

Cultural entrepreneurs believe in 'small is beautiful'. They generally run small, under-capitalised and quite fragile companies. They operate in fashion-driven markets that are open to new entrants and in which new technologies are driving down the costs of production but also the prices that independents can charge for their services. They often lack and do not know how to acquire the business skills and support they need to grow a company.

There is nothing soft about life in these industries. These sectors are often chronically unstable and unpredictable. Given these pitfalls it is quite rational for Independents to want to stay small, not just for creative reasons but to avoid over-committing themselves. Given the diversity of cultural businesses it is impossible to describe a typical lifecycle that all such businesses pass through. The career of many cultural entrepreneurs is punctuated by success and failure, with periods of business expansions sometimes followed by a return to self-employment.

Many Internet-based companies, for example, believe they have a shelf life of perhaps only three years before having to completely change their business model and service. A leading Internet entrepreneur, Steve Bowbrick of

Funmail, is a good example of the ups and downs an entrepreneur goes through in the new media industries. In the early 1990s Bowbrick created WebMedia, a successful website design company. But three subsequent ventures to create Internet information services failed and WebMedia folded, taking a substantial amount of venture capital with it. Bowbrick spent a year developing three ideas for Internet-based marketing products, none of which was successful, before hitting on the idea of Funmail, a new email product that proved hugely popular after its launch in the summer of 1999.

However, in general these entrepreneurs and the businesses they create seem to face three critical choices at critical junctures of their development.

## Gestation

Independents often spend a lot of time (perhaps several years) early in their careers sorting out what they want to do, what their distinctive skill is and how they might make money from it. This period of exploration can be chaotic and unfocused but it is vital because often it is only the sense of vocation formed at this early stage that carries them through the uncertainties they will face later on. In this period cultural entrepreneurs often do not need business skills or large investments. They need quite small sums to keep going. At this stage they need access to micro-credit. At the moment the only institution providing such credit on a large scale is the Prince's Business Youth Trust, although the National Endowment for Science, Technology and the Arts has also entered the field.

## Growth

Once a cultural entrepreneur has sorted out their marketable skill they have a chance to grow, usually by selling services and one-off projects. In this phase people can move from freelancing to setting up as sole traders and then create a micro-business.

Growth of these service-based businesses, in which people have to constantly find new customers, is difficult to sustain. It requires a considerable investment of time and management expertise to manage cashflow. That means cultural entrepreneurs – now perhaps several years out of higher education – need to acquire basic business skills. They need to start formulating business plans and budgets. Businesses based on service provision often go through periods of feast, when they have a lot of work, followed by a famine: they have been so busy delivering their current projects they cannot find the time to sell new ones. In television this is becoming more difficult as budgets per hour of programming have generally been cut with the advent of digital technology, which should make production cheaper. Getting beyond this feast and famine cycle requires more sophisticated management to smooth the peaks and troughs of cash-flow. In this phase cultural entrepreneurs either have to acquire more basic business skills themselves or to recruit people with those skills. The entrepreneurs we interviewed often found it hard to do either.

'We used to concentrate on making all the films and documentaries ourselves. But then we realised we could be creative with the company rather than with the product. Rather than pursue an ambition to be a big director I decided to focus on building the company. We want to be able to develop our own content and own the rights. We want to go from supplying a service to owning a product. But that is more complex, risky and time consuming.' (Hamish Barbour, co-founder Ideal World, television and film production company, Glasgow)

## How to Make it as an Independent

1  Be prepared to have several goes. You're unlikely to make it first time around. Learn from failure, don't wallow in it.

2  Timing is critical. Technology is moving so fast it's easy to be either too early or too late.

3  Don't have a plan: it will come unstuck because it's too inflexible.

4  Have an intuition and a feel for where the market is headed which can adapt and change with the consumers.

5  Be brave enough to be distinctive. If you are doing what everyone else is doing you're in the wrong business.

6  Be passionate: if you don't believe in what you are doing no one else will. At the outset only passion will persuade people to back you.

7  Keep your business lean. Buy top of the range computers but put them on second hand desks. Necessity is the mother of invention, not luxury.

8  Make work fun. If it stops being fun people will not be creative.

9  Give your employees a stake in the business: you may not be able to pay them much to start with so give them shares.

10  Pick partners who are as committed as you. To start with a business will only be sustained by a band of believers.

11  Be ready to split with your partners – often your best friends – when the business faces a crisis or a turning point. Don't be sentimental.

12 Create products that can become ubiquitous quickly, for example by being given away in a global market, thereby attracting huge stock market valuations.

13 Don't aim to become the next Bill Gates, aim to get bought out by him.

14 Take a holiday in Silicon Valley. You will be convinced anyone is capable of anything.

*Own product development*

The other option is to shift from providing a service to providing a product – films, music, designs, gadgets, computer games – from which a company can earn royalties. This process of investment in product development can be very risky without the backing of a major customer, and it can quickly consume a small company's resources.

The problems inherent in managing growth in a cultural business mean that most stay very small, rather than taking the risk and strain. Possibly 80 per cent of the Independents we interviewed were either self-employed or running a micro-business of no more than five people, with no ambitions for growth. A further 10 to 15 per cent were in the second phase: they were running a growing, service-based business. Only 5 to 10 per cent were in a position to contemplate going beyond that into own-product development and only a minority of these are likely to make it. The companies that can make it through these stages of development seem to be distinguished by these characteristics. They have:

• enough money to finance product development
• enough commercial discipline to make sure this investment is not wasted
• positions in potentially lucrative, international markets rather than small, national or niche markets
• unshakeable self-belief in their distinctive talent
• and last, but not least, luck.

This preponderance of self-employment, sole traders and micro-businesses in the cultural industries has important implications for policy-making. Government-sponsored business support programmes and arts funding is tailored toward fewer larger organisations. Developing an ecology of hundreds of micro-businesses requires a set of policy tools that most economic development agencies lack. The danger is that we are creating industries dominated by 'digital craft producers', which in turn will be dominated by larger international groups that will control distribution and publishing of their products. These sectors will continue to generate jobs primarily by spawning more small businesses, but they also need to create larger, stronger, faster growth businesses that can operate in international markets. And we need to create stronger institutions and intermediaries that can support independent producers and stand between them and the global markets in which they compete.

## Notes

1   *The Creative Industries Task Force Mapping Report*, Department for Culture, Media and Sport, October 1998, and mapping exercise prepared by Spectrum Strategy Consultants, February 1998.
2   *Cultural Production in Manchester: Research and Strategy*, report prepared by Justin O'Connor, Manchester Institute of Popular Culture, 1999.
3   This point is made by Angela McRobbie in her account of the lives of young fashion designers: *British Fashion Design; Rag Trade or Image Industry* Routledge, London, 1998. See also *Recommendations for Growth: UK Digital Media*, Digital Media Alliance report, available from Arts Council of England, prepared by Catalyst Media.
4   The role of cities as centres of creativity and innovation is highlighted in: P. Hall, 1998, *Cities and Civilization*, Weidenfeld & Nicolson, London; *The Richness of Cities* working papers, published by Comedia in association with Demos in 1998 and 1999; C. Landry and F. Bianchini, 1995, *The Creative City*, Demos, London; 'Cultural Industries and the City', presentation to European Union Culture Ministers, March 1998, Manchester Institute of Popular Culture.
5   Many of the figures in this section are drawn from *Cultural Production in Manchester* (see note 2) and its analysis of official statistics.

# 19    *Henry Jenkins*

# GAMES, THE NEW LIVELY ART

Over the past three decades, computer and video games have progressed from the primitive two-paddles-and-a-ball *Pong* to the sophistication of *Final Fantasy*, a participatory story with cinema-quality graphics that unfolds over nearly 100 hours of game play, or *Black and White*, an ambitious moral tale where the player's god-like choices between good and evil leave tangible marks on the landscape. The computer game has been a killer app for the home PC, increasing consumer demand for vivid graphics, rapid processing, greater memory and better sound. One could make the case that games have been to the PC what NASA was to the mainframe – the thing that pushes forward innovation and experimentation. The release of the Sony Playstation 2, the Microsoft X-Box, and the Nintendo Game Cube signals a dramatic increase in the resources available to game designers.

In anticipation of these new technological breakthroughs, people within and beyond the game industry began to focus attention on the creative potentials of this emerging medium. Mapping the aesthetics of game design, they argued, would not only enable them to consolidate decades of experimentation and innovation but would also push them forward towards greater artistic accomplishment. Game designers were being urged to think of themselves not simply as technicians producing corporate commodities but rather as artists mapping the dimensions and potentials of an emerging medium; this reorientation, it was hoped, would force them to ask harder questions in their design meetings and to aspire towards more depth and substance in the product they shipped. At the same time, the games industry confronted increased public and government scrutiny. If you parsed the rhetoric of the

"Games, the New Lively Art" from Henry Jenkins (2003), "Games, the New Lively Art". In Jeffrey Goldstein and Joost Raessens (eds.), *Handbook of Computer Game Studies*. MIT Press, Cambridge, Mass. Reprinted by permission of the MIT Press.

moral reformers, it was clear that their analogies to pollution or carcinogens revealed their base-level assumption that games were utterly without redeeming value, lacking any claim to meaningful content or artistic form. Seeing games as art, however, shifted the terms of the debate. Most of these discussions started from the premise that games were an emerging art form, one which had not yet realized its full potentials. Game designer Warren Specter, for example, told a *Joystick 101* interviewer, "We're just emerging from infancy. We're still making (and remaking!) *The Great Train Robbery* or *Birth of a Nation* or, to be really generous, maybe we're at the beginning of what might be called our talkies period. But as Al Jolson said in *The Jazz Singer*, 'You ain't heard nothing yet!'[1] In this context, critical discussions sought to promote experimentation and diversification of game form, content, and audience, not to develop prescriptive norms.

[ . . . ]

## The Lively Criticism of Gilbert Seldes

What I want to do in the following pages is revisit one important effort to spark a debate about the aesthetic merits of popular culture – Gilbert Seldes' *Seven Lively Arts* (1924) – and suggest how reclaiming Seldes might contribute to our current debates about the artistic status of computer and video games.

[ . . . ]

Games represent a new lively art, one as appropriate for the digital age as those earlier media were for the machine age. They open up new aesthetic experiences and transform the computer screen into a realm of experimentation and innovation that is broadly accessible. And games have been embraced by a public that has otherwise been unimpressed by much of what passes for digital art. Much as the salon arts of the 1920s seemed sterile alongside the vitality and inventiveness of popular culture, contemporary efforts to create interactive narrative through modernist hypertext or avant-garde installation art seem lifeless and pretentious alongside the creativity and exploration, the sense of fun and wonder, that game designers bring to their craft. As Hal Barwood explained to readers of *Game Developer* magazine in February 2002, "Art is what people accomplish when they don't quite know what to do, when the lines on the road map are faint, when the formula is vague, when the product of their labors is new and unique."[2] Art exists, in other words, on the cutting edge and that was where games had remained for most of their history. The game designers were creating works that sparked the imagination and made our hearts race. And they were doing so without the safety net that inherited modernist rhetoric provides for installation and hypertext artists. They can offer no simple, straightforward justification for what they are doing or why they are doing it except by way of talking about "the fun factor," that is, the quality of the emotional experience they offer players.

Although his writing was impressionistic and evocative, rather than developing a systematic argument or framework, one can read *The Seven Lively Arts* as mapping an aesthetic of popular culture, one which is broadly enough defined to be useful for discussing a wide range of specific media and cultural practices including many that did not exist at the time he wrote the book. Seldes drew a distinction between the "great arts," which seek to express universal and timeless values, and the "lively arts," which seek to give shape and form to immediate experiences and impressions. "Great" and "lively" arts differed "not in the degree of their intensity but in the degree of their intellect."[3] Seldes, in fact, often showed signs of admiring the broad strokes of the popular arts – where the needs for clarity and immediate recognition from a broadly defined audience allowed "no fuzzy edges, no blurred contours" – over the nuance and complexity of Great Art.[4] Seldes consistently values affect over intellect, immediate impact over long term consequences, the spontaneous impulse over the calculated effect.

Seldes defined art through its affective force, its ability to provoke strong and immediate reactions. As popular artists master the basic building block of their media, they developed techniques enabling them to shape and intensify affective experience. Creativity, Seldes argued, was all bound up with our sense of play and with our demands to refresh our sensual apparatus and add new energy to our mental life, which was apt to become dulled through the routine cognition and perception of everyday life. He wrote, "we require, for nourishment, something fresh and transient."[5]

From the start, games were able to create strong emotional impressions – this accounts for the enormous staying power with consumers. An early game of *Pac-man* or *Asteroids* could provoke strong feelings of tension or paranoia. The works of Shigeru Miyagawa represented imaginative landscapes, as idiosyncratic and witty in their way as the *Krazy Kat* comic strips or Mack Sennett comedies Seldes admired. Seldes wrote at a moment when cinema was starting to consolidate what it had learned over its first three decades of experimentation and produce works that mixed and matched affective elements to create new kinds of experiences. One could argue that recent games, such as *Deus X*, *Grand Theft Auto 3*, or *Shenmue*, represent a similar consolidation of earlier game genres, where-as games like *The Sims*,

*Majestic*, *Rez* or *Black & White* are expanding the repertoire of game mechanics and by doing so, expanding the medium's potential audience.

The great arts and the lively arts shared a common enemy, the "bogus arts," the middlebrow arts, which sought to substitute "refinement of taste" for "refinement of technique," and in the process, cut themselves off from the culture around them.[6] The popular arts, he warned, often promised more than they could deliver; their commercial imperative required that they leave us somewhat unsatisfied and thus eager to consume more, but in their straightforward appeal to emotion, they do not "corrupt." Middlebrow culture, however, often seduces us with fantasies of social and cultural betterment at the expense of novelty and innovation. Seldes wanted to deploy the shock value of contemporary popular culture to shake up the settled thinking of the art world, to force it to reconsider the relationship between art and everyday life.

[ . . . ]

The maturing of the cinematic medium may well have been what enabled Seldes to recognize its artistic accomplishments. However, in aspiring towards cultural respectability, cinema ran a high risk of losing touch with its own primitive roots. Seldes sounded a warning which would seem familiar to many contemporary observers of video and computer games, suggesting that the cinema was confusing technological enhancement with aesthetic advancement, confusing the desire to reproduce reality for the desire to create an emotionally engaging experience. What had given filmgoers the "highest degree of pleasure," he argued, was "escaping actuality and entering into a created world, built on its own inherent logic, keeping time to its own rhythm – where we feel ourselves at once strangers and at home."[7]

*Newsweek*'s Jack Kroll sparked heated debates in the gamer community when he argued that audiences will probably never be able to care as deeply about pixels on the computer screen as they care about characters in films: "Moviemakers don't have to simulate human beings; they are right there, to be recorded and orchestrated. . . . The top-heavy titillation of *Tomb Raider's* Lara Croft falls flat next to the face of Sharon Stone . . . Any player who's moved to tumescence by digibimbo Lara is in big trouble."[8] Yet countless viewers cry when Bambi's mother dies, and World War II veterans can tell you they felt real lust for *Esquire's* Vargas girls. We have learned to care as much about creatures of pigment as we care about images of real people. Why should pixels be different? If we haven't yet cared this deeply about game characters (a debatable proposition as the response to Kroll's article indicated), it is because the game design community has not yet found the right techniques for evoking such emotions, and not because there is an intrinsic problem in achieving emotional complexity in the medium itself. Kroll, like the respectable critics of early cinema whom Seldes battled, assumes that realism is necessary in order to achieve a high degree of emotional engagement. The art of games may not come from reproducing the world of the senses. As Steve Poole has written:

> Whereas film – at least naturalistic, "live-action" film – is tied down to real spaces, the special virtue of videogames is precisely their limitless plasticity. And only when that virtue is exploited more fully will videogames become a truly unprecedented art – when their level of world-building competence is matched with a comparable level of pure invention. We want to be shocked by novelty. We want to lose ourselves in a space that is utterly different. We want environments that have never been seen, never been imagined before.[9]

As I visit game companies, I see some of the industry's best minds struggling with this challenge. As they search for answers, they will need to avoid the temptation to port solutions over wholesale from cinema and other more established arts. Independent game designers, such as Eric Zimmerman, have argued that games need to return to a garage aesthetic, stripping aside fancy graphics and elaborate cinematics, to reclaim the core elements that make games distinctive from other expressive media. Protesting that games are more than simply "mutant cinema," Zimmerman warns that "mistaken attempts to apply the skills and methods of Hollywood to the world of electronic gaming resulted in CD-ROMs bloated with full-motion video sequences and lacking meaningful gameplay."[10] Similarly, Seldes warned that long intertitles substituted literary for cinematic values, seeking to "explain everything except the lack of action," and resulting in scenes devoid of visual interest.[11] The result was movies that no longer moved. Zimmerman and others warn that extended cinematics, often the favored mean of adding narrative and character to games, cuts the player off from the action and thus sacrifice those elements of interactivity which make games games. One could argue that a similar tension is at the heart of the ongoing debates among game scholars between the so-called narratologists and the ludologists. The ludologists fear that the narratologist want to impose an alien aesthetic sensibility onto games and thus cut the medium off from its basic building blocks in gameplay. Games should not achieve aesthetic recognition by giving themselves over to "cinema envy," they warn, but should remain true to their roots. Seldes's concept of the lively arts may, in fact, offer us a way out of this binary, since he focuses primarily on the kinetic aspects of popular culture, aspects that can operate inside or outside a narrative frame. Poole arrives at a similar conclusion:

A beautifully designed videogame invokes wonder as the fine arts do, only in a uniquely kinetic way. Because the videogame *must* move, it cannot offer the lapidary balance of composition that we value in painting; on the other hand, because it *can* move, it is a way to experience architecture, and more than that to create it, in a way which photographs or drawings can never compete. If architecture is frozen music, then a videogame is liquid architecture.[12]

## Memorable Moments

What Seldes offers us might be described as a theory of "memorable moments," a concept which surfaces often in discussions with game designers but only rarely in academic writing about the emerging medium. Writing about the German Expressionist film, *The Cabinet of Dr. Caligari*, Seldes [ . . . ] writes about the pleasures of finding peak experiences within otherwise banal works: "A moment comes when everything is exactly right, and you have an occurrence – it may be something exquisite or something unnameably gross; there is in it an ecstasy which sets it apart from everything else."[13] Such peak experiences seem fully within reach of contemporary game designers in a way that the development of complex causally-integrated yet open-ended narratives or psychological rounded yet fully interactive characters are not. If games are going to become an art, right now, rather than in some distant future, when all of our technical challenges have been resolved, it may come from game designers who are struggling with the mechanics of motion and emotion, rather than those of story and character.

As game designers evaluate games on the basis of their emotional appeal, their criteria often emphasize moments of emotional intensity or visual spectacle – the big skies that can suddenly open before you when you ride your snow board in *SSX*, the huge shots in a hockey game when the puck goes much further than it could possibly do in real life, the pleasure of sending your car soaring off a cliff or smashing through pedestrians in *Grand Theft Auto 3*. Increasingly, games enable us to grab snapshots of such moments, to replay them and watch them unfold from multiple angles, and to share them with our friends, pushing them to see if they can match our exploits and duplicate accomplishments. Game companies encourage their staffs to think of their designs in terms of the images on boxes or in previews, the way that the demo is going to look on the trade show floor. Yet, this may be to reduce the concept of memorable moments down to "eye candy" or spectacle, something which can be readily extracted from the play experience, something which can be communicated effectively in a still image. Other game designers would contest this understanding of the concept, arguing that memorable moments emerge when all of the elements of the medium come together to create a distinctive and compelling experience.

Often, in games, those memorable moments don't simply depend on spectacle. After all, spectacle refers to something that stops you dead in your tracks, forces you to stand and look. Game play becomes memorable when it creates the opposite effect – when it makes you want to move, when it convinces you that you really are in charge of what's happening in the game, when the computer seems to be totally responsive. Frequently, the memorable moment comes when the computer does something that follows logically from your actions, yet doesn't feel like it was prescripted and preprogrammed. As *Deus X* designer Warren Spector explains: "Great gameplay comes, I think, from our ability to drop players into compelling situations, provide clear goals for them, give them a variety of tools with which they can impact their environment and then get out of their way . . . That has to be so much more compelling for players – thrilling even – than simply guessing the canned solution to a puzzle or pressing a mouse button faster than a computer opponent can react."[14]

Seldes was one of a number of early twentieth century writers who sought to better understand the "mechanics of emotion" which shaped popular entertainment. The Italian futurist Filippo Marinetti saw within the variety theater "the crucible in which the elements of an emergent new sensibility are seething," describing it as an art which had "only one reason for existing and triumphing: incessantly to invent new elements of astonishment."[15] The Soviet film theorist Sergei Eisenstein developed a theory of "attractions," a term which he saw as broad enough to encompass any device – whether formal, narrative, or thematic – which could solicit powerful emotions from a spectator, arguing that film and theater should seek their inspiration from the circus and the music hall.[16] Inspired in part by Pavlovian refloxology, they tried to document and master basic "surefire" stimuli which could provoke a predictable emotional response from the spectator and then to streamline their works, cutting out anything that would obscure or retard that affective impact. Eddie Cantor warned, "A comedian in vaudeville . . . is like a salesman who has only fifteen minutes in which to make a sale. You go on stage knowing every moment counts. You've got to get your audience the instant you appear."[17] Theater critic Vadim Uraneff explained in 1923, "the [vaudeville] actor works with the idea of an immediate response from the audience: and with regard to its demands. By cutting out everything – every line, gesture, movement – to which the audience does not react and by improvising new things, he establishes unusual unity between the audience and himself."[18]

Game designers engage in a similar process as they seek to identify "what's not in the game," that is, to determine what elements would get in the way of the game mechanic or confuse the player. Game designers speak of "hooks" which will grab the consumers' attention and keep them playing, a concept which would have been familiar to vaudeville showman and circus barkers. Longtime game designers cite back to the challenges of developing games which played well in the arcades, which offered a compelling experience that could be staged in under two minutes and ramped up to an emotional high that would leave the player reaching for another quarter. Early console games also demanded economy, given the limited memory capacity of the early systems.[19] However, as consoles have developed greater capacity and thus enabled lengthier and more complex game experiences, some fear that game designers are adding too many features which get in the way of the core mechanics. The lengthy cut scenes of narrative exposition and character backstory, which academics praise for their aesthetic advancements, are often received with hostility by serious gamers because they slow down the play and result in a relatively passive experience. A great deal of effort goes into the first few minutes of game play, in particular, to insure that they offer a solid emotional payoff for the player rather than ending in frustration: an early moment of mastery or movement is to spark their appetite for bigger and better things to come.[20]

## Play as Performance

Seldes and the other early twentieth century critics saw the emotional intensity of popular culture as emerging from the central performer, whose mastery over his or her craft enabled them to "command" the spectator's attention. Seldes writes about the "daemonic" authority of Al Jolson: "he never saves up – for the next scene, or the next week, or the next show. . . . He flings into a comic song or three-minute impersonation so much energy, violence, so much of the totality of one human being, that you feel it would suffice for a hundred others."[21] [ . . . ]

One might well understand the pleasures of game play according to performance criteria but as we do so, we need to understand it as a pas de deux between the designer and the player. As game designer David Perry explains, "A good game designer always knows what the players are thinking and is looking over their shoulders every step of the way."[22] The game designer's craft makes it possible for the player to feel as if they are in control of the situation at all time, even though their game play and emotional experience is significantly sculpted by the designer. It is a tricky balancing act, making the player aware of the challenges they confront, and at the same time, insuring they have the resources necessary to overcome those challenges. If the game play becomes transparently easy or impossibly hard, the players lose interest. The players need to feel they can run faster, shoot more accurately, jump further, and think smarter than in their everyday life and it is this expansion of the player's capacity which accounts for the emotional intensity of most games. [ . . . ]

As many observers have noted, we don't speak of controlling a cursor on the screen when we describe the experience of playing a game; we act as if we had unmediated access to the fictional space. We refer to our game characters in the first person and act as if their experiences were our own. James Newman has argued that we might understand the immediacy of game play not in terms of how convincing the representation of the character and the fictional world is but rather in terms of the character's "capacity" to respond to our impulses and desires. A relatively iconic, simplified character may produce an immediate emotional response; a relatively stylized world can nevertheless be immersive. Once we engage with the game, the character may become simply a vehicle we use to navigate the game world. As Newman explains:

> Lara Croft is defined less by appearance than by the fact that "she" allows the player to jump distance x, while the ravine in front of us is larger than that, so we better start thinking of a new way round. . . . Characters are defined around gameplay-affecting characteristics. It doesn't matter that it's a burly guy – or even a guy – or perhaps even a human. That the hang glider can turn faster is a big deal; this affects the way the game plays. This affects my chances of getting a good score.[23]

A number of game designers have reminded me that Shigeru Miyamoto, whom many regard as the medium's first real master, designs his games around verbs, that is, around the actions which the game enables players to perform. He wants each game to introduce a new kind of mission, making it possible for the consumer to do something that no other game has allowed before. A close examination of Miyamoto's games suggests, at the same time, that he designs a playing space which at once facilitates and thwarts our ability to carry out that action and thus creates a dramatic context in which these actions take aesthetic shape and narrative significance.

Many contemporary games seek to expand that sense of player mastery beyond the game space

[ . . . ]

*Frequency* designer Alex Rigopulos describes the trajectory of a player through his game:

> When a gamer starts to play *Frequency*, he plays it using the gaming skills he already has: the ability to react to symbolic visual information with a precisely timed manual response. . . . What we noticed again and again in playtesting was that there is a certain point at which novice players stop playing entirely with their eyes and start playing with their ears (or, rather, their "internal ears"): they start to feel the musical beat; then, as a stream of gems approaches, they look at the oncoming stream, "imagine" in their ears what that phrase will feel like or sound like rhythmically, and begin to "play the notes" (rather than "shoot the gems"). As soon as players cross this threshold, they begin excelling much more rapidly in the game.[24]

[ . . . ]

## Mode of Production

If we are to see games accepted as a contemporary art form, game designers are going to have to stop using "market pressures" as an excuse for their lack of experimentation. True, game designers need to ship product and that can place serious limitations on how much innovation can occur within a single game. Yet, it is worth remembering that all art occurs within an economic context. The Hollywood filmmakers of the 1920s and 1930s often produced five to seven feature films per year, yet somewhere in that rush to the marketplace, they nevertheless came to more fully realize the potential of their medium and developed work that has withstood the test of time. Seldes describes popular art in terms of a careful balance between convention and invention: convention insures accessibility, invention novelty. What keeps the lively arts lively is that they are the site of consistent experimentation and innovation. No sooner are genre conventions mapped than popular artists start to twist and turn them to yield new effects. The constant push for emotional immediacy demands a constant refinement of the art itself, keeping creators on their toes and forcing them to acknowledge audience response into their creative decision-making.

Seldes worried whether the conditions that had led to an enormous flowering of popular arts in the early twentieth century could be sustained in the face of increasingly industrialized modes of production. He blamed the studio system for much of what was wrong with contemporary cinema, yet he ended the book with a prediction that the costs of film production are likely to decrease steadily as the core technology of film production becomes

HENRY JENKINS

standardized, thus returning filmmaking to its artisan roots. He predicts: "the
first cheap film will startle you; but the film will grow less and less expensive.
Presently it will be within the reach of artists . . . The artists will give back
to the screen the thing you have debauched – imagination."[25] Several decades later, in his book, *The Great Audience*, Seldes would be even more
emphatic that the rise of corporate media had strangled the aesthetic experimentation and personal expression which had enabled these "lively arts" to
exist in the first place.[26] With the coming of sound, the costs of film production had increased rather than decreased, further consolidating the major
studios' control over the filmmaking process, and thus delaying by several
decades the rise of independent cinema he had predicted.

What does this suggest about the future of innovation in game design? For
starters, the basic apparatus of the camera and the projector were standardized
by the turn of the century, enabling early filmmakers to focus on the expressive potential of the medium rather than continuing to have to relearn the
basic technology. Game designers, on the other hand, have confronted dramatic shifts in their basic tools and resources on average every 18 months
since the emergence of their medium. This constant need to respond to a
shifting technological infrastructure has shifted attention onto mastering tools
which could otherwise have been devoted to exploring the properties and
potentials of the medium. Secondly, despite a pretty rigorous patents war, the
early history of filmmaking was marked by relatively low barriers of entry
into the marketplace. Although many film histories still focus on a small
number of key innovators, we now know that the basic language of cinema
emerged through widespread experimentation amongst filmmakers scattered
across the country and around the world. The early history of computer
games, by contrast, was dominated by a relatively small number of game
platforms, with all games having to pass through this corporate oversight
before they could reach the market. The proliferation of authoring tools and
open-source game engines have helped to lower barriers of entry into the
game marketplace, paving the way for more independent and smaller game
companies. In such a context, those emerging companies have often been
forced to innovate in order to differentiate their product from what was
already on the market. The rise of the girls' game movement, for example,
can be explained in terms of female-run start-ups seeking to expand the
game market in order to create a niche for their product in the face of
competition with larger corporations.

At the same time as these new delivery technologies have loosened the
hold of the platform manufacturers over game content, the cost of game
development for those platforms has dramatically increased. We have seen
rising technical standards which make it difficult for garage game designers to

compete. Some have worried that the result will be an increased focus on blockbuster games with surefire market potential and the constant upgrading of popular franchises. What would contemporary cinema look like if it supported a succession of summer popcorn movies but could not support lower-budget and independent films. The situation is not totally hopeless. The sheer size of some of the major game publishers has encouraged them to diversify game design and content. A company like Electronic Arts, for example, draws on profits from its cash cow sports games to sustain a variety of smaller boutique companies, such as Maxis or Bullfrog, which are producing some of the most original and genre-breaking content.

## The Value of Criticism

How can we insure the continued creative evolution of games? What will games look like as a mature artform, given the extraordinary shifts it has undergone over the past few decades? What modes of production or forms of authorship will insure the diversification necessary to expand the core gaming market to reach a broader public? Seldes was quite clear that sustained and rigorous criticism of the "lively arts" was the key to their long-term development. Such criticism must start from a sympathetic position, one which takes the popular arts on their own terms, one which respects the defining properties of specific media and genres. This criticism offers a measure of success quite independent from, but every bit as important as, the results of the box office. As he explains, "the box office is gross; it detects no errors, nor does it sufficiently encourage improvement."[27] Criticism encourages experimentation and innovation; commercial pressures insure accessibility. The lively arts grow through a careful balancing between the two.

The nature and value of these aesthetic experiments warrant close and passionate engagement not only within the games industry or academia, but also by the press and around the dinner table. Even Kroll's grumpy dismissal of games has sparked heated discussion and forced designers to refine their own grasp of the medium's distinctive features. Imagine what a more robust form of criticism could contribute. We need critics who know and care about games the way Pauline Kael knew movies. We need critics who write about them with that same degree of wit, wisdom, and passion. Early film critics played vital functions in documenting innovations and speculating about their potential. As a new media, computer games demand this same kind of close critical engagement. We have not had time to codify what experienced game designers know, and we have certainly not yet established a canon of great works that might serve as exemplars. There have been real creative accomplishments across the first three decades of game design, but we haven't really sorted out what they are and why they matter.

The problem with many contemporary games isn't that they are violent but that so many of them are banal, formulaic, and predictable. Thoughtful criticism can marshal support for innovation and experimentation in the industry, much as good film criticism helps focus attention on neglected independent films. At the present time, game critics represent a conservative force on aesthetic innovation, with most reviews organized around pre-existing genre preferences. They are also mostly organized around technical elements as opposed to the game's emotional impact or its aesthetic statement. It is hard, in many cases, for truly innovative games to get the attention of consumers, though the success of products like *The Sims* suggest it is certainly not impossible.

Thoughtful criticism could even contribute to our debates about violence. Rather than bemoaning "meaningless violence," we should explore ways that games could not simply stage or simulate violence but offer us new ways to understand the place of violence within our culture. Moreover, game criticism may provide a means of holding the game industry more accountable for its choices. In the wake of the Columbine shootings, game designers are struggling with their ethical responsibilities as never before, searching for ways of appealing to empowerment fantasies that don't require exploding heads and gushing organs. A serious public discussion of this medium might constructively influence these debates, helping identify and evaluate alternatives as they emerge.

As Seldes grew older, his initial enthusiasm for the "daemonic" force of popular art gave rise to growing concerns that it could be used to negatively shape public opinion and he became a key supporter of Frederic Wertham's campaign to regulate comic books.[28] Seldes' career trajectory – from defender of *Krazy Kat* to persecutor of E.C. horror comics – suggests the ambivalence at the heart of his celebration of the "lively arts." We should recognize that ambivalence within our own response to games as an emerging medium and use our criticism to debate the merits of different approaches to representing violence in games.[29] The goal should be the creation of a context which supports more thoughtful game content rather than the promotion of censorship.

As the art of games matures, progress will be driven by the most creative and forward thinking minds in the industry, those who know that games can be more than they have been, those who recognize the potential of reaching a broader public, of having a greater cultural impact, of generating more diverse and ethically responsible content and of creating richer and more emotionally engaging content. But without the support of an informed public and the perspective of thoughtful critics, game developers may never realize that potential.

## Notes

1 Kurt Squire, "Educating Game Designers: An Interview with Warren Spector," http://www.joystick101.org/? op=displaystory&sid=2001/5/23/155255/302.
2 Barwood, "The Envelope Please?", *Game Developer*, February 2002.
3 Seldes, *The Seven Lively Arts* (New York: Sagmore Press, 1957), p. 272.
4 Ibid., p. 228.
5 Ibid., p. 293.
6 Ibid., p. 223.
7 Ibid., p. 288.
8 Jack Kroll, "Emotional Engines? I Don't Think So," *Newsweek*, February 27, 2000.
9 Steven Poole, *Trigger Happy: Videogames and the Entertainment Revolution* (New York: Arcade Publishing, 2000), pp. 218–20.
10 Frank Lantz and Eric Zimmerman, "Checkmate: Rules, Play and Culture," Merge, 1999, http://www.ericzimmerman.com/acastuff/checkmate.html. See also Eric Zimmerman, "Do Independent Games Exist?," in Lucian King and Conrad Bain (eds.), *Game On* (London: Barbican, 2002).
11 Seldes, *The Seven Lively Arts*, p. 286.
12 Poole, *Trigger Happy*, p. 226.
13 Seldes, *The Seven Lively Arts*, p. 186.
14 Squire, "Educating Game Designers."
15 Filippo Tommaso Marinetti, "The Variety Theatre," in Michael Kirby (ed.), *Futurist Performance* (New York: Dutton, 1971), pp. 179–86.
16 Sergei Eisenstein, "Montage of Attractions," *Drama Review*, March 1974, pp. 77–85.
17 Eddie Cantor as quoted in Mary B. Mullet, "We All Like the Medicine 'Doctor' Eddie Cantor Gives," *American Magazine*, July 1924, pp. 34 ff.
18 Vadim Uraneff, "Commedia Dell' Arte and American Vaudeville," *Theatre Arts*, October 1923, p. 326.
19 For a useful discussion of the aesthetics of early video games, see Van Burnham and Ralph H. Baer, *Supercade* (Cambridge, Mass.: MIT Press, 2001).
20 I am indebted to the participants of the Comparative Media Studies–Electronic Arts Creative Leaders workshop series for these insights into the game design process.
21 Seldes, *The Seven Lively Arts*, p. 175.
22 David Perry as quoted in Marc Saltzman (ed.), *Game Design Secrets of the Sages*, 2nd Edn. (Indianapolis: Macmillan, 2000), p. 18.
23 James Newman, "On Being a Tetraminoe: Mapping the Contours of the Videogame Character," paper delivered at the International Game Cultures Conference, Bristol, England, June–July 2001.
24 Alex Rigopulos, e-mail correspondence with the author, March 1, 2002.
25 Seldes, *The Seven Lively Arts*, p. 289.

26  Gilbert Seldes, *The Great Audience* (New York: Viking, 1950).
27  Seldes, *The Seven Lively Arts*, p. 303.
28  Seldes, *The Great Audience*, pp. 271–8, offer the fullest summary of his views on the comic book industry.
29  See James Cain and Henry Jenkins, "I'm Gonna Git Medieval on Your Ass: A Conversation about Violence and Culture," in Helaine Postner (ed.), *Culture of Violence* (Amherst: University of Massachusetts Press, 2002).

# 20    *JC Herz*

# HARNESSING THE HIVE

According to 20th-century entrepreneurial mythology, great ideas come, like divine providence, to those few special individuals who, by dint of extreme brilliance or business savvy, qualify as a distinct sub-species of Homo sapiens – Homo innovatus, as it were. Their creed is "Eureka!" And lo, they do burrow into garages, or bunker down in Stanford dorm rooms, or show up to work in black collarless shirts and tinted eyeglasses. Great companies are founded upon their genius. And when those companies grow large and bureaucratic, the Innovators do cluster in brightly colored playpens called R&D departments, where the Creative People are allowed to live, and vast coils of CAT-5 cable are run from their brain cavities into Product Development, Marketing and Strategy divisions, to irrigate the companies with precious new ideas.

The products of Homo innovatus are then received by grateful consumers, who wonder how we ever got by in the absence of turn-key, fully-integrated, global solutions that spring fully formed from the foreheads of the anointed, whose heroic exploits are trumpeted in *Wired, Business Week*, and *The Red Herring*. The next generation of Homo innovatus rises to fulfill their destinies, and the chain of insanely great ideas continues. Amen.

Homo innovatus is a great story: It's a hero story. We know how to hear it, and the media know how to tell it. VCs know how to fund it. The problem is that Homo innovatus doesn't explain a lot of leading-edge innovation, nor does it account for the dynamics that define a networked marketplace and the evolving relationship between companies and their customers in that marketplace. It does not account for the entrepreneurially

"Harnessing the Hive" from JC Herz (2002), "Harnessing the Hive: How Online Games Drive Networked Innovation." *Release 1.0* 20(9), October 18, pp. 2–8, 9–10, 11–12, 14–21. Reprinted by permission of edventure, www.edventure.com

perverse ecology of open-source software or for the robustness of eBay. More importantly, it doesn't give credence to the collective intelligence of the network – the fact that a million people will always be smarter than 20 people, and that there is business value in that differential.

As the technological spotlight shifts to the edge of the network, and to increasingly decentralized models for software and services, there is a counter-myth of innovation. To paraphrase Scott McNealy, the Network is the Innovator. This is the church of open, modular, extensible, distributed platforms for all manner of commercial and leisure activities. The creed is "let a thousand flowers bloom, as long as they sprout in our garden." In this paradigm, the innovative genius lies not in a creative singularity, but in the construction of systems that leverage the million monkeys theorem. The tide reverses, from one brilliant vision washing onto a million screens, to a situation where one shocked developer instant-messages his teammate, "You'll never believe what they're doing now – check this out."

In 2002, the bleeding edge of massively networked innovation is computer games, a pocket of the software industry whose lurid aesthetics mask transformational advances in technology and business practice. For years, games have been driving consumer sales of computer hardware. Unless you're in a video production studio, scientific research lab, or a military installation, computer games are the most processor-intensive applications on a desktop computer. Ultimately, the only reason to upgrade a home computer is the ever-escalating CPU requirements of the latest computer games, which is why Intel and Nvidia court game developers so assiduously: Ratcheting up the minimum spec of a hit computer game goes directly to Dell's bottom line. While hardware companies consolidate, gamers' rabid appetite for computer performance has buoyed both build-it-yourself web sites such as Tom's Hardware and niche manufacturers such as Alienware, which has carved out a profitable niche just furnishing high-end custom PCs tricked out for the ultimate computer game experience – the Lamborghinis of desktop computing.

More recently, games have been driving broadband adoption. Students who played *Quake* on university LANs in 1996 are now young professionals with zero tolerance for dial-up. In Korea, which has the highest per-capita broadband penetration in the world, online games are the dominant force driving the country's appetite for bandwidth. Earlier this year, a player survey conducted by Valve, an entertainment software company, of a million combat gamers revealed that 75 percent of them had upgraded from dial-up to broadband. But beyond hardware and connectivity, online games are the most highly leveraged kind of networked application – one that harnesses next-generation technology to basic patterns of human behavior: competition, collaboration, the tendency to cluster, and the universal appetite for peer acknowledgement. In other words, the forces that hone games, and gamers, have more to do with anthropology than with code. This kind of innovation is inextricably intertwined with the social ecology of the player population – the interpersonal conventions that define status, identity, and affiliation both within the games and in the virtual communities that surround them.

Unlike most technology products and platforms, an online game evolves in massive parallel between a company and its market. Profit is directly proportional to the community's sense that it owns the experience, and to the interaction among groups, rather than to the fabled "one-to-one" relationship between producer and consumer. To that degree, online games are a useful lens for the next generation of networked software designers and the people who bet money on them. Through this lens, four lessons about massively multiplayer innovation pull into focus:

- R&D estuaries: leveraging community-driven design
- Constructive ecologies: artifacts and social currency
- Beyond collaboration: group-to-group interaction
- Persistence and accretion

## R&D Estuaries: Leveraging Community-Driven Design

The development cycle for a computer game, circa 2001, is 18 months, from the generation of the design specification to the release of the product. (Production typically involves 12 to 20 people, with costs ranging from $5 to 7 million, or double both factors for a persistent online world.) But for many games, and particularly the stronger-selling PC titles, that process begins before the "official" development period and extends afterwards, with a continuous stream of two-way feedback between the developers and players.

Perhaps the most extreme example of front-loaded game design is the forthcoming multiplayer online world based on Star Wars, which is being built by Verant, the leading developer in this genre, and LucasArts. Verant's last online fantasy role-playing game, *Everquest*, has 440,000 subscribers paying $12.95 per month to live in a medieval fantasy world. Hosting 100,000 simultaneous players during prime time, *Everquest*'s server array requires a dedicated AT&T switching facility; *Star Wars Galaxies*, set to launch in late 2002 or early 2003, is expected by those in the industry to attract more than a million players. The virtual environment is massive – it will take weeks or months to traverse without "hyperspace" shortcuts – and will support a full-fledged economic and political system. Players will develop their characters by scaling a number of intersecting skill trees (engine mechanics, armor production, combat, knowledge in the Ways of the Force, etc.). As a design and engineering challenge, *Star Wars Galaxies* rivals the construction of a space station in sheer scale and complexity.

But even as the basic technology is built and the game mechanics are a mere glimmer in the developer's eye, players are a vital part of the design process. As soon as the development deal was signed, Verant set up a message board [see p. 341] both to communicate news about the game in progress and to solicit feedback from a hardcore player population with over 11 million man-hours of collective experience with games in this genre.

In a virtual environment as complex as a massively multiplayer online world (MMP), whose success depends entirely on player interaction, developers recognize the player base as a strategic asset. The dynamics of these games are rapidly evolving, and many of the parameters have yet to be defined. When in doubt, designers turn to message boards to tap players' perspectives on the pros and cons of specific features and aspects of game play that could be improved. These are, after all, the people who will inhabit this virtual environment on a week-to-week basis when the product is launched, and who will determine its success.

To a large extent, the players co-create the environment once the game launches; their satisfaction with the game hinges on their interactions with each other. They collectively author the human dynamics of the world, and the player-created objects within it – and they can leave if it doesn't suit them. The experience belongs to the players as much as to the developer. So it's in the developers' interest to keep players in the loop as the game takes shape and to leverage their experience. This is not just a marketing ploy ("Make them feel valued and they'll evangelize the product to their friends"), although it does also generate good will. It is part of the core design process on the bleeding edge of networked simulation.

Within existing technologies in well-established genres, the player base is even more actively involved in the design and evolution of computer games. "We put a lot of time and attention into making sure that there were clear and easy hooks for the fans who wanted to be involved in programming work to be able to add and integrate their own work into the game system," says Ray Muzyka, founder and co-CEO of Bioware, a Canadian game developer whose Dungeons & Dragons-inspired *Neverwinter Nights* gives players an unprecedented level of access to the underlying architecture of a fantasy role-playing game. "There's a very modular structure, where you can be a little bit involved in making things, or you can be really involved. Your own technical understanding can either take you into the depths of the code base or you can be very high-level, if you want to just use the easy-to-use *Neverwinter* tool set."

First-person shooters (FPS) were the first genre to exploit the creative energy of the player base, starting with *Doom* (1993), which was released on the Internet before its commercial debut, and whose tool kit encouraged a legion of college students to make their own levels and download other people's (remember ftp?). A few years (and a couple of sequels) later, id Software released the game's source code, endowing the creative commons with its first hulking beast of testosterone-soaked C++.

*Doom*'s successors, such as *Quake 3 Arena* and *Unreal Tournament*, are built on engines that have evolved for years, passed between programming teams and a population of gamers that customizes and often improves the game just as its sequel is being planned. Player innovations are thus incorporated into the next iteration of the product. A salient example of this phenomenon is in-game artificial intelligence, one of the great engineering hurdles in any game. In first-person shooters, there is a marked difference between real and computer-generated opponents: Human opponents are invariably smarter, less predictable, and more challenging to play against.

AI, however, like all engineering challenges, can be a beneficiary of the million-monkeys syndrome: Put a million gamers into a room with an open, extensible game engine, and sooner or later, one of them will come up with the first-person shooter equivalent of *Hamlet*. In the case of id Software's *Quake II*, it was a plug-in called the ReaperBot, a fiendishly clever and intelligent AI opponent written by a die-hard gamer named Steven Polge (who was subsequently employed by id's main rival, Epic Games, to write AI for Epic's *Unreal* engine). Polge's Reaperbot was far-and-away the best *Quake* opponent anyone (inside or outside id Software) had ever seen, and the plug-in rapidly disseminated within the million-strong player population, who quickly began hacking away at its bugs. Needless to say, these improvements in game AI were incorporated into the core technology of first-person shooters, a benefit to players and developers alike.

The point here is not that *Quake* has great AI, but how that AI came to be. *Quake*'s architecture, the very nature of the product, enables distributed innovation to happen outside the developer's walls. In essence, the player population is transformed from mere consumers into active, vested participants in the development and evolution of the game. Of course, not all players roll up their sleeves and write plug-ins. But even if only 1 percent contributes to the innovation in the product, even if they are making only minor, incremental improvements or subtle tweaks, that's 10,000 (unpaid) people in research and development.

JC HERZ

*Valve slashes the half-life of innovation*

In business terms, massively multiplayer innovation blurs the boundary between producer and consumer, between the company and its market. At the vanguard of this phenomenon stand companies such as Maxis (a subsidiary of Electronic Arts) and Valve (a Kirkland, WA-based game company), whose commercial success largely depends on the collective design intelligence of their player communities.

*Half-Life*, Valve's flagship first-person shooter PC game, was subjected to "hive attack" by beta testers. The end result has been called the greatest PC game of all time. But according to Mark Laidlaw, Valve's lead designer, *Half-Life*'s flawlessness "was a result of hundreds of hours of playtesting, and forcing ourselves to respond to every bit of feedback and criticism that came out of the playtesting sessions, and working it back into the game and then playtesting those areas over and over again . . . I don't think testing can be overstressed." (See p. 341 for a URL for this interview.)

Beyond play-testing products to within an inch of their lives, Valve's modus operandi, and its business model, is vitally dependent on the developers' ability to leverage the *Half-Life* "MOD" (short for "modification") community – players who use the game's power design tools to design new versions of *Half-Life* and distribute them on the Internet. Almost immediately after the game's commercial release, players began to re-engineer the game. Valve, in turn, began hosting MOD expos at Sony's Metreon – a San Francisco mall that caters to gamers and other pop-culture enthusiasts.

From this primordial pool of amateur MODs emerged a few masterpieces that arguably surpassed the original game. The first to surface was *Counter-Strike*, which converted *Half-Life*'s every-man-for-himself multiplayer death match into a squadbased combat game that cast players as members of either a terrorist or counter-terrorist team, each with unique weapons and capabilities. The game is played in a variety of maps/scenarios with varying objectives, including hostage rescue, assassinations, terrorist escapes and bomb defusing missions.

Originally envisioned by a player in Vancouver, BC, Minh "Gooseman" Le, *Counter-Strike* was, like all MODs, a labor of love. "My initial motivation was probably the same as anyone else involved in the MOD scene," he explained on one of the many MOD fan sites. "I just wanted to customize the game to fit my vision of what a game should be. First and foremost, it is MY vision . . . not anyone else's. I don't spend 10+ hours a week working on a MOD for free just to make a MOD that satisfies everyone, I make a MOD that I am happy with and if someone else happens to like it, then that's a bonus." (See p. 341 for a URL to this interview.)

When it turned out that lots of people did, in fact, like it, very very much, Le pulled together a team of fellow players happy to contribute time and energy to soup up the hottest MOD on the Net. His first recruit and project co-leader lives in Blacksburg, Virginia. CS mapmakers hail from England (one was studying geography at Cambridge University), Germany, South Africa, New Jersey, Colorado, and Irvine, California.

[ . . . ]

*Harvesting the honey*

The second difference, from a business perspective, lies in a game company's ability not only to cultivate this elite unpaid R&D community, but also to capture the best mutations of its product for direct commercial gain and *not* alienate the player community by doing so. "That's a challenge for us," says Valve ceo Gabe Newell. "These teams get formed in funny ways. It's not like they're setting out to do anything like this, and so ownership and people's roles can be kind of vague."

"Sometimes you just have to give them advice," he says. "They ask questions like, 'Should we get a lawyer?' And you say, 'YES, you should have a lawyer'. Or, 'Should we incorporate?' Well, it depends on where you are. A lot of times these are multinational groups; people working in different countries with different legal issues and taxation issues. So a lot of times we just try to help them understand what's going on. I mean, for us it's a really long-term investment, because it's a very social community. What goes around comes around. Everything you do follows you for a long time. So we try really hard to be helpful to these people. Within the *Half-Life* community, everything we do is very visible. We try to be very careful that everyone in the *Half-Life* forums isn't going to suddenly turn on us and savage us for something that we do."

Valve not only has a dedicated team to cultivate the MOD community, but it also underwrites the most promising MODs, which have significantly extended the life of the core product. In the wake of *Counter-Strike*'s success, Valve started a "grants" program to fund the best MOD development teams. Beyond money, the company provided in-house development support – artists and coders – to hone *Counter-Strike* for retail. In 2000, Valve released a commercial version of the game, packaged with other best-of-best MODs, as a retail product that succeeded despite the fact that it was still available on the Internet. "If you look at the time since *Counter-Strike* has come out, as an example of a product that came out of the MOD world," says Newell, "it's outsold every action game that shipped, and it's still a top seller for us, about 1.3 million units [to date]."

While the *Counter-Strike* team continued to operate in an independent fashion, Valve also managed to capture a MOD team in Australia whose *Quake* MOD, *Team Fortress*, was running on 40 percent of the *Quake* servers on the Internet in 1998. Valve hired the designers and brought the team in-house to develop *Team Fortress 2* as a new product. The value of this acquisition was two-fold. Not only would it fuel the *Half-Life* player base, but internally, it allowed Valve's coders to refine tools for the next wave of hot-MODders. Essentially, Valve hired MOD-makers to design tools for MOD-makers, operating at the membrane between the company's core staff and its player-developers.

[ . . . ]

## Constructive Ecologies: Artifacts and Social Currency

Most of the players who tinker with games aren't programmers. They don't have to be, because the editing and customization tools in today's games require no formal programming skill whatsoever. (Shades of high-level Web services.) Levels of combat games can be constructed in a couple of hours by anyone familiar with basic game play. Real-time strategy games offer similar capabilities. New maps, with custom constellations of opposing forces, can be generated with a graphical user interface. Objects, including custom avatars or "skins," can be constructed with photos wrapped around templates, sculpted with simplified 3D modeling tools, or bitmapped. Beyond the R&D dynamics discussed above, these crafting capabilities foster a constructive ecosystem around the making, enhancement and swapping of functional objects.

Unlike most online communities, games' constructive ecosystems are fueled by an innate human desire to make things, rather than talk about them. Consequently, the dynamics are radically different from the community interaction that occurs around text documents. Social currency accrues not to virtuoso talkers, but to people who make things that other people like to play with – Triumph of the Neato. Because the system runs on functional objects, rather than clever comments, there is greater real and perceived value in players' contributions. Downloading someone's level or map is more than a conversation. It's an acquisition. Similarly, player-creators are validated in a more meaningful way: People are using what they've made, not just agreeing with it. Use, not imitation, is the sincerest form of flattery.

## The Sims: virtual dollhouses, real profits

In a commercial context, this tool-based, user-driven activity has several important functions. It extends the life of the game, which both enhances the value of the product at no incremental cost and increases sales: The longer people play the game, the longer they talk about it – effectively marketing it to their friends and acquaintances. Will Wright, author of Maxis' best-selling *Sim City* series, compares the spread of a product in this fashion to a virus: "Double the contagious period," he says, "and the size of the epidemic goes up by an order of magnitude. If I can get people to play for twice as long, I sell ten times as many copies." Wright's formula bears out on the bottom line. His latest game, *The Sims*, has spawned four expansion packs (developed in response to the creations of its own R&D estuary of fans) and racked up nearly half a billion dollars in retail sales since its 2000 release.

*The Sims*, which scales Wright's Sim City down to the neighborhood level, is noteworthy because it illustrates the level of engagement a game can achieve when its designers incorporate crafting into the culture of the game. Four months before *The Sims* shipped, its developers released tools that allowed players to create custom objects for the game's virtual environment: architecture, props, and custom characters. These tools were rapidly disseminated among *Sim City* players, who began creating custom content immediately. In the months leading up to the game's release, a network of player-run Web sites sprang up to showcase and exchange "handcrafted" *Sims* objects and custom characters.

By the time the game was released, there were 50 Sims fan sites, 40 artists pumping content into the pipeline, and 50,000 people collecting that content. One quarter-million boxes flew off the shelves in the first week. A year later, there were dozens of people programming tools for *Sims* content creators, 150 independent content creators, half a million collectors, and millions of players reading 200 fan sites in 14 languages. While most of these sites are labors of love, a few are profitable as well.

At this point, more than 90 percent of *The Sims'* content is produced by the player population, which has achieved an overwhelming amount of collective expertise in all things *Sim*. The player population feeds on itself, in a completely bottom-up, distributed, self-organizing way; none of these people are on the Maxis payroll. So, if these people aren't being paid by game developers (in fact it's the reverse), why do they invest hundreds or thousands of hours whittling 3D models and maps?

[ . . . ]

JC HERZ

## Beyond Collaboration: Group-to-Group Interaction

In computer game culture, status is easily established, readily compared and (perhaps most importantly, for the core demographic) quantifiable. Every game ends with a winner and losers. Tournament players are ranked. Player-created content is not only reviewed, but downloaded and therefore measurably popular. The author of a game modification may have an internally driven sense of accomplishment, but he also knows that 18,431 people are playing his song; for a 19-year-old, that's a big deal, particularly when fan sites start pointing to his home page. He gets a few laudatory e-mails from strangers. His friends think he's cool and ask him for map-making advice. A level designer he's never met, but whose work he admires, asks if he'd be interested in teaming up on a *Half-Life* MOD.

It is this web of relationships between players – competitive, cooperative, and collegial – that sustains the computer game industry, no less than the latest 3D engine, facial animation algorithm, or high-speed graphics card. Game code disseminates and thrives because it is an excellent substrate for human interaction, not because it is technologically impressive. Behind every successful computer game is a surge of interpersonal dynamics, both on an individual level and on a group level; games elicit and enable the most basic kinds of human pack behavior.

These group dynamics are best represented by the vast network of self-organized combat clans that vie for dominance on the Internet. No game company ever told players to form clans; they emerged in the mid-90s, and have persisted for years. There are thousands of them listed in Google's clan directory. The smallest have five members; the largest number in the hundreds and have developed their own politics, hierarchies, and systems of governance. They are essentially tribal: Each has a name, its own history, monikers, and signs of identification (logos and team graphics). Clans do occasionally cluster into trans-national organizations, assuming a shared identity across national boundaries and adopting a loose federalist structure. Generally, however, clans comprise players in the same country, because proximity reduces network lag – a real factor in games that require quick responses.

[ . . . ]

The clan network may seem anarchic: It is fiercely competitive and has no centralized authority. But beneath the gruesome aesthetics and inter-mural bravado, it is a highly cooperative system that runs far more efficiently than any "official" organization of similar scale, because clans, and the players that comprise them, have a clear set of shared goals. Regardless of who wins or loses, they are mutually dependent on the shared spaces where gaming occurs, whether those spaces are maintained by gamers for gamers, like ClanBase, or owned and operated by game publishers, like Sony, Electronic Arts, or Blizzard Entertainment, the developer of hit games including *StarCraft*, *Warcraft*, and *Diablo II*.

*Designing multi-scale social context: small, medium, large, x-large*

In online worlds such as *Everquest*, *Asheron's Call* or *Dark Age of Camelot*, the environment itself demands group formation. With dangerous monsters roaming around, a solo player doesn't last long in the wild; parties of four to six form in the interest of sheer survival, and ripen into war buddies as battles are fought and won. In addition, larger groups of players agglomerate into guilds ranging from a few dozen to upwards of a hundred affiliated characters.

Like clans in the combat and strategy genres, these groups are tribal. They have their own rites of passage and leadership structures. They form alliances with or declare wars on other guilds. There is even third-party software for the local chieftains of these organizations, who in the real world would be called managers. For $20, GuildBoss furnishes "the *ultimate* guild and clan management utility for multiplayer games." It's integrated directly into Microsoft Outlook and ICQ, and helps a busy clan leader gauge the performance of all his elves, rogues, and warriors. For human resources management software (evaluation, promotion, presence awareness), you could do a lot worse.

[ . . . ]

"Many-to-many" is a common buzzword in technology circles. But it usually really means one-to-one-to-one: I can interact with many people, and so can other individuals. There's very little in the way of true group-to-group interaction. And yet this is one of the most compelling aspects of the online game experience – not me against you, but my team against your team, or my team playing something that your team built. The functional unit is not the individual; it's the pack. Group cohesion keeps players in the game, as in the real world: Clans, guilds, packs, teams, buddy lists, book clubs, the people you forward a joke to – that's where the leverage is.

Collaboration is part of it, but that's missing half the equation. Collaboration assumes that people interact across an inward-facing project circle. In contrast, games assume that groups face other groups. There is a lot of kinetic potential in that intersection. Perhaps it's because most software is engineered in the West, where the individual is the prime unit, but the discourse around online identity allows only for personal identity, with little or no acknowledgement of group identity. Games encompass both kinds of identity, in player culture and in the applications themselves (i.e. character names reflect their social affiliations). That creates another, very meaningful layer of context that's particularly resonant in non-Western cultures. It is not a coincidence that the capital of online games is not the United States or Europe, but Asia. As technology permeates the non-Western world, it would be useful to consider what applications might emerge from the more nuanced and complete set of social assumptions that are taken for granted in game design.

## Persistence and Accretion

The business value of social context is especially important for companies such as Electronic Arts, Sony, and Microsoft, which maintain persistent multiplayer worlds that support hundreds of thousands of gamers on a subscription basis. Unlike most games, whose playing fields exist only while participants are actively engaged, multiplayer online worlds such as *Everquest*, *Ultima Online* or *Asheron's Call* persist, whether or not any particular player is logged on at any given time. The virtual environment is not something that vanishes when you stop playing: There are forces (some internal, some resulting from other players' actions) continuously at work. This persistence gives the game depth and is psychologically magnetic: The player is compelled to return habitually (even compulsively) to the environment, lest some new opportunity or crisis arise in his absence.

Compared to transient multiplayer environments (i.e. combat and strategy games), the experience is qualitatively different. The world is dynamic, and therefore less predictable. More importantly, the game extends over days, weeks or months.

The persistence of the environment allows players to develop their characters' identities within these worlds, which all hew to the conventions of role-playing games (RPG). In an RPG, a player's progress is represented not by geographical movement (as in console adventure games such as *Mario Bros.* or *Tomb Raider*, where the object is to get from point A to point B, defeating enemies along the way), but by the development of his character, who earns experience points by overcoming in-game challenges. At certain milestone point-tallies, the character is promoted to a new experience level, gaining strength, skill, and access to new weapons and tactics – but also attracting more powerful enemies. The better the player becomes, the more challenging his opponents become. Thus, the player scales a well-constructed learning curve over several months as he builds his level-1 character into a highly skilled, fully equipped level-50 powerhouse. Not surprisingly, players are highly invested in the characters they have built up.

As in Slashdot's "karma" system or eBay's reputation ratings, "leveling up" is a big motivating factor for players: It's the game's way of validating their cumulative accomplishments with something quantifiable, if not tangible. It's not enough for players to amass knowledge and skill; they have to see those characteristics manifest themselves in the physics of the game. The accretion of value in persistent worlds changes the psychology of leisure: You haven't "spent" 1,000 hours playing a game; you've "built up your character." You've made progress! Accretion transforms idle time into something that feels industrious. It turns spending into earning. You see the same psychological dynamics with frequent flyer miles – and the same sort of behavior. Travelers go to great lengths – sometimes thousands of unnecessary miles – to build their characters up from Blue to Silver or Gold Elite in order to get double mileage, dedicated check-in and the mystical power of free confirmed upgrades.

Accretion elicits emotional investment. In the physical world, travelers cherish their stamp-filled passports as well as their frequent flyer miles. Scouts have badges; skateboarders and rock climbers proudly point to their scars; ballet dancers save their scuffed and worn toe shoes. But outside of games, there are very few online experiences that leave you with any sense of lasting value. You are only spending attention, not investing it. One reason the Web seems so rootless and superficial is the lack of accretion; there are very few mechanisms that render people's investment of time, attention, and emotional energy into persistent artifacts of quantifiable value.

Where those artifacts exist, they not only represent experiential value but are often parlayed into real-world financial value as well, as players monetize their time. The player accounts of high-level online game characters, which may be cultivated over years, sell for hundreds of dollars on eBay – itself a massively multiplayer game (like any market), and a role-playing game at that. Persistent world characters are, after all, statistical profiles of a player's cumulative experience in the world. When it comes to interaction design, eBay and MMPs are siblings separated at birth – which is why they mesh so well.

[In 2001], Edward Castranova, an assistant professor of economics at California State University at Fullerton, calculated the real-world value of each unit of *Everquest*'s currency, the platinum piece. Based on exchange rates between EQ platinum pieces and US dollars on eBay, he found that the value of the EQ currency was greater than the lira or the yen. Using the average players' rate of acquisition of platinum pieces in the game (i.e.

the treasure they gain by slaying monsters), the hourly "wage" in *Everquest* is convertible to $3.42. On an annual basis, an *Everquest* player's economic productivity – not the subscription fee he pays Sony, but what he "earns" as an errant adventurer, in convertible *Everquest* currency – falls somewhere between that of the average Russian and the average Bulgarian. If *Everquest* were a country, it would rank 77th in per-capita GNP.

Of course, not all of this MMP-to-real-world arbitrage is strictly legal under the games' end-user licensing agreements, and most people create characters to use rather than to sell. But the thing that divides persistent worlds from other online games is this: They're a service, not a product, and if the administrators crack down too hard, or make themselves look like jerks, players will leave and take their $12.95 a month with them. There's a recognition that if you allow people to build value in a persistent world, this sort of asset trading will occur on some level – *Ultima Online* has even started offering "buffed" characters as a premium service; for $29.95, you can buy an advanced level wizard straight from the company store. Other services include the ability to change your character's name for $29.99 (an implicit acknowledgement that characters are transferred to people who want to graft pre-established personas onto second-hand avatars). As long as players' activities aren't compromising the experience for others, MMP companies eventually let them wag the dog.

## Beekeeper Beware

Lest this magical mystery tour convey the impression that online games are a sort of fusion physics devoid of liability, one should remember that not all massively multiplayer innovation is positive. Gamers are notorious for exploiting every weakness of client software. If it can be hacked, they'll hack it, particularly if doing so conveys some in-game advantage (although they're not averse to reverse-engineering client software just for kicks). For example, the initial version of *Ultima Online* put lighting control on the client. It seemed fairly innocuous to the designers . . . until players with hacked clients started illuminating the dungeons on their own screens, while other players stumbled around in the dark. Radically mismatched mayhem and slaughter ensued. *Diablo II* players are highly inventive when it comes to duping objects (which are then sold on the open market). When it comes to exploiting loopholes in a distributed system, gamers' creativity knows no bounds.

For technologists who are still in the business of selling products, not online-all-the-time services, the community management issues can be daunting. Not only do you have to contend with how end-users interact with your code – you have to contend with how they interact with one another. Naturally, players expect high levels of responsiveness from administrators, even as they try to game the system. Pundits throw around buzzwords like "swarming" as if it's all upside. From the trenches, it can be a grueling experience: Ask a game designer who's being swarmed by angry players when his online world's economic system goes haywire shortly after launch. The amount of damage a group of malevolent or disgruntled players can do to a game's commercial prospects is significant. They can ruin the in-game experience for new players, forcing them to flee. They can rally their guilds to leave the system, ripping the game's social fabric apart on their way out. Positive feedback is a double-edged sword.

The great thing about these massively multiplayer systems is that players really care about them. The awful thing is that players really care about them. Keeping these social systems humming is as much an art as a science. The people harvesting honey have had their share of stings at some point. But then, biology is always messier than engineering – less pure, less predictable, but more productive. It takes a certain degree of humility to acknowledge the imprecision of social system design. As the designers of Lucasfilms' *Habitat* observed in their early forays into online world design, "In the most carefully constructed experiment under the most carefully controlled conditions, the organism will do whatever it damn well pleases."

The genius of online game design is that this open, organic condition is optimal, rather than disastrous. The loops are open. The universe is messy, and that's a Good Thing. And high above the teeming population of players fighting, building, trading, and pushing back against the world they've been given, the authors of the game are watching, to see where players lead them.

## Further Information and URLs

Verant's message board for *Star Wars Galaxies*: http://starwarsgalaxies.station.sony.com/starwars_dev_boards.html

Interview with Mark Laidlaw, Valve's lead designer, http://www.gamitopia.com/features/interviews/v/valve/3.php

Interview with Minh "Gooseman" Le, creator of *Counter-Strike*, http://www.digitalgunfire.com/cs/counterstrike/

# PART VI
# Creative Economy

# Terry Flew

# CREATIVE ECONOMY

## Creative Industries and the "New Economy"

At first glance, the words "creative" and "economy" don't seem to sit well together. The conjunction recalls the "Vocational Guidance Counselor" sketch on *Monty Python's Flying Circus*, about the chartered accountant who really wanted to be a lion tamer. Indeed, the history of the creative industries is replete with tales of creative people who have found themselves at odds with corporate structures. Yet there is clearly change in the air. The creative industries globally were estimated to have generated revenues of $US2.2 trillion in 1999, and to have accounted for 7.5 percent of global Gross National Product (Howkins 2001: 116). In the United States, creative industries were estimated to account for 7.75 percent of Gross Domestic Product in 2001, for 5.9 percent of national employment, and $88.97 billion in exports (Mitchell et al. 2003: 20). In "hot spots" such as London, the creative industries now rival business services as the key economic sector, with over half a million Londoners working directly in the creative industries or in creative occupations in other industries (*London: Cultural Capital* 2003: 42).

Moreover, the creative industries concept – associated with innovation, risk-taking, new businesses and start-ups, intangible assets, and creative applications of new technologies – has developed a wider provenance. There is much discussion worldwide about how to generate creative cities and regions, and strategies to develop the creative industries as part of a national innovation strategy are being developed in the United Kingdom, Canada, Australia, New Zealand, Taiwan, Korea, Hong Kong, and Singapore. Writers such as Charles Leadbeater (Leadbeater 2000), John Howkins (Howkins 2001), and Richard Florida (Florida 2002) have proposed that we are now in a *creative economy*, where capitalism is being transformed from within, as

Richard Florida puts it, "from an older corporate-centered system defined by large companies to a more people-driven one" where new ideas and innovation are paramount (Florida 2002: 6).

The concept of the creative industries draws a great deal from this rise of a creative economy. It is related to the rise of the *knowledge economy*, and to the growing importance of innovation, research and development, investment in ICTs, and education and training as the principal drivers of growth in twenty-first-century economies (OECD 2001a). Such developments draw attention to the relationship between creativity and innovation, with the latter understood as the development of new products, services, organizational forms, and business processes (OECD 2001b). The link between creativity and the knowledge economy is perhaps seen most clearly in the development of ICT software. The development of new forms of computer software involves creativity in its production, generates new forms of intellectual property, and conveys symbolic meaning to its users. There is a great deal of creativity embedded in computer code, and computer software programs are frequently both an input to and the output of artists and artistic works defined in a more conventional sense.

The rise of the creative industries is also associated with the growing significance being attached to the production and consumption of *symbolic goods*. As Chris Bilton and Ruth Leary (2002) observe:

> "Creative industries" produce "symbolic goods" (ideas, experiences, images) where value is primarily dependent upon the play of symbolic meanings. Their value is dependent upon the end user (viewer, audience, reader, consumer) decoding and finding value within these meanings; the value of "symbolic goods" is therefore dependent upon the user's perception as much as on the creation of original content, and that value may or may not translate into a financial return. (Bilton and Leary 2002: 50)

This definition of creative industries is useful as it acknowledges the often non-pecuniary dimensions of creative production, and its relationship with systems of meaning and symbol, as well as the growing importance of symbolic production and design to manufactured consumer goods as diverse as footwear, motor vehicles, and mobile telephones.

Developments in information and communications technologies (ICTs) in the 1990s, such as the rapid diffusion of the internet, generated claims that a *new economy* had emerged, whose laws and dynamics were qualitatively different to those of the twentieth-century industrial economy (cf. Stiroh 1999; Zappala 2002). Drawing upon US Federal Reserve Chairman Alan Greenspan's observation that the value of US economic output had trebled over the last 50 years while its volume – as measured in physical weight – had increased only marginally, Diane Coyle (1999) argued that we were now in a "weightless economy," increasingly based upon *dematerialized output* in the forms of computer code, media content, design, information, and services. Taking more of a historical perspective, Manuel Castells (1996) argued that there had been a fundamental transformation within the capitalist mode of production, from an industrial to an *informational* mode of development. The core dynamics of this economic system arose out of the fusion of technologies of knowledge generation, information-processing, and symbol communication with the processes of globalization, digitization, and networking, leading to the rise of the *network society* as the dominant form of social organization. Castells' arguments drew upon *long wave theories*, which argued that capitalism experiences 50-year cycles of technological and organizational innovation, and that the pervasive application of ICTs and growth in the information services sector constituted the basis for a "fifth long wave," that had become the way out of the crisis of the mass-production economy in the 1970s and 1980s (cf. Flew 2002: 58–64).

## The New Economy and the "dot.com" Crash

In the popular imaginary, new economy claims were best symbolized by the phenomenal stock market performance of newly-founded "dot.com" enterprises such as the web browser firm Netscape and the online bookseller Amazon.com, and by the rapid rise of the NASDAQ, the US-based index for high-technology shares. Suspicions that the NASDAQ boom was essentially a speculative bubble driven by hype and self-interest, and that "new economy" arguments were a form of "silicon snake oil" (e.g. Stoll 1995; Lovink 2002a), appeared to be validated by the sharp fall in the NASDAQ after April 2000, from above 5,000 points to 1,300. One-time dot.com darlings found it increasingly hard to raise venture capital, and many of the business plans of internet start-up companies were found to be not worth the paper they were printed on. The "magic bullet" qualities that had been attributed to electronic commerce were seriously questioned, the word dot.com gradually disappeared from respectable conversation, and corporate *mea culpas* became a new growth industry (e.g. Kuo 2001; Malmstein 2001; cf. Lovink 2002b).

New economy arguments are not, however, necessarily linked to "dot.com mania," just as electronic commerce does not in itself constitute the most significant implication of the rise of the internet. The existence of a new economy is not derived from the existence of new technologies alone,

**Table 1.** The "Old" and "New" Economies

| Issues | Old Economy | New Economy |
|---|---|---|
| **Economy-wide** | | |
| Markets | Stable | Dynamic |
| Scope of competition | National | Global |
| Organizational form | Hierarchical, bureaucratic | Networked |
| Structure | Manufacturing core | Services/information core |
| Source of value | Raw materials, physical capital | Human and social capital |
| **Business** | | |
| Organization of production | Mass production | Flexible production |
| Key drivers of growth | Capital/labour | Innovation/knowledge |
| Key technology driver | Mechanization | Digitisation |
| Source of competitive advantage | Lowering cost through scale | Innovation, quality, adaptiveness |
| Importance of research/innovation | Low-moderate | High |
| Relations with other firms | Go it alone | Collaboration, outsourcing |
| **Consumers/Workers** | | |
| Tastes | Stable | Changing rapidly |
| Skills | Job-specific skills | Broad skills and adaptability |
| Educational needs | One-off craft training or degree | Lifelong learning |
| Workplace relations | Adversarial | Collaborative |
| Nature of employment | Stable | Increasingly contract/ project-based |
| **Government** | | |
| Business–government relations | Impose regulations | Encourage new growth opportunities |
| Regulation | Command and control | Market-based, flexible |
| Government services | Welfare state | Enabling state |

*Source*: Coyle and Quah 2002: 6.

but from the growing importance of ideas and intangibles, and the role played by knowledge and creativity that can be subsequently applied through ICTs and networked media. Moreover, technological innovation should not be seen as "manna from heaven," but rather as arising from a cultural and institutional milieu that promotes innovation and experimentation. Geoffrey Hodgson (2000) has described this as a *learning economy*, where a shift occurs from an economy dominated by manufactured goods and manual labor to one where ideas, intangible assets, services, and relational skills predominate.

New economy arguments also receive support from recent developments in economic theory. One of these is *new growth theory*, which postulates that technological change and economic growth are intrinsically connected, since the wellspring of growth is innovation in products and processes, and new ways of combining inputs to generate new types of output. As economist Paul Romer puts it, "Human history teaches us . . . that economic growth springs from better recipes, not just from more cooking" (Romer 1993: 184). Romer also argues that the central economic change of the last two decades has been the shift toward what he terms the "Microsoft model," where "the whole economy will start to look like Microsoft, with a very large fraction of people engaged in discovery as opposed to production" (Romer 1995: 70). Economic historian Paul David concurs with this account, finding that intangible capital has become increasingly important as a driver in the US economy over the last 100 years, and that this is largely embedded in investment geared either toward the production and dissemination of information or improvements in human capital (David and Foray 2002; cf. Abramovitz and David 2001).

Diane Coyle and Danny Quah (2002) have provided a summary account of the distinctions that are made between the "old" and "new" economies, in terms of economy-wide characteristics, business behavior, work and consumption, and government policies (see table 1).

## Creativity and the "Culturalization" of Economic Life

There has been a growing interest in the importance of creativity in the knowledge economy. The argument that everyone is creative, or that everyone at least has creative potential, has increasingly become a staple of corporate management literature (e.g. de Bono 1995). Such arguments are, however, too often based upon a common but flawed understanding of creativity. The attribution of creativity to unique individual personalities loses sight of the extent to which creativity is best understood as being the outcome of a process rather than a *persona*, and how moments of creative discovery are characteristically the outcome of incremental processes undertaken as part of a team of people that possess diverse skills (Bilton and Leary 2002). Moreover, since creativity is frequently domain-specific – i.e. the creativity involved in mathematics differs from that of sculpture, and arises from very different forms of professional training – then the search for a singular creative archetype is bound to prove illusory. When it is applied in management training, the results are frequently disappointing, since the focus on creative individuals frequently comes up against the organizational barriers to realizing creativity.

Nonetheless, the growing interest in creativity outside of the traditional domains of culture is reflective of what has been termed the *culturalization of economic life*. This argument was proposed by Lash and Urry (1994), who argued that contemporary capitalism was marked by a growing degree of *reflexive accumulation* in economic life, that included a new degree of *aesthetic reflexivity* in the spheres of both production and consumption, as capitalist production became increasingly design-intensive and oriented toward niche consumer markets. Turning the "culture industry" thesis on its head, they argued that the production models of the cultural industries – based upon extensive research and development, a high level of failure among its many "prototypes," the development of a "star system" as a means of managing consumption, and an economy increasingly driven by the production of new ideas rather than the reproduction of established commodities – was increasingly permeating all sectors of advanced capitalist economies.

Du Gay and Pryke (2002) have usefully broken down the question of whether there has been a culturalization of economic life into three component elements:

- arguments that the management of culture has become the key to improving organizational performance, particularly when it can align organizational goals to feelings of self-realization among those working within the organization;
- the observation that economic processes inevitably possess a cultural dimension, particularly with the growth of the services sector, where economic transactions are often more directly related to interpersonal relations and communicative practice;
- the rise of the creative industries as employers of labor and sources of new wealth, and the adoption of practices throughout the economy that have their genesis in these industries.

## When Markets Give Way to Networks . . . Everything is a Service: Jeremy Rifkin

In *The Age of Access*, Jeremy Rifkin locates the rise of both the creative and service industries in a wider pattern of transformation of the nature of property and markets, including shifts:

- from *markets* and discrete exchanges between buyers and sellers, to *networks* based upon ongoing relationships between suppliers and users;
- from wealth based upon the *ownership of tangible assets* (plant, equipment, inventory, etc.), to the outsourcing of production, and wealth creation based upon *access to intangible assets*, most notably goodwill, ideas, brand identities, copyrights, patents, talent, and expertise;
- from the *ownership of goods* to the *accessing of services*;
- from *production and sales* to *customer relationship marketing*;
- from *production-line manufacturing* and long product cycles to *the Hollywood organizational model* of project-based collaborative teams brought together for a limited period of time.

For Rifkin, these changes together mark the rise of a new form of *cultural capitalism*, arising out of new forms of linkage between digital communications technologies and cultural commerce, where "more and more of our daily lives are already mediated by the new digital channels of human expression" (Rifkin 2000: 138). The creative industries are "the front line commercial fields of the Age of Access" (Rifkin 2000: 140), as they have pioneered networked organization, just-in-time production, heavy investment in prototypes, and the selling of access to lived experiences. Rifkin nominates tourism as the oldest cultural industry, and as "the most visible and powerful expression of the new experience economy" (Rifkin 2000: 146). He proposes that Thomas Cook's establishment of package tourism in the 1850s can be seen, in retrospect, as providing the template for the modern experience-based economy. In what he terms the Age of Access, Rifkin proposes that "cultural production is going to be the main playing field for high-end global commerce in the twenty-first century," and that it will constitute the "first tier" of economic life, above information and services, manufacturing and agriculture (Rifkin 2000: 167).

# Work in the Creative Industries: From Bureaucracies to Networks

The rise of the creative industries as a template for other areas of the economy, as part of what Rifkin terms cultural capitalism, raises important issues about the nature of work in these creative industries sectors. Miège (1989), Ryan (1992), and Hesmondhalgh (2002) have observed that work in the creative industries has been characterized by a high degree of autonomy for artists and other creative professionals, a relatively loose division of labor in the production process, and the existence of a wide "pool" of creative talent which can be drawn upon on a contract or project basis. Such sectors are also characterized by what Miège has termed "a permanent crisis in 'creativity' [where] producers must constantly be on the lookout for new 'forms' or new talent" (Miège 1989: 44).

Davis and Scase (2000) describe creative industries organizations as having developed a tripartite division of labor between creative personnel, technical personnel associated with creative production, and managers and administrators involved with control and coordination functions. They observe that since "modern cultural production is an interpretative activity with a premium on the ability to communicate ideas and emotions in a constantly shifting environment," roles and occupations associated with the creative function are typically characterized by "reflective, interactive and intuitive processes with an indeterminate outcome," where "the social organization of work tasks is implicit rather than explicit . . . [and] performance criteria are linked to evaluation by peers, critics and audiences rather than purely quantitative indicators" (Davis and Scase 2000: 53–4). This is in contrast to the performance of managerial tasks, which remain strongly linked to the objectives of the organization and to the use of rational means and standardized procedures for achieving these goals.

Davis and Scase identify two main ways in which this interface between creative and managerial tasks has been handled in creative organizations. The first is that of *bureaucracy*, which has historically prevailed both within large commercial creative industries organizations and large publicly funded organizations. In the bureaucratic model, the mechanisms of control are explicit and hierarchical, lines of accountability are predetermined, the mechanisms of coordination are explicit, and the performance of employees is monitored, measured, and appraised. Creative personnel enter into *employment relations* with commercial or public sector organizations, and are motivated both by the conventional measures of income and status within the organization, and by some degree of "internalized commitment" to the organization and its values. Such organizational structures are marked by a perpetual tension between the formal, rule-governed nature of bureaucracy and the autonomy, indeterminacy, and nonconformity that characterize creative work processes. The chronic danger is that creative personnel experience such processes as inhibiting the realization of their personal intellectual capital, and thwarting their intrinsic motivations in pursuing creative tasks. As a managing director of a large advertising company notes:

> People will stay in any place as long as they are getting out of that place what they want . . . For creative people, if they can get very, very good work out and be well paid, they will stay. And most creative people would rather earn 50,000 a year for doing good work than 100,000 a year and be doing shit. (Quoted in Davis and Scase 2000: 133)

The second approach, which is growing in significance, is that of *network organizations* (cf. Castells 2001). In the networked organizational model, self-employed individuals or small teams undertake creative work on a project or contract basis. Such structures allow for a high degree of autonomy, as they are based upon informal and tacit mechanisms of control and coordination; in such arrangements, it is *market relations*, rather than employment relations, that dictate the delivery of outcomes. Management by contract rather than control has been the historical norm for many areas of the creative industries, most notably book publishing and recorded music. It has increasingly been adopted by large commercial and public enterprises, who have seen virtues in outsourcing creative activities to independent subcontractors in order to maximize flexibility, reduce fixed costs, and achieve better outcomes through the ability to draw upon a "pool" of competing providers. The British Broadcasting Corporation explicitly adopted a purchaser–provider model in the 1990s through the "Producer's Choice" initiative, which required in-house BBC creative teams to compete with independent production houses for contracts to produce programs in areas of need identified by the BBC.

## Creative Work and Networked Organizations

The network organization model loosens considerably the control nexus between content creators and content distributors that had informed the large-scale cultural organization, replacing control through bureaucratic command with control through the market mechanism, directed toward a well-qualified and increasingly mobile creative workforce. Its growing significance can be seen in a recent European Union survey of employment in the

cultural sector, which found that employment growth rates in cultural occupations were four times the EU average (4.8 percent growth between 1995
and 1999, compared to overall employment growth in the EU of 1.2 percent) and that people working in cultural occupations were almost three
times as likely to be self-employed as the EU average (40.4 percent compared
to 14.4 percent for the EU as a whole) (MKW 2001: 84–6). The EU study
also indicates that workers in cultural occupations are twice as likely to have
a tertiary qualification as those in other sectors, and that higher degree qualifications are particularly pronounced among self-employed cultural workers
(MKW 2001: 87–8).

## Clubs to Companies: Angela McRobbie

Drawing upon her work on the arts, fashion, and music industries in
London, Angela McRobbie has associated the rise of the creative
industries with what she has termed the "Hollywoodization" of labor
markets, both in the sense that the perceived glamor of creative work
encourages people to accept long hours of work and low pay in the
hope of "making it," and because what Jeremy Rifkin terms the "Hollywood organizational model" – working as a part of creative teams in
short-term project-based activities – is increasingly seen as the norm in
cultural sector employment. The need to manage portfolio careers also
promotes a need for creative workers to develop business skills which
enable them to manage their career possibilities in highly fluid, networked environments.

McRobbie identifies five constitutive features of this new mode of
work in the creative industries. First, she notes the extent to which it
draws upon the "club culture sociality" of the "dance-party-rave"
music culture that rose to prominence in the 1990s, where clandestine
and rebellious elements of youth culture were fused with a highly
entrepreneurial approach to events marketing, establishing the club
promoter as a multi-skilled cultural entrepreneur. Second, she observes
that such multi-skilling is in many cases associated with people holding
multiple jobs, both within formal organizations and in more informal,
networked cultures. Third, McRobbie sees working long hours as
almost endemic to this model, as there is little or no regulation of
formal working hours, and because self-promotion and networking are
central to the gaining of new contracts and ongoing paid work.

Fourth, McRobbie argues that the highly individualized and competitive nature of this workforce, and the contract nature of work, discourages critique of potential employers and workplace politics, and that issues traditionally raised through trade unions lack a space in which to be heard in what she terms a "PR meritocracy." Finally, McRobbie questions the extent to which these new work patterns in the creative industries overturn existing power structures, as she argues that the need for ongoing work has increasingly led freelance workers into relationships with major distributors that look more like subcontracting and short-term contract work. McRobbie refers to the "loneliness of the long distance incubator," and observes that for many, such as women with children and those outside of major metropolitan centers, the opportunities to participate in such "club culture sociality," based on long working hours and night-time activities, are considerably diminished.

McRobbie's article can be read as a critique of the creative industries concept, particularly in the forms that have been associated with the "Third Way" ideologies of the Blair Labour government in the United Kingdom. The article raises important questions about the scope for exploitation for those working in the creative industries as a result of the "hourglass" structure of these industries, where the number of content creators so massively outweighs the number of content distributors and the scope for exploitation is therefore very high. McRobbie also observes that the groups least able to participate in "club culture sociality" are, not surprisingly, those most likely to be structurally disadvantaged in capitalist labor markets: women with young children; racial and ethnic minorities; people with disabilities; older workers; the long-term unemployed; and people living outside of major metropolitan centers.

The rise of the creative industries in the context of the new economy raises issues about the relative merits of the "social market" or "European" model of capitalism and what McRobbie terms American-style "fast capitalism." While the large inequalities, the pervasive sense of economic insecurity, and the adverse experiences of the working poor in the United States are well known and widely noted (e.g. Brenner 2000), the innovation and economic dynamism that have characterized the US economy since the early 1990s are also apparent, as is its relationship to rapid ICT take-up and development of the creative sectors. By contrast, a number of European economies, most notably France and Germany, have been experiencing high unemployment, slowing productivity, an aging population, and growing concerns about the impact of restrictive bureaucracy on the development of new enterprises and industries (Blackburn 2002; Baltho 2003). Moreover, extrapolating from the MKW study noted above, much of the dynamism of these economies is emanating from the creative sectors, outside of the traditional heartlands of "Fordist" industrialism. The challenge seems to be how to wed social capital formation and notions of collective security with the dynamism of the creative economy. Given this challenge, it is perhaps not surprising that debates about creative industries often get tied up with arguments about the nature of a "Third Way" between post-World War II social democracy and neo-liberal free market capitalism.

## Cultural Policy and Globalization

The funding of artistic and cultural activities, and the governance of culture more generally, has been commonly understood through the rubric of *cultural policy*. While cultural policy in the narrow sense has been understood as public funding for the arts and media through mechanisms determined by creative producers and their peers, cultural policy in a broader sense has been understood as the discursive and institutional frameworks through which culture is governed in order to develop cultural citizenship (Lewis and Miller 2002). Nationalism has been an important motivator of cultural policy, as Ernest Gellner noted when defining nationalism as "the striving to make culture and polity congruent, to endow a culture with its own political roof, and not more than one roof at that" (Gellner 1983: 43). With the development of globalizing media technologies such as film and broadcasting in the twentieth century, cultural policy has increasingly sought to incorporate the popular media into such nationalist projects, in part to resist the perceived "Americanization" of mass culture. National film policies, support for public broadcasters, and local content quotas for broadcast media can all be understood as applications of national cultural policy to these ends.

Creative industries and cultural markets operate on a global scale, and arguably have done so since the 1920s, when the Hollywood studios established the ascendancy of US films in European markets. The rapid worldwide expansion of television ownership and, more recently, the internet and multimedia, have further consolidated the ascendancy of US cultural product in global markets. While there is some evidence of "contra-flow" in global media (Thussu 2000), as well as the growth of "offshore" production in countries such as Canada and Australia (Miller et al. 2001), the overwhelming trend is toward expansion of the US share of global cultural markets, and

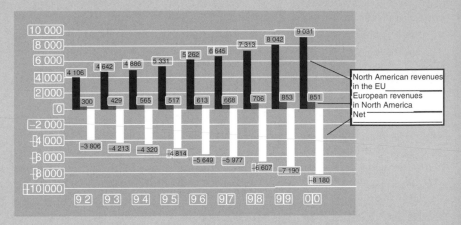

**Figure 1.** Balance of audiovisual trade between the European Union and North America, 1992–2000.
*Source:* European Audiovisual Observatory 2002.

an increase in cultural trade deficits between the US and most other regions of the world. This is seen clearly in the balance of audiovisual trade between North America and the European Union:

The globalization of cultural markets challenges cultural policy fundamentals as it points to an uncoupling of culture and polity. National governments face a declining capacity to regulate global media and communications flows, and engage in "cultural boundary maintenance" in the face of economic and cultural globalization. The General Agreement on Trade in Services (GATS) has generated further concerns about the impact of trade globalization on national cultural policy measures, with its potential requirement on member states to dismantle existing local content quota and domestic subsidy arrangements for film and television, and its capacity to preclude the development of new measures for convergent and digital media. As a result, the European Community and Canada have petitioned the World Trade Organization to develop a "cultural exception" to the disciplines of the GATS, arguing for the distinctiveness of culture and the need to preserve global cultural diversity (Footer and Graber 2000). Audiovisual services were the area where the most countries sought GATS exemptions in the Uruguay Round, completed in 1994. The conflict between the United States and Europe, led by France, was particularly fierce.

As cultural production is increasingly associated with the dynamics of creative industries in the new economy, there may be a case for rethinking the rationales underpinning support for cultural production. Traditional subsidy-based and quota-based models have assumed that the arts are different, and the media "not just another business," with both therefore requiring special treatment in policy terms. By contrast, it has been argued that policy approaches that draw upon government support for R&D as a catalyst of national innovation strategies, and place creative industries in the vanguard of new economy strategies, may generate more fruitful outcomes (see Stuart Cunningham's introduction to part V of this volume).

This chapter has observed the many ways in which the rise of the creative economy entails a shift in how we conceive of culture. We have been challenged to think about culture and creativity in their various forms as core elements of a creative economy. Creative industries sectors are key innovation sites in digital content production and distribution in an era of globalization and digital networked infrastructures, where there is a premium being attached to creativity and innovation as sources of competitive advantage for enterprises, cities and regions, and nations. This is different to the modernist paradigms of cultural policy as the preservation of a great tradition, or the integration of citizens into a common national culture.

---

## Culture and the Creative Economy in the Information Age: Shalini Venturelli

Shalini Venturelli argues that an understanding of the creative economy requires a significant rethinking of how we have understood culture. She observes that three traditions have dominated thinking about culture:

- the aesthetic tradition, and its association with excellence in the fine arts;
- the anthropological tradition, and its understanding of culture as a received and shared symbolic system, or a "whole way of life" of a society;
- the industrial or commercial tradition, which understands cultural products as industrial commodities sold to consumers.

In the context of the global information economy, Venturelli proposes that these traditions require substantial revision. As we recognize the distinctive features of informational and cultural products, it becomes apparent that the value of ideas and creative expression can be massively leveraged in networked digital environments, meaning that the value of these forms cannot be gainsaid independently of their use and application. Recognition of this new role of culture as a source of value-adding in the global information economy also requires a shift in

---

policy thinking away from questions of how to preserve cultural forms, practices, and institutions of the past – the "museum paradigm" of cultural policy – toward developing the environment that is most conducive to creativity and the generation of new cultural forms. This means extending the remit of cultural policy to all areas of economy and society.

An important implication of Venturelli's argument is that the case for national cultural policy in an age of globalization and international trade agreements rests, not in the need to protect national culture from global influences and competition, but in developing and maintaining the creative infrastructure through which new ideas and forms of creative expression can be developed, and distributed across global digital networks. There is thus a link between the vitality and health of artistic and cultural institutions, opportunities for creative expression and the development of new ideas, and competitiveness and dynamism in the global information economy. For Venturelli, the creative industries produce the "gold" of the information economy, and it would not be wise for nations to trade off too lightly their capacity to develop, distribute, and renew their creative infrastructure or the ideas and talents of their creative people.

# References

Abramovitz, M. and P. David (2001) *Two Centuries of American Macroeconomic Growth: From Exploitation of Resource Abundance to Knowledge-Driven Development*. Stanford Institute for Economic Policy Research Discussion Paper 01–05, August.

Australian Broadcasting Corporation (2001) This Time It's Different. Broadcast on *Four Corners*, April 30, <www.abc.net.au/4corners/dotcom/>.

Baltho, A. (2003) What's Wrong with Europe? *New Left Review* 22, 5–26.

Bilton, C. and R. Leary (2002) What Can Managers Do for Creativity? Brokering Creativity in the Creative Industries. *International Journal of Cultural Policy* 8(1), 49–64.

Blackburn, R. (2002) Symptoms of Euro-Denial. *New Left Review* 18, 131–40.

Brenner, R. (2000) The Boom and the Bubble. *New Left Review* 6, 5–43.

Castells, M. (1996) *The Rise of the Network Society*, vol. 1 of *The Information Age: Economy, Society and Culture*. Blackwell, Massachusetts.

Castells, M. (2001) *The Internet Galaxy: Reflections on the Internet, Business and Society*. Oxford University Press, Oxford.

Caves, R. (2000) *Creative Industries: Contracts between Art and Commerce*. Harvard University Press, Cambridge, Mass.

Coyle, D. (1999) *The Weightless World: Thriving in a Digital Age.* Capstone, London.

Coyle, D. and D. Quah (2002) *Getting the Measure of the New Economy.* iSociety, London.

David, P. and D. Foray (2002) *Economic Fundamentals of the Knowledge Society.* Stanford Institute for Economic Policy Research Discussion Paper 01–14, February.

Davis, H. and R. Scase (2000) *Managing Creativity: The Dynamics of Work and Organization.* Open University Press, Buckingham.

De Bono, E. (1995) *Serious Creativity.* HarperCollins, London.

Department of Culture, Media and Sport (2002) *Creative Industries Mapping Document 2001* <www.culture.gov.uk/creative/creative_industries.html>.

Du Gay, P. and M. Pryke (2002) Cultural Economy: An Introduction. In P. du Gay and M. Pryke (eds.), *Cultural Economy: Cultural Analysis and Commercial Life.* Sage, London, 1–19.

European Audiovisual Observatory (2002) *Focus 2002: World Film Market Trends.* European Audiovisual Observatory, Strasbourg.

Flew, T. (2002) *New Media: An Introduction.* Oxford University Press, Melbourne.

Florida, R. (2002) *The Rise of the Creative Class, and How it's Transforming Work, Leisure, Community and Everyday Life.* Basic Books, New York.

Footer, M. and C. B. Graber (2000) Trade Liberalization and Cultural Policy. *Journal of International Economic Law* 3(1), 115–44.

Gellner, E. (1983) *Nations and Nationalism.* Blackwell, Oxford.

Hesmondhalgh, D. (2002) *The Cultural Industries.* Sage, London.

Hodgson, G. (2000) Socio-Economic Consequences of the Advance of Complexity and Knowledge. In *The Creative Society of the 21st Century.* Organization for Economic Cooperation and Development, Paris, 89–112.

Howkins, J. (2001) *The Creative Economy: How People Make Money from Ideas.* Allen Lane, London.

Kuo, D. (2001) *Dot.Bomb: Inside an Internet Goliath – From Lunatic Optimism to Panic and Crash.* Brown & Co., New York.

Lash, S. and J. Urry (1994) *Economies of Signs and Space.* Sage, London.

Leadbeater, C. (2000) *Living on Thin Air: The New Economy.* Penguin, London.

Lewis, J. and T. Miller (2002) Introduction. In J. Lewis and T. Miller (eds.), *Critical Cultural Policy Studies: A Reader.* Blackwell, Malden, Mass, 1–9.

London: Cultural Capital (2003) The Mayor's Draft Cultural Strategy. Assembly and Functional Bodies Consultation Draft, February. <www.london.gov.uk/mayor/strategies/culture/index.jsp>.

Lovink, G. (2002a) The Rise and Fall of Dotcom Mania. In *Dark Fiber: Tracking Critical Internet Culture.* MIT Press, Cambridge, Mass, 348–69.

Lovink, G. (2002b) After the Dotcom Crash: Recent Literature on Internet, Business and Society. *Cultural Studies Review* 8(1), 130–54.

Malmstein, E. (2001) *Boo Hoo: A Dotcom Story from Concept to Catastrophe.* Random House, New York.

Miège, B. (1989) *The Capitalization of Cultural Production.* International General, Paris.

Miller, T., N. Govil, J. McMurria, and R. Maxwell (2001) *Global Hollywood*. British Film Institute, London.

Mitchell, W., A. Inouye, and M. Blumenthal (2003) *Beyond Productivity: Information Technology, Innovation and Creativity*. National Academies Press, Washington, DC.

MKW Wirtschaftsforschung GmbH (2001) *Exploitation and Development of the Job Potential in the Cultural Sector in the Age of Digitization. Final Report*. Module 2: Employment Trends and Sectors of Growth in the Cultural Economy. Commissioned by European Commission DG Employment and Social Affairs, June.

OECD (Organization for Economic Cooperation and Development) (2001a) *The New Economy: Beyond the Hype*. OECD, Paris.

OECD (2001b) *Cities and Regions in the New Learning Economy*. OECD, Paris.

Rifkin, J. (2000) *The Age of Access: How the Shift from Ownership to Access is Transforming Economic Life*. Penguin, London.

Romer, P. (1993) Economic Growth. In D. R. Henderson (ed.), *The Fortune Encyclopedia of Economics*. Warner Books, New York, 183–9.

Romer, P. (1995) Interview with Peter Robinson. *Forbes* 155(12), 66–70.

Ryan, B. (1992) *Making Capital from Culture: The Corporate Form of Capitalist Cultural Production*. De Gruyter, Berlin.

Stiroh, K. (1999) Is There a New Economy? *Challenge* 42(4), 82–101.

Stoll, C. (1995) *Silicon Snake Oil: Second Thoughts on the Information Highway*. Macmillan, London.

Thussu, D. K. (2000) *International Communication: Continuity and Change*. Arnold, London.

Zappala, G. (2002) The New Economy: Economic and Social Dimensions. In G. Argyrous and F. Stilwell (eds.), *Economics as a Social Science*, 2nd edn. Pluto Press, Sydney, 19–24.

# 21 *Jeremy Rifkin*

# WHEN MARKETS GIVE WAY TO NETWORKS . . . EVERYTHING IS A SERVICE

## The Hollywood Organizational Model ──────────

The Hollywood culture industries have had a long experience with network-based approaches to organization and, for that reason, are fast becoming the prototype for the reorganization of the rest of the capitalist system along network lines. To begin with, the entertainment industry has to deal with the risks that accompany products with a truncated life cycle. Each film is a unique experience that has to find a quick audience if the production company is to recoup its investment, making a network approach to doing business a matter of necessity.

That's not always been the case, however. The early film industry relied on the kind of "Fordist" manufacturing principles that were in vogue across a wide range of industries in the 1920s. So-called "formula" films were produced like automobiles coming off an assembly line. One of the pioneers of the field, the Universal Film Manufacturing Company, produced more than 250 films in a single year. In the early years, films were actually sold by the foot rather than by content, reflecting the bias toward a mass-production mode of operation.[1]

By the early 1930s, a handful of studio giants – including Warner Brothers, Paramount, Metro-Goldwyn-Mayer, and Twentieth Century Fox – controlled the film industry. Their organizations were hierarchically structured and designed to oversee and regulate every aspect of the production process, from scripts to distribution. Professor Michael Storper of the University of California at Los Angeles School of Public Policy and Social Research explains how the system operated.

> The major studios had permanent staffs of writers and production planners who were assigned to produce formula scripts in volume and push them through the production system. Production crews and stars were assembled in teams charged with making as many as thirty films per year. Studios had large departments to make sets, operate sound stages and film labs, and carry out marketing and distribution. A product would move from department to department in assembly-line fashion. . . . The internal organization – or technical division of labor – in each phase of the labor process became increasingly similar to that of true mass production, where routinization and task fragmentation were the guiding principles.[2]

In 1944, the big studios earned 73 percent of all domestic cinema rentals and owned or leased 4,424 theaters, or nearly one out of every four movie houses in the country. Moviegoing peaked in 1946, with more than 90 million tickets sold per week.[3]

In the late 1940s and early 1950s, the film industry was hit with two external shocks that forced it to reorganize along the network baselines currently in practice. The US Supreme Court – in a landmark antitrust case – forced the major studios to divest themselves of their cinema chains. No longer able to exercise control over the end user at the box office, film companies saw their revenues decline. The advent of television further cut into film company profits. Millions of former moviegoers preferred to stay home and be entertained for free. Box office receipts fell by 40 percent between 1946 and 1956, and the film audience declined by 50 percent. The gross revenues of the ten leading film companies declined by 26 percent, and profit declined by 50 percent.[4]

Faced with increasing competition from the new medium of television, the film industry responded by changing their approach to filmmaking. Realizing they couldn't successfully compete with a free medium pumping out similar formulaic cultural products, the studio leaders began to experiment with making fewer, more entertaining films, each a unique product that could vie for viewer attention. The new films were called "spectaculars" – later "blockbusters" – and they moved the film industry from mass production to customized production oriented toward creating a "movie experience" each time the moviegoer walked into the theater.

The new genre of films was more elaborate and expensive, and because each film was a unique product and therefore untested in the marketplace, large sums of money had to be invested in advertising and promotion. In short, the increasing cost involved in making fewer, more differentiated films brought with it greater financial risks and less sure returns on investments.

The network system of film production emerged in the 1950s partially in response to the need to bring together diverse talent to each unique film project and to pool risks in case any one product failed at the box office. The studio giants began to contract out for talent and services on a project-to-project basis. Independent production companies, made up of artisans and artists formerly under contract at the big studios, began to proliferate. Today, the remaining studio giants rarely produce films in-house. Instead, they act as financial investors, providing seed money to independent producers in return for the right to distribute the end product at movie houses and later on television and video.

Every film production brings together a team of specialized production companies and independent contractors, each with its own expertise, along with the talent. Together, the parties constitute a short-lived network enterprise whose life span will be limited to the duration of the project. Scripting, casting, set design, cinematography, costuming, sound mixing and mastering, editing, and film processing all are done by independent agents working in temporary partnership with an independent production company. By assembling expertise from a number of specialized companies, producers can find exactly the right combination of skills needed to make the specific film project a success. Independent contractors, in turn, minimize their risks by engaging in a number of projects simultaneously across industry lines. It's not unusual for a special-effects company, for example, to be working in several temporary networks at once, performing specialized tasks on any given day on a film, in a television commercial, or on location at a live stage event. At the same time, overall labor costs are kept at a minimum by utilizing skills on an "as needed" basis or by contract for the completion of specific services. From 1979 to 1995, the number of entertainment-related films tripled in Southern California. Most of the firms in the film industry, however, employ fewer than ten people.[5] Independent production companies, which produced only 28 percent of all US films in 1960, were making 58 percent of the films just two decades later, while the majors were producing fewer than 31 percent of the films.[6]

It should be emphasized, however, that although the network approach to commercial organization has brought an increasing number of smaller firms into the industry, the major studios and entertainment companies still exercise control over much of the process by their abilities to partially finance production and to control distribution of the product. In fact, film industry analysts Asu Aksoy and Kevin Robins make the point that vertical disintegration and the shift to network forms of organization were consciously pursued goals to allow the studio giants to better generate product while minimizing financial risks. The key to maintaining effective control over the industry, say Aksoy and Robins, has always revolved around controlling access to the distribution channels.

> By holding on to their power as national and international distribution networks, the majors were able to use their financial muscle to dominate the film business and to squeeze or to use the independent production companies.[7]

Robins and Aksoy contend that industry statistics are often misleading. Despite the fact that independent film companies produce the bulk of new films, the majors still reap most of the profit. In 1990, for example, the top five companies earned 69.7 percent of the box office returns.[8] The network approach to organizing commerce – as we will see repeatedly throughout the book – allows the biggest transnational companies to rid themselves of physical plants, equipment, and talent by creating strategic relationships with suppliers to produce content. In a world of increasing competition, more diversified products and services, and shorter product life cycles, companies stay on top by controlling finance and distribution channels while pushing off onto smaller entities the burdens of ownership and management of physical assets.

The Hollywood network approach to commercial organization is leading the way toward a new network-based economy in cyberspace, just as General Motors' hierarchical form of organization did at the onset of the second industrial revolution in the 1920s. In an article entitled "Why Every Business Will Be Like Show Business" in *Inc.* magazine, Joel Kotkin writes:

> Hollywood [has mutated] from an industry of classic huge vertically integrated corporations into the world's best example of a network economy. . . . Eventually, every knowledge-intensive industry will end up in the same flattened atomized state. Hollywood just has gotten there first.[9]

The Hollywood organizational model is quickly being adopted by a number of the cutting-edge industries of the twenty-first century. Andy Grove, former chairman of Intel, compares the software industry to the theater, where directors, actors, musicians, writers, technicians, and financial backers are brought together for a brief moment of time to create a new production. Even though the number of successes are few and far between, says Grove, the process also creates smash hits.[10] In his book *Jamming: The Art and Discipline of Business Creativity*, John Kao of the Harvard Business School urges CEOs to integrate the Hollywood network model into their long-term strategic plans. "You need to act like today's version of a Hollywood studio," says Kao.[11]

In the new network-based economy, Max Weber's idea of "organization" as a relatively fixed structure with set rules and procedures begins to disintegrate. In the fast-changing world of electronic commerce, enterprises have to be far more protean in nature, able to change shape and form at a moment's notice to accommodate new economic conditions. In geographic markets, structure still counts. In cyberspace, however, boundaries fall and process replaces structure as the standard operating procedure for survival. Organization becomes as ephemeral and fleeting as the electronic medium in which business is conducted.

Management consultant Tom Peters aptly describes the new network approach to commerce. In the future, says Peters, "networks of bits and pieces of companies will come together to exploit a market opportunity, perhaps stay together for a couple of years (though changing shape, dramatically, several times in the process), then dissolve, never to exist again in the same form."[12]

Everywhere in the world, companies large and small are in a frenzied scramble to become part of expanding commercial networks. In the Age of Access, a company's biggest concern is not being included in the commercial webs and relationships that create economic opportunities. Having access to networks is becoming as important in cyberspace commerce as enjoying market advantage was in the industrial era. Being left out of the loop can mean instant failure in this new world of ever changing alliances.

A final point needs to be made about the Hollywood organizational model that is too often glossed over or missed altogether in discussions of management strategies. It's no mere coincidence that other industries try to model the way the entertainment industry is organized. The cultural industries – including the recording industry, the arts, television, and radio – commodify, package, and market experiences as opposed to physical products or services. Their stock and trade is selling short-term access to simulated worlds and altered states of consciousness. The fact is, they are an ideal organizational model for a global economy that is metamorphosing from commodifying goods and services to commodifying cultural experience itself.

In cyberspace, the relationships between suppliers and users increasingly resemble the kinds of relationships that the culture industries have forged with audiences over the years. We are entering a more cerebral period of capitalism whose product is access to time and mind. The manufacture and transfer of physical goods between sellers and buyers (property), while still part of our day-to-day reality, especially in geographically based markets, will continue to migrate to the second tier of economic activity. The first tier will increasingly be made up of the selling and buying of human experiences. The movie industry is the front-runner in a new era in which each consumer's life

JEREMY RIFKIN

experience will be commodified and transformed into an unending series of theatrical moments, dramatic events, and personal transformations. As the rest of the economy begins to make the shift from geographic markets to cyberspace and from selling goods and services to commodifying whole areas of human experiences, the Hollywood studio model of organization will increasingly be looked to as a standard for organizing commercial activity.[13]

[ . . . ]

## The Birth of the Service Economy

Even as the production, exchange, and accumulation of property – in the form of both capital and consumer goods – was becoming a national pastime, other forces were at work in the evolving capitalist market that would eventually undermine private-property relations and the elaborate social system that had grown up around it.

The increasing complexity of large-scale business operations, more discretionary family income, and the entrance of large numbers of women into the workforce led to the introduction of business services and then later consumer services into the capitalist mix. At first, business services were an adjunct to the production and distribution of goods. Railroads, utilities, and other large-scale manufacturing concerns required ever more complex forms of coordination and organization. Business services, including accounting, financial planning, transportation, and communications, began to play an increasingly prominent role in the production and distribution of goods. At the same time, an affluent middle class began to spend more of its discretionary income on services of all kinds. The process accelerated as more and more women entered the workforce. Activities that women normally provided in the home, including child care, senior care, preparation of meals, health care, haircuts, and the like, were moved to the marketplace as paid commercial services. Between 1899 and 1939, the amount of flour consumed by commercial bakeries rose from $\frac{1}{7}$ to $\frac{2}{5}$ of the total produced. The production of canned vegetables increased fivefold; canned fruits twelvefold.[14] Braverman observes that "the source of status is no longer the ability to make things but simply the ability to purchase them."[15] Entertainment and leisure-time activities, which had been, for the most part, family affairs or public activities, also began to migrate to the marketplace, where they were made into commercial services of various sorts. Braverman summarizes the impact of this change in the structure of human relations in the first decades of the twentieth century this way:

Thus the population no longer relies upon social organization in the form of family, friends, neighbors, community, elders, children, but with few exceptions must go to market, and only to market, not only for food, clothing, and shelter, but also for recreation, amusement, security, for the care of the young, the old, the sick, the handicapped. In time not only the material and service needs but even the emotional patterns of life are channeled through the market.[16]

By the time Daniel Bell wrote his book *The Coming of Post-Industrial Society* in 1973, the performance of services had eclipsed the production of goods and become the driving engine of capitalism in both North America and Europe. Although "services" is a bit of a mercurial, catchall category and open to widely differing interpretations, it generally includes economic activities that are not products or construction, are transitory, are consumed at the time they are produced, and provide an intangible value. *The Economist*, partially in jest, once suggested that services are "anything sold in trade that could not be dropped on your foot."[17] They include professional work (legal, accounting, and consulting), the wholesale and retail trades, transportation, communications, health care, child care, senior care, entertainment and paid leisure activity, and government social programs.

In 1973, sixty-five out of every hundred workers were already engaged in services. In the European community, 47.6 percent of workers were in the service sector in the early 1970s.[18] Today, the service industries employ more than 77 percent of the US workforce and account for 75 percent of the value added in the US economy and more than half of the value added in the global economy.[19] Percy Barnevik, the former CEO of Asea Brown Boveri Ltd., predicts that by the year 2010, services will make up more than 90 percent of the US economy, and manufacturing activities less than 10 percent.[20]

The shift in primary commerce from goods to services makes property far less important in both business and personal life. In the Age of Access, we are more likely to measure economic activity in "MTBH – the mean time between haircuts" than by the number of widgets produced and sold, writes Peter Martin in the *Financial Times*.[21] Daniel Bell captured, at least in part, the significance of the transformation taking place in capitalist commerce when he observed that "if an industrial society is defined by the quantity of goods as marking a standard of living, the post-industrial society is defined by the quality of life as measured by the services and amenities – health, education, recreation, and the arts – which are now deemed desirable."[22]

Of course, what has been left unsaid in all of the discussions about the transition to a service economy, and what bears repeating, is that services do not qualify as property. They are immaterial and intangible. They are performed, not produced. They exist only at the moment they are rendered. They cannot be held, accumulated, or inherited. While products are bought, services are made available. In a service economy, it is human time that is being commodified, not places or things. Services always invoke a relationship between human beings as opposed to a relationship between a human being and a thing. Access to one another, as social beings, becomes increasingly mediated by pecuniary relationships.

**The metamorphosis** in the organization of human relations from the production and commercial exchange of propertied goods to access to commodified service relationships is transforming in nature. Yet our society continues to act as if property relations are fundamental when, in reality, economic forces are making physical property, at least, less relevant. Perhaps we have been reluctant to come to grips with a world in which the production and exchange of property is no longer the sole reference point for measuring economic activity because we are afraid of losing our moorings. Our codes of conduct, our civic values, indeed our deepest sense of who we are in relationship to the people, the institutional forces, and the world around us have for so long been mediated by property relations that the thought of being cast adrift in a new, less material, less boundaried, more intangible and ephemeral world of commodified services is unsettling. We'd have to rethink the social contract from beginning to end if we were to wrestle seriously with the impacts of a world based more on access than on ownership.

That day of reckoning, however, may be near because of two changes that Daniel Bell and other forecasters could not have anticipated. First, even goods themselves – the bulwark of a private property regime – are becoming transformed into pure services, signaling the end of property as a defining concept of social life. Second, the nature of services is changing. Traditionally, services have been treated more like goods and negotiated as discrete market transactions, each one separated in time and space. Now, with the advent of electronic commerce and sophisticated data feedback mechanisms, services are being reinvented as long-term multifaceted relationships between servers and clients.

# The Evolution of Goods into Services

As goods become more information-intensive and interactive and are continually upgraded, they change character. They lose their status as products and metamorphose into evolving services. Their value lies less in the physical scaffolding or container they come in and more in the access to services they provide. Taichi Sakaiya, the director-general of the Economic Planning Agency of Japan, understood the change taking place in the way we perceive of goods when he wrote, "The significance of material goods [will be] as containers or vehicles for knowledge-value."[23]

Companies are revolutionizing product designs to reflect the new emphasis on services. Instead of thinking of products as fixed items with set features and a one-time sales value, companies now think of them as "platforms" for all sorts of upgrades and value-added services. In the new manufacturing schema it is the services and upgrades that count. The platform is merely the vessel to which these services are added. In a sense, the product becomes more of a cost of doing business than a sale item in and of itself. The idea is to use the platform as a beachhead, as a way of establishing a physical presence in the customer's place of business or domicile. That presence allows the vendor to begin a long-term service relationship with the customer. For this reason, the platforms often are sold at cost in the expectation of selling more lucrative services to the customer over the lifetime of the product.

The toy maker Lego Group AS of Denmark is selling a new toy that combines a computer brain with Lego building blocks so that children can build robotic toys. The product can be plugged into a PC, and new commands that expand the number of things the toy can do can be downloaded from a central Web site.[24] Similarly, emWare, Inc., in Salt Lake City, has created a lawn-sprinkler system linked to the Internet. The sprinkler itself is really a platform for a range of upgraded services that can be integrated into it. For a service fee, the sprinkler can be programmed to automatically contact the National Weather Service Web site to check on weather conditions and forecasts and turn the spray on and off accordingly.[25]

Now, even the telephone itself is becoming a disposable service. In 1999, a new kind of telephone was patented that is so cheap, it is sold for a "fixed amount of air time" and then thrown away once the air time is used up. Its inventor, Randice Lisa Altschul, says the disposable phone will likely be used by harried mothers, children, and travelers who don't want to worry about losing a telephone. The same disposable technology could be used for a range of electronic devices, including hand-held electronic games. The point is, the physical container becomes secondary to the unique services contained in it. What the customer is really purchasing is access to time rather than ownership of a material good.[26]

*Encyclopaedia Britannica* is a good case study of how economic conditions are hastening the metamorphosis of conventional goods into pure services. Until very recently, a hardback set of the thirty-two volumes of *Encyclopaedia Britannica* cost $1,600 and was considered a major financial investment for most American homes. In the early 1990s, Bill Gates approached Encyclopaedia Britannica with the idea of creating a digital version of its product that could be delivered at a much cheaper retail price on CD-ROM. Worried that the cheap digital version would undermine sales of its printed volumes, Encyclopaedia Britannica declined the offer. Gates then bought Funk and Wagnalls and combined its contents with audio and visual material readily available in the public domain to create a digital encyclopedia called Encarta. The electronic form of the encyclopedia was put on a CD-ROM and sold for $49.95.[27] Besides selling for a fraction of the cost, Microsoft's Encarta was continuously upgraded and updated. As a result, within less than a year and a half it became the best-selling encyclopedia in the world.[28] Quickly losing market share, Britanica was forced to respond with its own online version. Subscribers could pay $85 for an entire year of "unlimited access to Britannica Online's vast resources."[29] The company then went a step further, providing free ongoing access to its entire database. The company's revenue now comes from advertisers, who place tailor-made ads at specific Encyclopaedia Britannica entry sites. *Encyclopaedia Britannica* has literally dematerialized into a pure service.

In recent years, a debate has been raging in the library world about the question of ownership of books and collections versus access to online publications. Librarians Eleanor A. Goshen and Suzanne Irving of the State University of New York at Albany note that "within the past decade in academic libraries, economic realities have caused a paradigm shift away from an emphasis on acquiring comprehensive research collections to an emphasis on developing effective methods for maintaining access . . . to research materials that are infrequently used in a particular institution."[30] Insofar as research libraries are concerned, much of the information can be accessed more readily from the Internet and other electronic data highways and at lower cost than purchasing the journals and books and holding them in inventory in large library facilities.[31]

Already, textbooks are being put online. John Wiley and Sons put two standard research reference books, the Kirk-Othmer *Encyclopedia of Chemical Technology* and the *Encyclopedia of Electrical and Electronics Engineering*, online in 1999. These books, which in the past were purchased and owned in the form of physical copies, are now accessible for a fee.[32]

While the demise of print has been forecasted for years, it appears that electronic-based access to material is finally becoming a reality for the first generation of young people who grew up with computers and feel more comfortable accessing information from a screen than viewing it on a printed page. Jeff Rothenberg, a senior computer scientist at the Rand Corporation, believes that the day is not far off when books printed on paper will be seen "more as objets d'art than things we use all the time."[33]

Books are not the only products dematerializing into electronic services in the new cyberspace economy. The same process is unfolding in diverse commercial fields. For example, the seven regional Bell telephone companies and other giant telecommunications companies now provide voice mail services. Rather than maintaining home answering machines, customers can access voice storage and retrieval systems. In this case, as in countless others, a product is being replaced by a service, and ownership is being eclipsed by access. Writing in the *Harvard Business Review*, Jeffrey Rayport and John J. Sviokla point out that the shift from a marketplace transaction to a marketspace service is occurring with increasing frequency as consumers come to feel more comfortable with access over ownership in their daily lives. They write, "If access can be acquired without the answering machine itself, the customer gains the benefits of the software-defined services without the nuisance of acquiring and maintaining the hardware-defined product."[34]

[ . . . ]

## Giving Away the Goods, and Charging for the Services

Perhaps the best evidence of the changing relationship between a product and the services that accompany it lies in the market value of each in relation to the other. Until recently, a service warranty was tacked on to a product, sometimes for a minimum additional charge, or, more often than not, provided free as an incentive to purchase the item. Now that relationship is being turned around. As noted earlier, a growing number of companies are giving away their products for free to attract customers, and then charging their clients for managing, upgrading, and otherwise servicing the products.

When Motorola introduced its Micro-Tac cellular phone in 1989, it retailed for $2,500. Just five years later, the same phone was priced at $100. Today, cellular telephone companies often give the Motorola phone away to new subscribers for free as an inducement to use their telecommunications services.[35]

In 1993, Computer Associates International, Inc., launched its new software accounting program, Simple Money, and priced it at zero. The company was banking on the belief that word of mouth about its generous offer would encourage widespread use and that it would recoup its initial offering by selling its new clients ongoing upgrades and services. (The cost of actually producing each additional diskette, with its software program on it, was so low as to be inconsequential.)[36]

In the information-technology industries, the race to give away products is gaining momentum and becoming standard commercial practice. Netscape gives away its Web browser. Microsoft gives away its Internet Explorer Web browser. Sun Microsystems distributes Java for free.[37] In the case of the software companies, the cost of producing and delivering each additional product approaches zero. At the same time, if the company can convince enough end users to switch to its programs, the firm can set an industry standard and in the process sell upgrades and services to its clients at significant margins.

Giving away software programs is a particularly effective strategy for information-technology firms because the more people who are linked together through a company's programs, the greater the benefits are to each participant and the more valuable the enterprise's potential services become. In the industry, this phenomenon is known as the "network effect." The larger the network, the greater the links, the more valuable the network becomes to those who are part of it. Giving away software helps build networks and is increasingly seen as a cost of doing business.

Again, the question is, how does a company make money when the costs of manufacturing products are declining toward zero in many fields, leaving little room for profit? How does one even price an item whose production cost is negligible? The answer is to give away the product and charge customers for the sophisticated services that accompany it.

*Business Week* glimpsed the far-reaching significance of this basic change in the relationship between products and services in an article appropriately entitled "The Technology Paradox." Its reporters wrote:

> The new rules require more than ingenuity, agility, and speed. They call for redefining value in an economy where the cost of raw technology is plummeting toward zero. Sooner or later, this plunge will obliterate the worth of almost any specific piece of hardware or software. Then, value will be in establishing a long-term relationship with a customer – even if it means giving the first generation of a product away.[38]

In the network economy, characterized by shorter product life cycles and an ever expanding flow of goods and services, it is human attention rather than physical resources that becomes scarce. Giving away products will increasingly be used as a marketing strategy to capture the attention of potential customers. Holding their attention will depend on the ability of companies to deliver effective services and create lasting relationships.

When virtually everything becomes a service, capitalism is transformed from a system based on exchanging goods to one based on accessing segments of experience. If, for example, one contracts for an air-conditioning service rather than buying the air conditioner itself, one pays for the experience of having air conditioning. The new capitalism, then, is far more temporal than material. Instead of commodifying places and things and exchanging them in the market, we now secure access to one another's time and expertise and borrow what we need, treating each thing as an activity or event that we purchase for a limited period of time. Capitalism is shedding its material origins and increasingly becoming a temporal affair.

## Notes

1   Benjamin B. Hampton, *History of the American Film Industry: From Its Beginnings to 1931* (New York: Dover, 1970).
2   Michael Storper, "The Transition to Flexible Specialization in the U.S. Film Industry: External Economies, the Division of Labor and the Crossing of Industrial Divides," *Cambridge Journal of Economics* 13 (1989), 278.
3   Ibid., pp. 278–9.
4   Michael Storper and Susan Christopherson, "The Effects of Flexible Specialization on Industrial Politics and the Labor Market: The Motion Picture Industry," *Industrial and Labor Relations Review*, April 1989, p. 334; Storper, "The Transition to Flexible Specialization," p. 279.
5   Joel Kotlin and David Friedman, "Why Every Business Will Be Like Show Business," *Inc.*, March 1995, p. 66.
6   Storper, "The Transition to Flexible Specialization," p. 286.
7   Asu Aksoy and Kevin Robins, "Hollywood for the 21st Century: Global Competition for Critical Mass in Image Markets," *Cambridge Journal of Economics* 16 (1992), 9.
8   Ibid.
9   Kotlin and Friedman, "Why Every Business Will Be Like Show Business," p. 66.
10  Geoffrey Owen and Louise Kehoe, "A Hotbed of High-Tech," *Financial Times*, June 28, 1992.
11  John Kao, *Jamming: The Art and Discipline of Business Creativity* (New York: HarperCollins, 1996), p. 124.
12  Tom Peters, *Liberation Management: Necessary Disorganization for the Nanosecond Nineties* (New York: Alfred A. Knopf, 1992), p. 12.
13  Walter W. Powell, "Neither Market Nor Hierarchy: Network Forms of Organization," *Research in Organizational Behavior* 12 (1990), 296–326: p. 308.
14  George Stigler, *Trends in Output and Employment* (New York: National Bureau of Economic Research, 1947), pp. 14, 24.
15  Harry Braverman, *Labor and Monopoly Capital* (New York: Monthly Review Press, 1971), p. 276.
16  Ibid., p. 248.

17    James Brian Quinn, *Intelligent Enterprise: A Knowledge and Service Based Paradigm for Industry* (New York: The Free Press, 1992), pp. 5–6.
18    Daniel Bell, *The Coming of Post-Industrial Society* (New York: Basic Books, 1973), pp. xvi, xix–xx.
19    Quinn, *Intelligent Enterprise*, p. 30.
20    Peter Martin, "Revolution Again," *Financial Times*, June 4, 1998.
21    Ibid.
22    Bell, *The Coming of Post-Industrial Society*, p. xvi.
23    Taichi Sakaiya, *The Knowledge-Value Revolution, or, A History of the Future*, trans. George Fields and William Marsh (Tokyo: Kodansha International, 1991), p. 60.
24    Thomas E. Weber, "Talking Toasters: Companies Gear Up for Internet Boom in Things That Think," *Wall Street Journal*, August 27, 1998, p. A1.
25    Ibid.
26    Teresa Riordan, "Throw Away That Cell Phone," *New York Times*, November 8, 1999, p. C4.
27    Carl Shapiro and Hal R. Varian, *Information Rules: A Strategic Guide to the Network Economy* (Boston: Harvard Business School Press, 1999), pp. 14, 19; Larry Downes and Chunka Mui, *Unleashing the Killer App: Digital Strategies for Market Dominance* (Boston: Harvard Business School Press, 1998), p. 51.
28    Downes and Mui, *Unleashing the Killer App*, p. 51.
29    Ibid.; Shapiro and Varian, *Information Rules*, pp. 19–20; Encyclopaedia Britannica, Inc., "Why Subscribe to BritannicaOnline?" http://www.eb.com/whysub.htm.
30    Eleanor A. Gossen and Suzanne Irving, "Ownership Versus Access and Low-Use Periodical Titles," *Library Resources & Technical Services* 39, no. 1 (January 1995); 43.
31    Roger Brown, "The Changing Economic Environment – Access vs. Ownership: Access Where? Own What? – A Corporate View," *Serials: The Journal of the United Kingdom Serials Group* 8, no. 2 (July 1995) 125–9.
32    Ethan Bronner, "For More Textbooks, A Shift From Printed Page to Screen," *New York Times*, December 1, 1998, p. A26.
33    Ibid.
34    Jeffrey F. Rayport and John J. Sviokla, "Managing in the Marketplace," *Harvard Business Review*, December 1994, p. 144.
35    Steven L. Goldman, Roger N. Nagel, and Kenneth Preiss, *Agile Competitors and Virtual Corporations* (New York: Van Nostrand Reinhold, 1995), p. 12.
36    Neil Gross, Peter Coy, and Otis Port, "The Technology Paradox: How Companies Can Thrive as Prices Dive," *Business Week*, March 6, 1995, pp. 76–7.
37    Kevin Kelly, *New Rules for the New Economy: 10 Radical Strategies for a Connected World* (New York: Viking, 1998), p. 57.
38    Gross et al., "The Technology Paradox," p. 77.

# 22    *Angela McRobbie*

# CLUBS TO COMPANIES

This article provides a preliminary and thus provisional account of some of the defining characteristics of work and employment in the new cultural sector of the UK economy, and in London in particular.[1] It also describes a transition from what can be labeled 'first wave' culture industry work as defined by the Department of Culture, Media and Sport's creative industries document published in 1998 to the more economically highly-charged and rapidly mutating 'second wave' of cultural activity that has come into being in the last three years. This latter development is marked by de-specialization, by intersection with Internet working, by the utilizing of creative capacities provided by new media, by the rapid growth of multi-skilling in the arts field, by the shrunken role of the sector that I would describe as the 'independents', by a new partnership between arts and business with public sector support, and by government approval as evident in the most recently published Green Paper from the DCMS (2001).[2] [ . . . ] The 'second wave' comes into being as a consequence of the more rapid capitalization of the cultural field as small scale previously independent micro-economies of culture and the arts find themselves the subject of intense commercial interest.

The expansion of these sections of employment also brings about, for a more substantial number of people, a decisive break with past expectations of work.[3] Given the extensive press and television coverage of these kinds of work, a wider section of the population has available to it new ideas about how working lives can or might now be conducted. Through the profusion of profiles and interviews with hairdressers, cooks, artists and fashion

"Clubs to Companies" from Angela McRobbie (2002), "Clubs to Companies: Notes on the Decline of Political Culture in Speeded Up Creative Worlds." *Cultural Studies* 16(4), pp. 517–31. Reprinted by permission of Taylor & Francis, http://www.tandf.co.uk/journals

designers, the public (especially young people) are presented with endless accounts of the seemingly inherent rewards of creative labour.[4] The flamboyantly *auteur* relation to creative work that has long been the mark of being a writer, artist, film director or fashion designer is now being extended to a much wider section of a highly 'individuated' workforce. The media has always glamorized creative individuals as uniquely talented 'stars'. It is certainly not the case that now, in post-industrial Britain, people genuinely have the chance to fulfil their creative dreams. Rather it is the case that there is a double process of individualization. First, this occurs in the obsessive celebrity culture of the commercial media, now thoroughly extended to artists, designers and other creative personnel, and second in the social structure itself, as people are increasingly disembedded from ties of kinship, community and social class. They are, in a de-regulated environment, 'set free', as Giddens would put it, from both workplace organizations and from social institutions (Giddens, 1991).

What individualization means sociologically is that people increasingly have to become their own micro-structures, they have to do the work of the structures by themselves, which in turn requires intensive practices of self-monitoring or 'reflexivity'. This process where structures (like the welfare state) seem to disappear and no longer play their expected roles, and where individuals are burdened by what were once social responsibilities, marks a quite profound social transformation as Bauman, Beck and others have argued (Bauman, 1999, 2000; Beck, 2000). In the British context, this process of individualization could summarily be defined as the convergence of the forcefulness of neo-liberal economics put in place by the Thatcher government from 1979 onwards, with mechanisms of social and demographic change that result in new social groupings replacing traditional families, communities and class formations. Individualization is not about individuals *per se*, as about new, more fluid, less permanent social relations seemingly marked by choice or options. However, this convergence has to be understood as one of contestation and antagonism. Individualization thus marks a space of social conflict, it is where debates about the direction of change are played out and where new contradictions arise. This is most apparent in the world of work since it is here that the convergence is most dramatically configured. Capital finds novel ways of offloading its responsibility for a workforce, but this relinquishing process is confronted no longer by traditional and organized 'labour'. Instead, the new conditions of work are largely being experienced by 'new labour'. By this I mean those sections of the working population for whom work has become an important source for self-actualization, even freedom and independence. This includes women for whom work is an escape from traditional marriage and domesticity, young people for whom it is increasingly important as a mark of cultural identity, and ethnic minorities for whom it marks the dream of upward mobility and a possible escape from denigration.

The cultural sphere provides an ideal space for young people to explore such individualized possibilities, just as it also offers the Government opportunities for a post-industrialized economy unfettered by the constraints and costs of traditional employment. The impact of this intersection accounts for what I want to propose here as an acceleration in the cultural realm. There is a much expanded workforce comprising of freelance, casualized and project-linked persons, and there is also a more fiercely neo-liberal model in place with the blessings of government for overseeing the further de-regulation and commercialization of the cultural and creative sector (DCMS, 2001). The culture industries are being 'speeded up' and further capitalized as the state steps back and encourages the privatization of previously publicly subsidized cultural provision. (For example, by buying in freelance arts administrators for single projects, rather than employing full-time staff.) Those working in the creative sector cannot simply rely on old working patterns associated with art worlds, they have to find new ways of 'working' the new cultural economy, which increasingly means holding down three or even four 'projects' at once.[5] In addition, since these projects are usually short term, there have to be other jobs to cover the short-fall when a project ends. The individual becomes his or her own enterprise, sometimes presiding over two separate companies at the one time.[6] To sum up, if we consider the creative industries in the UK as a kind of experimental site, or case study, or indeed 'arts lab' for testing out the possibilities for 'cultural entrepreneurialism' (see Leadbeater and Oakley, 1999), then I would suggest that we can also see a shift from first to second wave that in turn (ironically) marks the decline of 'the indies' (the independents), the rise of the creative subcontractor and the downgrading of creativity.

## On the Guest List? Club Culture Sociality at Work

Given the ongoing nature of these developments, the authorial voice of the following pages is tentative in that I am drawing on observations and trends emerging from my current work in progress on this topic. I propose a number of intersecting and constitutive features. First, imported into the creative sector are elements of youth culture, in particular those drawn from the energetic and entrepreneurial world of dance and rave culture. Second, the realm of 'speeded up' work in the cultural sector now requires the holding down of several jobs at the one time; third, that such working conditions are also reliant on intense self-promotional strategies, and, as in any business world, on effective 'public relations', and fourth, that where there is a new relation of time and space there is little possibility of a politics of the workplace. That is, there is little time, few existing mechanisms for organization, and anyway no fixed workplace for a workplace politics to develop. This throws into question the role and function of 'network sociality' (Wittel, 2001). Thus fifth and finally, we can see a manifest tension for new creative workers, highly reliant on informal networking but without the support of these being underpinned by any institutional 'trade association'. They can only find individual (or 'biographical' as Beck puts it) solutions to systemic problems (Beck, 1997).

The dance/rave culture that came into being in the late 1980s as a mass phenomenon has strongly influenced the shaping and contouring, the energizing and entrepreneurial character of the new culture industries. The scale and spread of this youth culture meant that it was more widely available than its more clandestine, rebellious, 'underground' and style-driven predecessors, including punk. The level of self-generated economic activity that 'dance-party-rave' organizations entailed, served as a model for many of the activities that were a recurrent feature of 'creative Britain' in the 1990s. Find a cheap space, provide music, drinks, video, art installations, charge friends and others on the door, learn how to negotiate with police and local authorities and in the process become a club promoter and cultural entrepreneur. This kind of activity was to become a source of revenue for musicians and DJs first, but soon afterwards for artists. It has meant that the job of 'events organizer' is one of the more familiar of new self-designated job titles. The form of club sociality that grew out of the ecstasy-influenced 'friendliness' of the clubbing years gradually evolved into a more hard-nosed networking, so that an informal labour market has come into being which takes as its model the wide web of contacts, 'zines', flyers, 'mates', grapevine and 'word of mouth' socializing that was also a distinctive feature of the 'micro-media' effects of club culture (Thornton, 1996). The intoxicating pleasures of leisure culture have now, for a sector of the under-35s, provided the template for managing an identity in the world of work. Apart from the whole symbolic panoply of jargon, clothes, music and identity, the most noted feature of this phenomenon was the extraordinary organizational capacity in the setting up and publicizing of 'parties'. Now that the existence of raves and dance parties has become part of the wider cultural landscape – having secured the interest and investment of major commercial organizations – it is easy to overlook the energy and dynamism involved in making these events happen in the first place. But the formula of organizing music, dance, crowd and space have subsequently proved to give rise to 'transferable skills', which in turn transform the cultural sector as it is also being opened up to a wider, younger and more popular audience.[7]

The example of the shaping-up influence of club culture, therefore, sets the scene for this article. And where patterns of self-employment or informal work are the norm, what emerges is a radically different kind of labour market organization. While the working practices of graphic designers, web-site designers, events organizers, 'media office' managers and so on inevitably share some features in common with previous models of self-employed or freelance working, we can propose that where in the past the business side of things was an often disregarded aspect of creative identities best looked after by the accountant, now it is perceived as integral and actively incorporated into the artistic identity. This is illustrated in the activities of the young British artists for whom the commercial aspect of the art world is no longer disparaged but is welcomed and even celebrated. Mentor and tutor to the Goldsmiths graduates (including Damien Hirst), Professor Michael Craig Martin reputedly encouraged the students to consider the partying and net-working they had to do to promote their art as a vital part of the work, not as something separate.[8] He also insisted that artistic values were not incommensurate with entrepreneurial values. To some extent this more openly commercial approach is also part of the logic of breaking down the divide between high and low culture. If, for example, art is not such a special and exceptional activity, if it ought not to see itself as superior to the world of advertising, then what is to stop the artists from expecting the same kind of financial rewards, expense accounts and fees as the art directors inside the big agencies? The new relation between art and economics marks a break with past anti-commercial notions of being creative. Instead young people have exploited opportunities around them, in particular their facilities with new media technology and the experience of 'club culture sociality' with its attendant skills of networking and selling the self and have created for themselves new ways of earning a living in the cultural field.

In this creative economy, older features of working life such as the career pathway, the ladder of promotion, the 'narrative sociality' of a life spent in a stratified but secure workplace have been rapidly swept away to be replaced by 'network sociality' (Wittel, 2001). Work has been re-invented to satisfy the needs and demands of a generation who, 'disembedded' from traditional attachments to family, kinship, community or region, now find that work must become a fulfilling mark of self. In this context, more and more young people opt for the insecurity of careers in media, culture or art in the hope of success. In fields like film-making or fashion design there is a euphoric sense among practitioners of by-passing tradition, pre-empting conscription into the dullness of 9–5 and evading the constraints of institutional processes.

There is a utopian thread embedded in this wholehearted attempt to make-over the world of work into something closer to a life of enthusiasm and enjoyment. We could also note that for young women, now entering into the labour market as a lifelong commitment instead of a part-time or interrupted accompaniment to family life as a primary career, the expectation that work is satisfying and inherently rewarding has a special significance alongside the need now to be one's own breadwinner.[9]

To have seemingly circumvented 'unhappy work' and to have come upon a way of earning a living without the feeling of being robbed of identity is a social phenomenon worthy of sociological attention. But the larger question of course is how this fits with the needs of a form of cultural capitalism that is currently re-inventing itself as innocuous or 'soft', at least in its Western forms. For the young woman fashion designer working 18-hour days and doing her own sewing to complete an order, 'loving' her work but self-exploiting herself, she only has herself to blame if things go wrong. After all she opted for this kind of unstable career choice.[10] This is exactly the scenario described by Bauman in his description of the stealthy ways in which the new capitalism seems to absolve itself from responsibility by creating invisible structures, and by melting down or liquefying the old social order (Bauman, 1999). Self-blame, where social structures are increasingly illegible or opaque, serves the interests of the new capitalism well, ensuring the absence of social critique.

A further defining feature of new cultural work is that its 'time and space' dynamics contribute to a marked absence of workplace politics in terms of democratic procedures, equal opportunities, anti-discrimination policies and so on. Maybe there can be no workplace politics when there is no work-place, i.e. where work is multi-sited. The necessity of speed and the velocity of transaction, along with the mobility and fluidity of individuals, throws into question a defining feature of this kind of work. This is its relation to the idea of 'reflexivity'. Underpinning both Giddens' and Beck's deployment of the concept is a traditional notion of the unified subject increasingly able – indeed called upon – to undertake self-monitoring activities. But in both writers' use of the term, reflexivity has retained an abstract character, requiring us to ask, what are the limits of reflexive practice? Is reflexivity applied primarily to the job in hand? Or to put it another way, the socially valuable outcome of reflexivity is yet to reveal itself. We would need some ethnographies of reflexivity before it would be possible to draw any conclusions, or indeed before the actual mechanisms of reflexivity could be assessed. What are its parameters? Under what circumstances does it lead to social critique? If we alternately consider reflexivity as a form of self-disciplining where subjects of the new enterprise culture are increasingly called upon to inspect themselves and their practices, in the absence of structures of social support (other than individualized counseling services), then reflexivity marks the space of self-responsibility, self-blame. In this sense, it is a de-politicizing, de-socializing mechanism: 'Where have I gone wrong?'

One way of explaining how and why things go wrong might involve turning to sociology. And, indeed, having recourse to specialist knowledge is how Beck understands reflexivity as operating. For him it is related to the wider dissemination and application of sophisticated sociological knowledge to the issues that sociology (or another academic field) has engaged with, usually as social problems and attempted to explain. (In the UK this is most apparent in the concept of the 'moral panic' in relation to youth culture; see McRobbie and Thornton, 1995.) Thus with an increasingly higher-educated population it might be surmised that critical reflexivity becomes a more widespread practice. But how does this tally with Bauman's argument that the more opaque the social structures of inequality and injustice, the less likely people are to understand how the society actually operates? At present, there is no obvious point of entrance for sociological explanations into these creative sectors since the trade media that covers these industries considers such knowledge as old-fashioned or irrelevant. This is partly the result of the pervasive success of neo-liberal values, their insinuating presence in the culture and media sector, and their successful discrediting of the political vocabulary associated with the left and with feminism (including equal opportunities, anti-discrimination, workplace democracy, trade union representation, etc.). The only site for the dissemination of these values is the academy, the place of training or education of the creatives. But whether or not these are remembered or acted upon or cast aside is an open question. Only anecdotal evidence exists.[11]

The extent to which the new world of work contributes directly to the decline of political antagonism is a clear gain for the free market economy. In the cultural sector, with its emphasis on the creative and expressive, it might be imagined that this could be the right place for social minorities to succeed and for women to achieve equal participation. However, it seems possible that quite the opposite is happening. What we see – in as much as it is possible to track these developments – is the emergence of working practices which reproduce older patterns of marginalization (of women and people from different ethnic backgrounds), while also disallowing any space or time for such issues to reach articulation.[12] In this case the club culture question of 'are you on the guest list?' is extended to recruitment and personnel, so that getting an interview for contract creative work depends on informal knowledge and contacts, often friendships. Once in the know about who to approach (the equivalent of finding where the party is being held), it is then a matter of whether the recruitment advisor 'likes you' (the equivalent of the bouncer 'letting you in'), and all ideas of fairness or equal representation of women or of black or Asian people (not to mention the disabled) fly out of the window.

In this new and so-called independent sector (see Leadbeater and Oakley, 1999) there is less and less time left in the long hours culture to pursue 'independent work'. The recent attempts by the large corporations to innovate in this sector means that the independents are, in effect, dependent sub-contracted suppliers. And where such contracts are to be had, in a context of increasing competition, it is hard to imagine that there is time and space for private reading never mind wider critical debate. (As Lash and Urry comment, 'information technology can . . . erode the critical crafts of reading and writing. What Agger calls "fast capitalism" undermines the power of the book' (1994: 324).) And after-hours, in the dedicated club/networking space, with free vodka on tap all night thanks to the sponsorship of the big drinks companies, who dares to ask 'uncool' questions about the minimal representation of women and non-white young people, about who the big clients are and what they do with the product, and about the downside of the 'talent-led' economy? In an atmosphere of businesslike conviviality overseen by accomplished 'PRs', the emphasis on presentation of self is incompatible with a contestatory demeanour. It's not cool to be 'difficult'. Personal angst, nihilism or mere misgivings must be privately managed and, for the purposes of club sociality, carefully concealed.[13] This is a 'PR' meritocracy where the question of who gets ahead on what basis and who is left behind finds no space for expression. Speed and risk negate ethics, community and politics.

## The Demise of the Indies?

Given the picture that I have been sketching, it is incumbent upon social scientists and cultural studies academics to develop a vocabulary and a methodology for tracing freelance pathways in the cultural sector. We need to be able to understand at the level of experience how this terrain is negotiated. There remains a chasm of difference between middle-aged academics for whom the university sector has provided a single sourced income more or less since graduation, and young people whose portfolio careers increasingly mean not serial jobs but multi-tasking. The latter becomes necessary partly because there is no cushion of welfare to cover periods between jobs, also because labour costs are falling in the cultural sector, and finally because creative work, as various studies have shown, is simply low pay work except for those at the very top.[14] Since 1998 I have been engaged in a tracking research study of freelance, self-employed and contract creative workers (a handful of whom are fashion designers who participated in my earlier study (see McRobbie, 1998) ). For them the kind of conditions which prevailed in the 'independent' cultural scene in London and in other UK cities between 1986 and 1996 are very much a thing of the past. Despite the hardship faced by the fashion designers I interviewed, including the long hours and the difficulties of maintaining a cash flow, the luxury they had, as my more recent respondents see it, was of being able to concentrate on their 'own work'. This sector of independent fashion design has been swept away as the high street chains are able to translate the catwalk styles into off-the-peg items literally within days. Likewise with the spiraling of urban property values there are fewer opportunities for finding cheap centrally located market stalls. By the end of the 1990s the only way to be 'independent' was to be 'dependent' on Kookai, Debenhams, Top Shop. Indeed the only way fashion design could survive was to sign up with a bigger company and more or less relinquish 'creative independence'. The corrosion of creativity was further achieved as the chain stores 'adopted' less than a handful of graduate stars a year and often discarded them within the year. State support for young and struggling designers working from tiny outlets is no longer available following changes to the benefits system. Voluntary sector support is also limited. The Prince of Wales Trust, for example, only offers a loan scheme for up to £5,000 for the under-30s. As a consequence fashion designers become a scattered and disconnected profession. They can no longer be found in key city centre locations. The small shops are all gone. An important outlet like Hyper Hyper, a unit space for up and coming designers situated in Kensington High Street, London, disappeared in 1998. What now happens to the annual crop of 4,000 fashion graduates who relied on this kind of space? The answer is that they are now advised to play safe and get a job with a high street retailer. A tiny number are recruited by the European fashion houses or by the American conglomerates, and one or two are awarded grants. Hence I think we can surmise that there is a decline in creativity, as the incubation period that was documented in my earlier research becomes increasingly unviable. There is nothing like the vibrancy and the collective (and competitive) spirit which characterized the earlier period. Fashion design graduates today must become multi-skilled. If they are doing a collection it will be at weekends, or perhaps in the odd day they can find between other jobs. Typically magazines like *i-D* find ways of celebrating this new scenario. In a recent article published in the magazine, the journalist wrote, 'Fashion multi-taskers: suddenly they're everywhere. . . . And its addictive. Once you've tried doing four jobs you'll never want anything less. . . . It's no longer necessary to be a full time anything to be successful and respected' (Rushton, 2001).

The substance and tone of this article reflects the kind of upbeat business-minded euphoria which is a characteristic of the sector. So much for reflexivity. When it is inconceivable that the main trade magazine shows itself capable of seriously reflecting on conditions in the sector, then magazines like *The Face, i-D* and *Dazed and Confused* demonstrate themselves to be remarkably disengaged and complicit with the changes affecting the industry. These changes come from the increased presence of the big brands. The large companies need to innovate and to develop a more experimental youth-driven image and this is provided by the second wave of young cultural entrepreneurs hiring out their services on a contractual basis. But what is squeezed out in this process is independence and socially engaged, critical creativity. The same is true for many other of the creative sectors. Freelance economies in the field of film or video production cannot, for example, take the strain of turning down work to free up time to make, let us say, a short documentary film uncommissioned and with no apparent destination. Instead cultural production is increasingly driven by the imperatives of market and consumer culture, and the banality of pop promos, TV and cinema advertising is concealed by the technological euphoria, the association of newness and youthfulness, and of course by the parties, the celebrity culture and the cheque in the post. Granted there are still fashion designers, architects, writers, musicians and other creative occupations, but being a specialist rather than a multi-skilled 'creative' is becoming a thing of the past and a mark of being over 35.[15] The norm now is a kind of middle-class 'ducking and diving'. In the shift from the first to the second wave of creative economy in the New Labour enterprise culture, the kind of small-scale economies of the decade from the mid-1980s to mid-1990s have all but disappeared. Thus we could say that the cultural entrepreneurialization set in motion during the Thatcher years has in the Blair period been almost fully accomplished. Of course it is important to avoid a crude determinism. It is not, therefore, my intention to engage here with questions of cultural value, but rather to point to a process of creative compromise. There is more and more culture, more visual work, more novels being published, more music being produced, more magazines being launched and at the same time the shift from there being 'independent work' to there being any number of freelance workers is also a shift in the balance of power from a social 'milieu of innovation' to a world of individual 'projects'.

# The Loneliness of the Long-Distance Incubator ———

Let me conclude by rehearsing some of the features that serve to consolidate the new (and rarely spoken about) structural divides in the cultural economy. If the club is the hub, then age and domestic responsibilities define patterns of access and participation. While sociologists have pointed to the increasing impact of age in changing labour markets (especially for women; see Walby, 1997) in the creative sector, there is simultaneously a stretching out of the contours of youthfulness (such as 'middle youth') through the marketing of lifestyle goods to the under-50s, and also a retrenchment and re-marking of boundaries, in that the new ways of working bear the hallmark of the rave culture generation. The night-time economy of club culture translates directly into the long hours culture of new media and creative work. This is obviously incompatible with having children, and certainly incompatible with being, for example, a single parent. Work merges with leisure and when a deadline must be met friends might lend their support and work through the night (McRobbie, 1998). The assumed youthfulness and the impregnable space of the club suggests that these are not such 'open-minded' spaces. Of course, all occupational groups develop their own ways of working, and nor is the club a novelty for artistic and creative persons *per se*. But there is an irony in that alongside the assumed openness of the network, the apparent embrace of non-hierarchical working practices, the various flows and fluidities (see Lash and Urry, 1994), there are quite rigid closures and exclusions. The cultural and creative sectors have in the past in the UK been led and administered by the public sector. Academics have also had a role to play. But a close reading of the recent Green Paper 'Culture and Creativity Ten Years On' (DCMS, 2001) implies that this will change dramatically, as artists and creative individuals are freed from the constraints of bureaucracy and 'red tape'. As the whole sector is more thoroughly entrepreneurialized there will be less need for the infrastructure of state, indeed it is argued that it will be to the advantage of the artists that administration will be cut. The result? Artists and cultural personnel will be free to carry on with what they do unhindered. Academics will be kept well out of the picture; indeed if the recent Cultural Entrepreneur Club is a model, their presence will be occasional and by invitation only. What warrants the presence of those who are not 'good for business'?[16]

The second structural dynamic is that of qualification. The conventions associated with the traditional CV and the job application process are nothing short of overturned in the network culture, and yet patterns do re-emerge. Top or 'branded' universities promise graduates better access to big companies seeking to outsource creative work, and the same holds true for appointments with venture capitalists. Universities and colleges become key sites for developing the social skills for the network (once again often as party organizer), so, for the 45% of young people who at present do not enjoy three years of higher education, this is a further absence of opportunity. (It is also unlikely that mature students who are concentrated in poorer universities are in the position to immerse themselves in the hedonistic and expensive culture of networking.) Third, there is the spatial dynamic, with only a few urban centres providing anything like the cultural infrastructure for gainful employment in creative fields. With a handful of private–public partnerships now replacing the kind of city cultural policies for regeneration pursued in the 1980s and into the early 1990s, there is the appearance of shadow culture industries in Glasgow, Manchester and Nottingham (all of which are have large student populations) while, as Leadbeater reports (1999), Cardiff Bay has also seen the development of a thriving new media sector. But this leaves vast tracts of the country more or less untouched by the work opportunities provided by the cultural and creative network and it creates an enormous imbalance between London where, at least in the short term, freelance curators and art project managers can have five jobs on the go at once (and thus juggle the bank balance around the cash-flow) and elsewhere where 'portfolio income' is replaced by at best 'one job at a time', usually with spaces of no work in between. (Is London also disembedded and individuated, a city state with its own speeded up economy? What distortions occur as a result of this 'lifted out' status?)

Age, gender, ethnicity, region and family income re-emerge like phantoms (or in Beck's terminology 'zombie concepts', dead but still alive) from the disguised hinterland of this new soft capitalism and add their own weight to the life chances of those who are attempting to make a living in these fields (Beck, 2000). As Adkins (1999) argues, new forms of re-traditionalisation begin to have an impact on the participation of disadvantaged social groups and minorities. Adkins is suggesting that where state-provided supports disappear and community weakens, and where individuated persons operate on a more self-reliant basis, in this case in the new cultural economy, then there will almost inevitably be a process of having to fall back on traditional forms of support. This can mean a return to more rigid gender roles for women, for example, being excluded from the network because of children, or finding it difficult to avoid reproducing traditionally patriarchal family forms. Such changes are also the result of the double process of neo-liberal successes in the field of work and the negating of the values of the left and the women's movement. Finally there is the sheer incommensurability of working patterns in the creative network with existing official, governmental and social science paradigms. (Even the recent Green Paper fails to appreciate the growth of multi-taskers in the arts.) There is as yet no category for the curator/project manager/artist/website designer who is transparently multi-skilled and ever willing to pick up new forms of expertise, who is also constantly finding new niches for work and thus inventing new jobs for him/herself (e.g. incubator/creative agent), who is highly mobile moving from one job or project to the next, and in the process also moving from one geographical site to the next. Social interaction is fast and fleeting, friendships need to be put on hold, or suspended on trust and when such a non-category of multi-skilled persons is extended across a whole sector of young working people, there is a sharp sense of transience, impermanence and even solitude (Augé, 1995).

Research on these areas would have to consider the specifically gendered and ethnic consequences of individualization. The existing methodologies of the social sciences might well be brought into crisis by the fluidity and hyper-mobility of these agents. There are a number of other points of tension or ambivalence that also throw our older political paradigms into crisis. In the past I have taken issue with those who have (often with a sneer) considered the ambition and energy, the glamour and desire for success on the part of these young people as evidence of their either being complicit with the aims and ambitions of the project set in motion by Mrs Thatcher, or else of their being ideologically bludgeoned into believing the Hollywood dream (McRobbie, 1999). My argument was that it was quite possible to adhere to principles of social justice, and gender and racial equality while working in the seemingly glamorous world of the culture industries. Of course, in the absence (yet again) of studies that systematically tracked creative employment with political sensibility, my comments were based on working closely with students who would be entering or who already had entered these fields. The accelerated speed of cultural working in the second wave, however, marks an intensification of individualization, a more determined looking out for the self. At this point the possibility of a revived, perhaps reinvented, radical democratic politics that might usefully de-individuate and resocialize the world of creative work is difficult to envisage.

To conclude, if the instruments of the social sciences are challenged by the flows of creative individuals, and likewise the vocabularies of social democratic practice seem ill-equipped for the new mobile work-sites of cultural capitalism, so also is it the case that the identity of these cultural workers as bounded by the characteristics of 'British creativity' is a quite profound misnomer. The creative work that central government in the UK wants to flag up is less British than is assumed.[17] Many are producing for a global market, as mobile subjects the political peculiarities of the nation state begin to look either insular, or restrictive, for example in relation to work practices and migration law. This undermines the value of a vocabulary of political culture bound by nation. The second wavers are redescribing culture and creativity as we know them, transcending and traversing a multiplicity of boundaries that come tumbling down in an 'ecstasy of communication'. We cultural studies academics might teach these young people in the relatively fixed space of the seminar room, but once they enter the world of work, our encounters with 'incubators' and others are increasingly estranged and contingent.

# References

Adkins, L (1999) 'Community and Economy: A Retraditionalisation of Gender'. *Theory, Culture and Society*, 16(1), 119–41.

Augé, M. (1995) *Non-Places: Introduction to an Anthropology of Supermodernity*. London: Verso.

Bauman, Z. (1999) *Liquid Modernity*. Cambridge: Polity Press.

—— (2000) *The Individualised Society*. Cambridge: Polity Press.

Beck, U. (1997) *Risk Society*. London: Sage.

—— (2000) Unpublished lecture. LSE, February, London.

DCMS (1998) Creative Industries: Mapping Document, London.

—— (2001) Creative Industries Mapping Document, London.

Giddens, A. (1991) *Modernity and Self Identity*. Cambridge: Polity Press.

Hanspal, J. (2000) 'Good Character and Dressing for Success'. Unpublished MA thesis, Goldsmiths College, London.

Lash, S. and Urry, J. (1994) *The Economy of Signs and Spaces*. London: Sage.

Leadbeater, C. (1999) *Living on Thin Air*. London: Viking.

Leadbeater, C. and Oakley, J. (1999) *The Independents*. London: Demos.

McRobbie, A. (1998) *British Fashion Design: Rag Trade or Image Industry?* London: Routledge.

—— (1999) *In the Culture Society*. London: Routledge.

McRobbie, A. and Thornton, S. (1995) 'Rethinking "Moral Panic" for Multi-Mediated Social Worlds'. *British Journal of Sociology*, 66(4), 559–75.

Rushton, R. (2001) 'Fashion Feature'. *i-D Magazine*, February.

Sassen, S. (1995) *The Global City*. Oxford: Blackwell.

Scott, A. (2000) *The Cultural Economy of Cities*. London: Sage.

Thornton, S. (1996) *Club Culture*. Cambridge: Polity Press.

Ursell, G. (2000) 'Television Production: Issues of Exploitation, Commodification and Subjectivity in UK Television Labour Markets'. *Media, Culture and Society*, 22(6), 805–27.

Walby, S. (1997) *Gender Transformations*. London: Routledge.

Wittel, A. (2001) 'Toward a Network Sociality'. *Theory, Culture and Society*, 18(6), 51–77.

## Notes

1   For London as a global city see Sassen (1995); for cultural economies and urban areas see Scott (2000).

2   By 'independents' I mean small-scale micro-economies primarily in music and fashion and related fields, which emerged as post-punk phenomena in the mid-1980s in response to unemployment and to government endorsement of 'enterprise culture'. Generally, these groupings presented themselves as radical, critical, innovative and loosely collective, e.g. the fashion duo Body Map, the 'indie' record label Rough Trade and the magazine *The Face* in its early days.

3   The DCMS Mapping Document (1998) indicates employment rates in culture and communication at over 1 million persons, the DCMS Mapping Document of 2001 puts the figure at 1.3 million.

4   In an earlier article on this subject I quoted a hairdresser interviewed in the *Independent* who said he was 'classically trained' (McRobbie, 1999).

5   This kind of comment is emerging from current interviews with respondents working in the cultural sector. They repeatedly tell me of small companies undercutting others by offering virtually no cost for jobs that will help their profile.

6   Another respondent currently runs one tiny TV production company, another media consultancy and alongside this she also teaches two days a week.

7   Rave culture is a much-cited influence on the entrepreneurial activities of artists including Damien Hirst.

8   Personal communication from former MA student, Goldsmiths College London.

9   Young women are increasingly encouraged to consider work and employment as lifelong activities as partners can no longer be relied upon as breadwinners.

10   The Minister for Culture, Media and Sports, the Rt. Hon. Chris Smith, actually suggested in a panel debate (Royal Television Society, February 1999) that the young people working in the industry 'do it because they love it, they know what they are letting themselves in for'.

11   An unexpected consequence of my study of UK fashion designers is that I have been visited by a stream of aspiring young fashion graduates who have come across the book and, as a result, seek my advice.

12   Cultural Entrepreneurs Club (September/October/November 2000) comprised a majority of white males from 'good' universities.

13   This point is made clearly in 'Good character and dressing for success' by Jesh Hanspal, unpublished MA thesis, Goldsmiths College (2000).

14   This is the result in my study McRobbie (1998), and also Ursell (2000).

15   At the above-mentioned Cultural Entrepreneurs Club I was introduced to a trained architect working as a time-based arts agent, a photographer working as a curator/administrator and a graphic designer working as a website editor.

16  Again, on both occasions I attended this club I was the only academic present. Unlike the business mentors and venture capitalists also present, I found no immediate role to play other than to talk with former students.

17  The nominations for the Turner Prize 2000 included three non-UK artists, one German, one Dutch and another Japanese all based in London, and two of whom trained in London art colleges. In fact, a pattern is emerging where European and overseas students train in UK art colleges and then go on to enjoy better support for their creative activities from their own governments than is available in the UK. Hence the prominence of the new Dutch, Belgian and South Asian fashion designers.

# 23   *Shalini Venturelli*

# CULTURE AND THE CREATIVE ECONOMY IN THE INFORMATION AGE

## Redefining Culture in the Global Information Economy

The globalization of the information economy and the internationalization of cyberspace makes it imperative that concepts of culture and creativity be reassessed and repositioned at the center of public policy. This requires a recognition that the cultural and creative challenges of the Information Economy be approached in terms of policies governing the production, distribution and exploitation of expression. Both these arguments form the basis of a set of recommendations, guidelines and principles for national and international policy.

Some have recently argued, such as Thaler (2000), for example, that the future study of economics ought to consider the flaws in economic theory of the post-war period, particularly the reliance on rational mathematical models devoid of social and psychological factors. Models that account for social factors are much harder to develop, of course, suggesting that Homo sapiens is not so rational after all. Not just economics, but notions of culture also call for some fundamental reassessments in the new century. Theories that inform much of our thinking on the information revolution and the Global Internet need to evolve beyond accounts of the uses and functions of information, and begin to integrate factors that are social, political and most of all, cultural.

"Culture and the Creative Economy in the Information Age" from Shalini Venturelli (2002), *From the Information Economy to the Creative Economy: Moving Culture to the Center of International Public Policy*. Center for Arts and Culture, Washington, DC, pp. 3–16, 37–8. Reprinted here under the title of "Culture and the Creative Economy in the Information Age" by permission of Shalini Venturelli.

We have inherited ideas regarding the cultural dimensions of modern life from three traditions, which, taken together, shape the entirety of our approach to cultural problems and policies. The first is the aesthetic tradition which runs deep in the genesis of civilization, especially Western. It unfolds over two thousand years from, for example, Aristotle's formal taxonomies in the *Poetics*, to Heidegger's existential search for being as art in *Poetry, Language, Thought* (1971). This tradition, while still relevant to the creation, study, and contemplation of art, has long ceased to inform social debates and public policy. In the US and other Anglo-Saxon legal and political systems, at least, naturalism and positivism have displaced the power of art to reveal social truth or reality, giving rise to scientific and statistical verification as the unassailable basis of collective self-determination and public policy. Yet there still persist many modern and developing societies that measure the vigor of collective identity by aesthetic productivity in the fine arts and by the historically inherited corpus of artistic achievements that define the national culture.

A second form of cultural understanding has been the legacy of the modern social sciences, more precisely, the anthropological tradition. From Frazer's *Golden Bough* (1922) with its enthralling survey of primitive life and Malinowski's study of New Guinean social organization and kinship systems in *Argonauts of the Western Pacific* (1922), the tradition spans the last century and gives rise to a symbolic approach with Geertz's pioneering mapping of the symbolic basis of culture in the *Interpretation of Culture* (1973) and Bourdieu's ethnographic dissection of modern cultural taste in *La Distinction* (1979). Anthropology has revealed that culture is more than the general body of the arts; rather, in Raymond Williams' words, it is "a whole way of life" (1958), or a complete meaning system. Nevertheless, the anthropological tradition continues to assume that culture is in the nature of artifact, a received symbolic system inherited and passed on in human societies, both modern and premodern, from one generation to the next. Cultural inquiry becomes then a task of decoding and deconstruction, unlocking the unique hidden meaning system which holds together the turbulent forces of a particular society.

The third tradition that drives our understanding of culture is industrial and commercial. This approach, as Adam Smith first suggested in *The Wealth of Nations* (1776), casts manufacturing and productive institutions as the collective basis of social life, thus recognizing modern industrial institutions as a new cultural system. At the same time, cultural products, especially popular culture, can be treated as any other category of industrial good and mass produced for ever widening consumer markets. The industrial economy is the foundation of modern culture, while culture itself becomes an industrial product. The industrial marketplace subjects all goods, whether cultural or non-cultural, to the same forces of supply, demand, and economies of scale. For these reasons, among others, the study of economics begins to assimilate the cultural to the agricultural, to commodity markets and manufactured goods sectors. No separate models are required to explain contraction or expansion in the production of different types of cultural products since they, like all other product sectors, are subservient to one single and ineluctable economic force – consumer demand (see Venturelli, 1998a). To the extent this tradition affirmed the marketplace as the arbiter of all cultural preferences, it underscored the democratic basis of both culture and the industrial market. Using basic assumptions in industrial and classical liberal economics, the characteristics of creative ideas and cultural products prevailing at any given time in a particular market can be explained quite simply as a factor of consumer demand. Thus largely unexamined assumptions of twentieth-century economics that regarded the market for widgets identical to that for books, film, and television programs, led to poor conceptualization of creative marketplace. Policymakers have worked from industrial assumptions to decide the fate of the information and creative marketplace, with scant intellectual or empirical grounds to assess how and in what manner the production and distribution of creative ideas and intellectual/cultural products are qualitatively different from the production and consumption of widgets, automobiles, appliances and other industrial products.

Modern notions of a "national culture" draw from the aesthetic and anthropological traditions in laying claims to a body of art, a way of life, and a symbolic meaning system. The industrial approach to culture is also useful to the policy of a national culture, allowing for widespread diffusion and standardization of language and national cultural products. Yet all three historical traditions, I argue, are inadequate to the demands and challenges of the Global Information Economy or Information Society, and have been for some time.

## Culture and the New Information Space: Shifting the Debate

There are at least two reasons why our conventional understanding of culture must be revised.

The need to re-examine our approach to culture has actually been apparent for some time. Since the information revolution of more than a century ago (with the emergence of the telegraph, telephone, photography, cinematography, commercial publishing and broadcasting), we ought to have known, though would not recognize, that information and cultural products are, in fact, not like other products at all. By a few substantive oversights, industrial or rather post-war economics has been reluctant to accept that the economics of ideas and cultural expression cannot be explained by the economics of mining, metals, minerals, agricultural commodities, or manufactured consumer products. Unlike automobiles, toothpaste, appliances, or textiles, information products are not consumed one unit at a time. Rather, each product unit is designed to be utilized repeatedly by many, thus becoming more valuable with use. While the value of a single industrial product such as an automobile, refrigerator, or computer decreases with usage, the precisely opposite effect applies to an information or cultural product. A film, book, television program, or software product increases its value disproportionately the more it is used, viewed, or applied by increasing numbers of people. This has been the case since commercial publishing began and certainly since the age of mass-distributed audio-visual products such as popular music, film, and television programs. While we have had ample evidence of this economic phenomenon from the dawn of film and broadcasting, an appreciation of the unique characteristics of cultural products went largely unacknowledged in public policy and research.

Today, that recognition is unavoidable, for the boosting of value based upon repeated usage is even further accelerated in a network environment such as the Global Internet. In fact, the rift between industrial economics and information economics has grown even wider with the introduction of infrastructure networks for facilitating distribution of ideas. The inherent tendencies of information economics to leverage the value of creative ideas with use have been steadily heightened in the deployment of networks such as theater networks, giant book store chains, and cable television. But with the Internet it is now possible to cultivate worldwide audiences in the millions with well-designed forms of intellectual and creative ideas – audio, video, text, or data – distributed digitally in cyberspace. The economic value of individual creative expression can now be augmented exponentially to a degree unknown in the economic history of nations. This is largely because, as a networked information system levitates the value of ideas and forms of expression, it causes even further heightening of demand for the same expression, thus creating an upward spiral in the spread of a specific form.

This multiple leverage capacity of information in cyberspace casts the meaning of monopoly in an entirely different light from that conceived in conventional economics, providing far more acute evidence of the special character of information monopoly and cultural monopoly. Anti-trust or competition law whose fundamental legal and regulatory assumptions derive from industrial economics of supply, demand, and control over the factors of production, is ill-equipped to deal with the prospect of rapid acceleration in the monopolization of knowledge and ideas within very brief windows of time. As proprietary control over ideas spreads through the information network, the ability to work with existing ideas to innovate new forms becomes reduced, thus creating the economic and social irony of information scarcity coexisting within an environment of enlarged access to information technology. These processes in an Information Society simply cannot be accounted for by aesthetic, anthropological or industrial explanations of culture.

Second, the conventional, one may say, "legacy" approaches are deficient in their tendency to confine the consideration of culture to a received, inherited, or cumulative body of art, aesthetic forms, symbolic meaning systems, practices and institutions. Yet the most significant question about any culture is not the legacy of its past, but the inventive and creative capacities of its present. The real issue is also less about the handful of giants that dominate the history of art (the aesthetic claim to culture), or the essentialist qualities of cultural practices (the anthropological claim), or the size of markets for mass produced cultural products (the industrial claim). Instead, the most significant issue confronting us today concerns the possibilities available for most people in a society to participate in originating new cultural forms. Hence, the environmental conditions most conducive to originality and synthesis as well as the breadth of social participation in forming new ideas comprise the true tests of cultural vigor and the only valid basis of public policy.

This is not to say that the cultural legacy of the past is irrelevant; rather, that the protection of cultural traditions must not comprise the sole aim of cultural policy. In the Information Society it has become a matter of fundamental urgency to promote a climate of creative development throughout economy and society. In a "museum paradigm" of cultural policy, works of art and artistic traditions are revered and cultural traditions closely guarded and defended. But when these become the predominant measure of cultural resources and the notion of legacy occupies the sole definition of the creative spirit, ultimately the development of that spirit would be undermined. Such a recipe for creative stagnation is bequeathed us in the Mayan temples and the Parthenon whose creative societies are dead while artifacts remain. A culture persists in time only to the degree it is inventing, creating, and dynamically evolving in a way that promotes the production of ideas across all social classes and groups. Only in this dynamic context can legacy and tradition have real significance.

## Cultural Wealth of Nations: Key to the Information Economy

On this basis, culture can be seen as the key to success in the Information Economy, because for the very first time in the modern age, the ability to create new ideas and new forms of expression forms a valuable resource base of a society and not merely mineral, agricultural, and manufacturing assets. Cultural wealth can no longer be regarded in the legacy and industrial terms of our common understanding, as something fixed, inherited, and mass-distributed, but as a measure of the vitality, knowledge, energy, and dynamism in the production of ideas that pervades a given community. As nations enter the Global Information Society, the greater cultural concern should be for forging the right environment (policy, legal, institutional, educational, infra-structure, access, etc.) that contributes to this dynamism and not solely for the defense of cultural legacy or an industrial base. The challenge for every nation is not how to prescribe an environment of protection for a received body of art and tradition, but how to construct one of creative explosion and innov-ation in all areas of the arts and sciences (see Venturelli, 2000a, 2000b, 1999, 1998b). Nations that fail to meet this challenge will simply become passive consumers of ideas emanating from societies that are in fact creatively dynamic and able to commercially exploit the new creative forms.

Several considerations are paramount in this cultural debate. Nation states opposed to the protection of cultural industries, whether in Europe or else-where, are about to discover, if they have not already, that the cultural conflict over media and audiovisual content is not a superficial, high-diplomacy power play between the US and France. It is, instead, about the fate of a set of enterprises that form the core, the so-called "gold" of the Information Economy. In a feudal agricultural and a mercantile economy, land, agricultural products, and natural resources such as tea, spices and gold formed the basis of wealth. Gold, in particular, has been the objective cur-rency of wealth across cultures and nations since ancient times. In the indus-trial age, the basis of wealth shifted to other mineral resources such as oil, and to the creation of capital in plant, equipment, and mass-produced products manufactured from natural raw materials such as iron, oil, and wood. Con-trol over these resources and of the means of transforming them into mass-produced products for distribution to ever wider markets has been the basis of economic power since the industrial revolution. The Information Society is now changing that equation. The source of wealth and power, the "gold" of the information economy, is found in a different type of capital: intellec-tual and creative ideas packaged and distributed in different forms over infor-mation networks. One might even say that wealth-creation in an economy of ideas is derived far less than we imagine from the technological hardware and infrastructure, since eventually most nations, such as China, will make investments in large-scale infrastructure technologies. Rather, it is dependent upon the capacity of a nation to continually create content, or new forms of widely distributed expression, for which they will need to invest in creative human capital throughout the economy and not merely in gadgets and hardware.

For these reasons, every nation will need to have, for example, a vibrant and diverse audiovisual industry, publishing industry, intellectual industry, and a dynamic arts community if it is to "grow" its other multimedia content and cultural sectors. In this respect, nations which attempt effectively to prevent the total erosion of content industries will have an advantage over those that simply give up the struggle to diffuse and diversify knowledge and creative enterprises to the growing consolidation of international content producers and distributors.

It is no small irony, then, that many countries impervious to the cultural protection argument are now scrambling to find schemes and mechanisms to revive their publishing, film and broadcast sectors, even as they seek ways to encourage the growth and expansion of new content sectors such as software and information services. Mechanisms of cultural revival include, for example: lottery systems to subsidize film production (UK), taxes on cinema receipts (France), differential postal rates to encourage domestic magazine content (Canada), tax levies on commercial publishers to subsidize small-scale independent publishers (Germany), and structural funds and tax breaks to encourage private investment in content enterprises (Canada, France, Australia, India, among others). As many have yet to discover, the gap in creative productivity does not derive from lower levels of national creative talent or content quality attributes; rather, the gap lies in the power to distribute through advertising, marketing, control of multiple networks, and from horizontal and vertical concentration with other media such as broadcasting, cable, satellite, wireless, and the Internet (Venturelli, 1998a).

Undoubtedly the Global Internet is already revolutionizing how cultural forms, including audiovisual products, are distributed and consumed. Cultural enterprises and information industries have made this assumption, or they would not be actively positioning themselves for the transformation. At the same time, the new information industries are rediscovering the importance of traditional content sectors such as print publishing and film because these enterprises form the creative foundation and feeding line into all the on-line content forms. In short, a nation without a vibrant creative labor force of artists, writers, designers, scriptwriters, playwrights, painters, musicians, film producers, directors, actors, dancers, choreographers, not to mention engineers, scientists, researchers and intellectuals, does not possess the knowledge base to succeed in the Information Economy, and must depend on ideas produced elsewhere.

In an unexpected way, this changing reality has vindicated the arguments of societies that sought to protect their content enterprises in the name of cultural survival and sovereignty. They were right, though I suggest for the wrong reasons, since it is not the cultural legacy that is at stake, but the capacity to invent and create new forms of culture. Few nations had any notion, even five years ago, that the fate of economy and society would be dependent on cultural resources and the capacity to contribute original forms of expression in the Information Society. From this standpoint, then, all nations will need to regard their content and creative enterprises, including the creative work force, with at least the same value they once ascribed to their metals, mining, minerals, agricultural and heavy manufacturing industries.

## References

Bourdieu, Pierre (1979). *La Distinction: Critique sociale du jugement*. Paris: Les Editions de Minuit.

Frazer, Sir James G. (1922). *The Golden Bough*. London: Macmillan.

Geertz, Clifford (1973). *The Interpretation of Culture*. New York: Basic Books.

Heidegger, Martin (1971). *Poetry, Language, Thought*, translated by Albert Hofstadter. New York.

Malinowski, Bronislaw (1922). *Argonauts of the Western Pacific*. New York: Dutton.

Smith, Adam (1776/1986). *The Wealth of Nations*, introduction by A. Skinner. London: Penguin.

Thaler, Richard H. (2000). "From Homo Economicus to Homo Sapiens." *Journal of Economic Perspectives*, 14(1), 133–42.

Venturelli, Shalini (2000a). "Ownership of Cultural Expression: The Place of Free Speech and Culture in the New Intellectual Property Rights Regime of the European Union," *Telematics & Informatics: An International Journal on Telecommunications & Internet Technology, Special Issue: The Socio-Cultural Consequences of the European Information Society*, 17(1–2), 9–38.

—— (2000b). "Inventing E-Regulation in the US and EU: Regulatory Convergence and the New Information Space." Keynote Address presented at the Conference on Regulating the Internet: EU and US Perspectives, European Union Center and Center for Internet Studies, University of Washington, April 27–29.

—— (1999). "Information Society and Multilateral Agreements: Obstacles for Developing Countries," *Media Development, Key Issues in Global Communication*, 46(2), 22–7.

—— (1998a). *Liberalizing the European Media: Politics, Regulation and the Public Sphere*. Oxford: Oxford University Press.

—— (1998b). "Cultural Rights and World Trade Agreements in the Information Society," *Gazette: The International Journal for Communication Studies*, 60(1), 47–76.

Williams, Raymond (1958). *Culture and Society*. London: Chatto & Windus.

# Index